For Dummies
BESTSELLING BOOK SERIES

Mutual Funds For Canadians For Dummies, 2nd Edition

by Andrew Bell

Cheat Sheet

D0565281

Andrew's Top Ten Investing Commandments

1. If they don't have clean water, think long and hard before investing there. Fibre-optic stocks count as not having clean water.

2. To be safe, lend money only to people who print their own money and employ uniformed professional killers.

3. If your fund invests in "e"-anything, cultivate a sophisticated, ironic sense of humour. It'll help you chuckle as your cash melts away.

4. Every extra colour in the brochure costs you 1 percent of your portfolio annually. Same goes for each mumbling PhD on the management team who's figured out "strategic asset allocation."

5. Invest now — you're not going to win the lottery. And that thing you bought in Cozumel isn't even a rabbit's foot.

6. Do as the boring flabby pros do and hold index funds, bonds, and cash.

7. If you or I have already heard about a hot investment opportunity, it's too late. Same goes for fund managers.

8. Biotechnology promises rich rewards for patient investors — the ones who are willing to wait forever.

9. Get your money into a registered retirement savings plan as soon as possible. And then leave it there.

10. Three words: Manager over 35.

Favourite Mutual Fund Manager Excuses for Bad Returns — And What They Really Mean

"Valuations are now more reasonable." — The fund has dropped like a rock.

"It's a stock picker's market." — Buying everything didn't work so now we'll try this.

"We're conservative." — We can't make up our minds.

The Eigh[...] Successful Investing

1. The only investments that are suitable for most of your long-term savings are high-quality global stocks, which are tiny portions of ownership issued by big international companies, and high-quality bonds from stable governments, which are loans to that government in a particular currency.

2. Pretty well everything that's worth investing in is also easy to explain and understand. That's why tech stocks have been such a great way to lose money.

3. The most important things to look for in a mutual fund are low and easy-to-understand annual expenses, top-quality holdings, and a broad mix of investments. Reliably selecting future hot performers is impossible — and worrying too much about past returns is wandering into a swamp.

4. The more bells and whistles attached to the fund, or the fancier the concept, the higher the expenses. And that reduces your return.

5. Star fund managers almost invariably go into a slump and either drop back into the pack or even become underperformers. Also beware of the "curse of the front cover" — as soon as a fund gets praised in the media, it's nearly certain to turn into a dog.

6. Buy a bond fund. With just about every stock and share in the market dropping like a rock, it's a great time to own bonds.

7. When you're buying funds, ask to see a sample account statement. If you can't understand it, or if they don't have one to show you, then shop elsewhere. Because if you can't tell how much your funds are earning for you, how do you know if they're doing their job?

8. Own index funds that mindlessly track the Canadian, U.S., and international stock markets, plus a couple of regular Canadian and global equity funds. That way, if some of your funds go into a slump, you'll probably still have a few winners.

...For Dummies®: Bestselling Book Series for Beginners

Types of Mutual Funds — Defined!

Equity funds: These give you a tiny stake — in the form of stocks and shares — in lots of companies. They're available in a vast array of flavours, from sensible to downright silly. Owning equity funds is the best way to get rich over the years, but watch out for dips along the way — sometimes lasting for years — when the stock market goes into one of its regular hissy fits.

Money Market funds: Almost as dull as that hilarious story you tell about your cute kid. Buy one of these and you're lending money for short periods to the government or to big companies. Park your money in one and watch it grow slowly. Your savings aren't at risk — as long as a giant meteor doesn't land on our nation's capital.

Bond funds: An essential ingredient in just about anyone's fund arsenal, these funds hold longer-term government and corporate loans. You earn plenty of interest and a steady return. But watch out for inflation: It'll cut through these suckers like a hot machete through butter.

Balanced funds: A little bit of everything for bone-lazy mutual fund customers. Just dump your money in and let somebody else worry about how to invest it. Not such a bad plan if you're too busy with your Scottish dancing to fool around with funds — but beware of high costs and returns that can be hard to judge.

Index funds: The elegant kings and queens of funds — and something that every investor should own. These beauties simply give you a return that's in line with the entire stock and bond market by holding just about every share and bond that matters. No muss, no fuss, and nice low annual expenses for you. They'll never top any performance leagues, but they won't crash and burn in a plume of black acrid oily smoke either.

Segregated funds: Mutual funds with belt, braces, and a parachute strapped on. This gang guarantees to at least refund your investment if you hang onto the fund for ten years — or to pay the cash to your heirs if you die. Sounds like a great deal but watch out for high expenses and complicated rules.

Clone funds: Miracles of engineering, these let you move your retirement savings outside Canada and still get a nice tax holiday. But watch out for financial nuts and bolts that haven't been fully tightened — most of these funds are still new, after all. Costs can be high, and then there's the devilish question of currencies. So don't bet your whole wad on these things, sailor.

Dividend funds: A collection of high-quality conservative shares that produce a stream of lightly taxed payments, ideal for investors who want to get regular income from their funds. What could be nicer? Well, clearer definitions and lower expenses would help.

Labour-sponsored funds: A handy way to invest money in obscure spotty computer geniuses and get a serious tax break. Lots of these funds' weird holdings go bust — but who cares, when some also explode in value? A good way to invest a little cash that you don't mind tying up for years, or even losing, in hopes of getting a rich payoff.

Fund packages: Nourishing stews of funds (if a little dull) with impressive-sounding names and, usually, complicated rules. A useful solution if you want to just buy a grab-bag of investments and forget about them. But as ever, watch out for those sneaky annual costs.

WILEY

...For Dummies®: Bestselling Book Series for Beginners

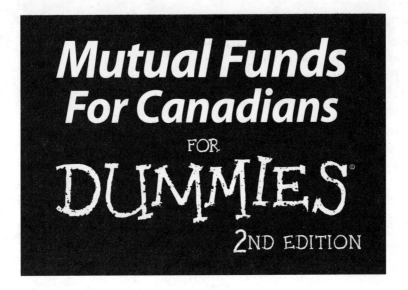

Mutual Funds For Canadians

FOR

DUMMIES®

2ND EDITION

by Andrew Bell

John Wiley & Sons Canada, Ltd

Mutual Funds For Canadians For Dummies,® 2nd Edition

Published by
John Wiley & Sons Canada, Ltd
22 Worcester Road
Etobicoke, ON M9W 1L1
www.wiley.ca

National Library of Canada Cataloguing in Publication

Bell, Andrew, 1960–

Mutual funds for Canadians for dummies / Andrew Bell. — 2nd ed.

Includes index.
ISBN: 0-470-83251-7

1. Mutual funds — Canada. I. Title.

HG5154.B44 2002   332.63'27   C2002-904930-X

Printed in Canada

1 2 3 4 5 TRI 04 03 02 01 00

Distributed in Canada by John Wiley & Sons Canada, Ltd.

For general information on John Wiley & Sons Canada, Ltd, including all books published by Wiley Publishing, Inc., please call our warehouse, Tel 1-800-567-4797. For reseller information, including discounts and premium sales, please call our sales department, Tel 416-646-7992. For press review copies, author interviews, or other publicity information, please contact our marketing department, Tel: 416-646-4584, Fax 416-236-4448.

For authorization to photocopy items for corporate, personal, or educational use, please contact Cancopy, The Canadian Copyright Licensing Agency, One Yonge Street, Suite 1900, Toronto, ON, M5E 1E5 Tel 416-868-1620 Fax 416-868-1621; www.cancopy.com.

About the Author

Andrew Bell, 42 but still fairly alert and strong, was an investment reporter and editor with the *Globe and Mail* for 12 years. He joined Report on Business Television as a reporter in 2001.

Bell, an import from Dublin, Ireland, was for 10 years the main compiler of Stars & Dogs in Saturday's *Globe*. The roundup of hot and damp stocks and mutual funds was an invaluable therapeutic aid in relieving his own myriad jealousies, regrets, and resentments. He has also taken to the stage, where he practises a demanding "method" that involves getting the audience and other performers as off balance and upset as possible.

He lives in an unfinished and perhaps unfinishable construction project in Cabbagetown, Toronto, with his wife, daughter, and very rare brown-and-black tabby cat.

Dedication

For Tara and Sasha. And my dad, Cecil Bell.

Author's Acknowledgements

Thank you to my colleagues for their support and indulgence, especially Eric Reguly, Lori Vanden Bergh, Steve Northfield, Mike Den Tandt, and Dave Pyette. My wife, Tara Ellis, cheerfully put up with months of whining, procrastination, and self-pity. And so did talented editors Joan Whitman and Melanie Rutledge. Thanks also to Ellen Roseman, who first got me writing about funds.

Publisher's Acknowledgements

We're proud of this book; please send us your comments at canadapt@wiley.com.

Some of the people who helped bring this book to market include the following:

Acquisitions and Editorial

Executive Editor: Joan Whitman

Editor: Melanie Rutledge

Copy Editor: Kelli Howey

Cover Photo: © Jose Luis Pelaez, Inc./CORBIS/MAGMA

Production

Publishing Services Director: Karen Bryan

Project Manager: Elizabeth McCurdy

Project Coordinator: Abigail Brown

Layout and Graphics: Kim Monteforte, Heidy Lawrance Associates

Proofreader: Allyson Latta

Indexer: Belle Wong

John Wiley & Sons Canada, Ltd

Bill Zerter, Chief Operating Officer

Robert Harris, Publisher, Professional and Trade Division

Publishing and Editorial for Consumer Dummies

Diane Graves Steele, Vice President and Publisher, Consumer Dummies

Joyce Pepple, Acquisitions Director, Consumer Dummies

Kristin A. Cocks, Product Development Director, Consumer Dummies

Michael Spring, Vice President and Publisher, Travel

Suzanne Jannetta, Editorial Director, Travel

Publishing for Technology Dummies

Andy Cummings, Acquisitions Director

Composition Services

Gerry Fahey, Executive Director of Production Services

Debbie Stailey, Director of Composition Services

Contents at a Glance

Table of Contents

Part III: The Fund Stuff: Building a Strong Portfolio 153

Chapter 10: Equity Funds: The Road to Riches 155

Chapter 11: Heirloom Equity Funds: The Dull Stuff that Will Make You Wealthy 173

Chapter 12: Las Vegas–Style Equity Funds: Trips You Don't Need . . .185

Chapter 13: Balanced and Asset Allocation Funds 205

Introduction

Believe it or not, mutual funds still work. And they work excellently. Yes, stock markets have crashed from their insane highs of 2000, dragging mutual funds down with them. Yes, plenty of corporate executives have been shown to operate with all the moral qualms of a starving jackal, and mutual fund managers and other professional investors have turned out to be sheep waiting to be fleeced. But conservative funds that invested in high-quality companies — and cautious investors who made sure they didn't risk all of their money in the stock market and in stock funds — have survived the past three years with manageable losses. As of June 2002, the average Canadian balanced fund — which owns a bit of everything — had still made money for its investors over three and five years. And over longer periods of five years or more, stock funds were also still in profit. But here's the great part: Picking conservative funds with good returns and putting them together in a smart financial plan isn't that hard or time-consuming. Just follow the simple (and often obvious) guidelines in this book, and you'll do fine.

Life is short and we're all overloaded. So much mud-wrestling, so little time. I've written *Mutual Funds For Canadians For Dummies* as though the two of us are sitting in a coffee shop and I'm giving you the basic facts on mutual funds and investing — only the essential stuff you need to earn a decent return on your money. I hope you never feel, while reading this book, that I'm droning on about something that doesn't affect your life. Most people relegate mutual funds to the grey parking lot of their lives that's reserved for stuff like plumbing or Bulgaria. Something to think about if you have to, but otherwise no thanks. That's a pity; funds really can make a difference in your financial picture.

They aren't very complicated either — a mutual fund is really just a handy invention that allows hordes of people to pool their cash into a professionally managed investment vehicle that handles the bookkeeping. It then buys things such as shares in companies and bonds issued by governments, things that a lot of ordinary people find confusing. Funds are so powerful and simple that they've helped to transform the economy of the capitalist world.

Until the mass-market mutual fund came along, investing in shares and buying bonds was mostly a privilege of the rich, just like tax evasion and dull conversations about the unreliability of nannies. These days, mutual funds have helped millions of ordinary people, especially in North America, to gather unprecedented wealth.

This book is meant to help you be part of that phenomenon. With a little education you too can jump on the bandwagon and make yourself some cold, hard cash. There are important reasons to understand the funds you do end up buying. Getting up to speed about mutual funds doesn't take long and it can be sinfully profitable. For more and more Canadians — especially the self-employed or those working for small companies — the returns they get from their funds will determine when they can stop working and what kind of retirement income to expect.

Some Basic Truths about Funds

It would be nice to think that all funds are created equal, but life isn't quite that simple.

Right off the bat you need to know that many funds are over-priced; in other words, their annual charges, often used to pay the very people who sell you funds, are too high to allow you to end up with a decent return. Many funds are little better than marketing ploys and still more just drag their hapless customers through years of lousy returns.

But don't panic. And don't give up or buy the first thing a salesperson shoves your way. Excellent funds that offer good value for the money are easy to buy if you stick to a few simple rules. Together we'll sift through all the options and come up with the right funds for you. Pass the cream and sugar, it's coffee time.

How this Book Is Different

Pick up nearly any book or article about investing and you'll probably see a picture of the author — a fresh-faced thing with cute tousled hair or a solemn corrupt senator type trying to look prosperous. Oh, there's nothing more glamorous than the hectic, glittering life of the investment author!

And then there are the promises: The special formulas, the daring analysis, the hinted-at guarantee that at last you've found the route to riches. But what we all-knowing money gurus rarely get around to explaining is: How come, if we're such fantastic investors, we have to do something as wretched as write a book?

Why aren't we striding the trading floor at RBC Dominion Securities, barking orders over a cell phone at quivering central bankers and restructuring the South Korean steel industry before lunch?

The evidence shows that hardly anybody, including investment professionals, is consistently good at picking shares and bonds that go up in price. Despite all the fancy talk and arcane theories, stock and bond prices move in unpredictable patterns — like the weather or the population of porcupines in New Brunswick.

So it's time to come clean: This book contains no magic, just some plain logic and simple facts that you could find out for yourself by fooling around with mutual funds for a few years. But lots of people don't have the time or inclination to do that — this book is for you, folks.

Besides, the investment market can be an awfully expensive place to learn investing lessons. So read on and gain the benefit of my (often painful) experience.

How this Book Is Organized

The best first move is to look at the table of contents to get an idea of what's here. If you already know the basics, just jump to the topics you have trouble with. In the case of subjects with lots of further complications, like official rules and so on, I've given you Web addresses.

The book is supposed to be like a set of Russian dolls, nesting inside each other. The smallest doll is Chapter 1, What Is a Mutual Fund? If you're not quite clear on the basics of investing in funds, you can read that chapter and get all of the truly important information. It's designed to be a brief primer that gives you the essential core of mutual fund investing. The next level, providing more information on the drawbacks and advantages of funds, is Part 1, which was written as a complete introduction to mutual funds. It provides more detail on each topic than Chapter 1 alone. Then, to explore any aspect of funds in yet more depth, you can simply start jumping around the book. The whole thing is pretty flexible. And like Monty Python, you can take it all in a rather silly order.

So don't worry about reading every chapter. You should be out partying anyway. Jump to any section, because each is understandable without reading others first. Throughout the book, I've avoided jargon wherever possible — where I'm forced to use a technical term, I explain it right away.

The sections that follow describe the parts in this book and what they cover.

Part I: Meet the Mutual Fund

This first section is a summary of how funds work and the reasons to buy them, as well as what type to buy. Packed with definitions and plain English explanations, this part is built for the novices who has been left scratching their heads about fund basics. Every investor needs to get his financial house in order before diving into the fund pool, so this part also features a crash course on financial planning and much, much more.

Part II: Buying Options: Looking for a Helping Hand

In Part II we walk through all the possible sources of help you might consider, from your friendly neighbourhood bank to a discount broker. Packed with inside information about who does what, this part will help you figure out exactly what you're looking for in terms of financial advice, and how much that advice should set you back.

Part III: The Fund Stuff: Building a Strong Portfolio

Here is the industry's entire menu of funds, give or take a handful. These days there are funds for every type of investor, the daredevil who would just as soon go the race track and the notorious mattress stuffer who can't part with a single dime. This part runs through them all, defines the many types and helps you match your financial goals to what these beasts have to offer. All the biggies are here — equity funds, money market funds, and index funds, plus a look at funds packages. Each chapter boasts my picks for winning funds.

Part IV: The Nuts and Bolts of Keeping Your Portfolio Going

Getting started in funds may seem like the hard part, but keeping your portfolio humming along and turning a profit is a challenge all its own. In this part I offer some valuable advice on tracking your progress, optimizing the mighty combination of your registered retirement savings plan and mutual funds, and take a long hard look at taxes and your funds.

Part V: The Part of Tens

The Part of Tens is a collection quick factoids about funds. I list ten famous foul-ups in funds, which I hope you'll find entertaining, yet slightly horrifying — and there's more horror when I go through ten gimmick funds. Also featured are the warnings — ten signs you need to fire your adviser and ten tough questions to put to anyone who wants to manage your cash.

Icons Used in this Book

Ever go over one of those speed bumps — the British call them "sleeping policeman" — at full throttle? Catches your attention. This finance stuff can get heavy after the 200th page. So to keep you alert, throughout the book there are icons in the margin to wake you up and tip you off that here comes important information that's too good to miss. It might be a grim admonition, a neat piece of advice, or a nugget of wisdom. Here's what to look out for.

Warning icons appear when there's a dangerous reef that you have to skirt. Something that could cost you lots of money, either by hitting you with excessive fees and expenses, leaving you vulnerable to nasty losses, or dragging down your overall returns.

Remember icons flag an important piece of information that's like the crucial clue in an Agatha Christie novel. The bit where the jealous sister-in-law couldn't possibly have heard the 1 a.m. time check on the radio when she said she did — *because the clocks went forward that night.* My turning points won't be so complicated. They're simply realities about mutual funds that you should always bear in mind.

These Tip icons point to methods or suggestions that save you money, improve your returns, or reduce your risk. They're also quick-and-dirty shortcuts. Or they mark practicalities that fund companies may not mention.

Relax: You can get away without reading this stuff. But for those who like a good conspiracy story, this icon denotes interesting if throwaway information. It flags a place where I talk about the internal workings of a fund. But you can invest in funds perfectly well without reading it. In practice, Technical Stuff usually involves the money that fund managers and salespeople get from the funds they market. That's the thing that kind of drives the whole show forward.

This icon — judiciously used — denotes a product or particular fund that does a good job and offers you benefits. But watch out — funds have an annoying habit of dropping to the bottom of the performance table right after writers recommend them. In part that's because the type of investments that the fund buys have already shot up in value.

That's Almost All, Folks

Things are getting better for you, the mutual fund buyer. For example, new index funds and fund-like products that follow smaller sections of the stock market are coming out and they can be bought cheaply from discount brokers. But once you start trying to pick narrow baskets of stocks, you're back to the old problem of trying to outguess the market. Mutual fund expenses aren't coming down, in fact there are signs they're going up, but Internet trading and discount brokers are making it easier to buy great funds with low expenses. It is an exciting time to get into funds, and between the two of us I'm sure we'll pick some winners. Let's get started.

Part I
Meet the Mutual Fund

"The first thing we should do is get you two into a good mutual fund. Let me get out the 'Magic 8-Ball' and we'll run some options."

In this part . . .

Just read this and you can go and pass out on the couch again, I promise. Here's all you need to build a perfectly good mutual fund portfolio. I explain why you almost certainly should own at least some funds. I also describe how funds work and I set out the basic mechanics of buying funds and using them to make money. I also look at how funds fit beautifully into just about everyone's financial plan, and I show you some of the alternative investments you can buy. After reading this part, you'll be armed with all the essential facts needed to launch a solid investing program.

Chapter 1

What Is a Mutual Fund?

*U*nless you've been living as an ascetic hermit on top of a pillar in Turkey for the past decade, railing against the evils of humankind, you've heard a lot about mutual funds. Chances are you or someone in your family has already bought some. Mutual funds seem complicated, so — even though they are incredibly popular — lots of people shy away. They're not sure where to start or they just buy the first fund that their banker or financial planner suggests. And too often Canadians end up disappointed with the performance of their funds, because they've been sold something that's either unsuitable or just too expensive. It's a shame, because building a portfolio of excellent funds is easy if you follow a few simple rules and your own common sense. This stuff isn't complicated — a mutual fund is just a money-management service that operates under clear rules. Yes, there's a lot of marketing mumbo-jumbo and arcane terminology, but the basic idea could be written on a postage stamp. In return for a fee, the people running the fund promise to invest your money wisely and give it back to you on demand. The fund industry has become competitive and sophisticated, which means that there are plenty of good choices out there.

In this chapter, I'll show how funds make you money — especially if you leave your investment in place for several years. I'll also quickly describe the main places you can go to buy funds, and touch on the different types available. Later on in the book I'll go into more detail on these topics, but after you've read the first chapter, you'll know the basics.

Mutual Fund Basics

So exactly what is a mutual fund? Truth be told, a mutual fund is pretty straightforward.

A *mutual fund* is a pool of money that a company gets from investors like you and me and divides up into equally priced *units*. Each unit is like a tiny little slice of the fund. When you put money into the fund or take it out again, you either buy or sell units. For example, say a fund has *total assets* — that is, money held in trust for investors — of $10 million and investors have been sold a total of 1 million units. Then each unit is worth $10. If you put money into the fund, you're simply sold units at that day's value. If you take money out, the fund buys units back from you at the same price. [Handling purchase and sale transactions in units makes it far simpler to do the paperwork.] And there's another huge advantage to the system: As long as you know how many units you own, you can simply check their current price to find out how much your total investment is worth. For example, if you hold 475 units of a fund whose unit price is listed in the newspapers at $15.20, then you know that your holding has a value of 475 times $15.20, or $7,220.

Owning units of a mutual fund makes you, you guessed it, a *unitholder.* In fact, you and the other unitholders are the legal owners of the fund. But the fund is run by a company that's legally known as the *fund manager* — this is the firm that handles the investing and also deals with the fund's administration. The terminology gets confusing here because the person (usually an employee of the fund manager) who chooses which stocks or bonds the fund should buy is also usually called the fund manager. To make things clear, I'll refer to the company that sells and administers the fund as the *management company* or *fund sponsor.* I'll use the term *fund manager* for the person who picks the stocks and bonds. His or her skill is one of the main benefits you get from a mutual fund. Obviously, the fund manager should be experienced and not too reckless — after all, you're trusting him or her with your money.

Under professional management, the fund invests in stocks and bonds, increasing the pool of money for the investors and boosting the value of the individual units. For example, if you bought units at $10 each and the fund manager managed to pick investments that doubled in value, then your units would grow to $20. In the world of mutual funds, just like almost everywhere else, you don't get something for nothing — in return, the management company slices off fees and expenses. They usually come to between 0.3 percent and 3 percent of the fund's assets each year. Confused? Don't be, it isn't rocket science. This example should help. Units in Canada's biggest mutual fund, Templeton Growth Fund, were bought from and sold to people like you and me at $9.68 each on June 30, 2002. So if you invested $1,000 in the fund that day, you owned 103.3 units ($1,000 divided by $9.68. The price you pay for each unit is known as the fund's *net asset value* per unit. The net asset value is the fund's assets minus its liabilities, hence the "net" (which means after costs and debts are taken away), divided by the number of units outstanding.

So a fund company buys and sells the units to the public at their net asset value. This value increases or decreases proportionally as the value of the fund's investments rises or falls. Let's say in February you pay $10 each for 100 units in a fund that invests in oil and gas shares, always a smelly and risky game. Now, say, by July, the value of the shares that the fund holds has dropped by one-fifth. Then your units are worth just $8 each. So your original $1,000 investment is now worth only $800. But that August, a bunch of companies in which the fund has invested strike oil in Alberta. That sends the value of their shares soaring and lifts the fund's units to $15 each. The value of your investment has now grown to $1,500.

Where can you go from here? You've made a tidy profit after a bit of a let-down, but what happens next? Well, that depends on you. You can hang in and see if there is more oil in them there hills, or you can cash out. With most funds, you can simply buy or sell units at that day's net asset value. That flexibility is one of the great beauties of mutual funds. Funds that let you come and go as you please in this way are known as *open-end funds*, as though they had a giant door that's never locked. Think of a raucous Viking banquet where guests are free to come and go at will because one of the end walls of the dining hall has been removed.

That means most mutual funds are marvellously flexible and convenient. The managers allow you to put money into the fund on any business day by buying units, and you take money out again at will by selling your units back to the fund. In other words, an investment in a mutual fund is a *liquid asset*. A liquid asset is either cash or it's an investment that can be sold and turned into good old cash at a moment's notice. The idea is that cash and close-to-cash investments, just like water, are adaptable and useful in all sorts of situations. In investment jargon, the ability to get your cash back at any time is called *liquidity* and professionals prize it above all else. More than they prize red Porsches with very loud sound systems or crystal goblets in lovely velvet-lined boxes with their initials engraved in gold.

The other type of fund is a *closed-end fund.* Investors in those are sold their units when the fund is launched, but to get their money back they must find another investor to buy the units on the stock market like a share, often at a loss. The fund usually won't buy the units back, or may buy only a portion. You can make money in closed-end funds, but it's very tricky. As craven brokerage analysts sometimes say when they hate a stock but can't pluck up the courage to tell investors to sell it: "Avoid."

Now that you're feeling flush with cash, let's see how funds make it all happen.

The Nitty Gritty: How a Fund Makes You Money

We'll stick with the example of Templeton Growth, a well-run huge fund that's widely available (just about any discount broker, financial planner, or stockbroker in the country, no matter how sad and disorganized, can probably sell it to you). Templeton Growth's $8.7 billion in assets as of mid-2002 made it Canada's biggest mutual fund. That's $1 million 8,700 times over, or about $290 for each of the approximately 30 million people living in Canada. The fund is free to invest in stock markets anywhere in the world, and since November 29, 1954, it has been buying shares in blue-chip, conservative companies in just about any country you care to name (not much in Bhutan or Tajikistan yet, but give them time).

Like most other mutual fund companies, sponsor Franklin Templeton Investments of Toronto sells units of Templeton Growth to the public every business day, and buys them back from other investors at the same price.

The somewhat sleazy dawn of the mutual fund

The modern mutual fund evolved in the 1920s in the U.S. In 1924, one Edward Leffler started the world's first open-end fund, the Massachusetts Investors Trust. It's still going. Mr. Leffler's fund had to be purchased through a broker, who charged a sales commission, adding to an investor's cost. Four years later, Boston investment manager Scudder Stevens & Clark started the first no-load fund — a fund that you buy with no sales commission — First Investment Counsel Corp. The fund was called no-load because instead of purchasing it through a commission-charging broker, investors bought it directly from the company.

There was nothing wrong with those early open-end funds. They were run well and they survived the Great Crash of 1929 and subsequent Depression, in part because the obligation to buy and sell their shares every day at an accurate value tended to keep managers honest and competent. But closed-end funds were the main game in the 1920s. (Closed-end funds don't buy back your units on demand, meaning that you're locked into the fund until you find another investor to buy your units from you on the open market.) And a crooked game it was. By 1929, investors were paying ridiculous prices for closed-end shares. Brokers charged piratical sales commissions of 10 percent, annual expenses topped 12.5 percent, and funds kept their holdings secret. Needless to say, most collapsed in the Crash and ensuing Depression.

Following that debacle, mutual funds in Canada and the United States were far more tightly regulated, with laws forcing them to disclose their holdings at least twice a year and report costs and fees to investors. There are still plenty of badly run funds, and plenty of greedy managers who don't put their unitholders' interests first, but at least there are clear rules that protect investors who keep their eyes open.

With most companies' funds you're free to come and go as you please, but companies often impose a small levy on investors who sell their units within 90 days of buying them. That's because constant trading raises expenses for the other unitholders and makes the fund manager's job harder. The charge, which should go to the fund and usually does, is generally 2 percent of the units sold, but it can be more. Check this out before you invest, especially if you're thinking of moving your cash around shortly after you buy.

Returns — what's in it for you?

The main reason people buy mutual funds is to earn a *return*. A return is simply the profit you get in exchange for either investing in a business (by buying its shares) or for lending money to a government or company (by buying its bonds). It's money you get as a reward for letting other people use your cash — and for putting your money at risk. Mutual fund buyers earn the same sorts of profits but they make them indirectly because they're using a fund manager to pick their investments for them. The fund itself earns the profits, which are either paid out to the unitholders or retained within the fund itself, increasing the value of each of its units.

When you invest money, you nearly always hope to get:

- ✔ **Trading profits** or *capital gains* (the two mean nearly the same thing), when the value of your holdings goes up. Capital is just the money you've tied up in an investment, and a capital gain is simply an increase in its value. For example, say you buy gold bars at $100 each and their price rises to $150. You've earned a capital gain of $50, on paper at least.

- ✔ **Income** in the form of interest on a bond or loan, or dividends from a company. *Interest* is the regular fee you get in return for lending your money, and *dividends* are a portion of a company's profits that's paid out to its shareowners. For example, say you deposit $1,000 at a bank at an annual interest rate of 5 percent, then each year you'll get interest of $50 (or 5 percent of the money you deposited). Dividends are usually paid out by companies on a per-share basis. Say, for example, you own 10,000 shares and the company's directors decide to pay a dividend of 50 cents per share. You'll get a cheque for $5,000.

You also hope to get the money you originally invest back at the end of the day, which doesn't always happen. That's part of the risk you assume with almost any investment. Companies can lose money, sending the value of their shares tumbling. Or inflation can rise, which nearly always makes the value of both shares and bonds drop rapidly. That's because inflation eats away at the value of the money, which makes it less attractive to have the money tied up in such long-term investments where it's vulnerable to steady erosion.

Here's an example to illustrate the difference between earning capital gains and dividend income. Say you buy 100 shares of a company — a Costa Rican crocodile farm, for example — for $115 each and hold them for an entire year. Also, say you get $50 in dividend income during the year because the company has a policy of paying four quarterly dividends of 12.5 cents, or 50 cents per share, annually (that is, 50 cents times the 100 shares you own — $50 right into your pocket).

Now imagine the price of the stock rises in the open market by $12, from $115 to $127. The value of your 100 shares rises from $11,500 to $12,700, for a total capital gain of $1,200.

Your capital gain is only on paper unless you actually sell your holdings at that price.

Add up your gains and income, and that's your total return — $50 in dividends plus a capital gain of $1,200, for a total of $1,250.

Let's work through another example to make this crystal clear, using a loss this time. Templeton Growth units that were sold to the public at $10.68 on the last day of 2000 fell to $10.40 in the rocky stock markets of 2001, for a decline of 28 cents a unit during the year. In June of 2001, Templeton Growth also paid out a *distribution*, a payment to unitholders, of 20 cents per unit. So at the end of the year, a unitholder in this fund had lost 8 cents on every unit he or she held — comprising a 28-cent capital loss that was almost entirely compensated for by the 20-cent distribution. Distributions are made when a fund has earned capital gains, interest, or dividends from its investments.

On a per-unit basis, the investor in Templeton Growth started the year with $10.68 at risk, and during 2001 she suffered a loss of 8 cents. That represented about 0.7 percent of the starting figure of $10.68, so the percentage *return,* the amount your money earned or lost by being invested, was a loss of 0.7 percent, or just less than $\frac{1}{100}$ of the investor's original stake. Calculating the return is actually a little more complicated than that because most investors would have simply reinvested the mid-year distribution in more units, which actually rose a little in price during the second half of the year. In fact, returns for mutual funds always assume that all distributions are reinvested in more units. Templeton Growth's official return for 2001 was a loss of 0.7 percent. (Unitholders didn't have much to gripe about, by the way. A lot of rival global stock funds had bet far more heavily on overpriced technology and telecommunications shares, which collapsed in 2001. Most funds in the group left their unitholders with a loss of 13 percent or more during the year.)

Returns as a percentage

Returns on mutual funds, and nearly all other investments, are usually expressed as a percentage of the capital that the investor originally put up. That way you can easily compare returns and work out whether you did well or not.

After all, if you tied up $10 million in an investment to earn only $1,000, you wouldn't be using your cash very smartly. That's why the return on any investment is nearly always stated in percentages by expressing the return as a proportion of the original investment. In the example of the crocodile farm, the return was $50 in dividends plus $1,200 in *capital appreciation,* which is just a fancy term for an increase in the value of your capital, for a total of $1,250. At the beginning of the year you put $11,500 into the shares by buying 100 of them at $115 each. To get your *percentage return,* the amount your money grew expressed as a percentage of your initial investment, divide your total return by the amount you initially invested and then multiply the answer by 100. The return of $1,250 represented 10.9 percent of $11,500, so your percentage return during the year was 10.9 percent. It's the return produced by an investment over several years, however, that people are usually interested in. Yes, it's often useful to look at the return in each individual year — for example, a loss of 10 percent in Year 1, a gain of 15 percent in Year 2, and so on. But that's a long-winded way of expressing things. It's handy to be able to state the return in just one number that represents the average yearly return over a set period. It makes it much easier, for instance, to compare the performance of two different funds. The math can start getting complex here but don't worry, we'll stick to the basic method used by the fund industry.

Fund returns are expressed, in percentages, as an *average annual compound return.* That sounds like a mouthful, but the concept is simple. Let's say you invested $1,000 in a fund for three years. In the first year, the value of your investment dropped by 10 percent, or one-tenth, leaving you with $900. In Year 2, the fund earned you a return of 20 percent, leaving you with $1,080. And in Year 3, the fund produced a return of 10 percent, leaving you with $1,188. So over the three years, you earned a total of $188, or 18.8 percent of your initial $1,000 investment. When mutual fund companies convert that return to an "average annual" number, they invariably express the number as a "compound" figure. That simply means the return in Year 2 is added (or compounded) onto the return in Year 1, and the return in Year 3 is then compounded onto the new higher total, and so on. A return of 18.8 percent over three years works out to an average annual compound return of about 5.9 percent. As we saw in the example, the actual value of the investment fluctuated over the three years, but let's say it actually grew steadily at 5.9 percent. After one year, the $1,000 would be worth $1,059. After two years, it would be worth $1,121.48. And after three years, it would be worth $1,187.65. The total differs from $1,188 by a few cents because I rounded off the average annual return to one decimal place, instead of fiddling around with hundredths of a percent. There are some important points to remember when looking at an average annual compound return.

- ✔ **Average:** That innocuous-looking average usually smooths out some mighty rough periods. Mutual funds can easily lose money for years on end — it happened, for example, when the world economy was hurt by inflation and recession in the 1970s.

- ✔ **Annual:** Obviously, this means per year. And mutual funds should be thought of as long-term holdings to be owned for several years. The general rule in the industry is that you shouldn't buy an equity fund — one that invests in shares — unless you plan to own it for five years. That's because stocks can drop sharply, often for a year or more, and it's silly to risk money that you might need in the short term (to buy a house, say) in an investment that might be down from its purchase value when you go to cash it in. With money you'll need in the near future, it's better to stick to a super-stable short-term bond or money market fund that will lose little or no money (more about those later). Of course, mutual fund companies sometimes use the old "long-term investing" mantra as an excuse. If their funds are down, they claim that it's a long-term game and that investors should give their miraculous strategy time to work. But if the funds are up, the managers run hysterical ads screaming about the short-term returns.

- ✔ **Compound:** This little word, which means "added" or "combined" in this context, is the plutonium trigger at the heart of investing. It's the device that makes the whole thing go. It simply means that to really build your nest egg, you have to leave your profits or interest in place and working for you so that you start earning income on income. After a while, of course, you start earning income on the income you've earned, until it becomes a very nicely furnished hall of mirrors. Here's another example: Mr. Simple and Ms. Compound each have $1,000 to invest, and the bank's offering 10 percent a year. Now, let's say Mr. Simple puts his money into the bank, but each year he takes the interest earned and hides it under his mattress. Simple-minded, huh? After ten years, he'll have his original $1,000 plus the ten annual interest payments of $100 each under his futon, for a total of $2,000. But canny Ms. Compound leaves her money in the account so that each year the interest is added to the pile and the next year's interest is calculated on the higher amount. In other words, at the end of the first year, the bank adds her $100 in interest to her $1,000 initial deposit and then calculates the 10-percent interest for the following year on the higher base of $1,100, which earns her $110. Depending on how the interest is calculated and timed, she'll end the ten years with about $2,594, or $594 more than Mr. Simple. That extra $594 is interest earned on interest.

How funds can make you rich

The real beauty of mutual funds is the way they can grow your money over many years. "Letting your money ride" in a casino — by just leaving it on the odd numbers in roulette, for example — is a dumb strategy. That's because the house will eventually win it from you because the odds are stacked in the casino operator's favour. But letting your money ride in a mutual fund over a decade or more can make you seriously rich.

From its launch in 1954 through to the end of June 2002, an investment in Templeton Growth produced an annual average compound return of 14.1 percent. If your granny had been prescient enough to put $10,000 into the fund when it was launched, instead of blowing all her dough on sports cars and wild men, it would have been worth $5.4 *million* by mid-2002.

The main reason why Canadians had more than $416 *billion* in mutual funds in mid-2002 is that funds let you make money in the stock and bond markets almost effortlessly. By the way, that $416-billion figure, which worked out to an incredible $13,900 or so for everyone in the country, doesn't even include billions more sitting in *segregated* funds, which are mutual fund–like products sold by life insurance companies. They're called segregated because they're kept separate from the life insurer's regular assets. You can read more on seg funds in Chapter 19.

Of course, there's no law that says you have to buy mutual funds in order to invest. You might make more money investing on your own behalf, and lots of people from all walks of life do. But it's tricky and dangerous. So millions of Canadians too busy or scared to learn the ropes themselves have found that funds are a wonderfully handy and reasonably cheap alternative. The Canadian fund industry association, the Investment Funds Institute of Canada, said in July 2002 that the public had 52.9 million accounts with its member firms. Buying funds is like going out to a restaurant compared with buying food, cooking a meal, and cleaning up afterward yourself. Yes, eating out is expensive, but it sure is nice not to have to face those cold pots in the sink covered in slowly congealing mustard sauce.

What mutual funds buy

There are really only two long-term investments that mutual funds and other investors put their money into:

- **Stocks and shares:** Tiny slices of companies that trade in a big, sometimes chaotic, but reasonably well-run electronic vortex called, yes, the stock market.
- **Bonds:** Loans made to governments or companies, which are packaged up so that investors can trade them to one another.

Folk memories run deep, and after ugly stock market meltdowns in the 1920s and 1970s, mutual funds and stocks in general had unhealthy reputations for many years. The same may happen after the great market slide of 2001 and 2002, but it's too early to say. Canadians, like people all over the world, for generations preferred to buy sure things, usually bonds or fixed-term deposits from banks, the beloved guaranteed investment certificate (GIC). But as inflation and interest rates started to come down in the 1990s, it became harder and harder to find a GIC that paid a decent rate of interest — most people are truly happy when they get 8 percent, research shows. As you can see from Table 1-1, the Canadian mutual fund industry really started growing like a magic mushroom on a wet morning in Victoria, B.C., in the mid-1990s, once rates on five-year GICs dropped well below that magic 8 percent. At that point, Canadians decided that they were willing to take a risk on equity funds. Table 1-1 shows the growth of the Canadian mutual fund industry from 1970 to mid-2002.

Table 1-1	Growth of the Mutual Fund Industry in Canada		
Year	*Total Assets ($Billions)*	*Year*	*Total Assets ($Billions)*
1970	2.5		
1971	2.5	1987	20.4
1972	2.7	1988	20.8
1973	2.2	1989	23.5
1974	1.6	1990	24.9
1975	1.8	1991	49.9
1976	1.8	1992	67.3
1977	1.8	1993	114.6
1978	1.9	1994	127.3
1979	2.7	1995	146.2
1980	3.6	1996	211.8
1981	3.5	1997	283.2
1982	4.1	1998	326.6
1983	5.8	1999	389.7
1984	6.7	2000	418.9
1985	10.2	2001	426.4
1986	17.5	2002 (June)	416.6

Industry statistics provided by The Investment Funds Institute of Canada.

Types of Funds

Mutual funds fall into four main categories. Later in the book there are chapters devoted to each type, but this is a quick breakdown. Here I'll give you just the bare facts. The four main types of mutual funds are:

- ✔ **Equity funds:** By far the most popular type of fund on the market, equity funds hold stocks and shares. Stocks are often called "equity" because every share is supposed to entitle its owner to an equal portion of the company. In June 2002 Canadians had $97 billion in Canadian stock funds, about the same in global stock funds, and another $29 billion in U.S. equity funds. These funds represent an investment in raw capitalism — ownership of businesses.

- ✔ **Balanced funds:** The next biggest category is balanced funds. They generally hold a mixture of just about everything — from Canadian and foreign stocks to bonds from all around the world, as well as very short-term bonds that are almost as safe as cash.

- ✔ **Bond funds:** These beauties essentially lend money to governments and big companies, collecting regular interest each year and (nearly always) getting the cash back in the end.

- ✔ **Money market funds:** They hold the least volatile and most stable of all investments — very short-term bonds that are issued by governments and large companies and usually provide the lowest returns. These funds are basically savings vehicles for money that you can't afford to take any risks with. They can also act as the safe little cushion of cash found in nearly all well-run portfolios.

Where-to-Buy Basics

In Chapter 3, I go into detail about some of the legal and bureaucratic form-filling-out involved in buying a fund (don't worry, it's not complicated). In essence, though, you hand over your money and a few days later you get a "transaction slip" or "confirmation slip" stating the number of units you bought and what price you paid. You can buy a mutual fund from thousands of people and places across Canada, but there are four basic ways to go about it.

- ✔ **Buying from professionals:** The most common method of making a fund purchase in Canada is to go to a stockbroker, financial planner, or other type of adviser who offers watery coffee, wisdom, and suggestions on what you should buy. These people will also open an account for you in which to hold your mutual funds. They are essentially salespeople and they nearly always make their living by collecting sales commissions on the funds they sell you, usually from the fund company itself. Their advice may be excellent and they can justifiably claim to impose needed discipline on their clients by getting them into the healthy habit of saving. But always remember that they have to earn a living: The funds they offer will tend to be the ones that pay them the best commissions. Examples of fund companies that sell exclusively through salespeople, planners, and stockbrokers are Mackenzie Financial Corp., Fidelity Investments Canada Ltd., AIM Funds Management Inc., CI Fund Management Inc., AGF Management Ltd., and Templeton, all based in Toronto. Investors Group Inc. of Winnipeg, Canada's biggest fund company, also sells through salespeople, but the sales force are all affiliated with the company.

✔ **Bank purchases:** The simplest way to buy funds is to walk into a bank, or call your bank's 1-800 number. Banks never charge sales commissions to investors who buy their funds. The disadvantage to this approach is limited selection, because most bank branches are set up to sell only their company's funds. And not all bank staff are equipped or trained to give you detailed advice about investing. But the beauty of this approach is that you can have all your money — including your savings and chequing accounts and even your mortgage or car loan — in one place, making it simple to transfer money from one account to another. Buying your mutual funds at your bank can also earn you special rates on loans.

✔ **Buying direct from fund companies:** For those who like to do more research on their own, there are excellent "no-load" companies that sell their funds directly to investors. They're called no-load funds because they're sold with no sales commissions. No-load funds can avoid levying sales charges because they don't market their wares through salespeople. Because these funds don't have to make payments to the advisers who sell them, they often come with lower expenses. Examples of no-load companies include Phillips Hager & North Ltd. of Vancouver, Altamira Investment Services Inc. of Toronto (which was bought by National Bank of Canada in 2002 but is still independently run), and McLean Budden Ltd. of Toronto. Once again, limited selection of funds is a drawback.

✔ **Buying from discount brokers:** Finally, for the real do-it-yourselfers who like to make just about every decision independently, there are discount brokers that operate over the phone or the Internet. Mostly but not always owned by the big banks, they sell every fund from nearly every company, usually free of commissions and sales pitches. Such *fund supermarkets* are a huge force in the United States and they've gained popularity in Canada. The advantages, and they're huge ones, are low costs and a wide selection of funds. But service from some big discount brokers has at times been spotty to pathetic, and horror stories abounded in late 1999 and early 2000 of investors who couldn't raise anyone on the phone to take orders or answer questions. Those problems seem to have been fixed, but don't expect lots of personal help or advice from a discounter.

So let's recap. You know what a mutual fund is, how it makes you money, the general types, and how to get your hands on some funds. It'll soon be time to dive in and start buying. In Chapter 2 we look a little closer at the things you should seek out and the things you should beware of.

Chapter 2

Buying and Selling Basics

. . . .

In This Chapter

▶ Exploring reasons to choose mutual funds

▶ Looking at potential drawbacks of funds

▶ Considering load versus no-load funds — the great divide

. . . .

A s 1999 drew to a close, business reporters in a dusty forgotten corner of the *Globe and Mail*'s newsroom were ordered to come up with retrospectives of the millennium. One of the themes to be considered was significant business inventions.

We agreed that mutual funds were one of the 20th century's great wealth-creating innovations. Funds have transformed stock and bond markets by giving people of modest means easy access to investments that were once limited to the rich. They are likely to continue for years, letting ordinary and not-so-ordinary people build their money in markets that would otherwise intimidate them. That's because the idea of packaging expert money management in a consumer product, which is then bought and sold in the form of units, is so brilliantly simple. Even journalists can understand it. In this chapter, we'll take another look at funds, assessing their great potential as well as their nasty faults. We'll wrap up with a chat about the great debate over no-load and load funds.

Reasons to Buy Funds

In Chapter 1, I discuss how and why mutual funds work and why they make sense in general. Here I'll give you some specific, significant reasons to make them a big part of your financial plan.

Public scrutiny and accountability — safety in numbers

Perhaps the best thing about mutual funds is that their performance is public knowledge. When you own a fund, you're in the same boat as thousands of other unitholders, meaning that there's pressure on the fund company to keep the performance up. If the fund lags its rivals for too long, unitholders will start *redeeming,* or cashing in their units, which is the sort of thing that makes a manager stare at the ceiling at 4 a.m., sweat rolling down his or her grey face. Fund companies are obliged to let the sun shine into their operations — and sunlight is the best disinfectant — by sending unitholders clear annual *financial statements* of the fund's operations at least once a year. These statements are tables of figures showing what the fund owns at the end of the year, what expenses and fees it paid to the management company, and how well it performed. Statements are audited (that is, checked) by big accounting firms. The management company must also at least offer to send you the semi-annual statements, showing how the fund was doing halfway through the year. (To get the semi-annual statement, you often have to mail back a fiddly little card requesting it. Make sure you do. It costs you nothing, and knowing that investors are interested in what's happening to their money helps to keep fund companies on their toes.) There's more on the financial statements for funds in Chapter 3. A lot of the information in the statements is hard to understand and not particularly useful, but there's one thing you should always check: Look at the fund's main holdings. If you bought what you thought was a conservative Canadian stock, for example, then you want to see lots of bank stocks and other companies that you've at least heard of.

Don't mix up the *financial statements* — which describe how the fund is doing — with your own individual *account statement.* Your account statements are personal mailings that show how many units you own, how many you've bought and sold, and how much your holdings are worth. Companies usually must send you personal account statements at least twice a year. Some fund sellers, such as banks, send quarterly statements, and discount brokers often mail them monthly. Many fund companies even have Internet-based and telephone-based services that let you verify the amount of money in your account every day. There's more on account statements in Chapter 3.

Returns for nearly every big fund are published once a month in the mutual fund reports of major newspapers. In the *Globe and Mail* it's on the third Wednesday of every month.

How often should you check your fund's performance? Unfortunately, there's no easy answer to this one. But it's a good idea to look every three months or so to see how your manager is doing. Even if you bought your funds through a financial planner or other salesperson — who's supposed to be looking out for your interest — it never hurts to keep an eye on how well the recommendations are turning out.

This next section helps you decipher monthly and daily mutual fund reports. When you know what to look for, you can accurately track your funds' performance. I'm not saying that your fund manager won't give you the straight story, but getting a second opinion is never a bad plan, especially when it comes to your cash.

How to read a monthly mutual fund report

Figure 2-1 is a sample from the *Globe and Mail*'s monthly report showing the returns for the Templeton Growth Fund. The first thing to note is that funds that buy the same sorts of investments are listed together. We know that Templeton Growth invests in stocks in just about every country, so it's listed under the "global equity" category along with other funds that do the same thing. There's a separate group for funds that concentrate on Canadian stocks, or science and technology companies, and so on.

Rating	Fund name	RRSP RRIF	Assets ($M)	NAVPS	Dist.	MER	Fees	Percentage return 1mo	3mo	1yr	3yr	5yr	10yr
	Keystone Prem Glo Elite 100 Cp	F	5.4	5.91		2.00m	O	-7.0	-17.5	-22.6	-	-	-
	Keystone Premier Glo Elite 100	F		2.72		2.00m	O	-6.8	-17.2	-21.9	-	-	-
	Keystone Prem RSP Gl Elite 100	R		2.89		2.00m	O	-6.7	-17.2	-22.3	-	-	-
★★★★	Keystone Reg Max Equity Growth	R		60.58		0.10m	O	-5.7	-9.1	-6.1	1.5	-	-
★★	Laketon Global Equity	N	41.3	133.19	1.169		N	-6.4	-16.8	-20.4	-10.0	-3.5	-
	London Life Foreign Equ (MF)	F	12.4	10.09		3.02	R	-6.3	-8.8	-	-	-	-
★★	♣London Life Global Equ (MX)	F	45.7	8.61		3.28	R	-7.3	-16.9	-24.0	-7.8	-	-
★★★	♣London Life Global Equity (L)	F	184.2	8.71		2.91	R	-5.9	-12.4	-13.5	-6.8	-	-
	London Life Global Equ Profile	F	3.4	9.02		3.27	R	-6.8	-14.4	-	-	-	-
★★★★★	Templeton Global Smaller Co.	F	393.9	14.85		2.80	O	-3.4	-0.7	12.9	10.5	7.6	12.6
★★★★	Templeton Growth Fund Ltd.	F	8724.9	9.68		2.21	O	-6.9	-10.0	-6.5	-0.6	2.8	10.0
★★★★	Templeton Growth GIF	F	95.9	5.83		2.65	O	-7.0	-10.2	-7.0	-1.1	-	-
★★★★	Templeton Growth RSP	R	442.5	4.57		2.25	O	-7.1	-10.2	-7.7	-	-	-
	Templeton Growth Tax Class	F	54.5	4.71		2.01	O	-6.9	-9.9	-6.2	-	-	-
★★★★	♣Tradex Global Equity	F	4.2	8.74		3.24	N	-6.8	-5.9	-7.9	-0.6	-	-
	Trans AGF Int Value GIF 75/100	R	2.2	4.44		3.67m	O	-11.1	-14.8	-	-	-	-
	Trans AGF Intl Value GIF 75/75	R	1.6	4.45		3.27m	O	-11.1	-14.7	-	-	-	-
	Trans CI Global 75/100	R	0.1	4.67		3.37m	O	-4.2	-10.9	-	-	-	-
	Trans CI Global 75/75	R	0.1	4.67		2.92m	O	-4.2	-10.8	-	-	-	-
	Trans Fid Intl Port 75/100	R	0.5	4.61		3.27m	O	-5.7	-12.3	-	-	-	-
	Trans Fid Intl Port 75/75	R	0.4	4.67		2.82m	O	-5.6	-11.9	-	-	-	-
	Trans TOP Glo Mgr Port 75/100	R	1.7	4.63		3.52m	O	-7.6	-12.5	-	-	-	-
	Trans TOP Glo Mgr Port 75/75	R	1.8	4.69		3.22m	O	-7.5	-12.4	-	-	-	-
	Trans TOP Glo Mgr Port 100/100	R	4.2	4.68		3.67m	O	-7.6	-12.5	-	-	-	-
	Trident Global Opportunities	F	31.2	105.84		2.25m	O	-1.4	-0.7	-0.3	6.9	-	-
★★★★★	Trimark Global - DSC	F	490.9	32.30		2.62	D	-5.6	-7.4	-	-	-	-
★★★★★	Trimark Fund - SC	F	3622.2	31.27		1.63	F	-5.5	-7.2	7.9	9.8	9.1	15.4
★★★★★	Trimark RSP Select Growth	R	972.4	5.37		2.46	O	-5.8	-7.7	5.9	-	-	-
★★★★★	Trimark Select Growth	F	6278.8	16.92		2.43	O	-5.8	-7.5	7.1	8.9	8.1	13.7
	Trimark Select Growth Class	F	140.8	10.21		2.50	O	-6.0	-7.9	5.5	-	-	-
★★★★★	Trimark Select Gwth Seg (AIG)	F	51.8	7.06		4.26	O	-5.9	-7.9	5.1	7.9	-	-
★★★	University Avenue World	F	1.9	8.36		2.75	O	-6.4	-8.0	-21.4	-0.7	-	-
	Wickham ETF	F	0.3	8.45		2.50	F	-7.9	-18.7	-	-	-	-
★★★	Zurich Clarington Global Eqt	F	2.5	10.11		3.63	D	-7.1	-13.7	-14.4	-	-	-
★★★	Zurich International Equ Index	F	0.9	7.45		2.98	D	-4.6	-7.6	-12.1	-9.2	-	-
★★★	Zurich Scudder Global	F	0.5	8.44		3.63	D	-6.3	-12.0	-16.6	-	-	-
■ HIGHEST IN GROUP						4.93		3.8	12.7	13.7	18.7	23.4	15.4
■ MEDIAN IN GROUP						2.84		-6.5	-11.9	-15.0	-5.4	0.8	7.8
■ AVERAGE IN GROUP						2.84		-6.5	-11.7	-14.0	-3.9	1.7	8.1
■ LOWEST IN GROUP						0.17		-12.7	-22.2	-36.3	-20.9	-11.4	-7.6

Figure 2-1: An extract from the *Globe*'s monthly fund report, showing returns for global equity funds.

In the first column on the left, there are usually between one and five stars. These stars indicate how good the fund's return has been, taking risk into account, compared with the performance of similar funds. Five stars is good and one star is bad. This is a handy way of seeing at a glance how the fund has done in comparison with the funds in its group or category — but there's no guarantee that a fund manager's hot streak will continue. After the column showing the fund's name, there's a letter indicating what the fund's status is in registered retirement savings plans (RRSPs), registered retirement income funds (RRIFs), and similar tax-deferred savings schemes. These are special accounts used for retirement savings, in which your investment income and capital gains pile up tax-free. Contributions to the plans can also be used to create a tax deduction. The money in the plan is usually taxable as income when you take it out, though. In other words, the plans let you defer or postpone paying taxes. Because the federal government provides such generous tax breaks for RRSPs and other tax-deferred plans, it requires that most of the investments held in the plan be Canadian. That way, the bulk of the money stays in Canada. In the *Globe*'s listing, an **R** in the RRSP/RRIF column means the fund is 100-percent eligible — that is, it counts as Canadian content for your RRSP. An **F** means that it counts as foreign content. An **N** indicates a rare fund whose structure or investment goals means it legally can't be put into your RRSP. There's more on RRSPs in Chapter 24.

Then come columns showing the fund's assets in millions of dollars, its unit price or net asset value per share at the end of the latest calendar month, any distributions paid in the latest month, and the annual *MER (management expense ratio)*.

The management expense ratio is one of the most important concepts in mutual fund investing and it's a subject we'll be returning to over and over in this book. That's because the lower the management expense ratio, the more money you're likely to make in the fund. The MER simply means the total in management fees and expenses charged by the fund's management company. For example, the typical Canadian equity fund carries a yearly management fee of 2 percent — that's the fee levied by the management company for going to the trouble of organizing, selling, and running the fund. In other words, the company helps itself to 2 percent of the fund's assets each year, whether unitholders have made any money or not. But nearly all fund companies also make their funds pay a bunch of legal, bookkeeping, and general administrative expenses. They're tacked onto the management fee to give you the management expense ratio. In the case of Canadian equity funds, the average fund has an MER of 2.6 percent.

What can you do with this jumble of numbers? The unit price is useful information because by multiplying the price by the number of units you own, you can work out the value of your holdings. You can also make sure that the unit price in the newspaper matches the price shown on the statement you get from your broker or fund company, in order to double-check their bookkeeping. Keep the newspaper's mutual fund reports for June 30 and December 31 in your little sequined satchel until you've done your checking, because you'll be getting reports from your fund company showing the value of your holdings as of those dates.

The unit price is also handy if you're hazy on which fund you actually own. Don't laugh — a lot of smart people aren't always sure. With more than 4,800 funds, versions of funds, and fund-like products available in Canada, it's easy to get confused. With many international equity funds, for example, there are four different versions on sale: the plain fund, the U.S.–dollar version, the "guaranteed" version that promises under certain circumstances not to lose you any of your original investment, and the "RSP" or "clone" version that counts as Canadian content for RRSPs even though it's a foreign fund. If your account statement shows you own a fund whose unit price is $10.95, for instance, and the newspaper reports the same price, chances are you're talking about the same fund.

After the management expense ratio, the letter in the next column indicates what sort of sales commissions are imposed when you buy the fund. There's more on that subject later in this chapter. Don't worry — it's perfectly possible to invest in excellent funds without wading through the tangled details of sales charges. Just for the record, here's what the letters mean — along with one word of warning. Mutual fund companies and insurers use so many confusing terms, many of which mean almost the same thing, when they're talking about commissions that you shouldn't take these letters as gospel. Always check thoroughly to see what sort of sales charge — known as a sales "load" — you're on the hook for.

- ✔ **N — No load:** No sales fees — bank funds and funds from no-load companies such as Altamira Investment Services Inc., which sell directly to the public, fall into this group.

- ✔ **F — Front-end load:** A commission is payable when you buy the fund.

- ✔ **D — Deferred load:** A commission is due when you sell the fund, but it usually declines to zero over a number of years.

- ✔ **O — Optional:** You choose between a front-end load and a deferred load — most funds sold by brokers and financial planners fall into this group.

- ✔ **R — Redemption fee:** A fee is payable when you sell the fund — unusual.

- ✔ **B — Both:** Usually includes a front-end load and a deferred load — also unusual.

At last we get to the meat of the subject. The next columns of the *Globe*'s fund report show the fund's performance over one month and three months, and then provide annual returns over one, three, five, and ten years.

These returns are after the fund's fees and expenses have been deducted. There are some exceptions to this practice in the monthly report — that is, funds that levy extra charges that reduce the performance shown — but the returns for all of the biggest companies are after charges. The companies that deduct fees and expenses *after* the returns shown in the paper are generally fund companies that sell funds as part of a comprehensive financial package. Clients get a customized statement that lists their fees separately, instead of lumping the charges in with the fund's overall return. Always check whether the returns you're being shown are before or after the deduction of all charges and costs.

Remember that the report lists funds together if they have a similar investment objective. At the bottom of the listings for each fund category is another useful set of data: The performance of the average, best, worst, and median funds in the group. You can use it to see if your fund has been a sumo wrestler or a weak sister.

There's another handy feature in the *Globe*'s report — when a fund's return for a particular period is above the average, the number is shown in bold, letting you scan quickly for strong performers. Always remember, though, that a fund may have what looks like a strong long-term record but its performance could easily have been inflated by one short hot run. See Chapter 10 about equity funds for a more in-depth discussion of this topic.

The difference between the average and the median

Sometimes figuring out whether a fund has done better than other funds in its group is harder than it looks. When you look at a newspaper fund report, you'll come across two terms used to describe the typical fund's performance: The *average* and the *median*. The average and the median are both numbers that attempt to show how funds in a particular category have done. That way, if you're interested in a fund you can compare its performance with that of its rivals. For example, if you're considering buying your bank's U.S. equity fund, it's a good idea to see how it has done compared with other funds in the U.S. equity category. However, sometimes the average can be distorted upward or downward by a few extreme cases, so the median acts as a middle-point, giving a good idea of what the typical return for funds was. Here's how it works:

✔ The **average** is calculated by simply adding up the return figures for all funds for a particular period and then dividing by the number of funds involved.

✔ The **median** is the halfway mark. Half of the funds fell below that point and half were above.

Normally, the two numbers are very similar, but a sprinkling of very high or low returns in the sample can pull them apart. Let's look at an extreme example: labour-sponsored venture capital funds, a volatile type of fund that's supposed to invest in tiny companies. In 1999, the average labour fund in Canada made 17.9 percent but the median return was only 4.7 percent. Why the huge difference? Because the average was pumped up by enormous returns — as high as 99.1 percent — from a handful of funds that happened to ride some red-hot little shares. But most funds didn't do nearly so well and, in fact, half of them made less than 4.7 percent.

How to read a daily fund report

Every day that stock and bond markets are open, most mutual funds calculate and publish a value for their units. Some small or very specialized funds do this only monthly or weekly, and some take a day or two getting the information out to the newspapers, but a unit price for most widely available funds appears the next day in major newspapers. The listing also usually shows the change in unit price from the previous day. See Figure 2-2 for a Saturday listing for Templeton Growth from the *Globe*.

fund	latest value	dollar chg	% chg	weekly high	low	% chg
FRNKLN TMPLTN - TEMPLETON C$						
Balanced	7.82	+.01	+.13	7.90	7.81	-2.37
Cdn Asset All	6.82	+.01	+.15	6.89	6.80	-2.57
Cdn Asset All-T	13.30	+.02	+.15	13.44	13.26	-2.49
Cdn Stock	8.90	+.03	+.34	9.02	8.84	-3.58
Emerg Mkt	6.68	-.05	-.74	6.93	6.68	-4.30
Emerg Mkt RSP	3.69	-.03	-.81	3.83	3.69	-4.40
Glo Bal	6.35	-.02	-.31	6.40	6.34	-2.31
Glo Bal RSP	4.45	-.01	-.22	4.48	4.44	-2.20
Glo Bond	9.55	-.01	-.10	9.57	9.50	+1.17
Glo Sm Co RSP	5.21	-.02	-.38	5.28	5.20	-2.80
Glo Small	13.51	-.06	-.44	13.69	13.50	-2.81
Growth	8.75	-.04	-.46	8.83	8.73	-3.63
Growth RSP	4.13	-.02	-.48	4.17	4.13	-3.73
Int'l Stock	13.01	-.13	-.99	13.36	12.98	-5.59
Int'l Stock RSP	3.75	-.04	-1.06	3.85	3.74	-5.54
Int'l Stock-T	12.61	-.13	-1.02	12.95	12.58	-5.61
FRNKLN TMPLTN - TEMPLETON U$						
Emerg Mkt U$	4.22	-.05	-1.17	4.40	4.22	-7.05
Glo Bal U$	4.01	-.04	-.99	4.12	4.01	-5.20
Glo Bond U$	6.03	-.04	-.66	6.11	6.03	-1.79
Glo Small U$	8.53	-.09	-1.04	8.80	8.53	-5.64
Growth U$	5.52	-.06	-1.08	5.68	5.52	-6.60
Int'l Stock U$	8.21	-.14	-1.68	8.59	8.21	-8.37
FRONT STREET CAPITAL						
Casurine PF 07/25	16.84	-1.74	-9.36	16.84	16.84	—
Multiple Opp	1.86	-.07	-3.46	2.03	1.86	-10.5
Special Opp	1.37	-.08	-5.19	1.51	1.37	-10.2
GBC FUNDS						
Bond 07/23	11.45	+.12	+1.06	11.45	11.45	—

Figure 2-2: A Saturday mutual fund listing from the *Globe*.

It shows the price and change from the previous day in terms of cents and percentage, but the Saturday listing also includes some bonus information: It gives the percentage change in unit price from the previous week, plus the high and low price the units set during the week just passed. In Chapter 22 I'll show you how you can use numerous Web resources to track how your fund is doing so far this year, this month, and so on.

Putting your eggs in many baskets

Another good reason to buy mutual funds is the fact they instantly mitigate your risk by letting you own lots of stocks and bonds, ideally in many different markets. *Diversification,* spreading your dollars around, is the cornerstone of successful investing. Diversifying means you won't be slaughtered by a collapse in the price of one or two shares.

Some people learn about diversification the hard way. Investors think they've lucked into the next big thing, hand over their entire fortune, and then lose it all in a cruel market correction. Pinning your hopes on just one stock or handful of stocks is never a wise move, so don't let this happen to you.

Mutual funds let ordinary investors buy into faraway markets and assets. It would be difficult and expensive for most ordinary people to purchase shares in Asia or Europe, or bonds issued by Latin American governments (go easy on those, though), if they couldn't buy them through mutual funds. In recent years, markets everywhere have tended to go up and down in unison, driven by the Great American Interest Rate Outlook. But history demonstrates that a portfolio with lots of different and varied asset classes will tend to suffer fewer speed bumps.

Most equity mutual funds own shares in at least 50 companies — fund managers who try to go with more "concentrated" portfolios have been known to get their fingers burned. In fact, academic research suggests that only seven stocks may be enough to provide adequate diversification for an investor, but seeing dozens of names in a portfolio offers a lot more reassurance.

Good returns from professional management

One of the most entertaining and informative books ever written on the subject of investing is *A Fool and His Money: The Odyssey of an Average Investor* by John Rothchild. First published in 1988, the book describes Mr. Rothchild's own abject failure in the market and includes his observation that most amateur investors are less than frank about how they've actually done. Even if they've had their heads handed to them, they tend to claim that they ended up "about even." The moral of the story: Even if your relatives and pals claim to have made a fortune in the market, treat their boasts with a goodly dose of skepticism.

Yes, bad funds abound. But chances are that you'll do better in a mutual fund than you would investing on your own. At least the people running funds are professionals who readily dump a stock when it turns sour, instead of hanging on like grim death, as we amateurs tend to do. The habit of selling quickly and taking the loss while it's still small is said to be one of the main traits that distinguishes the pro from the amateur.

Easy does it — funds are convenient

Funds are just so darned handy, it's no wonder hundreds of millions of people around the world buy them. Yes, you could make your own lip balm. You could gather the eucalyptus bark and the deer's eyelid secretions, and boil them up in a big copper pot for days while chanting your head off. But it's easier just to walk into the drugstore and buy a stick. Likewise, it's a snap to sign a cheque or let the fund company deduct cash from your bank account regularly — a lot easier than worrying about the market and finding out the difference between investing in a long-dated strip bond and an exciting newly listed Internet solutions startup with scalable technology. Critics of funds claim, with some justification, that the industry has brainwashed members of the public into thinking they're too stupid to invest for themselves. And it does seem fund companies want us to believe that it's necessary to have some 25-year-old pup in a suit do it for us, in return for a fat fee. But the reality is that most people are just too busy, confused, or plain lazy to figure out the investing game. This book will make you an educated fund investor, whether you choose to deal with that young pup or go it alone. In Chapter 4, I list a few sample portfolios that are about as easy to buy as a candy bar, and a lot better for you.

Why dollar-cost averaging may be a fairy tale

Pick up nearly any fund company's colourful and relentlessly upbeat brochure (they're written by chipmunks and tiny bluebirds that are cruelly force-fed a diet of snack cakes and fuchsia blossoms). Just before you pass out with boredom, you'll almost certainly see a phrase along these lines: "Investing small amounts regularly means you buy more units when prices are low and fewer units when they're high, reducing the average cost of the units you purchase." Well, maybe. But that's about as useful as saying it's a bad idea to go up to muscular guys in Sudbury, Ontario, and imitate them in a mocking, mincing way. Sort of obvious. The industry even has a name for the strategy — dollar-cost averaging.

Don't get me wrong: Putting small amounts into a decently run mutual fund over many years is a great way to build wealth. But independent researchers are skeptical as to whether dollar-cost averaging actually means better returns. If the strategy worked, you'd expect it to produce the best results with volatile funds — those whose unit prices bounce around the most — because you'd be buying lots when they were in the dumps and very few when they were riding high. In 1999, Chicago-based researcher Ibbotson Associates, famed for compiling widely used figures on investment returns, looked at ten pairs of funds with the same compound annual returns over a decade but very different volatility. Even using the fund industry's beloved dollar-cost averaging strategy, the less volatile fund produced the better return, seven out of ten times. So invest small amounts regularly, because it's a great way to grow your money. But don't assume you're getting units at bargain basement prices. The evidence seems to be that the best way to make money in the stock and bond markets is simply to invest your cash as early as possible — and let time and compound returns work their magic.

Funds offer a lot of convenience. The company keeps your money safe, handles the record-keeping for your savings, and deals with dreary stuff such as checking that your RRSP doesn't have too much foreign content. Most fund companies get you to nominate a Canadian fund that is used as a spillover tank if your non-Canadian assets exceed their limit. Some of your foreign fund units are simply redeemed and put into the Canadian fund instead. It all leaves you free and clear to get on with your first love, naked samba dancing.

Investing without breaking the bank

As I mentioned above, the typical Canadian stock fund rakes off about 2.6 percent of your money each year in fees and costs. That's a hefty charge, but the fund company also relieves you of a lot of drudgery and tiresome paperwork in return.

Mutual funds are a positive bargain if you're just starting to invest. Quite a few companies will let you put as little as $500 into their funds, and you can often open up a regular investment plan — where the money is simply taken out of your bank account — for as little as $50 a month. That's a pretty good deal when you realize that fund companies actually lose money on small accounts. If an investor has, say, $1,000 in an equity fund with a management expense ratio of 2.6 percent, then the company is collecting only $26 in fees and expenses, barely enough to cover postage and administration costs, let alone turn a profit. Even the cheapest "discount" stockbroker in Canada will let you do only one trade for about 25 bucks. The costs of a mutual fund investment are buried in the MER and the relatively incomprehensible statement of operations, but at least you can work them out with a bit of digging. Try asking traditional full-service stockbrokers for a clear explanation of their commission rates. You'll get a lot of mumbling and long sentences containing the phrase "it depends," but no clear answers.

Not for your eyes only — tight surveillance

Mutual fund companies are pretty closely watched, not only by overworked provincial securities regulators but also, believe it or not, by rival companies. Competing companies don't want a rotten peach spoiling the reputation of the whole barrel. The Investment Funds Institute of Canada (IFIC), the industry lobby group, is a mouthpiece for the companies, naturally. But it also generally keeps an eye on things. And Toronto, where most of the industry is based, is a village where everyone knows everyone. You'd be surprised how many industry executives tell reporters about skullduggery *off the record* — always about competing fund sellers, of course. Yes, greed abounds. Fees are too high, reporting to unitholders is often vague to useless, salespeople are given goodies, and funds are sometimes used as a horn of plenty when managers divert their trading, and the resulting flow of commissions, to their brokerage buddies. But most companies are simply making too much money honestly to risk it all by running scams.

The stocks and bonds a fund buys with your money don't even stay in the coffers of the fund company: Under provincial securities laws, the actual assets of the fund must be held by a separate "custodian," usually a big bank or similar institution. You're most likely to get swindled by your salesperson, but in Chapter 8 I set out some of the best ways to protect yourself. Just stick with regular mutual funds, those that come with a document called a "simplified prospectus" and are managed by an IFIC member, and you should be okay.

Cashing out — getting your money if you need it

If you decide to move your hard-earned cash out of a fund, your fund company will normally have a cheque in the mail to you within three days. Getting your money out of a fund effortlessly whenever you like may not seem like a big deal — but in the world of investing, being able to do so whenever you want to, with no hassles or questions, is as good as a torrid fling with Leonardo DiCaprio or Shania Twain, your choice. No, not both, you greedy beast.

Don't forget that lots of other investments, including guaranteed investment certificates, hit you with a penalty if you take your cash out early. Selling a stock invariably costs you a brokerage commission and there's no guarantee you'll get a decent price for your shares. Sell a bond and you're often at the mercy of your dealer, who can pluck a price out of the air.

Perils and Pitfalls of Funds

So now that you're convinced that funds are the right place to be, I'm going to throw you for a bit of a loop. An informed investor is a wealthy investor, after all, and it's important to realize that funds aren't perfect. None of these disadvantages means you shouldn't buy mutual funds. But keeping them in mind will help you stay out of overpriced and unsuitable investments.

Excessive costs

Once you start amassing serious money in mutual funds, your costs can get outrageous. For example, if you invest $100,000 in a set of typical equity funds with a management expense ratio of 2.6 percent, the fund company is siphoning off $2,600 of your money every year. The math gets truly chilling when you extrapolate the cost of management fees over long periods. Over 20 years, at an MER of 2.6 percent, the fund company will end up with an incredible 52 percent or so of the total accumulated capital. How so? Simply by slicing that little 2.6 percent off the top each year.

In a study done for discount broker E*Trade Canada, Chris Robinson, an associate business professor and expert on personal financial planning at Toronto's York University, looked at the question of when it becomes cheaper to invest in a well-diversified basket of stocks through E*Trade rather than buy a mutual fund with (relatively low) total annual expenses of 2 percent. He found that depending on the number of stock trades each year, an investor with a portfolio as small as $60,000 could reduce his or her annual expenses by investing directly in stocks rather than funds. However, he also found that low-cost *index funds* with MERs of only 0.5 percent or so — such as those from Altamira Investment Services Inc. — seem to be the cheaper way to go until a portfolio gets up to $100,000 or more. Index funds are funds with low expenses that simply track the whole stock or bond market by producing a return in line with a market index, such as the Standard & Poor's/Toronto Stock Exchange index of just under 300 well-known companies. There's more on index funds in Chapter 15.

Style drift — when managers get lost in the jungle

It always makes me think of doomed forgotten schooners, listlessly floating on remote seas, but this is a mutual fund failing that can cost you thousands of dollars. It happens when managers *drift* or depart from the type of investments they told you they'd buy when you signed on, usually because they're chasing hot returns or because they're scared. The problem is that it's often difficult or impossible to get up-to-date information on what is actually in your fund. Some companies post reasonably current holdings on their Web sites — more on that in Chapter 22 — but your only legal entitlement to a full list of all of the portfolio holdings is when the company sends you annual and semi-annual financial statements for the fund. And they normally don't arrive until weeks after December 31 or June 30.

Sometimes the drift is a matter of opinion: In early 2000, quite a few Canadian funds with "value" in their name held lots of shares in soaring Nortel Networks Corp., even though Nortel was trading at an incredible 100 times its projected earnings over the next year (it subsequently crashed from record highs of more than $120 to less than $2 in 2002). In saner times, a manager who promised to buy "value" stocks was supposed to seek out beaten-up pipeline shares and the like, but managers in recent years have claimed to have discovered "new value" rules that apparently let them buy a stock at whatever price they like.

Just because a fund has a word like "value" in its name, don't rest assured that your fund manager is seeking out only investments that fall under that category. Always be on the look for drifting — ultimately, it's your responsibility to make sure you're headed in the right direction.

When bad managers attack

They may be smart and they may be professionals, but fund managers sure can blow it, leaving behind nothing but a lot of little scraps of grey polyester and a bunch of ugly minus signs in front of their returns. Put down whatever you're eating — what you're about to see would make a 400-pound wild boar queasy — and have a look at Table 2-1. It shows some of the worst-performing Canadian equity and Canadian large-company equity funds in the 1990s, with assets over $50 million. If you hung around with any of these lads for the whole of the decade, you missed out on a lot of fun. (The figures for mutual fund returns in this book are from www.globefund.com, the *Globe and Mail*'s mutual fund Web site, or from Globe HySales, a mutual fund database that the *Globe* sells to mutual fund salespeople.)

Table 2-1	Slow Lane: Canadian Equity Underperformers in the Ten Years to June 2002 % Returns		
Fund Name	**1-Year Return**	**5-Year Annual Return**	**10-Year Annual Return**
Canada Life Canadian Equity	−17.9	−1.3	6
Mackenzie Growth	23.6	−0.2	6.6
Elliott & Page Equity	−16.4	−1.6	6.7
Scotia Canadian Blue Chip	−10.1	2.9	6.7
CIBC Core Canadian Equity	−8.1	3.1	7
Renaissance Canadian Growth	−11.6	1.2	7.4
National Bank Canadian Equity	−7.8	0.7	7.5
Ethical Growth	−5.1	−0.1	7.6
Average Canadian equity fund	**−4.2**	**3.6**	**9.3**
S&P/TSX total return	**−6.1**	**3.7**	**9.9**

It's very rarely as terrifying as that, though. Companies usually replace managers of big funds after just a couple of years of bad performance. Having a decent Canadian equity fund, in particular, is a marquee attraction for a company. It's the fund category carrying the most prestige, partly because it wins the most attention from the media. You can be sure that just about every manager running a large equity or balanced fund, Canadian or global, is working his or her silk socks off trying to top the performance league. Every so often, companies get in bidding wars for managers with a great reputation. So everyone running a fund is trying to get public notice for earning hot returns, because it increases his or her market value.

Can't see the forest for the funds

By mid-2002, Canada had an unbelievable 4,881 funds and fund-like products, counting U.S.-dollar editions, different versions with varying sales charges, and "guaranteed" funds with endlessly changing small print. There were funds that could be traded without racking up taxable capital gains, "market-neutral" funds that were supposed to shake off the effects of a bad stock market, funds that stuck to the safe and predictable world of Internet companies, and funds that really didn't seem to have any very good reason for existing, to be honest. Table 2-2 tells the tale of this proliferation. The figures are from the Investment Funds Institute of Canada, the fund industry trade group, which offers a raft of statistics at its Web site, www.ific.ca.

Table 2-2	The Number of Mutual Funds Exploded from 1990–2002
Year	*Number of Funds*
1990	539
1991	580
1992	716
1993	840
1994	1,127
1995	1,283
1996	1,563
1997	1,886
1998	2,443
1999	3,057
2000	3,765

Year	Number of Funds
2001	4,685
2002 (June)	4,881

There are several reasons for this ridiculous profusion of products:

✔ Fund companies have learned the folly of relying too much on just one or two funds. The danger, for them, is that if performance goes in the tank then investors head for the door, pulling out tens of millions of dollars. Better to offer many varied funds so that if one turns cold, the others are still cooking.

✔ Like acting, the fund business is, well, glamorous, and everyone wants in. But unlike pulling on the black tights, running a mutual fund is also profitable. Once a fund company can get its assets above $100 million or so, it's difficult to lose money because those 2-percent management fees keep rolling in. And all sorts of newcomers have been coming into the fund industry, including insurance companies and even financial planning chains. But they love to offer their own house-brand funds because they get to keep all of the fees instead of splitting the take with a separate name-brand fund company such as Mackenzie Financial Corp. or AGF Management Ltd. Clients are often happier with a name they've heard of, though, so insurance companies have taken to hiring well-known mutual fund companies as managers of their funds. However, the fund remains the insurance company's own product — and the insurer gets to keep the lion's share of the management fee.

✔ The investment game, with its hype and image obsession, is essentially a branch of showbiz. Every year you have something new to keep the salespeople awake and the investors hungry.

✔ Finally, in fairness to the industry, some of the new funds are meant to satisfy consumers' demands. After Canadian stocks dismally lagged U.S. and overseas shares in 1998, for example, there was a hunger for foreign funds that count as Canadian for RRSPs, so the industry obliged with newfangled clone funds. There's more on this type of fund in Chapter 20.

Vague explanations of poor performance — oh yes, we always report in Aztec rope language

No matter how badly a fund did, the analysis given to investors is frequently a languid description of the stock or bond market and a few of the manager's choice reflections on the future of civilization. All written in a sort of Old

Etonian detached and refined tone, as thought the person running the fund was really just dabbling, old chap. Don't really have to work at all, don't-you-know, what with the estate in Scotland and the trust funds. Only really drop by the office for half an hour every two weeks or so, dash it all. Damn busy with the golf and usually comatose by 5 p.m.

What unitholders deserve, but too often are denied, is an honest discussion of whether their fund kept up with the market and its peers. Securities regulators are putting the squeeze on companies to improve their reports, but it'll take time. You shouldn't have to pull on a grubby deerstalker hat and smoke a smelly pipe to discover what went wrong with performance and what the manager plans to do about it.

In the meantime, if your fund lags the market and other funds in the same category, ask for a clear explanation from your broker or financial planner if you got advice when buying funds. If you bought a no-load fund, you should get a written set of reasons in the company's regular mailings to unitholders. Because no-load companies deal directly with their investors — instead of going through a salesperson — their reports are often clearer than the information provided by companies that market their funds through advisers.

Another big problem in the reporting of performance is that all too often it's not at all clear who is actually running your fund and how long they've been doing it. Fund companies rarely, if ever, print the length of a manager's tenure, and they usually don't warn investors in a timely way if he or she quits or is fired. Yes, there are a few veteran managers who've been running the same fund for years. And some companies such as Fidelity Investments Canada Ltd. make it reasonably plain who's actually calling the shots. But at many companies, managers come and go with such unpredictable frequency that it's difficult if not impossible to keep track of them. Rather than worry about finding a genius to pick your stocks, you're much better off looking at the fund itself. Make your decision about investing with an eye to how the fund has performed and what it currently holds, rather than trying to figure out who is in the top spot.

Getting a report card — did you keep up with the market?

It's often hard to tell from a company's promotional handouts, and even from its official reports to unitholders, whether the returns from its funds have been any good. That's because most companies, incredibly, still don't show their performance against an appropriate market benchmark, such as the Standard & Poor's/Toronto Stock Exchange composite index (S&P/TSX) for

Canadian equity funds or the Morgan Stanley Capital International World index for global equity funds. There are some honourable standouts: For years, Altamira Investment Services Inc. has compared its returns with those of the market in general. And things have gotten better with the fund industry's new generation of *prospectuses*. A prospectus is the document that must be given to the purchasers of a fund, describing its rules and risks. The new prospectuses must compare a fund with a benchmark, such as the S&P/TSX for Canadian equity funds. The new breed, which started coming out in 2000, are still of only limited usefulness because they don't say *why* the fund has lagged or outperformed its benchmark. The new prospectuses also give the fund's returns on a calendar year-by-year basis, which is invaluable for checking whether unitholders have enjoyed steady returns or suffered through insane swings. If you're trying to compare a fund's performance with that of the broad market, check your newspaper's monthly mutual fund listings. Fortunately, the newspapers print a set of benchmark returns each month that can help you decide whether a fund is a star or a schnauzer.

Too many funds and too few long-term results

Fund managers love to talk about how investing is a long-term game, especially when they're losing money, but have you noticed how many ads you see touting performance over periods as short as one year? And companies seem unable to resist launching new funds that invest in the hottest new asset class — just in time to lose money for investors when the bubble bursts. It happened with resources and emerging markets in the 1990s, and in 2000 it happened again with science and technology funds. By late 2000, there were more than 120 technology funds and new versions of existing technology funds. Did Canadians really need that many? They arguably didn't need any of the wretched things: Most tech funds lost at least 34 percent in 2001 and then fell an average 35.5 percent in the first half of 2002, leaving the category with an average three-year annual loss of 21.8 percent.

It's easy to get dizzy amid the flashing lights and loud music, and jump aboard the fund industry's carousel of new products. But steer clear of the fancy stuff and stick to plain old conservative equity and bond funds with your serious long-term money, and you'll end up ahead. In Chapter 27, I talk about gimmick funds and list the sort of funds you should beware of.

Load versus No-Load — The Great Divide

There are two main ways to buy mutual funds:

- ✔ **Through a professional seller:** You can get a salesperson such as a broker or financial planner to help. The broker has to earn a living so you'll almost certainly end up buying load funds — a load is a sales charge or commission that's paid to the broker, either by you or by the fund company.

- ✔ **Going it alone:** You can pick your funds on your own, with perhaps some advice from a bank staffer or mutual fund employee. In that case, you'll often end up buying *no-load* funds, which don't levy a sales commission.

Grey areas abound. You can buy *load* funds on your own and pay no commissions (through a discount broker, which will provide little or no advice). Some brokers will sell you no-load funds or load funds on which they waive commissions. And banks can fall in between the two stools. But those are the two essential methods.

Load funds — the comfort zone

Most mutual funds in Canada are sold to investors by a salesperson who is in turn paid by way of a sales commission. Millions of people love the feeling of having an advocate and adviser who seems to know his or her way through the jungle of investing. And why not hire a professional? After all, you probably don't fix your plumbing yourself or remove your own appendix (too hard to get the stains out of the kitchen tiles).

Your adviser might work for a stockbroker, a financial planning firm, or an insurance brokerage — or he or she might be self-employed. But the important point is this: If you buy funds through a salesperson, your primary relationship is with them, not the fund company.

Any fund company should be able to answer your questions about your account and you should always make sure you get a regular account statement from the fund company itself (unless you're with one of the big stockbrokers; the big brokers usually handle all of the record-keeping). But load companies, such as Mackenzie Financial Corp. and Fidelity Investments Canada, won't even sell you funds directly. You have to open an account with a broker or planner, who will then put the order through for you. The companies' systems and much of their marketing are designed to deal with salespeople, not members of the public, so your buy and sell orders must come from your broker.

Table 2-3 shows Canada's biggest 20 mutual fund companies at the end of June 2002 and the method they use to sell their funds. The figures are from www.ific.ca. As you can see, 11 of the 20 giants were load companies. Of the nine no-load companies, six were banks and one sells funds only to doctors and their families. Only Phillips Hager & North and Altamira were non-bank, no-load companies — and Altamira was bought by National Bank of Canada in 2002.

Table 2-3	Canada's Biggest 20 Fund Companies and How They Sell their Funds	
Company	Assets (as of June 2002 in $Billions)	Selling Style
Investors Group	39.9	Load
Royal Bank of Canada	36.1	No-load
AIM Funds Management Inc.	35.5	Load
Mackenzie Financial Corporation	32.3	Load
TD Asset Management	32.2	No-load
Fidelity Investments Canada Limited	30.8	Load
AGF Management Limited	26.2	Load
CIBC Securities Inc.	25.5	No-load
CI Mutual Funds Inc.	19.2	Load
Franklin Templeton Investments	18.7	Load
BMO Investments Inc.	15.1	No-load
A.I.C. Limited	13.4	Load
Scotiabank	11.9	No-load
MD Management Limited	9.5	No-load
Phillips Hager & North Ltd.	8.9	No-load
Spectrum Investments Inc.	6.4	Load
Dynamic Mutual Funds	5.7	Load
National Bank Mutual Funds	5.0	No-load
CM Investment Management (CIBC)	4.6	Load
Altamira Investment Services Inc.	4.4	No-load

Decoding sales commissions

Sales commissions on load funds come in a bewildering number of variations and forms. And discount brokers have dreamed up even more ways to make the whole thing even more complicated (see Chapter 6 for details). But when you buy a load fund from a broker or planner, you have two basic options:

- You can negotiate and pay an upfront commission — known as a *sales charge* or *front load* — to the salesperson. Savvy investors usually pay only 2 or 3 percent. That entitles you to sell the fund at any time with no further charges, and it sometimes gets you lower annual expenses.

- Or you can buy funds with a *back-end load* or *redemption charge*. In that case, the fund company itself pays the commission to the broker — usually 5 percent in the case of an equity fund or a balanced fund and less for a bond fund. However, you the investor are on the hook for a "redemption charge" if you sell the fund within a set number of years. Table 2-4 shows the redemption charge formula for equity and balanced funds at Mackenzie.

Table 2-4	Selling Periods and Redemption Charges at Mackenzie
Sell During	*Applicable Redemption Charge*
First year	5.5%
Second year	5.5%
Third year	4.5%
Fourth year	4%
Fifth year	3.5%
Sixth year	2.5%
Seventh year	1.5%
After that	0%

The redemption charge is based either on the original purchase cost of the units you're redeeming or their value at the time you sell. The policy varies by company (Mackenzie charges it on the value at the time of redemption). The first option is slightly better for you because, presumably, the value of your units will have increased by the time you redeem. For example, say you invest $10,000 in a fund on a back-end load basis and the fund gains 20 percent, leaving you with $12,000. Say you decide to redeem half of your holding, incurring a 4.5-percent back-end load. If the redemption charge is based on your original investment, then you pay $225 (which is 4.5 percent of $5,000), but if it's based on the current market value then you pay $270 (4.5 percent of $6,000).

But there's a difficulty, for the fund industry, with back-end loads. If the adviser doesn't have to wangle a commission out of the client every time he or she buys a fund, there's more of a temptation for brokers and planners to switch customers from fund to fund, collecting commissions from the fund companies along the way. So the fund industry borrowed a technique from the life insurers, who have been dealing with salespeople's naughty tricks for generations, and introduced the *trailer fee* or *trail commission*. Trailers are essentially yet another commission — usually between 0.5 percent and 1 percent of the value of the client's holding annually — that's paid by the company to the salesperson each year as long as his or her customer stays in the fund. It's a payment for loyalty. The trailer comes out of the management fee, not out of your account, so you never see it.

Mackenzie, like many load companies, pays a higher trailer to salespeople when they sell the fund on a front-load basis, getting their sales commission directly from the investor. That's because the company itself hasn't had to pay the charge. So on front-load fund sales, where the investor negotiates and pays the commission, Mackenzie pays a generous trailer of 1 percent of the client's holding of equity funds each year; but on deferred-load sales, where Mackenzie paid the original sales commission, the trailer is just 0.5 percent. It all gets pretty confusing — and it gets more complicated as you go further in — but that's the basis of the commission structure in mutual funds. In Chapter 8, there are tips on how to deal with salespeople.

No-load funds — the direct approach

The other great branch of the fund industry is the no-load sector — funds that sell directly to the public with no sales commissions. Here, life is much simpler. These companies will open an account for you when you contact them and there's no need to involve a broker, planner, or any other kind of adviser. There are no charges to buy or sell a fund, although remember that there's often a penalty of 2 percent if you dump a fund within three months of buying, to discourage in-and-out trading.

The banks dominate the no-load fund business, through their vast customer bases, discount brokerage arms, and branch networks. But so far, they have had difficulty building a strong record, and big market share, in equity funds.

Because no-load funds usually don't pay sales commissions to brokers — although they sometimes pay trailer fees to persuade advisers to sell their funds — their annual expenses and fees should be much lower than those of load funds. Should be, but aren't. Bankers aren't known for cutting fees where they can get away with keeping them high, and most no-load funds in Canada are only slightly cheaper than broker-sold funds. In other words, you can expect to part with more than 2 percent of your assets each year when you invest in most equity or balanced funds, no matter where you buy them.

There are some great low-priced funds in the no-load world, though. They are:

- ✔ **Index funds:** This type of fund, available from the big banks and Altamira, tracks the whole market while hitting investors for fees and expenses of less than 1 percent each year. Because index funds generate such small fees for the management company, load companies can't afford to sell them and also pay commissions to brokers. So no-load companies are the only sellers of index funds. There's more about index funds, which are a wonderful invention, in Chapter 15.

- ✔ **Actively managed funds:** Some no-load companies, such as Phillips Hager & North Ltd. of Vancouver, sell excellent "actively managed" funds with expenses of less than 2 percent. Actively managed funds, unlike index funds, buy and sell particular stocks in an attempt to beat the market and other managers. However, these bargain funds often have relatively high minimum investments in order to keep costs low (servicing tiny accounts isn't profitable, remember). PH&N requires a minimum account size of $25,000 with the company. There's more on dealing directly with no-load companies in Chapter 9.

How an Irish charmer revolutionized the mutual fund

Until the late 1980s, investors had to cough up the sales charge for load mutual funds themselves — it ran as high as 10 percent of the investor's money in some iniquitous cases. But in 1987 a brilliant fund marketer named Jim O'Donnell at Mackenzie Financial had a brainwave: Consumers loathed having to part with cash off the top just to pay a salesperson; they wanted to see all of their money going to work for them right away. So why not have the *company* pay the commission to the broker and get the money back through the management fee?

There was at least one problem with the strategy. Investors who hadn't paid a sales charge upfront might be inclined to simply dump the fund whenever they wanted. They hadn't paid a sales load, after all, so they wouldn't feel like they were wasting the commission. So Mackenzie also introduced its redemption charges, which kicked in if you cashed out early. The back-end idea was a smash hit and the company's first back-end load fund, the Industrial Horizon Fund, attracted hundreds of millions of dollars within months of its launch in 1987. The rest of the load fund industry soon copied it.

Chapter 3

Paperwork and Your Rights

. . . .

In This Chapter

▶ Making a fund purchase

▶ Checking on how your investment is growing

▶ Figuring out a prospectus in a few seconds

. . . .

*E*ver get work done on your house and notice how contractors talk? They use expressions such as "six of one and half a dozen of another" or "you could do that" and they'll pound 'em out in a barrage that leaves you more confused than before. People in the investment business like to drone on in the same way. They produce documents that explain every angle and aspect, but skip the stuff you really want to know: Is this fund any good and how has it done?

Investors hate getting piles of paper in the mail but the glossy brochures keep coming. To some extent, the verbiage isn't the companies' fault. Securities law obliges those selling investments to disclose trivia their clients couldn't care less about it. Still, it's pretty simple to filter out the noise in the mailings you get from a fund company — and cut straight to the information that really matters. And the documents from fund companies have improved, especially prospectuses, the all-important fact sheets that tell you about the promise and perils of a fund before you buy it. In general, the documents and forms you have to deal with are straightforward. Mutual fund forms are set up to be easy to fill out. There are also some special questions to open a registered retirement savings plan or sections of your tax return to fill in to report investment income and gains for taxes, but they tend to be simple.

In this chapter I go over the important paperwork, to demystify your account statement (the regular mailing that shows how you're doing) and walk you through the prospectus (the brochure that describes the fund). As always, the thing to watch out for is the costs loaded on your account — and I show you where to sniff around.

Sign Me Up

The big thing to decide straightaway is whether you're investing inside a registered retirement savings plan — a special tax-sheltered account in which investment profits pile up tax-free — or in an ordinary, taxable account in which your money is subject to taxes (see Chapter 23 for more on how RRSPs work). You can expect to fill out three main types of form when you buy or sell mutual funds.

- An account application form — which may just be called a "retirement savings plan" form if it's for an RRSP.

- The lines for reporting investment income and capital gains on your tax form — this doesn't apply if you're investing in an RRSP. (There's more on taxes in Chapter 24.)

- If you've decided to start a regular investing program, a form allowing the fund company to take fixed amounts out of your bank account for investment in funds. People usually have the money taken out monthly, but some fund companies allow you to use different periods, such as every week.

Starting a program of regular investments of small amounts into even a conservative mutual fund is one of the best ways of getting rich painlessly. For example, putting just $100 each month into the Royal Bank of Canada's biggest balanced fund (which holds a relatively stable mixture of stocks and bonds) from mid-1992 to mid-2002 left an investor with almost $16,000.

Your account application form (or RSP application form)

When you decide to buy a mutual fund, the first thing you'll be asked to fill out is an "account application" form — which tells the company who you are, what you want to buy, and how much you want to spend. An account is like a little shelf on which all your investments are kept at the broker's or the mutual fund company's office.

The account application is the document that gives the fund company your name, address, and level of investment knowledge, plus the amount of money you want to put into each fund. For investors, it's actually one of the most useful and informative documents that a mutual fund seller prints. That's because it contains hard information that the fund company needs itself, so the new account form is free of vagueness and verbosity. For example, in the space where the form asks how much you want to invest in each fund, it will nearly always clearly state the minimum investment.

Before you agree to buy anything, have a good look at the application form. And if you have any questions at all, approach your seller for a clear explanation. The form will also sometimes disclose what extra fees — such as charges for administration — you're expected to cough up. That's not a sudden attack of candour on the company's part — it's simply that the bureaucrats need to know how you'll be paying, directly or by having it taken out of your account.

The form for opening a new account includes some odd-looking questions. The fund company or broker wants to know:

- ✔ How experienced you are as an investor
- ✔ Your income
- ✔ Your *net worth* (the value of your personal assets after your debts are taken away)

They're not just being nosy here. One of the pillars of the provincial securities laws is a requirement that people selling investments should recommend only securities that are suitable for the customer — a principle referred to in the jargon as *Know Your Client* or KYC. In fact, the new account application form is often just referred to as the KYC. The idea is this: An elderly investor on a limited income shouldn't have a big chunk of his or her portfolio rammed into a Low-Coupon Speculative High-Yield Unsecured Sub-Saharan Junk Bond Fund.

The KYC can be a useful protection for you if it turns out later that your adviser put you into funds that were too risky for your circumstances, but it also works to the salesperson's advantage. He or she has an automatic out if you lost money on a volatile fund but you claimed when you opened the account that you knew a fair bit about investing. This is no place to put on a brave face — if you're a complete novice, say so and be proud of it. Pretending to know more than you do could really get you into hot water here if there is a dispute between you and your broker about an investment that went sour.

If you're investing with a bank or other direct fund seller such as Altamira Investment Services Inc., the application form will be issued by the company and it'll be clear that your deposit's going straight to them. But if you're buying funds through a financial planner, or independent fund salesperson, make sure that you fill out an application form that was issued by the fund company itself. For your own security and convenience it's important that you're recorded as a customer on the books of the fund company, giving you an extra measure of protection if the dealer or financial planner makes an error or even runs into cash-flow or regulatory problems. For example, if you're investing in Mackenzie Financial Corp. funds, see that the form you fill out is a Mackenzie form.

When money is held on the books of the mutual fund company itself, the account is said to be *in client name*. In other words, the account bears the name of the individual investor at the head office of the fund company. It's a good arrangement for you because that way, if there's ever a dispute with your broker or you want to move your account elsewhere, your units and your name are in the fund company's records, making it much easier to shift your money. Nearly every big financial planning chain and mutual fund dealer is set up so that mutual fund units are held in client name on the books of the fund company. That means you should get statements at least twice a year from both the dealer and the fund companies you've invested with; always check them against each other. However, with traditional stockbrokers such as RBC Dominion Securities Inc., or with discount brokers such as TD Waterhouse, your money may be held only on the broker's books. In that case, the fund company may have no record of your account. Wherever you invest, it usually pays to keep an eye on the securities listed for your account and the transactions shown.

Discount brokers and traditional stockbrokers tend to have sophisticated *back offices* or administration systems because their clients usually own stocks and bonds as well as funds. That means mutual funds are held in the same big pot as other securities, so these brokers don't pass their client's name on to the mutual fund company. Unfortunately, that means the fund company may have no record of your investment and isn't able to send you an annual and semi-annual statement of your personal holdings. That could make it harder to resolve any disputes with your broker over what you bought and how much it's worth. And very early in your investing career, someone is certain to get an order wrong. In my dealings with discount brokers, mutual fund companies, and fund dealers, there have always been mistakes. However, the good news is that the discount brokers and stockbrokers are large organizations that have the resources to fix errors. But get everything in writing, retain photocopies of all of the forms you fill out, and keep brief notes of the orders you issue over the phone.

Getting confirmed

You also should get a *confirmation* or *transaction slip* in the mail from the fund company a few days after your purchase, confirming that you've bought units, the amount, and whether you bought them with an upfront or "front-end" commission or with a *back-end load* or redemption charge (assuming it's a fund that's sold with commissions). A back-end load or redemption charge applies when you sell fund units. Once again, read this very carefully and if you spot any errors, immediately contact the salesperson to get the mistake fixed.

Also, when writing out your cheque to pay for your funds, make it payable to the fund company. Or, if the dealer says it must be made out to him or her, write "in trust" on the cheque. That gives you extra protection if the dealer hits financial problems, potentially tying your money up in bankruptcy proceedings.

The main thing, when you've decided what fund to buy, is keeping a brief note of what you asked for and what you were told. And hang onto copies or photocopies of everything. If a dispute arises, an investor who can calmly produce notes from his or her meetings with the adviser, along with copies of documents, will be taken far more seriously.

Prospectuses — Not Always Your Friend

A mutual fund prospectus is the document that must be given to you when you buy a mutual fund. It's the crucial method that the fund industry uses to set out the purpose of the fund, describe the fees, costs, and charges, and warn buyers of the risks involved in investing in the fund. Always ask to see the prospectus before you buy a fund (the salesperson should offer it) and then make sure you read at least these two sections:

- The investment objectives of the fund — that is, the sort of things it invests in.
- The charges and fees — if they aren't clearly explained, then get your salesperson to help.

Unfortunately, prospectuses have traditionally been written using such vague language, or with so many technical terms, that it used to be impossible to figure out whether a fund was worth buying. But new securities rules have metamorphosed prospectuses into clear and concise summaries that allow investors to put their finger on important information quickly.

You've been warned

I once asked a famous lawyer, renowned for his courtroom wiles and enormous fees, what I should do if I were ever arrested. Assuming I was innocent. You can probably guess what he told me: Keep your mouth shut. Try it — any lawyer will tell you the same. The point I'm trying to make here is that, innocent or guilty, the cops are not your friend when you're a suspect. They defend society; they do a tough and thankless job and I'm glad they're there to take a bullet for me. But if you're arrested, the cops are not on your side. Your lawyer is your friend, as long as you pay your bill, so say nothing until he or she arrives. The mutual fund prospectus is not entirely your friend, or at least it's not a true do-anything-for-you hoops-of-steel give-you-her-last-smoke type of friend. The prospectus, the document describing a mutual fund that's given to purchasers, is designed to inform you, but it's also there to protect the fund salesperson and fund company. Because once you've been given it, the law assumes that you've been adequately warned about the dangers and disadvantages of the fund. No point whining about the losses on funny foreign currencies when you were told of the danger right there on page 137.

Mutual fund prospectuses — which usually cover all or at least several of the funds in a company's lineup under one cover — have always contained the following information:

✔ **The name of the fund and its investment objectives:** For example, providing a steady income while preserving capital for a money market fund, or capital gains for a stock fund. Usually it's a bland motherhood statement that tells you little — after all, it would be an odd equity fund that didn't seek capital gains. Perhaps some day, they'll invent a fund that tries to *lose* as much money as possible, and also dream up a way to get investors to buy it. I hope I'm alive to see it: I bet the wretched thing finds itself stuck with shares that go up like a rocket. And I bet I end up owning it.

✔ **The risks of investing in the fund:** A good prospectus will warn of the dangers of losing money in bonds if inflation returns or interest rates turn up. And there's sure to be a warning that an equity fund will be vulnerable if the stock market tanks. There are almost always special warnings about the dangers of foreign funds, such as the chance of currency losses if the Canadian dollar climbs relative to overseas currencies. And small-company fund prospectuses invariably point to the unpleasant volatility and unique dangers of small stocks. But once again, the risks section usually consists of stating the bleeding obvious, as our Australian friends would say.

✔ **The company's ideal of an appropriate investor:** Look for clues as to the sort of investor that should buy the fund and the sort that should avoid it. For example, Franklin Templeton Investments — one of the more conservative fund companies — used to print a commendably honest line in the prospectus for its emerging markets fund. It said an investment in the fund "may be considered speculative." After reading that, you had no cause to go whining if you got beaten up. And sure enough, Templeton Emerging Markets lost money for two years running, in 1997 and 1998, shot up 42.9 percent in 1999, and then fell again in 2000 and 2001.

✔ **The costs and fees imposed on investors:** By law you'll find the management fees for a fund and the expenses that have recently been charged to investors. You'll also see any sales charges or commissions. Since most load funds can be bought with a front-end or a deferred load, you'll usually find both options explained. Along with the charges to investors, the prospectus must also list the commissions, annual fees, and other incentives given to salespeople. In principle, that's a great idea because it tells fund buyers how their advisers may be biased or influenced. Unfortunately, though, disclosure of commissions is often hedged around with "up to" or "may," leaving most investors no wiser than before.

Prospectuses for bank-sold funds will also talk vaguely about "incentives" given to their employees, and nearly all mutual fund companies will reserve the right to "participate" (as one fund seller delicately puts it) in advertising by brokers and "conferences" for salespeople. In other words, the fund managers hand over money to help brokers pay for these things. The good — or bad — old days of flying to Maui for a "seminar" at a fund company's expense are over. The public, media, and regulators just got so sick of the piggery that the fund industry agreed to introduce a "sales code," which bans the worst of the excesses.

You should always remember that a fund company often has two sets of customers: not only its unitholders (the people who actually own the funds) but also the brokers and financial planners who sell its wares. If a broker-sold fund company doesn't keep them sweet, it's in trouble.

More charges to look for

Here are some of the other charges that the prospectus must disclose:

- ✔ **Fees for administering registered retirement savings plans, registered retirement income funds, and registered educational savings plans:** These range from zero to about $75 annually. Ask if you can pay them separately by cheque — especially where it'll save your precious RRSP dollars — but some companies claim that their systems are set up only to take the money directly out of your account (which is handier for them).

- ✔ **Fees for closing your account and moving the money to another institution:** You should expect to pay $40 or $50.

- ✔ **Fees for short-term trading:** If you sell a fund within a short period of buying it, usually one or three months, you'll often face a penalty of 2 percent of the amount you sold. That's because funds are supposed to be a long-term holding, and investors who hop on and off over and over again increase costs for everyone.

Pulling out of the deal

A mutual fund prospectus (the term comes from a Latin word meaning "view") is one of the central pieces of mutual fund regulation. In fact, it's considered so important that in most provinces you have two business days after you get the prospectus to cancel your purchase of a fund *for any reason.* So even if you pull on a clown costume and dance around, chanting in a nerve-grating Belfast accent, as you demand your money back, they have to pay up, no matter how silly your explanation. Interestingly, in many provinces you also have the right to cancel your mutual fund purchase within 48 hours of getting your order confirmation. But don't expect the fund company or broker to welcome your business in future if you cancel your order without a reasonable justification. The law assumes that until you've had a chance to read the prospectus, you haven't been properly told about the fund. But once you've read it, you're pretty well on your own. Unless you can show that the fund isn't sticking to the promises made in the prospectus, the people selling and running the fund can reasonably argue that all of the risks and expenses have been explained to you — and you'll have a tough time cancelling your agreement to buy the fund.

How prospectuses are improving

For years, mutual fund prospectuses were rather useless documents because they didn't deal with the two questions any investor really wants answered: Has the fund been any good in the past, and how has it stood up against other funds?

The "new" prospectuses, which started coming out in 2000, are a thousand — no, make that a million — times better. For the first time they include all of the above information, but the big improvement is that they also feature a nice tight summary of costs and returns to investors.

In the past, the prospectus for a Canadian equity fund would almost invariably mumble some reassuring but weasel-like incantation along the lines of "the manager will seek long-term growth of capital by investing in high-quality Canadian companies with above-average growth prospects whose share price, in the opinion of the manager, doesn't reflect the company's long-term above-average growth prospects as a high-quality Canadian company." Big deal. But to actually find out how the fund had performed over the years, you had to pick up marketing handouts from the fund company or buy a newspaper's monthly fund report. To discover what was actually in the wretched fund, you had to go burrowing through its glossy brochures (which at least usually listed the main holdings) or look up its lugubrious financial statements. And to learn how the fund had done against its rivals and against the market, you almost always had to buy a newspaper's fund report. Whew.

In fairness to fund companies, securities laws limited what they could put in the prospectus. When I started writing about mutual funds in the mid-1990s, prospectuses looked like instruction manuals for badly made home appliances: lots of dreary expressions such as "continuous distribution" or "adjusted book value." And nothing about what the actual returns for the funds had been and how well the fund had done against the market. Fund companies valiantly tried writing the things in plain English but they were so hamstrung by legal requirements that their attempts at "investor-friendly" prospectuses turned out to be more annoying than informative. Lots of "we've" and "what this means for you," but very few hard facts.

Provincial securities cops realized it was a waste of time for companies to produce prospectuses that were too boring, vague, and incomprehensible for anyone to actually read. So they finally got the industry to agree, after much badgering and years of unspeakably dull meetings, to produce a prospectus with some useful information.

Figure 3-1 shows pages from a prospectus. This one, a crisp and well-produced example, is for Bank of Montreal's Special Equity Fund, which invests mostly in small Canadian companies. The following elements are circled:

- ✔ **Top-ten holdings:** The big holdings of an equity fund represent the manager's true loves and they're a reliable guide to the personality of the fund. Check 'em out — if they're natural resource producers or small companies you've never heard of, or bonds issued by technology outfits or developing nations, you're in for interesting times, as the old Chinese curse puts it. The top holdings of this fund are all reasonably solid medium-sized companies. Their shares aren't likely to shoot up ten times in value, but they're not likely to go bust either.

- ✔ **Year-by-year returns:** These are great for letting you know what kind of swings in value you can expect. Shares in small companies are volatile beasts, as you can see from this chart. Notice how in 1994 and 1998 the fund lost more than 17 percent — that's more than $1 of every $6 investors had riding on it — but it had a couple of blowout years to compensate, rising more than 20 percent each time.

- ✔ **Overall past performance:** This shows the overall past performance of $10,000 invested in the fund at its launch in 1993 compared with the performance of the same wad invested in the Toronto Stock Exchange 300-share index (Canada's stock market benchmark, now named the Standard & Poor's/Toronto Stock Exchange composite index) and the Nesbitt Burns Small Cap Index. The small-cap index is a widely used yardstick for small-company stocks, compiled by the bank's giant broker, BMO Nesbitt Burns Inc. There are other small-cap indexes — and some people say the Nesbitt index has too many little oil stocks in it to be truly representative of the small-cap market — but there's no point getting worked up about it. Notice how this fund has kept up with the

76

BMO SPECIAL EQUITY FUND

BMO Special Equity Fund

Fund details

Type of fund	Canadian small and mid-capitalization fund
Date started	August 3, 1993
Securities offered	Units of a mutual fund trust
Eligible for registered plans	Yes
Foreign property	No
Management fee	2.00%
Portfolio manager	Jones Heward Investment Counsel Inc.

What does the fund invest in?

Investment objectives

This fund's objective is to provide above-average growth in the value of your investment over the long term by investing in small and mid-sized Canadian companies.

The fundamental investment objective may only be changed with the approval of a majority of unitholders at a meeting called for that purpose.

Investment strategies

These are the strategies the portfolio manager uses to try to achieve the fund's objective:

- examines the financial statistics of each company it's considering, to determine if the company's stock is attractively priced
- may emphasize specific industry sectors with high potential return or companies that may benefit from trends like an aging population
- reviews company operations and research and development to assess the company's potential for growth
- interviews senior management as needed to assess the company's less tangible assets, like the quality of leadership
- continuously monitors the companies the fund invests in for changes that may affect their profitability
- may invest up to 30% of the purchase cost of the fund's assets in foreign securities
- may use derivatives like options, futures and forward contracts to:

- protect the fund against potential losses from changes in interest rates. For example, a portfolio manager may be concerned about the impact that rising interest rates may have on the fund. By using index futures, the portfolio manager can reduce the security price fluctuations,
- reduce the impact of currency fluctuations on the fund's holdings. For example, by buying an option to sell a currency at a specified price, the portfolio manager can reduce the fund's potential loss if the currency drops in value,
- gain exposure to securities instead of buying the securities directly.

The fund will only use derivatives as permitted by Canadian securities regulators.

The portfolio manager may frequently buy and sell investments for the fund. This can increase trading costs, which may lower the fund's returns. It also increases the chance that you may receive a distribution of capital gains in the year. If you hold the fund in a non-registered account, distributions are taxable.

Top ten holdings at January 31, 2002

Astral Media Inc	3.60%
Standard & Poor's Mid-Cap 400, Depository Receipts	3.20%
Kingsway Financial Services	2.90%
Industrial Alliance Life Insurance Co	2.90%
Cott Corp	2.90%
Goldcorp Inc	2.60%
Meridian Gold Inc	2.50%
Forzani Group Ltd	2.00%
Dorel Industries Inc	1.80%
CGI Groupe Inc	1.80%

What are the risks of investing in the fund?

These strategies may involve the following risks, which we explain starting on page 142:

- equity risk
- liquidity risk
- foreign investment risk
- currency risk
- securities lending, repurchase and reverse repurchase transaction risk
- derivative risk.

Figure 3-1:
Prospectus showing information for the BMO Special Equity Fund.

Who should invest in this fund?

Consider this fund if:

- you're looking for a fund that invests in smaller Canadian companies with high growth potential
- you're comfortable with medium-to-high investment risk.

Past performance

It's important to remember that past performance is no indication of future performance.

Year-by-year returns

This chart shows the fund's annual historical return, which changes each year. Annual return is the percentage change in the value of an investment from January 1 to December 31.

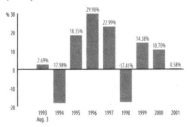

Overall past performance

This chart compares the growth of a $10,000 investment in the fund with the returns of:

- the Toronto Stock Exchange (TSE) 300 Total Return Index, which reflects the price movements of the 300 largest companies (by market capitalization) on The Toronto Stock Exchange
- the BMO Nesbitt Burns Small Cap Index, which reflects the stock performance of small to mid-size Canadian companies.

Annual compound returns

This chart compares the historical annual compound return of the fund with the TSE 300 Total Return Index and the BMO Nesbitt Burns Small Cap Index.

		Since Inception	Past 5 years	Past 3 years	Past year
BMO Special Equity Fund	%	6.31	5.28	8.39	0.58
TSE 300 Total Return Index	%	11.16	6.95	7.34	(12.57)
BMO Nesbitt Burns Small Cap Index	%	6.84	3.24	10.12	3.44

Distribution policy

The fund distributes any income and capital gains in December. Distributions are automatically reinvested in additional units of the fund, unless you tell us in writing that you prefer to receive cash distributions. Please see page 155 for more information.

Financial highlights at September 30

Distributions and net asset value per unit

		1997	1998	1999	2000	2001
Distributions from net income	$	–	–	–	–	–
from realized gain	$	–	–	–	–	–
return of capital	$	–	–	–	–	–
Total annual distributions	$	–	–	–	–	–
Net asset value	$	16.76	11.90	13.20	19.62	14.72

Ratios and supplemental data

		1997	1998	1999	2000	2001
Net assets (000's)	$	351,000	333,807	334,908	380,751	293,946
Number of units outstanding (000's)		20,939	28,052	25,380	19,408	19,970
Management expense ratio	%	2.31	2.40	2.38	2.35	2.40
Portfolio turnover rate %		100.00	92.10	115.40	142.20	122.45

Fund expenses indirectly borne by investors

See *Fund expenses indirectly borne by investors* on page 6 for the assumptions we're required to use in this table. The assumptions do not reflect the actual performance of the fund.

		One Year	Three Years	Five Years	Ten Years
Fees and expenses payable over	$	24.60	77.55	135.93	309.42

Nesbitt index but, like other small-company funds, it seriously lagged the broad market in 1999 and 2000. That's not really the fault of the fund: Big company stocks, especially the banks and Nortel Networks Inc., dominated the stock market in the second half of the 1990s.

✔ **Annual compund returns:** Next, the BMO prospectus shows the familiar compound returns for the past one, three, and five years. Once again, there's a comparison with the Nesbitt index and the S&P/TSX Index.

✔ **Financial highlights:** This section starts by showing the *distributions* by the fund for each of its past five financial years and its net asset value (or unit price) at the end of each period. Distributions are payouts of interest income, dividends, or capital gains that the fund has earned — most unitholders just take them in the form of more units. Notice that this fund has a financial year-end of September 30, which is unusual. Most funds have a financial year that simply ends on December 31. If you plan to put the fund in a tax-sheltered account such as an RRSP, the size and frequency of the distributions don't matter much. But if you're on the hook for tax each year on the capital gains and interest income you earn, watch out. A fund that throws off lots of distributions leaves you vulnerable to lots of taxes, even if you reinvest the distributions in more units. There's an explanation of the strange world of fund distributions in Chapter 24.

This section also shows how the fund's assets have changed over the past five years. As you can see, this fund's assets have shrunk in recent years as investors shunned small-company stocks.

Also shown is the management expense ratio for the past five years. This is useful information when you're looking for low-cost funds (and you should be). Simply checking the expense ratio for the latest year could be misleading because one-off factors could have affected the figure. But seeing the expenses for five years gives you a good handle on what to expect. It may also help to put some pressure on the fund industry to bring down expenses because it'll be clear that with many funds, even though their assets soar, costs aren't reduced. In mutual funds, economies of scale don't seem to apply.

Showing the *portfolio turnover* rate is an idea that Canada has adopted from U.S. prospectuses. It measures the speed at which the manager changes the fund's holdings — a 100-percent turnover rate is high, indicating that trading equivalent to the value of the entire fund took place during the year. Often, high turnover means lots of distributions if managers spin out their trading profits to unitholders (otherwise, the fund itself must pay taxes). But this fund, despite its high turnover rates, hasn't paid any capital gains distributions in recent years. That's probably because its trading profits have been cancelled out by trading losses, eliminating the need for distributions.

What is the S&P/TSX composite index?

The S&P/TSX composite is Canada's main stock market barometer, measuring the value of nearly 300 of our most important publicly traded companies, such as Royal Bank of Canada or Trans-Canada PipeLines Ltd. It's a fine way of checking how good the returns from stocks in general have been. For example, the index climbed above 11,000 in 2000, up from 5,000 at the start of 1996, more than doubling the money of an investor with a portfolio identical to the index. But by mid-2002, it had sagged to less than 7,000 again, for a loss of almost 40 percent from those record highs.

Actually, calculating the return from the index and from any portfolio of stocks is a little more complicated because the stocks also paid dividends — meaning that a "total return" index for the S&P/TSX, which includes dividends, is often used. But that's the general idea. Every country has benchmarks for measuring returns from its local stock market. In the United States there's the old-fashioned Dow Jones Industrial Average,

a relic of the 1800s, which contains 30 giant companies. But there's also the more representative Standard & Poor's index of 500 companies and the technology-heavy Nasdaq Stock Market Composite Index. The wildest index name I've come across is Finland's: The Hex index. One of the fun things about being an investment reporter these days is noticing more and more countries starting up stock markets, each with its own benchmark. Malta, Ghana, anyone?

The S&P/TSX composite used to contain a fixed 300 companies — it was known as the TSE 300 — but the Canadian market turned out to be too small to produce 300 companies large enough for big pension funds and mutual funds to invest in. After persistent criticism that the index was full of little stocks that were hard to trade, the exchange brought in Standard & Poor's Corp. of New York to redesign the market benchmark. The revamped edition was launched in 2002. These days, the index has no fixed number of stocks — as of mid-2002, it contained just 275 companies.

Finally, there's another idea taken from U.S. prospectuses — a hypothetical total of expenses and fees that an investor in the fund could expect to pay over periods ranging from one to ten years. They're called "indirect" because they're simply taken out of the value of your holding in the form of the management expense ratio, instead of being billed to your account directly. The information is meaningless until you read the explanation, at the beginning of the prospectus, of how the example is calculated. In fact, it assumes the investor put $1,000 into the fund, that it earned only 5 percent a year, and that the fund carried the same 2.4-percent management expense ratio in all years as it did in its latest period. As you can see, an investment of $1,000 in the fund ten years ago under those circumstances would have generated just over $309 in total fees and expenses for the bank. It's a fairly useful indication as to how much mutual fund investing can cost: Say your investment had been $5,000, then you would have ended up handing over more than $1,500 during the ten years.

The mysterious annual information form

Pick up any mutual fund prospectus and you'll notice that it's referred to as the "simplified" version. As you get further into mutual funds, and hopefully more interested in them, you might get a hankering to look at the "complicated" version. Well, actually there's no such thing. The prospectus that's given to investors is called "simplified" because it's only part of the full prospectus document: The rest of it, technically speaking, is the fund's annual and semi-annual statements and a little-known document called the "annual information form." The AIF is available if you ask for it (the prospectus should provide a contact address or phone number) or you can download it from the Internet at www.sedar.com, the central clearing house where just about all Canadian public companies and mutual funds must file their reports and other required disclosure documents. The AIF contains things like the names of the trustees for the funds, who are supposed to be looking out for the interest of the investors, more detail on the commissions paid to brokers and other salespeople, and a bit more information about the outside portfolio managers hired to help run the funds.

The new prospectuses are a huge step forward, because for the first time they actually include the fund's performance and an indication of how well it did versus a recognized benchmark. One of the big ideas behind the new documents is simplicity and brevity, and they certainly meet that goal. But in fact the information is a bit too concise. It would be helpful to have some discussion of *why* the fund beat or underperformed its benchmarks and also a comparison with the returns of rival funds.

Your Account Statement

Account statements, which show how much your holdings are worth and how much you've bought and sold since the last report from your fund company, are one area where the fund industry still needs to make progress. Investors often have trouble understanding what they actually own and even more difficulty figuring out their rates of return. Every company uses its own system and layout, and jargon such as "book value" isn't much help.

You may get an account statement only twice a year if you invest through a stockbroker or financial planner. The broker or planner and the fund company you've used will often both send you statements for the six months ending June 30 and for the year ending December 31. Usually the people who invest through a salesperson aren't interested in monitoring their investments frequently (that's why they hired someone to advise them), so twice-yearly statements are fine. Sometimes, a company will agree to send you statements more frequently — so try asking — but the fund seller's system may not be set up to do this. If you hold your funds directly with a bank or no-load company, then you'll probably get a statement every quarter. That's because investors who go directly to their bank or to a fund company usually enjoy making their own decisions about investing — so they want to check their holdings more frequently. Finally, if you invest through a discount broker, your statement will often arrive monthly, especially if you've done some buying or selling in your account during the previous month. Discount brokerage customers tend to be very interested in investing, so they insist on regular updates. All companies still send out account statements, but just about every large fund seller also now lets you check your account and recent transactions over the phone or at their Internet site.

Besides your name, address, account number, and the nature of your account (that is, taxable or tax-deferred), your statement will almost certainly show the following:

- ✔ The total value of your investment in each fund you hold, plus a total value for your account.

- ✔ The number of fund units you held and their price or net asset value at the end of the reporting period. Remember to check these against the unit value shown for the fund in your newspaper's monthly report for the period — and it's not a bad idea to verify that the number of units matches the number shown in your previous statement, adjusting for any sales or purchases you may have made or for any distributions (in the form of new units) that the fund declared.

- ✔ Any purchases or redemptions of units, and at what prices.

Beyond that, statements vary, but many big fund companies also provide the following information:

- ✔ The change in the value of your account, and ideally of your investment in each fund, since your last statement.

- ✔ The book value of your holdings. This technically means the amount that you've ever put into the fund, which is useful for calculating whether you're using up your complete foreign content limit in a tax-sheltered plan. That's because the foreign content is calculated as a percentage of the book value, not the current market value.

Annual and Semi-annual Financial Statements (or Annual Reports)

At least once a year, a glossy brochure shows up at your house filled with rows of dull-looking figures and dry terms such as "statements of operations" or, my favourite, "net realized gain (loss) on sale of investment (excluding short-term notes)." These are the fund's financial statements, which, like the prospectus, usually group several funds into one document. Fund companies produce the statements twice a year. They have to send the report for the fund's financial year-end to all unitholders, but they're generally allowed to send the half-year report only to investors who actually request it. There should be a mail-in card for you to do this. Unless this stuff really sends you to sleep, you should ask to have the six-month report mailed to you. You'll be reminding the fund company that you take your money seriously. There's no point getting worked up about the financial details in the statements, but there are some things you should check:

✔ The report must show the complete portfolio for the fund, not just the top holdings. It's worth it, and interesting, to glance down the list to see if the manager has any funny-looking stuff that may be an attempt to jazz up performance while taking on more risk. The full portfolio listing will also show what the fund paid for each stock and bond and what it's worth now: It's always fun to see which investment has proved to be a disaster for the fund, although managers often "window dress" by dumping a turkey so that it doesn't show up in the report.

✔ The statements often contain a commentary by the manger or fund company on what went right or wrong for the fund. As usual with mutual fund handouts, these tend to be bland and boring descriptions of the market or economic outlook, rather than an honest discussion of the manager's good and bad moves. But there are some important clues to look for: If the portfolio manager has been replaced or if the fund's strategy is being changed in a major way, it may be time to dump it. And keep an eye on the top holdings. If they look riskier than you want, or if they leave out major sectors of the economy, then the fund company may be rolling the dice in order to jack up returns and attract more investors.

Don't throw the book value at your manager

Be careful when comparing the book value of your investment in a fund with its market value. The book value is the total sum that's been put into the fund, so in that sense it represents your total investment. But it also includes the value of any distributions made by the fund, in the form of new units, even though they weren't real investments that came out of your pocket. The reinvested distributions have the effect of increasing the book value, and they can make it grow larger than the market value — making it appear that the fund has lost you money when it may have been a winner. For example, say you originally invest $10,000 in a fund that produces a return of 20 percent, leaving you with a market value of $12,000. But say the manager is an active trader and she pays out $4,000 in capital gains distributions along the way. Then your fund could have a book value of $14,000, or $2,000 more than its market value on your statement, even though the manager has done a good job.

Chapter 4

Building Your Very Own Financial Plan

So we're going right back to basics here — are funds for you? The key is that mutual funds, when selected carefully, are great for almost everyone and work best as part of an overall financial plan. There are some important factors to consider before jumping right in. The most important is taking a frank look at your financial health.

Never plant day lilies in your garden. Oh yes, they cover the bare patches nicely and the flowers smell wonderful in May. But they're just so aggressive, sending out sinister tentacles and jumping up among other plants like scary alien invaders. Here's another annoying species that seems to have popped out of nowhere: the financial planner. Human beings got through millennia without needing them but now we have thousands, lecturing us about our reckless spending and hectoring us about our feckless lack of preparation. But good financial planning isn't rocket science and doesn't have to be scary. It doesn't even really begin with mutual funds — it starts with getting your debt under control and buying enough insurance. Still, for those who have their act together and want to save and invest money, funds are a powerful ally.

Mutual funds are ideal for building retirement savings. Make sure you buy plenty of funds that invest in high-quality shares and bonds, and you've found a simple and painless way of taking advantage of the high returns earned by most professional investors. Yes, share and bond prices drop from time to time, but if you don't need the money for years, you have long enough to ride it out. Funds aren't just for retirement savings, however: They're also ideal if your life is in a holding pattern — trying to find someone special (hint: perhaps tone down that annoying bray of a laugh) or figuring out whether to move to another country for a while. In that case, you simply buy a less-volatile set of mutual funds and sit tight. Funds are also just the ticket for building your short-term savings in order to make a big purchase, maybe your first home. In that case, you want no risk and a nice steady return. Whatever you're chasing in life, funds are a valuable ally above all for their convenience and ease of record-keeping — although you should always keep an eye on your statement.

Mutual funds are also perfect if you're working toward early retirement but haven't yet made up your mind when to quit — that's because they can be shuffled and changed around with ease as your plans change. Funds are perfect for almost any financial plan because they're such a maintenance-free and relatively low-cost way of storing and accumulating wealth. Running your own business or buying real estate properties might produce higher returns and lucrative tax write-offs. But being self-employed represents a 24-hour commitment — and whining tenants who call about the drains at 4 a.m. get annoying after a while. Funds are problem-free and easy to monitor, and they produce excellent returns if you keep management fees and costs down.

In short, funds are for dealing with your savings, the money you have left over after feeding, housing, and clothing your family and taking care of your own bloated desires. Most people want to do one of three things with their savings, or at least a mixture of these three: Grow a big nest egg for retiring, put money in safe-keeping with a reasonable return because they don't know what their ultimate plans will be, or, finally, save money for a short-term purpose like buying a first home. In other words, they want funds to grow their money over the long term, for several years or more; give them a reasonable rate of return while avoiding big losses; or simply hold their money safely with a modest annual payoff. In this chapter, I'll walk you through using funds to achieve each of the three goals. I'll outline the best way to set your objectives, help you identify what kind of investor you are, and show you how to start building a suitable portfolio of funds.

Looking at Your Long-Term Financial Future

The first thing to do is to relax, grab a giant plate of fries with gravy, and remember you live in the best country in the world. If you're working and paying into the *Canada Pension Plan (CPP)* — and have a reasonable prospect of doing so until you're 60 or so — then you're unlikely to end up in absolute poverty. If you're in a pension plan sponsored by a company, union, or professional association, so much the better. If you can build even some modest savings on top of that — a lump sum equivalent to your final year's income, say — then you really shouldn't have any problems getting by in retirement. But you're no doubt planning to buy something nice near the water or take some agreeable cruises and, for that stuff, just "getting by" won't cut it. So even if you have a good pension and full government benefits coming your way, you'll need cash to kick-start things. And if you're not in a pension plan, you certainly want to be accumulating your own rainy day fund. There's no clear-cut science here, but you don't want to find out that you hugely underestimated your needs. Don't panic: The government may reduce benefits, but seniors are a powerful, organized lobby and, most of all, they vote. So it's a near-certainty that there'll be some kind of pension from the government when you retire. The greying baby-boomers will see to it. But unless you want to spend a lot of time kicking around the local mall, like you do now, then a lump sum will come in handy.

How much will you need in retirement?

Many experts claim that you should try to generate an after-tax income — including all pensions and government benefits — equal to about 70 percent of your present net income.

And the conventional assumption for many planners is that you ignore the value of your home, if you own it, of course, when calculating your wealth in retirement. That's because planners often treat the value of an investor's home as an insurance policy that might be needed for medical expenses and so on.

Mind you, those guidelines are pretty extreme. Many people get by on much less than 70 percent of their former net income when they quit work. And a lot of people will be able to sell their family home for a tidy sum, leaving them with a healthy tax-free profit when they move into something smaller. Still, the rules represent an ideal to aim for.

Just about everybody in Canada with a paying job, including the self-employed, is covered by the CPP. That's the federal government-sponsored pension plan, which you pay for through contributions throughout your working life. For those working in Quebec, there's the very similar Quebec Pension Plan.

For 2002, the maximum monthly benefit payable under the CPP for those aged 65 was $788.75, payable for life and increasing in line with inflation.

On top of that, there's Old Age Security, a pension provided to all Canadians over 65 who've lived in this country long enough. As of July 2002 it was $443.99 a month. And for seniors with no other savings, there's the Guaranteed Income Supplement, a maximum of $527.66 in mid-2002.

Meet the Cleavers: Last-minute savers who did just fine

Actuaries — pension and life insurance experts who work on cheerful questions such as when you can expect to die — get a lot of ribbing for being dull. Even accountants, not exactly known for their excess of personality, like to make jokes about them. Q: How do you know you're talking to a bunch of actuaries? A: They look at *their own* shoes throughout the conversation.

But some actuaries are a lot of fun. Especially Malcolm Hamilton, a retirement expert with the consulting firm William M. Mercer Ltd. in Toronto. He accuses the investment and savings industries of scare tactics, especially with their pious assertion that you'll need 70 percent (or even 80 percent) of your pre-retirement income when you retire. Mr. Hamilton says that's a load of bull, and that people get by on as little as one-third of their gross working income. That's because living costs such as employment expenses, kids, mortgage, and, most of all, taxes disappear. Here's an example of what he means, adapted from his description of a typical Canadian couple.

Take the Cleavers, a couple who just got married at 25.They have a combined income of $50,000, roughly in the middle for Canadians. Of that, $20,000 goes in taxes, employment expenses, and savings for their first home. This leaves the Cleavers with $30,000 to spend on themselves.

Ten years later, the Cleavers have two kids and a $200,000 home. They now make $79,000 each year, of which taxes, employment expenses, and mortgage payments eat up $34,000. The kids cost them another $17,000, $3,000 of which goes to registered education savings plans. That leaves the Cleavers with the same $30,000, or slightly less, to spend on themselves. They save nothing for retirement. Ten more years later, in their mid-forties, they can finally begin diverting money to their RRSPs, accelerating the pace when the children go to college. And all of those RRSP contributions generate huge tax savings. By age 54, the Cleavers are earning $100,000 annually, of which $54,000 goes to RRSPs (they're able to put such large quantities into their plans because they have years of unused contributions). Taxes and employment expenses consume $16,000. On themselves, the Cleavers spend the same old $30,000. So at 55, with a house and $450,000 of retirement savings, the Cleavers retire. They reckon that their savings, the CPP, and Old Age Security will give them an inflation-protected income of $32,000 per annum. Does that mean they're living in poverty? No, says Mr. Hamilton, and here's where he starts having fun.

In his words: *"Financial planners warn that the same fate awaits others who don't save millions. 'Look at the feckless Cleavers,' they say. 'They used to earn $100,000 per annum; now they subsist on $32,000.'*

"For the record, the Cleavers' finances . . . are remarkably simple after retirement:

"$32,000 of income, less $2,000 of income tax, leaves $30,000 for the Cleavers to spend on themselves, just as they always have — just as they always will. The Cleavers' version of Freedom 55 is not the one you see on television. They will not winter in the Caribbean, nor will they enjoy that sunset view of the Pacific. Their riches are measured in leisure time, not dollars. And since the government hasn't found a way to tax leisure, the Cleavers live well and pay little or no tax."

The moral of the story: Your costs will fall off a cliff when you retire, so don't get spooked into diverting every spare penny into your RRSP. Sure, saving is good — and it'll get easier as the kids leave and the house is paid off. But always question the assumption that you'll need 70 percent of your pre-retirement income.

Now, obviously you'd be hard-pressed to live off those amounts from the government. But look at seniors all around you. Especially at your parents, relatives, and friends. Notice how they seem to be, well, comfortable? That's largely because, once they retired, their expenses were significantly reduced. More specifically:

- ✔ When you stop working, your house will almost certainly have been paid for, leaving you free of accommodation costs apart from utilities and maintenance.

- ✔ Your employment expenses, including transportation, parking, and clothing, will fall to nothing.

- ✔ Sure you'll want to travel, but now you can take advantage of off-peak discounts and other special reductions. And let's face it, you'll be slowing down.

- ✔ Your kids will almost certainly have flown the nest and their education will be just about paid for. No more pimple-faced, sullen . . . well, you know.

In other words, before you assume that there's an old age of penury ahead — meaning that you automatically have to put the very maximum into your wretched registered retirement savings plan — remember that you'll have spent a lifetime living frugally already, earning enough to pay your taxes and mortgage and bankroll the kids' hockey skates and education. That said, the best way to ensure that you'll be free of financial worries in the years to come is to plan carefully and pay attention to your finances. By using investment options like mutual funds, you can make your retirement a better experience. You'll feel more flush with cash and be able to travel, shop, and generally relax in high style. Plus, investing isn't all about your day in the sun; sound investments can help you meet many of your life goals like educating yourself and your children, buying your dream home, starting your own business, and much, much more.

Start saving now, today, because the younger you are the more powerful the effect of buying mutual funds. Yes, you'll probably get by in retirement, but starting a regular contribution plan to a fund at an early age can earn you thousands of dollars. Let's say you'd put $100 monthly into Bank of Nova Scotia's Scotia Global Growth Fund for five straight years, from June 1997 to June 2002: you'd have ended up with $4,776. But if you'd started five years earlier, you'd be sitting on $12,347, or almost three times as much.

Setting Your Financial Priorities

Pick up any of the piles of unwanted personal finance books in the store and they all begin by saying the same thing, mainly because it's true: Pay your debts.

I gave at the office: Making a contribution at work

If you're working for a large company or for the government, and they offer a traditional defined benefit plan, it's usually a good idea to sign on for it. A defined benefit plan is a pension plan that promises to pay a percentage of your salary when you leave. A typical generous scheme might offer 2 percent times years of service times the average of your best (or last) 5 years of income. So if you worked for 35 years, with the best 5 years averaging $50,000 each, your annual pension would be 2 percent times 35 times $50,000, which works out at $35,000 a year. When you're negotiating with a new employer, look for a pension that's at least this good — or seek compensation for not getting it.

Sure, you might do better investing on your own rather than making contributions to the pension scheme — and being in a pension plan reduces the amount you can put into your own RRSP. But for people who are poor savers, a pension scheme is a wonderful backup. It's especially important to get into a pension plan if you're over 40 and certainly if you plan to stay with the employer after age 50. That's because the actual value of being in a defined-benefit plan shoots up exponentially as soon as you reach middle age (because your quitting date is drawing closer).

And if you're leaving a job early, it's frequently a good idea to stay in the plan rather than take a lump sum. Pension benefits are often increased in line with inflation, either formally or by way of goodwill payments, and pension schemes also may bring you health benefits. At least ask the human resources people to explain how much you'll get in dollar terms if you leave your accrued contributions in the scheme and then collect a reduced pension later at 55, 60, or 65. If you can, show the projections to an accountant who's knowledgeable about pensions or, better yet, call up a firm of actuaries. See if you can persuade one to give you an hour or two of advice for an agreed fee of, say, $300 or $400. It'll be money well spent. Just as you should always have your lawyer by your side before you talk to the cops, it's good to have your own expert looking out for you when dealing with something as complicated as a pension. A corporation is happy to see you take a lump sum and stumble off into the night, with no more claim on them. But it could be a lot better for you to stay in line for a pension down the road, at 55, for example. So ask the other old codgers at work what they're doing (they're usually pretty savvy) and stick around in the scheme if you can.

That's the first step for anyone, and often the most difficult. Remember that if you're shelling out $100 in credit card interest each month and you're in a 50-percent tax 'n' deductions bracket on your uppermost income, then it takes $200 in earnings to pay for that sucker.

It's impossible to build wealth with debt bleeding you dry, so with the exception of your home mortgage, becoming borrowing-free is the first move. That's difficult, as many of us know from painful experience, but it's the first step toward freedom.

Fund salespeople and even banks will often suggest that you borrow money to buy mutual funds. This works out fine as long as the funds go up, but remember that if the funds drop in value, you'll still be on the hook for every penny you borrowed to buy them. So think long and hard before taking out a loan in order to buy mutual funds that invest in stocks and bonds.

Here, roughly in order, are the priorities you should set on your road to fiscal responsibility:

✔ **Pay off your debts:** Start with the high-interest and non–tax-deductible kind.

✔ **Get life insurance:** Buy enough insurance to provide for your loved ones if they lose you, and buy fire and theft coverage for your home and property.

✔ **Set up an emergency fund:** Make sure you have access to some cash if an emergency hits. Traditionally, experts advise six months' income.

✔ **Have a will drawn up:** Save everybody a lot of hassle and delay (at a horrible time) by biting the bullet and getting this done. A lawyer will handle it for about $250.

✔ **Hire an accountant or some other fee-charging expert:** For a charge that can be as low as $200 or $300 they will look over your tax situation, unless your income is so low you can't afford it. If you do any kind of freelance work or earn any sort of self-employment income this step is essential.

Only when you've completed the steps above should you think about saving and investing money, including buying mutual funds. And here you'll run into one of the main problems with the way mutual funds are sold: They're a wonderful product, but financial planners and other advisers who earn commissions from funds don't get paid for telling clients to cut their debts and buy insurance. So they see buying funds as the solution to just about everybody's problem, at the risk of leaving customers underinsured or paying far too much in interest on their debts. That's why you should remember that anyone who sells mutual funds for a living has a natural in-built bias. So in Part II, where I take a close look at financial planners, I recommend that you think strongly about going to a fee-charging financial planner or accountant who doesn't get commissions for selling products.

Get quotes on disability insurance. This insurance will provide at least some income if you can't work. If your job doesn't provide any coverage, then it's a must, especially if there's only one wage earner in the household.

Understanding what type of investor you are

Let's say that you have decided to build some capital. Mutual funds are the most convenient way to do it. The next question is what you'll need the money for. And here's where you can build funds into your financial plan. Once your debts and spending are under control, and you've bought adequate insurance and tax advice, the next step is to set goals. Most people have financial objectives that fall into one of these three groups. Chances are that your situation fits one of the following descriptions, or it's a blend of two of them:

- **Growth investors** are building a portfolio of long-term savings that are supposed to last through retirement or through an extended and far-off period of not working. In that case, it doesn't really matter if the stock market goes into long slumps — it can even be to your advantage if you're steadily investing all the while, because you get to buy stocks cheaply. The real danger is having your money eroded by inflation. So the goal is maximum growth, and that means lots of equity funds with a relatively small proportion of the portfolio in bonds in order to spread your risk. Growth investors are the greediest of all: They typically chase annual returns of 9 or 10 percent and are willing to expose their portfolio to danger in order to get it.

- **Balanced investors** aren't sure what's likely to happen in their life, but it could include buying a home, moving to oceanside Nova Scotia (let me have my little dreams), or starting a family. But whatever the eventual goal is, it's definitely going to require a few thousand dollars. In that case, caution is the watchword. You might need the money soon, and it would be awful to have to sell your mutual funds straight after the stock market collapsed, scything into their value. So the best formula is lots of money market funds and bond funds, with a modest equity component if you're comfortable taking on some risk. Balanced investors are generally happy with returns of 6 to 8 percent per year.

- **Savers** are amassing a pile of money to buy a home or car within the next few years, or building a war-chest so they can stop working for a while, perhaps to go back to school or to dig for ancient pornographic mosaics in old Thrace. If you're one of these people, then you want to keep risk to a minimum, because this is money you'll be needing very soon. That means no stocks, or hardly any, and lots of short-term bonds and money market securities. Savers traditionally will settle for annual rates of return of 5 percent or less as long as their money isn't at risk.

For all three types of investor, mutual funds are a wonderful tool. They're cheap or free to buy, flexible, and convenient. The fund company handles all of the record-keeping (but check your statement carefully), which means funds require little or no thought or attention from the investor. And funds offer attractive rates of return. So decide which goal matches yours, and then look at the suggested sample portfolios at the end of this chapter for some ideas.

Learning from my mistakes — investing is an inexact science

Okay, so I'm going to give you the straight goods. Even reporting on financial markets daily doesn't shield me from the inevitable hits and misses every investor encounters when he throws his hat in the ring. My investing career began in the mid-1990s, when I opened a self-directed RRSP at Toronto-Dominion's discount brokerage, then called Green Line Investor Services but now known as TD Waterhouse. I'll spare you all of the details of my expensive education, but here are a few lowlights:

- ✔ I thought a company called Pallet Pallet — which was trying to consolidate the vibrant and exciting market for wooden warehouse "pallets" — was a turnaround possibility. The company's stock had plunged to pennies after it tried to grow too fast and ran into soaring costs. Needless to say, the pallet industry turned out to be fragmented into tiny mom-and-pop operations for some very good reasons. (I never really found out what they are, though. I'm sure there's a sitcom there somewhere.) And I ended up selling my Pallet Pallet shares at a loss.

- ✔ I decided that flying basket-case Canadian Airlines was another recovery candidate — but being the greatest market strategist of the late 20th century, I was too clever to bother with the company's boring common stock. No, I bought *warrants*, a speculative sort of certificate that only gains real value if the underlying shares climb. Climb a lot, that is. They didn't and I lost more money.

- ✔ I reckoned Asia was in for a major bounce back from its sell-off of 1994, when the average Asian fund dropped 11 percent. So I plunged into madcap Asian mutual funds. Asian markets promptly went into a four-year slump, culminating in the near economic meltdown of 1998. After a while, I stopped looking at my returns.

Okay, I had a couple of successes in technology stocks that actually popped up like they were supposed to. But I've found that funds are the way to go, for me anyway. My mainstream Canadian equity funds — which I once despised as ballast in my scheme for world financial control — have proved to be my best investment. And even my speculative resource and Asian funds have finally bounced back to something like the price at which I bought them — once I stopped looking at them. I wish I'd bought dull global equity funds instead; I would have made a lot more money.

For some reason, my portfolio seems to thrive when I ignore it and get on with my life. When I attempt to fiddle and fuss and apply my master strategies, it all goes wrong again. So now I do what most Canadians do: just check my statement and file it in a drawer. Periodically, I look at my funds' performance and main holdings, but otherwise I let the pros get on with their jobs. After all, why hire a plumber and then go around yourself with droopy pants hanging off your backside? The moral of this story: Prepare yourself for the fact that your best-laid plans, including can't-miss investments, can suddenly go awry. Prepare yourself for this probability and you'll not only sleep better, you'll be able to afford a more expensive mattress.

What pieces of mail from your broker and fund company should you keep? Here's the rule: If it didn't arrive by first-class mail — known as letter-mail — throw it out. Everything that comes at cut-price postage rates is basically marketing bumph.

Brokerage statements and transaction slips are all that you really need to keep from your broker. Going back several years is best, especially if there are taxable transactions involved. The mailings are easy to clip together with a big bulldog pin, in order by date. Use one pin for the current year and then attach all the previous years together using another.

Borrowing to invest can be a good idea if you plan to put the money into your RRSP — that's because contributions to an RRSP can be used to reduce your taxable income, generating lucrative tax savings for you. You can then use the tax refund you get to pay off some of the loan: Banks even have RRSP loan-marketing schemes based on this strategy. And remember that once in the RRSP, the money grows tax-free. Still, even though taking out an RRSP loan offers advantages, experts often advise that you should limit your borrowing to an amount that you can pay off in one or two years. If you're borrowing money to invest outside an RRSP, then the interest you pay on the loan can be written off as an expense for tax purposes, even if your investments tank. But because the government considers RRSPs to be such a generous tax break, interest you pay on a loan taken out for an RRSP contribution can't be used as a tax deduction. Don't let the tax sweetener blind you to the fact that playing with other people's money in this way, by borrowing money to invest, is a risky strategy: you still have to pay them back.

How Various Investments Have Performed

Always remember that when you're saving and investing money, you have a fundamental choice. You can settle for low risk and low return by buying things like bonds or guaranteed deposits. The returns are thin but the fluctuations in the value of your holdings tend to be small. Or you can gamble on high risk plus (you hope) high return. That involves buying stocks. They can make a lot more for investors but the price swings are wild. There just ain't no such animal as a low-risk high-return investment. Sorry. But low-return investments carry their own special risk: the danger that you'll see the value of your savings devoured by inflation, which is the long-term decline in the value of money. It all gets a bit confusing, but here are some examples to help you figure out your choices.

Have a look at Figure 4-1, which shows the rate of return from four different sorts of investments over two decades, to get an idea of what your options are. In each case, the example assumes that an investment of $100 was made each month from mid-1982 to the end of June 2002.

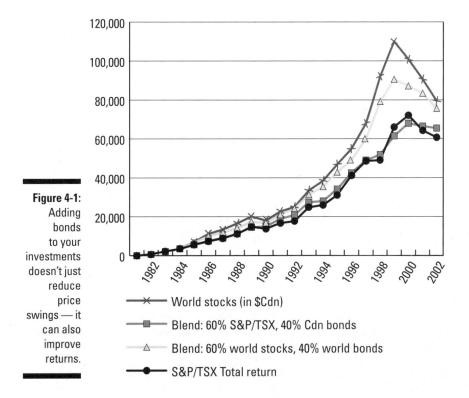

Figure 4-1:
Adding bonds to your investments doesn't just reduce price swings — it can also improve returns.

Of the four strategies, the biggest return for Canadians by a thin margin came from buying into pure global stocks. The most lucrative of the four investment options was owning the blue-chip shares that make up the Morgan Stanley Capital International (MSCI) World Index, which tracks the performance of every major stock market on the planet. From mid-1982 to mid-2002 it produced an average annual return of 10.9 percent in Canadian-dollar terms. That was enough to build a $79,401 nest egg for an investor who put in $100 each month. When I wrote the first edition of this book in

2000 — when the stock market was only beginning to turn bad — the 20-year return on the MSCI World Index was a huge 17.1 percent, and a $100-a-month investor would have ended up with more than $168,000 over 20 years, or twice as much money. In other words, stocks may be a great long-term investment but it depends whose long-term we're talking about — which period you use for measuring. The bottom line is that you may get lucky with stocks if you cash out at the right time, when the market is surging. But who's that lucky? (Not me, let me tell you.) The only sensible course is to own lots of bonds (loans to companies and governments) as well as shares — that way your portfolio has a chance to produce the steady returns that retirement saving is all about. Remember too that a good chunk of the gains from foreign stocks came from currency changes, mainly because the Canadian dollar slumped against the U.S. dollar in the late 1990s. That produced a bonus for Canadian investors: the value of overseas holdings grew steadily because they were denominated in foreign currencies. Investors in the MSCI World Index who made all of their investments in U.S. dollars earned a bit less, about 9.5 percent annually for a nest egg of $67,453, because they didn't profit from the drop in the Canadian dollar.

Next, I've shown the return for a more cautious, balanced portfolio, the sort just about every investor should own, which had 60 percent of its assets in the MSCI World Index (that is, pure stocks) and the rest in a basket of U.S.-dollar bonds. It generated almost as much: 10.4 percent, leaving an investor with $75,678 after 20 years.

The next return is for a patriotic investor who doggedly put $100 each month into the Standard & Poor's/Toronto Stock Exchange composite index, the benchmark for Canada's stock market. Canadian stocks had trouble keeping up with overseas markets in the 1990s, partly because of the drop in our currency. So the TSE 300 produced an average return of only 8.6 percent, leaving our investor with accumulated capital of around $60,698.

Finally, I've shown how an investor with a cautious balanced Canadian portfolio would have done. Quite nicely. This time it's a mixture of the S&P/TSX stocks (60 percent of the portfolio) and the Scotia Capital Markets "Universe" index of Canadian bonds — the sort of investment mix that lots of Canadian pension fund managers and other professionals hold. Over the two decades, the balanced approach produced an annual return of 9.2 percent, ahead of the pure stock portfolio, for an ending value of about $65,388.

For those building a mutual fund portfolio, this reveals some interesting things:

   ✔ Over the two decades, portfolios with lots of bonds performed as well as or even better than 100-percent equity portfolios. Admittedly, that was against a backdrop of falling inflation and interest rates worldwide, always great for bond prices. But cautious investors who took the balanced approach kept up nicely with the ears-pinned-back all-stocks-or-be-damned gamblers. So own some bonds.

✔ Canadian stocks have dramatically underperformed overseas shares, in part because we don't have many of the big giant global companies that made so many investors so rich in the 1980s and 1990s. That means a portfolio that has most of its assets in Canada is exposed to a small market that may be less likely to produce big winners. Up to 30 percent of a registered retirement savings plan can be invested in foreign shares and bonds, so make sure you take advantage of the foreign-content maximum. (Still, remember that at least some of your long-term savings should remain in Canada if you plan to retire in this country. That's because in retirement, you'll need Canadian dollars to draw on. And if our dollar has climbed a lot versus other currencies, it'll reduce the value of your foreign investments.) The fund industry has come up with scores of "clone" or "RSP" funds that let you play foreign markets but also count as Canadian for RRSPs. In Chapter 20 there's more on using these foreign funds to get more foreign property into your RRSP.

✔ Portfolios with bonds suffered much smaller price plunges during the 20 years. At the end of 1999, the all-global-stock portfolio was worth more than $110,000 but it lost more than $30,000 by mid-2002, despite its regular $100-a-month infusion of cash. The mixed global portfolio, by contrast, shrank by less than $15,000.

Portfolios for Your Type of Investing

Let's look at three suggested mutual fund portfolios that offer a good prospect of achieving the different goals of a short-term saver, a balanced investor, and a growth investor. In the case of the balanced and growth portfolios, I've provided both RRSP and non-RRSP versions. The savers' portfolio consists mostly of Canadian assets (no point speculating on currency changes if you're just saving for a Volvo), so it can be held both within and outside an RRSP. Virtually any professionally designed pre-mixed fund package will offer roughly the same proportions of cash (that is, money market funds), bonds, and stocks. Are these the very best portfolios that could ever be designed? No, because the future can't be predicted with complete accuracy. Distrust any financial professional who says he or she can tell you what the markets will be up to, or down to, in the years to come. These portfolios represent a cautious guess as to what the global economy will do and they amount to a forecast that the world isn't likely to slide into either hyperinflation or bitter deflation (a prolonged fall in prices).

The portfolios include lots of so-called *index funds* — funds that simply track a stock or bond market average or index by essentially buying every stock in the market. For example, most Canadian equity index funds are designed to produce a return in line with the S&P/TSX index. Index funds offer huge advantages to investors, such as low costs (less than 1 percent of your money each year compared with well over 2 percent for traditional equity funds) and the reassurance that your fund won't badly underperform the market. But in the late 1990s and in 2000, market indexes just about everywhere were taken over by a few highly priced glamour stocks. That meant index investing itself had become something of a risky proposition — so half of the stock market money in these portfolios has been allocated to traditional-style "actively managed" funds, which have managers who attempt to predict which stocks will go up and which will drop. There's more on index funds in Chapter 15.

Note that international equity funds usually invest in stocks outside of North America, so the international index funds mentioned here don't track the U.S. market. That's why I've also included U.S. index funds. However, global equity funds buy stocks everywhere, including the United States. The actively managed funds in these portfolios are global so there's no need to include separate U.S. equity funds.

Some experts will look at these suggested portfolios and complain that there are no specialized funds here that invest in small companies. In the past, shares in small companies have occasionally produced huge returns and there's evidence that they sometimes do well when big-company stocks are languishing. Traditionally, that has happened in very hot stock markets, when investors are willing to buy risky little stocks in pursuit of big gains. In other words, buying shares in lesser-known companies provides something called *diversification* — the strategy of spreading an investor's risk among different investments. But small-company shares also have a nasty habit of stagnating for years and their returns tend to be highly volatile: Big gains one year and then nothing for several years. So to keep things simple, I've left small-company funds out of these sample portfolios. You might miss out on a percentage point or two of returns every few years, but you'll be avoiding a lot of risk. As you get more comfortable with investing, you may decide to add some small-stock funds to your portfolio. Just make sure that you buy at least two, because different types of small stocks tend to thrive at different times. For example, in 1999 investors went crazy for obscure little technology outfits but they didn't want to know about established small businesses that did dull stuff like fix drilling equipment. It's frustrating to find yourself stuck with a manager who bought just the wrong sort of small-company shares.

In Part III there are chapters on each type of fund, explaining its advantages and drawbacks in detail.

A penny earned is a penny saved

The first portfolio, shown in Table 4-1, is ideal for savers. It includes small quantities of regular bonds, even though their prices can be volatile, to increase its interest income. And the global bonds provide a small amount of protection against a plunge in the Canadian dollar because they're bought and sold in foreign currencies. In fact, you could make this portfolio even simpler by just putting half of the money into a money market fund and the rest into a short-term bond. Money market funds are very unlikely ever to lose money for their unitholders (it would probably take a major financial dislocation before one did). Short-term bond funds are a little more dangerous, but they're also slightly more lucrative to own than money market funds. The average short-term bond fund produced an average annual return of 5.5 percent during the ten years ended June 2002, compared with 4.1 percent for the average money market fund.

Table 4-1	Suggested Portfolio for Savings (20% Money Market and 80% Bonds)
Fund Type	**Percentage of Total Portfolio**
Money market fund	20%
Canadian short-term bond or short-term bond index fund	50%
Canadian bond or bond index fund	20%
Global bond or global bond index fund	10%

Balancing act

The next two portfolios, Tables 4-2 and 4-3, for balanced investors, are truly ones you can just buy and forget. Yes, they will go into a slump if inflation returns and interest rates surge. But that's true of virtually any investment except for cash (usually held in the form of bonds and other debt instruments with less than a year to go before they mature). With their large 30-percent proportion of cash and cash-like short-term bonds, they are portfolios that are unlikely to lose more than 10 percent in a single year, unless there's a sharp uptick in inflation, the economy slides into a recession, or some national or global mishap sends the bond market into a downward spiral.

Table 4-2	Suggested RRSP or RRIF Portfolio for Balanced Investors (55% Bonds and 45% Stocks)
Fund Type	**Percentage of Total Portfolio**
Money market fund	5%
Canadian short-term bond or short-term bond index fund	25%
Canadian bond or bond index fund	15%
Global bond fund or global bond index fund	10%

(continued)

Table 4-2 *(continued)*

Fund Type	Percentage of Total Portfolio
Canadian equity index fund	8%
Conservative Canadian equity fund A	4%
Conservative Canadian equity fund B	3%
Conservative global equity fund A	7%
Conservative global equity fund B	8%
RSP international index fund	10%
U.S. equity index fund	5%

Table 4-3 **Suggested Non-RRSP or RRIF Portfolio for Balanced Investors (55% Bonds and 45% Stocks)**

Fund Type	Percentage of Total Portfolio
Money market fund	5%
Canadian short-term bond or short-term bond index fund	25%
Canadian bond or bond index fund	15%
Global bond or global bond index fund	10%
Canadian equity index fund	8%
Conservative Canadian equity fund A	4%
Conservative Canadian equity fund B	3%
Conservative global equity fund A	7%
Conservative global equity fund B	8%
International equity index fund	10%
U.S. equity index fund	5%

One for the risk-takers

Finally, there's the Ferrari, for those who relish the cold taste of fear, the brutal snapping and the terrible slashing of the stock market. Check out Tables 4-4 and 4-5. You could easily make these portfolios more exciting and dangerous by reducing the bond weighting even more, or by buying emerging markets funds and narrow regional funds that invest in Asia or Europe. Arguably, every aggressive portfolio should contain a small weighting in developing countries (because of their huge growth prospects), but I've left out emerging markets funds to keep the portfolios as simple as possible. In any case, at least one of your conservative global equity funds is certain to own a few companies in emerging nations. You could also step on the gas by going into volatile sector funds that track just one type of company, such as technology outfits or oil and gas producers. However, once again, your index funds and actively managed funds are almost certain to own these companies and industries anyway. In short, a portfolio like this is certain to do well as long as stock markets stay strong. It's very broadly diversified, and its big index fund component means that you'll end up owning lots of huge, well-run companies.

Table 4-4	Suggested RRSP or RRIF Portfolio for Growth Investors (25% Bonds and 75% Stocks)
Fund Type	*Percentage of Total Portfolio*
Canadian bond fund or bond index fund	15%
RSP/non-RSP global bond fund	10%
Canadian equity index fund	10%
Conservative Canadian equity fund A	5%
Conservative Canadian equity fund B	5%
RSP/non-RSP international index fund	20%
RSP/non-RSP U.S. equity index fund	10%
Conservative global equity fund A	13%
Conservative global equity fund B	12%

Table 4-5	Suggested Non-RRSP or RRIF Portfolio for Growth Investors (25% Bonds and 75% Stocks)
Fund Type	**Percentage of Total Portfolio**
Canadian bond fund or bond index fund	15%
Global bond fund	10%
Canadian equity index fund	10%
Conservative Canadian equity fund A	5%
Conservative Canadian equity fund B	5%
International index fund	20%
U.S. equity index fund	10%
Conservative global equity fund A	13%
Conservative global equity fund B	12%

As you become more knowledgeable about and interested in investing, you may want to start adding to or altering these suggestions. But they're a good place to start when you're adding the power of mutual funds to your financial plan.

Chapter 5

Beyond Mutual Funds

. . . .

In This Chapter

▶ Considering Canada Savings Bonds

▶ Checking out old reliable — guaranteed investment certificates

▶ Looking at regular bonds and strip bonds

▶ Taking stock of stocks

▶ Sniffing out income trusts

▶ Catching up with the new Exchange Traded Funds

▶ Investigating hedge funds and other managed products

. . . .

So you've got your debt under control and your insurance taken care of. Time to start saving money. But what are you going to do with those vast piles of cash? Think of this chapter as an investment primer, a rundown on the drawbacks and attractions of the different types of financial assets you can buy with your savings. If you're certain by now that funds are the way to go for you, then feel free to skip to Part II, where I explain where you can go to buy them. But it's useful to know about the other investment choices you have — including Canada Savings Bonds and guaranteed investment certificates, which can't be bought through mutual funds at all.

Don't worry, though. The decisions you need to make are fairly simple when you come down to it. The investment business is an incredibly conservative industry. For all the dot-com flash and techno-trading systems, your basic investment options are the same as they were in the 1920s or even the 1820s — stocks, bonds, or cash. Here's what's out there: everything from the mundane to the manic. In this chapter, I take you for a stroll down Risk Road, moving from the very safest choices to the most unpredictable. Along the way, I point out some of the dangers and delights of each investment — so that even if you end up handing your money over to a fund company to manage, you'll at least have an idea of what they're going to do with it.

Canada Savings Bonds: Dull Yet Dependable

Every fall, Ottawa starts running ads in the newspapers and on the TV, touting the wonders of lending money to the government by buying Canada Savings Bonds and their flashier-sounding cousins, Canada Premium Bonds. Some provinces sell their own versions. Actually, these things aren't really bonds at all since their market value never fluctuates in line with prevailing interest rates. That's because they can be cashed in at virtually any time by simply selling them back to the government at the purchase price plus accumulated interest. With most normal bonds, you have to find a buyer to take them off your hands and there's no certainty as to the price you get. If interest rates have gone up, making other bonds more attractive, you'll have to accept a lower price than the one you paid.

The ability to get your cash back easily makes CSBs and CPBs like a sort of savings voucher, entitling the holder to a stream of interest payments and the return of his or her capital on demand. That flexibility is one of the great virtues of Canada Savings Bonds, and it's a good reason to consider buying them for your short-term savings needs — but the low interest rates on offer mean they're unsuitable for the lion's share of your savings. Meanwhile, the reassuring government guarantee makes CSBs suitable for the "cash" or no-risk portion of your investment portfolio. CSBs and CPBs currently have a *term to maturity* of ten years — that is, you have to take your money back after that time or roll it into another set of bonds. They can be bought at nearly all banks, credit unions, stockbrokers, and trust companies. Or you can buy them from the government itself: Go to the Web site at www.csb.gc.ca or call 1-888-996-8899, Monday to Friday from 8 a.m. to 8 p.m. Eastern time. Thousands of employers across Canada offer them to their staff by way of direct deductions from their pay.

The interest rates paid on the bonds are announced at the time of sale but the government is free to increase the rate above those minimums if interest rates in the broad market have increased enough (if the rate is too low, the public have an annoying habit of cashing in all of their CSBs). Canada Premium Bonds pay slightly more interest but carry more limitations on when you cash them in. Canada Savings Bonds can be sold back to the government at any time (although you get no interest if you cash them in within the first 90 days), but Premium Bonds are redeemable once a year, on the anniversary of the issue date or during the 30 days afterward.

Apart from the ability to get your investment back easily (a wonderful convenience), CSBs and CPBs come with some major advantages for investors. They are:

✔ **Easy to buy:** You can make small investments of as little as $100, or $500 when the bonds are bought under the "RSP option" for inclusion in a registered retirement savings plan. You can put the bonds in your own "self-directed RRSP" — an account that you run yourself at a stock-broker or discount broker — or in a special RRSP for Canada Savings Bonds and Canada Premium Bonds. It's called the Canada RSP.

✔ **Available in two appealing types:** These bonds can be purchased in *regular interest* form, with the annual interest payments going directly into your bank account. Or you can buy no-brainer *compound interest* bonds, where the income is added to your investment and thus starts generating interest of its own.

✔ **Safe and secure:** The money is safe as long as the federal government's credit remains good. And you always know exactly how much your *principal* — the money you have tied up in an investment — is worth. That's not the case with a stock, bond, or mutual fund, whose value may have slumped by the time you go to sell it.

However, there are some major drawbacks to CSBs and CPBs:

✔ **Low returns:** The price of security and convenience is a return that's a lot lower than the potential payback from bonds or stocks. The Canada Savings Bonds that went on sale from March 2 to April 1, 2002 carry an interest rate of 1.30 percent for the first year, 2.75 percent for the second, and 4 percent for the third year, for an annual compound rate of return of 2.67 over three years. The Canada Premium Bonds that went on sale during the same period carry an interest rate of 2 percent for the first year, rising to 6 percent for the fifth year, which works out at an annual compound rate of 3.99 percent if held for the five years.

As you can see from Table 5-1, an investor who invested $10,000 in Canada Savings Bonds and left it there from mid-1982 to mid-2002 ended up with just under $40,000. He or she would have gotten almost exactly the same 7.2-percent annual return by buying one-year guaranteed investment certificates at a bank. However, an investor who took on more risk and put her money into AGF Management Ltd.'s big $1.4-billion AGF Canadian Balanced Fund, a typical and fairly cautious balanced portfolio of stocks and high-quality bonds, would have finished with almost $74,000 — or 84 percent more. (The investment returns were calculated using Globe Hysales, a mutual fund database that the *Globe and Mail* sells to investment advisers.)

Table 5-1	Comparison Growth of $10,000 Invested for 20 Years		
Time Period	*One-year GIC*	*Canada Savings Bonds*	*AGF Cdn. Balanced*
Initial investment (1982)	$10,000	$10,000	$10,000
After 5.5 years (1987)	$16,778	$17,226	$23,710
After 10.5 years (1992)	$26,534	$27,205	$32,871
After 15.5 years (1997)	$33,330	$34,741	$63,917
After 20 years (2002)	$38,887	$39,844	$73,382

> ✔ **Lack of long-term projections:** Because the rates on CSBs and CPBs are periodically re-set to keep them in line with competing interest rates, it's impossible to know exactly what you'll earn over the life of the bond beyond the announced years. By contrast, if you buy a GIC or ordinary bond, and hold it until it matures, you know exactly what you're getting.

CSBs and CPBs are really more of a savings vehicle than a true investment. There's nothing wrong with that — but the price you pay for simplicity and peace of mind is a low return.

Go ahead and buy them if you want a safe investment that you can choose and then forget about. CSBs are great for people who want simplicity and security. The government takes care of the record keeping, and the return you get will always be better than that of a bank account. But the interest rate on CSBs and CPBs is so low that with a little homework it's easy to find investments that will make your money work harder.

The Good Old GIC: You Know Where You Sleep

You've no doubt noticed that most banks offer miserable rates of interest — 1 percent if you're lucky — on money dumped in a "savings" account. You can do better, though, if you leave the cash with the bank, insurance company, or trust company for a fixed period by buying a *guaranteed investment certificate*. A GIC is a deposit that a financial institution accepts on the understanding that the money will be returned after a set number of years plus a guaranteed amount of interest. The interest is calculated on an annual basis and each year's interest is usually added or "compounded" onto the total for the purpose of calculating the next year's interest — so you earn interest on interest. For example, a $10,000 deposit for three years at a rate of 5 percent will be worth $10,500 after one year, $11,025 after two years, and

$11,576.25 after three years. A drawback is that you may not be able to get the deposit back before the term is up or, if you can, you might have to forfeit the interest earned. In other words, these deposits aren't as *liquid*, cashable, as you might think. That means GICs are less flexible than Canada Savings Bonds. The great beauty of GICs, though, is that you know exactly where you stand: for example, a five-year deposit of $10,000 at a rate of 5 percent compounded annually will give you $12,762.82 after 60 months, no more and no less.

For years, generations even, the GIC was Canada's favourite investment and it's still the number-one choice of many Europeans. And why not? As recently as 1990, when interest rates were high and prices for food and shelter were rising fast, you could leave money on deposit at a big safe bank and come back a year later to collect a lump sum that had magically grown by 12 percent. Well, it wasn't magic, actually. Banks had to offer those kinds of rates to attract any money because inflation was rising. But as you can see from Table 5-2, a steady drop in the rate of inflation during the 1990s meant a remorseless decline in GIC rates. And once rates slumped below the 7- to 8-percent mark in the early part of the decade, the stage was set for a flood of hundreds of billions of dollars into mutual funds as Canadians demanded a decent return on their money.

Table 5-2	One-Year Average GIC Rate 1990–Mid-2002												
One-Year Average Return													
1990	1991	1992	1993	1994	1995	1996	1997	1998	1999	2000	2001	2002
12.2%	8.66%	6.1%	4.8%	5.87%	6.25%	3.64%	2.82%	3.69%	3.89%	4.77%	2.67%	1.66%

A mild outbreak of inflationary fears in 1999 and early 2000 lifted interest rates and the returns on GICs above their 1997 and 1998 lows. But as of mid-2002, returns on one-year GICs at big banks had slumped below 2 percent. No bonanza. Or bonzana.

A quick way to find out the various GIC rates on offer from a wide variety of institutions is to buy the *Globe and Mail* on Mondays. It lists rates for mortgages, deposits, and savings rates at a range of lenders and deposit takers, from the biggest bank to the most obscure trust company. You can get a higher rate by going to a smaller company, but dealing with the little outfit may be more troublesome because it won't have the same branch network and resources.

Don't spurn the humble GIC out of hand. They never lose money, while the majority of Canadian equity mutual funds dropped in value during three of the ten calendar years from 1992 to 2001 — and the average fund lost 4.3 percent in the first half of 2002. GICs offer other advantages:

✓ **Simplicity:** They're simple and quick to buy, with no extra fees or complicated forms to fill out. Just about any bank, insurance company, or stockbroker will sell you one.

✓ **Income generating:** They're a useful planning tool if you need your portfolio to throw off a regular stream of income. That can be done by "laddering" GICs — putting the money into deposits with separate terms, each maturing on a different date to match your spending needs. Even if you don't need the money for income, having your GICs come due at different times is also handy for reducing "reinvestment risk." That's the problem of getting a pile of money to reinvest from a maturing bond or deposit just as interest rates are low. If the money comes up for re-investment at different times, you can re-invest it at a variety of interest rates.

✓ **Safe and secure:** If you buy a GIC from a bank, trust company, or loan company, as long as the GIC's term to maturity doesn't exceed five years, your money is protected by insurance provided by the federal government's Canada Deposit Insurance Corporation. If the financial institution fails, CDIC will cover an individual for up to $60,000 in deposits (including chequing accounts and the like but *not* mutual funds) at that institution. When buying a GIC, always make sure that the company you're dealing with has CDIC coverage. Go to the Web site at www.cdic.ca for more information, including the "Quiz on Deposit Insurance"— at last, a fun activity for guests at one of your interminable soirees.

But before you abandon all thoughts of buying mutual funds and plunge into GICs instead, remember that fixed-rate deposits are a dangerous investment in one important sense. Their rates of return can be so low that they do little to protect you against inflation. As Table 5-3 shows, even quite modest rates of inflation eat away alarmingly quickly at the real value of your savings. The U.S. dollar, still the world's main store of wealth, lost its value at an average of about 5 percent during the 1980s and 1990s — in other words, prices in the United States rose by about 5 percent per year. Inflation of just 5 percent a year wipes out one-quarter of the value of your money in about six years. In Canada, inflation in mid-2002 stood at just over 2.1 percent, but the Bank of Canada was raising interest rates, which it usually does when worried that inflation rates will climb. The curse of inflation means that, as an investor, you're constantly clambering up a slippery, moving staircase covered in rotting mackerel and parts of Scotsmen. Stand still or go forward too slowly, and you end up sliding backward.

Table 5-3	How Inflation Destroys Money over Time
Time Elapsed	*Approx. Value of $10,000 at 5-Percent Inflation*
Initial amount	$10,000
One year	$9,500

Time Elapsed	Approx. Value of $10,000 at 5-Percent Inflation
Two years	$9,025
Three years	$8,574
Four years	$8,145
Five years	$7,738
Six years	$7,351
Seven years	$6,983
Eight years	$6,634
Nine years	$6,302
Ten years	$5,987

Types of GICs

GICs come in a sometimes-bewildering range of shapes and flavours, so always make sure you understand all of the mechanics before you buy one. Get the employee of the financial institution to write down the value of the deposit when it matures (except in the case of GICs, whose returns are tied to the stock market). Here are some common variations:

✔ **Index-linked GICs:** These pay you little or no fixed interest but they promise to return your initial investment and pay a return that's linked to the performance of a stock market index — always a bit watered-down, though, in order to pay for the guaranteed return of capital and leave a profit margin for the bank. In other words, your money is safe from loss but your potential return isn't as good as it would have been investing directly in stocks. For example, a typical GIC linked to the Canadian stock market might pay no guaranteed interest but give the investor a return identical to the change in the Standard & Poor's/Toronto Stock Exchange composite index — subject to a maximum of 30 percent. So if you invested $10,000 and the market went up 40 percent, you'd get back $13,000, not $14,000. Index GICs were popular in the late 1990s, when interest rates on ordinary one-year GICs fell below 3 percent. The problem with these products is that their rules and terms are so complicated that it can be difficult or impossible to know how well you're doing as you go along. Yes, they offer some stock market action for investors who would otherwise be too nervous to go into equities, but most investors will do better with an index fund and a couple of conservative equity funds, especially if they can ride out downturns in the market over a few years.

- ✔ **Cashable GICs:** Traditional GICs tie your money up or at least reduce the interest you get if you cash out early. But cashable GICs let you take all or part of your money out early with no penalty. Expect to get a lower annual rate, though. It can be a full percentage point lower than the return on a normal non-cashable GIC.

- ✔ **Convertible GICs:** RRSP marketing season is the first 60 days of the calendar year, when money put into your RRSP can be used to reduce taxable income for the previous year. For example, if you earned $50,000 during 2002 but managed to put $5,000 into a plan by March 1, 2003, then you'd have to pay tax on income of only $45,000 for 2002. During that two-month period, institutions offer flexible GICs that let you invest your money at the one-year rate, but then allow you to switch to a longer-term deposit or to the company's mutual funds.

- ✔ **Escalating-rate GICs:** These GICs also don't lock you in. You can cash out without penalty after one or two years, but if you stay on, the interest rate gets higher.

Bonds and Strip Bonds

Bonds are loans to governments or corporations that have been packaged into certificates that trade on the open market. They usually pay a fixed rate of interest, often twice a year. And they "mature" or come due after a set number of years, when the holder of the bond gets back the value of the original loan, known as the "principal." But don't bother buying individual bonds until you've got $10,000 or so to spend, because the cost of buying a cheap bond index mutual fund is so low. Index funds, which just earn a return in line with an entire bond market or index, are particularly suitable for the bond market because normal human managers find it very difficult to earn much more than their rivals without taking risks. Bond index funds from CIBC or Toronto-Dominion Bank can be held for less than 1 percent a year. That's less than $100 out of a $10,000 investment, so you're doing fine.

If you're comfortable buying and selling on the stock exchange, it's worth thinking about buying a *bond exchange-traded fund* — bond ETFs are units in a simple trust that give you ownership of bonds but trade on the exchange like a share. There's a section on exchange-traded funds — which are perhaps the best deal of all for small investors — later in this chapter. The big advantage to buying bonds or a bond ETF is that you save on fees. Most Canadian bond funds hit their investors for at least 2 percent in annual charges and expenses, so buying bonds directly means you get a far better yield. But one problem is that the brokers aren't yet geared to offering competitive *order execution* for large numbers of retail investors who want to buy bonds — people can find it hard to get information or do trades. It's just not a popular product and profit margins for the dealer are thin, so the brokers haven't bothered doing much. There's information on trading bonds at `www.ebond.ca`, a Web site with full listings of current bond yields.

If you want to put, say, $25,000 into bonds you're getting rich, so it's time to hire an accountant to help with your investments. Watch out for fund sales-people, though. If you invest $25,000 in a regular white-bread broker-sold bond fund with expenses of 2 percent and up, you'll be paying $500 in annual fees and costs. Of course, you may just decide it's worth it to pay the cost. You're busy, after all, weaving your hair into those wonderful intricate little ringlets. And here's more good news: in Chapter 14, Bond Funds: Boring Can Be Sexy Too, I suggest funds that offer better deals on annual expenses.

The trouble with bonds is that, unlike stocks, they don't trade in a central market place where the prices are posted. If you buy stocks, your broker usually just acts as an "agent" who connects you with the seller's broker, collecting a commission for the service. But your broker generally buys and sells bonds as a "principal" — that is, the firm actually owns the bonds it trades, holding them in "inventory" like a store. That means when you're trading bonds, you generally have to ask your broker what the firm's price quote is for a bond you want to buy or sell. And then you more or less have to accept the price that's offered.

There can be even bigger problems buying and selling *strip bonds*, which are bonds that have been modified by brokers to reflect the fact that many long-term buyers who hold bonds until maturity aren't interested in collecting periodic interest payments. In fact, such dribs and drabs of interest are a liability because they must constantly be reinvested. So strip bonds pay no interest until they mature — the interest payments have been "stripped" away. Instead, they're bought at a deep discount to their face value, maturing at full value or "par" like a normal bond. For example, you might pay your broker 50 cents on the dollar for a strip bond maturing in ten years. That will give you an annual compound yield of about 7.2 percent. In other words, an investment of $5,000 becomes $10,000 after a decade. Because strip bondholders are prepared to wait until they get any of their money back, they're rewarded with a higher yield to maturity. It's often .5 to 1 percentage point of extra yield yearly compared with a regular bond with a similar term to maturity.

Strip bonds can be difficult to get rid of. They're volatile, losing their market value quickly when interest rates rise. That's because higher rates offer better interest-earning opportunities in the here and now, so they rapidly devalue money you don't get for a long time. And strip bonds are all about waiting for a faraway payoff. Because strip bonds are often sold as a retail product, your broker may be reluctant to buy one back from you at a decent price if the firm has no demand for strips from other clients. So if you're buying a strip, plan on holding it to maturity.

You can put through a regular bond order at discount broker TD Waterhouse for as little as $5,000 , but the yield you get won't be as good as the one you see listed in the newspapers. Table 5-4 shows a typical listing for a government bond and one for a big blue-chip corporation in summer 2002. These are approximate rates for large trades of bonds and you could expect to pay a higher price, and get a smaller yield, with a small order. Notice how in each case the bond was producing an annual yield lower than its annual stated interest rate, or *coupon*. That's because, with interest rates so low, investors hungry for income were trading the bonds at a premium to their face value. When the bonds mature, at their face value, the buyers who paid a premium will take a small loss on the extra they paid. Notice also how the Royal Bank bond offers a higher yield than the federal government issue: corporate bonds yield more than government bonds because they're slightly more risky (the government can print its own money, after all). But it's harder to trade corporate bonds because the market is smaller, and if you want to get out of a bond you could find it hard to sell the thing at a decent price.

Table 5-4	Yield on Ten-Year Canadian Government and Nine-Year Royal Bank Bonds			
Issuer	*Interest Rate*	*Maturity Date*	*Price per $100 Face Value*	*Annual Yield (to maturity)*
Canada	5.25%	June 2012	$100.77	5.2%
Royal Bank of Canada	7.2%	June 2011	$105.37	6.4%

So if you have at least $10,000 to play with, buy bonds and hold them to maturity by all means. You know exactly what yield you're getting and how much money you'll have when the bonds mature. With a bond mutual fund, which is constantly rolling over its holdings, you won't have nearly that much certainty. For much more on bond funds, have a look at Chapter 14.

If you plan to try trading bonds, remember that making money in this market ("going forward," an annoying expression that Bay Street types like to use a dozen times before breakfast) is going to be tougher in the long run. That's because bond prices usually only go up when interest rates and the rate of inflation fall — if inflation stays unchanged, then all you're likely to get from a bond is its yield to maturity at the time of purchase. The fact that inflation has been in a more or less steady decline since 1990 means the good times may be over for the bond market, for now at least. As of mid-2002, as we've seen, ten-year Canadian government bonds offered a yield of only about 5 percent a year, and that may well be all the buyers end up getting.

Stocks — Thrills, Spills, and Twisted Wreckage

The stock market is insane. While it is possible to spot stocks trading at crazy prices and make money buying those individual shares, it's also hard, so hard as to be damned near impossible. Unless you plan to spend quite a bit of time tracking stocks and reading the financial press, you're probably best off in equity funds. The easiest strategy of all: just climb aboard the madness by putting a chunk of your money into stock index funds — which track the whole stock market — and you'll be doing what a lot of smart pros do. The indexes themselves go crazy from time to time, as they did in 1999 and 2000 when technology and telecommunications stocks dominated the market benchmarks, but when you look at the long-term record of U.S. stocks, for example, it's hard to stay away from the index-fund party. You're only alive three times, after all, and the last two times you come back as something in the sea, so why not have fun now?

As Figure 5-1 shows, an investment of $10,000 in Canadian dollars in U.S. shares in the summer of 1973 — when the great 1970s bear market was still very much alive and biting — multiplied your money almost 40 times over by mid-2002. The final total was an impressive $393,000, down from well over half a million dollars at the end of tech-crazy 1999. But for most investors, the reality has been a bit more prosaic. A lot more, in fact. The same $10,000 put into Asian stocks (excluding Japan) grew to about $160,000, while Canadian stocks left you with a similar $157,000.

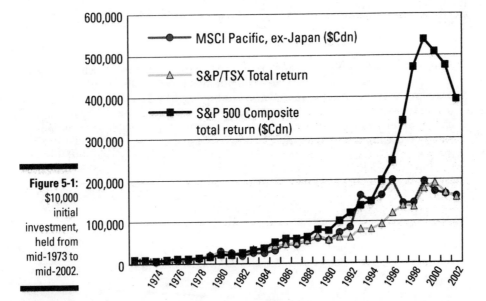

Figure 5-1: $10,000 initial investment, held from mid-1973 to mid-2002.

Think you can beat the market? Go ahead and dive into the shark . . . er, whatever . . . water where loads of sharks are swimming around. Picking good stocks consistently is really, really hard. You also need a broker to put through your trades. Your shares get held in the brokerage's computer system under an account in your name. Always check your statement and transaction confirmation slips carefully, because mistakes happen.

If you want to buy individual stocks, you will need a bit of money to make it worth the trouble and expense — say, at least $10,000 — unless you're just throwing a few thousand at the market for laughs (and it is enjoyable, so try it when you get a chance). Most trades go through in "board lots" of 100 shares at a time, for efficiency. If you're dealing in blue-chip companies, buying 100 shares can add up — it costs $2,500 for 100 shares trading at $25 each. Buying less than 100 shares at a time is generally inefficient because it means dealing in an "odd" or "broken" lot of less than 100. If you deal in odd lots, you'll often get a lower price when you sell and have to pay more per share when you buy.

And, as usual in investing, you must make a choice between having a sales-person take care of all of the humdrum stuff at a cost, or doing it yourself at less expense. The price of buying stock through a full-service traditional stockbroker is usually shrouded in black curtains and dry ice. A *Globe and Mail* columnist, Rob Carrick, wrote an entertaining piece in May 2000 noting that establishing commission rates is like bargaining in a grim, sweaty bazaar on the edge of a poisoned desert — in other words, full-service brokerage commissions are completely negotiable. But his piece quoted commission rates, before "discounts," at two brokers that ranged up to 3.5 percent for a small trade. That's quite a haircut to take when you buy and again when you sell, but most frequent traders could haggle for much less. But don't expect a full-service broker to be too thrilled about your business unless you've got at least $50,000 to throw into the market, because with any less than that you're more of an annoyance than a revenue stream.

So investors with modest means are left with a discount broker, which may impose no minimum account size at all but also provides little or no advice or help. Their commission rates vary, but buying, say, 100 shares at $25 each would typically cost you between $25 and $50, depending on whether you use the Internet or a live human to do your trade. That's between 1 percent and 2 percent of your trade but it's a one-off expense until you sell again, so there's no point getting worked up about it. There's plenty more on discount brokers in Chapter 6.

Buying and selling stocks profitably and reliably is difficult, maybe impossible, but there seems to be evidence that ordinary investors can do well by investing in a few well-run, growing companies and simply holding them for years. Mind you, that's emotionally tough to do. Take Bombardier Inc., a Montreal company that sells planes, trains, and other transportation equipment all over the world. If you'd bought Bombardier shares in the summer of 1995, you'd have multiplied your money more than five times over by early 2000. But it was a scary ride — the stock took a hiding in 1998, for example, after the company reported rotten results from its consumer division, which makes Ski-Doo snowmobiles and Sea-Doo watercraft. And the shares tanked again after the terrorist attacks of September 11, 2001, as investors worried about a huge downturn in the global aviation industry. So to succeed at the tough game of equity investing, you need not only luck but also the intestinal fortitude to hold on through nasty losses. There's much more on the stock market in Chapter 10. Have a look at Figure 5-2 to see the steep rise and fall of Bombardier.

Figure 5-2: Bombardier's share price over five years.

Source: www.globeinvestor.com

For those who find even stocks too staid, options, warrants, futures, and rights are the wonder drug of investing — volatile ways to play or speculate on a share, market, or commodity. They're structured to offer faster price changes than the underlying asset itself. The general principle is that for a little money you get to "buy risk" from someone who doesn't want it. But the downside is that your wild party has a time limit because the speculative instrument always expires after a set period. That's a huge drawback: Many a market veteran will testify that picking the right investment is tough enough, without having the clock ticking against you. Only buy these things with money you don't care about.

Income Trusts — Er, Why Does this Cheque Have a Faint Smell of Sardines?

Insulin, the snowmobile, Trivial Pursuit — here's another great Canadian invention. Since the late 1990s, Bay Street has led the world in creating income trusts for small investors. *Income trusts* are businesses that have been turned into a sort of fund that pays out regular — usually monthly — distributions to holders of their units. In mid-2002, the *yield,* or yearly payout to investors per dollar you paid to own it, was 10 percent on most trusts. In other words, per $10,000 investment, you could expect $1,000 in income payments, or one-tenth annually, versus less than $500 on government bonds. Plus, shareholders get tax benefits which let them delay having to pay some of the tax on the payments they receive.

Trusts hold a lot of promise, along with some risk, for small investors. Financiers have taken regular companies and essentially turned them inside out so that the cash the businesses generate is paid directly to investors in the form of a frequent cheque. That replaces the regular corporate system in which businesses generate a profit that is then taxed before they can pay out a dividend to their owners.

Canadians have taken to the idea with wild enthusiasm — with interest rates so low, any investment that produces regular income is welcome. And the public clearly appreciates the fact that you know where you stand with an income trust. If the distribution gets cut or omitted, then management is on the hook to explain what's gone wrong. Income trusts trade on the stock exchange like an ordinary share, so they're simple to buy and sell. Look for them under "trust units" in the *Globe and Mail's* stock market listings.

As of June 2002, big broker CIBC World Markets estimated that income trusts listed on the Toronto Stock Exchange were worth a total of more than $24 billion. Almost half were in oil and gas, electricity, and pipelines: oil and real estate companies were the first to use this type of financing vehicle. But in the past two years, income trusts have popped up in a bewildering variety of forms. There's a fund that pays out cash flow from international sardine producer Connor Brothers. two frozen-food warehouse funds, a pet food fund, and a fund that pays income from A&W burger restaurants — plus another fund for The Keg steakhouse chain.

So far — and I must stress that it's the early days for this type of investment — the funds have generally kept their distributions flowing as promised (oil and gas trusts have had to cut theirs when commodity prices fall, but that was obvious to investors all along). CIBC estimated that for buyers in mid-2002, oil and gas trusts were likely to produce yields of about 12.5 percent in 2003, while the other varied trusts were poised to provide yields of between 8 and 11 percent.

Now, those are pretty generous income streams (remember that ten-year government bonds were yielding only 5 percent or so), but income trusts are riskier than a bond. In fact, many professional investors say you should treat them like a stock. There's no guarantee that the underlying businesses will indeed be able to keep up the profits or revenue needed for the distributions — even though the brokerage firms selling these things say they've selected stable, predictable companies for the trusts. The structure of the trusts tends to be horrendously tangled, with corporate diagrams that would make your hair stand on end — complexity is always a red flag in investing. And there's the danger that the necessity to pay out cash will in fact bleed some of the businesses dry. But the small investor who buys a trust has one thing on his or her side: mutual funds are also investing in them. Anxious to get in on the act, mutual fund companies have started funds that buy the trusts. I'm a little skeptical here: when you combine the trusts' management fees with the fees on the new funds (the average "Canadian income trusts" mutual fund has an annual management expense ratio of 2.2 percent), you end up paying a lot of money to a lot of people. But at least professional investors are keeping an eye on the folks running the trusts.

The bottom line here is that income trusts are too new and potentially volatile to go overboard on, but the generous yield means they're a reasonable bet for many investors. Just make sure you buy at least three or four to spread your risk.

Exchange Traded Funds: Perhaps the Best Thing Yet

This new investment vehicle has the potential to seriously damage the mutual fund industry if they catch on in a big way. That's because for investors, they're a simple concept that offers great returns, simplicity, and low expenses. They're also an investment idea that Canada played a major role in developing.

Exchange Traded Funds are funds that trade on a stock exchange like shares, but have nobody in the driver's seat. All they do is simply own all of the stocks in a market benchmark — such as the Standard & Poor's 500-share index of America's big companies — or in an industry group. That means ETFs give investors the same returns as a particular market or group of stocks, but they do so at a much lower cost than practically any mutual fund. The idea is catching on — as of 2002, more than U.S.$110 billion worth of ETFs was trading on world markets.

Let's use Canada's biggest Exchange Traded Fund as an example. As of late summer 2002, just over Cdn$3.3 billion worth of "i60" units traded on the Toronto Stock Exchange, under the symbol XIU, at around $37 each. The buyer of one of these units was acquiring a tiny slice of each of the stocks in the S&P/TSX 60 Index of 60 big blue-chip Canadian companies, with a dividend cheque arriving in the mail every quarter. The i60s give their investors returns in line with the S&P/TSX 60 Index, which lost almost 10 percent in the year ended June 30, 2000. Sure enough, i60s dropped from $45 to around $40 in the same time frame. But i60s carry management expense ratios of only 0.17 percent, which is less than one-tenth of the average 2.6-percent expense burden carried by the average Canadian large-cap equity fund (the sort that invests in big companies). The holder of i60s is just tracking the index, but he or she, over time, is almost certain to end up ahead of the average mutual fund buyer. See Chapter 15, where I describe index funds and explain why it's so hard for most regular mutual funds to beat the market.

Not all ETFs just give you ownership of a broad market index, though. In Canada, for example, you can buy "iEnergy" units that track oil and gas stocks, "iFin" units that track financial shares, or "iGold" units that give you ownership of gold stocks, all with much lower costs than the specialized mutual funds that invest in those industries.

Here's another neat idea — you can buy "iG5" units on the TSX that are designed to give you the same return as government of Canada five-year bonds and "iG10" units that give you ownership of ten-year bonds. Again, the management expense ratio is rock-bottom, at only 0.25 percent annually, compared with almost 2 percent on the average Canadian bond fund. The mathematics of how these bond ETFs calculate their interest payments and so on is daunting. But, like all of the ETFs I've mentioned so far, they're run by Barclays Global Investors, a huge international investment manager with the resources to do the job properly and a reputation that would be damaged by any foul-ups. You can get good information on Exchange Traded Funds at the Barclays Web site, at www.iunits.com. Toronto-Dominion Bank is also a player in ETFs — check out www.tdassetmanagement.com.

Wouldn't you know it, though, ETFs do come with some disadvantages. There are brokerage commissions to pay when you buy and sell them, and they're less convenient to invest in than mutual funds — you usually can't set up regular investments of small amounts each month, for example. And unlike mutual funds, ETFs generally don't offer automatic reinvestment of your dividends in more units (although your broker might) — forcing you to reinvest the cash yourself.

Managed Products — A Fee Circus

Every year, the investment industry comes up with warehouses full of glittering new nougat-flavoured candy-coloured "managed" investment products, each holding out the prospect of riches and implying that your savings will be exposed to only the barest smidgein of risk. And pretty well every year, a lot of these exciting innovations fail to deliver the golden eggs. The problem is that when investments are done up in such fancy packages, somebody has to pay for all of the frills and gorgeous ribbons — and it's always the retail buyer. The investment may be called a *unit trust,* a *structured* or *hybrid fund,* a *royalty trust,* a *closed-end fund,* a *partnership,* or an *income trust* — but whatever the name and no matter how wonderful the sales spiel, never forget that if someone's trying to sell the thing to you, they're collecting a fee somewhere down the line.

Buyer beware

In Chapter 27, I list ten types of investment funds that I think you should avoid, but here are some other investments that you may be tempted by. Some may be well managed, underpriced, and lucrative to own, but all carry disadvantages.

- **Limited partnerships:** These things are so complicated that you need to have a lawyer look them over for you, and even then you're vulnerable. They usually produce tax breaks for the buyers by investing in risky things such as movies or natural resources, but unless you have money to burn don't consider these highly speculative investments.

- **Hedge funds:** These began as privately run funds for the very rich, but there's now a campaign worldwide to sell hedge funds to the small investor. And there are fears that (as a witty *Canadian Business* magazine headline writer put it) hedge funds will be the "Next Big Ding." Hedging is the practice of protecting your investments against loss — by selling borrowed shares at the same time as you buy others, for example. And that's what the rich are mostly interested in when it come to investing: protecting what they have. Hedge funds are no longer all about avoiding losses, though. Some, although not all, use exotic or risky techniques to chase high returns. Hedge funds are available in Canada for as little as $25,000, and some retail funds have emerged that offer hedge fund management for a few thousand dollars. Make sure you get professional advice before putting any serious money into this type of product.

- **"Structured" or "hybrid" funds:** These things were not Bay Street's finest hour. Investors plowed hundreds of millions of dollars into the funds in 2001, attracted by their promise of a high yield plus the guaranteed return of capital after ten years. The typical fund sold units at $25 each with the pledge to refund that purchase price at the end of a decade — while also trying to pay a rich yield in the range of 8 to 10 percent annually. The funds planned to pull off the neat trick by financial engineering — it involved a risk-free strategy of selling options to other investors that gave *them* the right to buy the fund's stock holdings. Didn't work. The market for options turned tail, which forced many of the funds to reduce their hoped-for distributions to unitholders. The promise to repay investors' purchase price still looks safe because it's generally bankrolled by a major bank. But investors expecting a stream of fat cheques have been disappointed.

The bottom line is this: In your investing career, you should stick to the things that the professionals buy — bonds and stocks and simple mutual funds that invest in bonds and stocks. Buying a fancy, managed product adds a level of costs and complexity that can only reduce your returns. It's also risky to buy a stock or a royalty or income trust at the issue price when it's first sold to the public, even though you traditionally get it commission-free. Grab it later when the price has fallen, because there's always a good chance it will eventually. The issue price has often been inflated to pay for brokerage commissions and other marketing expenses, not to mention general hype — so let some other poor investor pay for all those shiny new Infinitis and Lexuses you see pulling into Toronto's First Canadian Place.

Part II

Buying Options: Looking for a Helping Hand

In this part . . .

Next time someone tries to sell you a mutual fund, you'll know exactly what's going on in their thick little skull. But first, you have to decide whether you're a resolute do-it-yourself investor or a person who needs a person. Humanity can be divided into two groups: Those who want help with their investing and those who want to do it on their own. Funds are perfect for either approach. In this part, I list and describe the different companies and people you can go to for advice on selecting funds . . . or simply to have your purchase orders carried out. I point out a few of the advantages and drawbacks of each method of buying funds and I talk about the selections of funds that each salesperson or company will offer.

Chapter 6

Discount Brokers: Cheap Thrills

Discount brokers are about the closest you can get, as yet, to investing heaven — they're cheap and simple. A discount brokerage account is a great place to build wealth for the long term because you can put almost any kind of investment into it — including mutual funds, shares, bonds, Canada Savings Bonds, or even your own mortgage. Next to the invention of the mutual fund itself, discount brokers have done more than any other financial innovation to open up the stock and bond markets to ordinary people. And best of all, discount brokers are great for keeping costs down, which is one of the most important determinants of investment success. Discounters are firms set up simply to carry out your buy-and-sell orders — charging low commission rates — and provide an account in which you can hold your investments. They sometimes purport to offer lots of flashy services and information, some of which can actually be useful. But essentially, a discounter is just a bare-bones order-taking service.

In Canada, a minor price war broke out among discounters in the late 1990s as firms vied to come up with special offers, dancing dogs in neck ruffs, free trades, and extra services — which usually added up to a better deal for customers. Since then, though, the special promotions have died down — discounters have given up expensive gimmicks, sometimes even raised their rates, and concentrated their marketing more narrowly on getting the clients they really want, folks with plenty of cash. Picking a discount broker can be tricky, though. In this chapter, I give you the whole story — how discounters work, how they can save you more of your hard-won cash, how to pick the right one for you, and, finally, a few warnings about the horrible problems that some discount brokerage customers have run into.

What Discount Brokers Are

A *discount broker* is a true broker in the sense that it's a firm set up simply to act as agent. It collects a *commission* — that is, a transaction fee — when you buy or sell stocks, bonds, funds, and other investments. Yes, financial planners, insurance agents, and traditional stockbrokers also take your orders in this way, but they also bill themselves as advisers and experts who get a fee for helping out. Nothing wrong with that as such — but their fees eat into your returns. A Canadian discount brokerage firm is nearly always an arm of a big bank, taking most orders over the phone or the Internet. In the United States, discounters execute your share-buying transactions for as little as U.S.$10. In Canada, minimum charges for a single trade are generally Cdn$25 and up. Discounters are perfect for mutual fund investors because they sell a huge range of funds with low sales commissions.

If you're absolutely certain that you're going to want personal advice from someone when you pick your funds, then skip this chapter and jump to the next chapter, where we talk in detail about banks and the services they provide. Discount brokers don't provide much advice, so if you feel you need help picking funds, you won't enjoy using one.

A discounter is like a toothless dealer at a seedy Romanian horse market — an evasive mildewed character with bushy eyebrows, smelling faintly of cheap plum brandy. You wouldn't expect him to hold your hand (wouldn't really want to touch him, in fact). Just sell me a horse and go away. In the same way, there's little or no "advice" or "financial planning" on offer from a discount broker. Just a bare-bones account to hold your investments, and rock-bottom fees to buy and sell. The discounters may offer to sell you fancy packages of pre-selected funds, but there's not much personal advice about your situation.

Discounters, then, essentially offer a commodity. They employ a bunch of youngsters who are paid a wage for covering the phone and who don't traditionally get extra pay for persuading customers to buy things. In return for charging low commissions, discounters hope to attract enough business to turn a profit. That's why they're so keen to turn as much of their business as possible over to the Internet, where it can be automated.

In the past, discounters were subject to the provincial securities rule that obliges brokers to ensure that trades are suitable for the client. Like other people in the investment business who accept your money, they were supposed to follow the Know Your Client rule. (See Chapter 3 for more.) However, in the year 2000, securities regulators in Canada began relaxing the requirement that trades through a discount broker must be vetted to see if they fit with the customer's risk tolerance and investment knowledge. That was after lobbying by the discounters, who claimed that having a human being check every trade slowed up the process too much. The message, for those who may have missed it, is this: When investing through a discounter, you're on your own, Dennis.

Who is discounting in Canada?

This is an industry where you have to be large to make money. That's why the big banks dominate the discount brokerage sector in Canada, because they already have vast customer bases. Each of the big banks has a discount brokerage arm, giving the banks a lock on the business, but there are also a couple of U.S. interlopers — including E*Trade Canada, the Canadian unit of giant U.S. discount broker E*Trade Group. Toronto-Dominion Bank's discount broker, TD Waterhouse, dominates the market. Proper figures aren't released, but Waterhouse may have two-thirds of the discount brokerage business in Canada. This means that other banks don't earn huge profits from their discount brokerage arms, but banks usually feel obliged to push into every business they can.

Investing on the cheap?

How much cheaper are the discounters? Well, their commissions for trading stocks are usually only half the fees levied by traditional stockbrokers, or even less, at least for small trades. And discounters publish their rates openly. In May of 2000, *Globe and Mail* personal finance columnist Rob Carrick described the mystery surrounding commission rates at traditional brokers. He noted that:

- Trading 100 shares priced at $25 each would cost you $85, or 3.4 percent of the value of the trade, before discounts, at RBC Dominion Securities Inc., the full-service stockbrokerage arm of Royal Bank of Canada (larger trades would involve much lower percentage commission rates).

- The same trade at Royal Bank Action Direct, Royal Bank's discount brokerage arm, would cost only $38 in commissions.

Getting set up with a discounter

Setting up an account with a discount broker is simplicity itself. You don't have to sit through a sales spiel or show that you have thousands to invest — just call them up, sign a few forms, open an account, and put some money in. Here are the basic steps:

- Call the discount broker you picked and ask for a new account application form or an RSP application form. You can usually print it right off the firm's Web site. (Chapter 3 has more details on these. Or go to the TD Waterhouse site at www.tdwaterhouse.ca for an example.)

- Sign and fill in the form, and send it back.

✔ Notice the dense pages of conditions that they make you sign. Guess what? They're not in your favour. But just about all discount brokers impose these convoluted terms — which essentially say that in the event of a disagreement the broker is always right — so you can't really escape.

✔ A discounter will pretty well accept your business no matter how poor you are. But you'll have to have the necessary cash in your account, Jack, before you make the first trade. For a fund, the minimum buy is nearly always $1,000.

✔ You never have to meet anyone face-to-face. The anonymity is relaxing, although you'll almost certainly get put on hold for a good stretch when problems occur in your account. And you'll get used to shouting at dazed teenage Waterhouse slaves in a harsh barking tone.

✔ After that, just phone in your orders and check your account statement carefully. Always have them mail the trade-confirmation slip to you and check it against the order you placed.

Most discounters let you call up your account on the Internet, so just take a printout of the page and date it when you want a permanent record of your holdings and their value. They'll also mail you a monthly statement if you place orders or a quarterly one if you don't. Check these against your own records.

Using a discount broker is investing for grown-ups. There's no one around to hold your tiny hand or coo into your tight little rosebud of an ear that "the market always comes back." In return for the low commissions they charge, discounters are geared to provide little or no personal service.

Why Discount Brokers Are the Best Place to Buy Funds

A discount broker is the best place to buy and hold mutual funds. Discounters let you buy certain mutual funds for no upfront charge when other brokers would demand a commission. They also carry a vast selection of hundreds of mutual funds (more than any broker does), lots of bonds, and just about any stock you care to name. That means you can hold funds from a multitude of different companies — including some low-cost no-load funds that are hard to buy from a broker or financial planner. And a discount brokerage account also lets you combine funds with your other investments, such as stocks or guaranteed investment certificates, so that all of your holdings show up on one convenient statement.

Discounters are the perfect source for mutual funds because the choice is so huge and the charges are so low. There's more on their low costs later in this chapter but here's a rundown of the other main reasons you should strongly consider leaving your money with a discounter.

Your one-stop shop — convenience

Discount brokers are just extremely convenient. You can be on top of a mountain in Nepal, or in a jail cell in Ballydehob (say hello to Liam but don't let him "arm wrestle" you), but as long as you can get to a phone, you should be able to raise someone to sell or buy funds, stocks, and bonds in your discount brokerage account. By contrast, a full-service broker may be out of the office, ill, or busy, creating a delay if the backup person is slow. Another reason to love discounters: they've embraced the Internet wholeheartedly, with many letting you look at your account, and place orders, at any time over the Web. So if you enjoy surfing the Web, then a discounter is the place for you. With a discounter, you have control over what happens in your account. No salespeople are there to interfere or offer advice that may be tainted by the desire to earn sales commissions — or by orders from higher up, brutal Stalinist-style commands that blare from a cracked loudspeaker inches from the poor broker's ear, to push a particular stock or fund.

Access to a broad selection of options

Wide selection is a powerful reason to go with a discount broker, because discounters sell just about everything. A bank branch or no-load fund company can generally sell you only its own funds, and a broker is likely to have a "select list" of funds with which he or she is most familiar. But a discount broker will let you buy hundreds of funds, as well as thousands of stocks and bonds, in North America and often on overseas markets as well. That means you can have the luxury of just one central portfolio that holds all of your investments, instead of spreading them all around town.

Discounters have to carry every major fund because otherwise their competitors will beat them on selection. Having every fund available can be very useful for you if you want to leave an underperforming fund. It means you have somewhere to move the money. If you're with a broker who doesn't sell the funds you want to switch to, however, you're in trouble.

Many firms proclaim that they carry hundreds of funds, and in fact they probably do. But you'll find that some low-cost funds from independent providers come with high minimum purchases of $5,000 and up. Always ask if the fund you're interested in is available and find out about any conditions.

A wealth of investing information

Finally, discount brokers can be useful channels for getting hold of investing information. Check out their Web sites and you'll see offers of investment newsletters and books at cut-rate prices. Some have tried selling research reports from stock analysts at full-service brokerages — sometimes it's the brokerage that the discounter's parent bank owns.

Research shows that most investment newsletters fail to beat the market over time. And brokerage analysts are notorious for seeing the world through rose-coloured glasses (they rarely say a stock is a Sell because that's certain to enrage the company's management. Angry corporate managers are likely to cut the critical analyst off from information and may even blacklist his or her firm in future when it comes to picking brokers to handle a stock issue or other deal).

At Last — A Break on Costs

One of the big pluses with discounters is the fact that most let you buy funds on a *front-load* basis at no initial cost to you. Front-load means that the fund buyer pays an upfront commission directly to the broker or financial planner at the time of purchase — the exact rate is negotiable, but it's usually 3 percent or less these days. The advantage to paying a front load is that the funds can then be sold at any time with no further charges.

The discounters aren't being particularly generous with their zero-load offer on front-load funds, mind. Fund companies love it when their wares are sold front-load because they don't have to pay any commission to the broker. So they pay an especially generous annual *trailer commission* — typically 1 percent of the client's holding in an equity fund — to the broker that sold the fund when it was bought on a front-load basis. Trailer commissions are ongoing commissions that a salesperson or their firm gets as long as the client stays in the fund or funds sold by the manager. Paid by the fund company itself, trailer commissions ultimately come out of the management fee your fund is charged. Big fat trailers on mutual funds sold on a front-load basis (even if the investor actually paid no load) are the reason why discounters are happy to let you have front-load funds at what looks like no charge — they're often indirectly collecting 1 percent of your money each year from the fund company.

A word on commissions

Table 6-1 shows the major discounters, their toll-free contact numbers, and their Web sites. Going online is the best way to check out commissions, which change as discounters jostle for market share. By the time you read this, they'll no doubt have come up with new special offers and dancing kittens in little kilts. Check out the Web sites listed for all the latest and greatest. Discounters need to recruit new clients because this is a volume-driven industry: if you're not No. 1 or No. 2, you're really an also-ran, limping down the home stretch with the glue-factory van waiting beside the stables. . . .

When looking at these prices, keep a few things in mind:

- Bank-owned discounters usually levy no fees at all if you're buying or selling funds managed by their parent banks. So, for example, if you're dealing with Royal Bank of Canada's discounter, Action Direct, you can sell Royal Bank's no-load funds for free.

- Discounters generally require a $1,000 minimum investment if you're buying mutual funds. It's a low-margin business, after all, and tiny orders are just more trouble than they're worth for the firm.

- Higher commission rates often apply if you place your order by talking to a person over the phone. For Internet and automated-telephone orders, the commissions are usually lower by about 30 percent.

Table 6-1	How to Contact the Discounters
Discount Broker	**Contact Information**
BMO InvestorLine (Bank of Montreal)	1-800-387-7800 www.bmoinvestorline.com
CIBC Investor's Edge	1-800-567-3343 www.investorsedge.cibc.com
E*Trade Canada	1-888-872-3388 www.canada.etrade.com
Merrill Lynch HSBC	1-866-865-4722 www.mlhsbc.com
National Bank Discount Brokerage	1-800-363-3511 www.invesnet.com
Royal Bank Action Direct	1-800-769-2560 www.actiondirect.com
Scotia McLeod Direct Investing	1-800-263-3430 www.scotiamcleoddirect.com
TD Waterhouse	1-800-465-5463 www.tdwaterhouse.ca

In Chapter 2 we discuss the other type of mutual fund sales commission — the *redemption charge,* or *back-end load.* Funds sold on that basis charge you nothing upfront, but levy a commission if you sell the fund within six or seven years. Most discounters simply treat back-end loads like regular brokers do. When a client buys an equity fund on a redemption-charge basis, the broker collects a 5-percent commission directly from the fund company (not the client). The firm then extracts any applicable redemption charges from the proceeds if the customer sells the fund early. Some discount brokers have tried "rebating" a portion of that 5-percent commission back to clients who buy

Back-end-load rebates and bonuses: As if life wasn't complicated enough

Listen, I'm sorry to keep burdening you with all this commission stuff. And by now you're probably wondering: Why is everyone in the fund industry obsessed with sales charges? Why do they create myriad different classes of the same fund, each sold with a different commission, and drape them with incomprehensible rules and names? Well, the bottom line is that selling expenses — particularly the cost of paying commissions to brokers and financial planners — are an enormous cost of business for mutual fund companies. Let's look at this example — equity-fund salespeople, as a general rule, get 1 percent of the client's assets each year, either upfront or payable as an annual "trailer" commission. Well, most equity funds charge a management fee (MER) of 2 percent (extra costs usually bring total expenses for unitholders up to 2.5 percent or more), so half of the management fee revenue is going to the broker or financial planner who sold the fund.

But anyway, here's just one more commission complication before we leave the subject. Some discount brokers have tried taking the 5-percent commission they get from the company for selling a deferred load fund and "rebating" some of it to the customer in the form of a bonus. For example, if you invest $10,000 in a fund on a back-end-load basis, and the discounter pays you

a 2-percent bonus, then $10,200 would immediately show up in your account. Seems like you're getting money for nothing. These rearload rebates have ranged from 2 to almost 3 percent depending on which broker you're dealing with — as long as you meet their many conditions.

Getting a bonus straight off the top like that sounds like a great deal, but it hasn't proved popular with discount brokerage customers. That's because with a deferred-load fund, you're "locked in" by the commission that you must pay to the fund company if you cash out within about six years. Discount brokerage customers are independent souls who don't like having their hands tied in any way. So they have steered clear of rear-end-load funds carrying rebates, even if they looked like a real bargain at first glance.

The bottom line? Sure, take advantage of a rebate if you're certain that you want to stay in the fund for several years (until the deferred load no longer applies), but don't lose dollars just to save cents. If you think there's a possibility that you'll want to sell the fund again while the back-end load is still in effect, then go with the front-load version to keep life simple and your investment strategy unencumbered.

deferred-load funds. It's a nice little bonus but it also makes the whole exercise more complicated. You'll do fine without it if you just buy front-load funds.

How to Pick a Discounter

Don't get in a lather comparing the discounters' commissions and totting up their special offers. It's wonderful to see people in the investment business

---

Hell on hold

The reason why you should be careful about your selection of a discount broker is that their service has long tended to be spotty, with orders and requests sometimes going through incorrectly or after long delays (of course, traditional "full-service" brokers and financial planners often get orders wrong too). In late 1999 and early 2000, the discounters were swamped with business as Canadians went mad for technology stocks and trading on the Internet. Frustrated *Globe* readers e-mailed and called us with gory tales of having to wait on the phone for hours to place an order. Some people claimed that they hadn't been able to sell or buy for *days*. And there are other drawbacks of going with a discounter: the people answering the phone don't know you (unless you're a high roller who's given special attention), so you can forget about getting much personalized advice. Yes, some discounters are offering more research and information, but they'll always be the port-of-call for resolute independent souls who want to make all of their investing decisions for themselves.

---

offering to cut their prices, but over the long term saving $100 on a one-off basis doesn't amount to much. If you plan to simply buy and hold high-quality funds and stocks, it doesn't make a lot of difference if you've spent $100 or $200 in commissions building the portfolio. Yes, cheaper is always better, but fast and polite responses to your orders or questions, and investments that suit your needs, are all just as important as low rates.

At your service

The important thing is efficient, accurate, and prompt service — something that, sadly, discounters seem to have had a problem providing in the past. After a debacle in the hectic stock market of early 2000, when some clients said they were left on the phone for up to a week, the discount firms embarked on a hiring frenzy aimed at ensuring that they had enough staff to handle soaring demand.

If you've got the time and energy, you could pick a firm by opening two or even three separate accounts at different discounters at first — there are usually no fees for signing up as a client. After a year or so, you'll get a good feel for which discounter is most reliable and the easiest to use and you can transfer all of your assets there. Be sure to ask your family, friends, and work mates about their experience with discounters. If you keep coming across horror stories about a particular firm, then shop elsewhere.

Apart from commissions, the fee you're most likely to face at a discount broker is an annual administration fee of about $100 for a registered retirement savings plan (often the fee is waived if your account is big enough).

Don't worry too much about picking the right discounter. If you make the wrong choice, you can switch later at the cost of a few weeks' wait and a fee of about $100. It's messy — and watch out for mistakes while they transfer your investments — but you have a right to move.

Finding the right discounter for you

A good source of information on discount brokers (and low-cost investing in general) is the Stingy Investor Web site, at www.stingyinvestor.com. Run by avid number-cruncher Norman Rothery of Toronto, it offers a rundown of discounters' rates (although some of the information was out of date as of August 2002).

Don't become obsessed with commission rates when choosing a discounter. Some have decided to market themselves as cut-price providers, offering minimum commissions for a stock trade that can run $25 or even less. That's a tremendous deal for investors; but remember that if you don't plan to trade stocks frequently, it's only of limited value. Look at the whole picture — including mutual fund commissions, service standards, and special options — before you make your choice.

Try calling the company a couple of times with questions. If you can't seem to get decent answers, then consider going somewhere else.

Some experts advise that you should use a discount broker not owned by your usual bank. That way, if there's ever a dispute over a trade, the broker can't just dip into your bank account and extract money.

How about a mutual fund discount broker?

Apart from the true discount brokers, which are licensed to deal in stocks and bonds as well as funds, investors also can choose from among dozens of "no-load" or "discount" mutual fund dealers that sell only mutual funds. These companies, which are often happy to buy and sell funds over the telephone, usually charge no commission on front-load funds, living off the rich trailer payment instead. Individual stockbrokers and financial planners also frequently offer to sell funds with no load.

Discount dealers will clearly save you money, and there's no reason not to go with one if you're happy with the level of service available and the selection of funds. But once again, don't let cost be the only deciding factor. There's no point saving yourself a one-off expense of 2 percent if the dealer subsequently doesn't give you enough advice and choice of products. Personally, if I were looking to save money, I'd stick to a regular discount broker who's able to sell me shares and bonds as well as funds while also offering low commissions. And call me a scaredy-cat, but I'd rather deal with a discounter that's a large multi-billion dollar organization. That way, I know the systems are in place to administer my account properly.

What's Wrong with Discount Brokers

The major problem with discounters, especially for investors who are just getting going, is that they're not set up to provide advice on your personal financial situation or to help you create a financial plan. A discounter is essentially a tool for doing transactions — but buying and selling investments is only part of getting rich. A good planner or full-service stockbroker will also provide tips on tax and wealth-management — using life insurance, for example — that you won't get from a discounter.

Seduced and abandoned?

Discounters leave you on your own to make all of the decisions, but freedom can bring problems. Some research seems to show that retail investors who work without an adviser don't do well because they're prone to buying high and selling low. That is, they euphorically buy shares and equity funds when the market has soared and then dump them when prices have already crashed. That may be true or just a self-serving myth fostered by the brokerage industry. But a good fund salesperson can impose valuable discipline in two ways: by getting you to save money in the first place and by persuading you to hang on when things look bleak. So if you're a nervous or impulsive type, holding your stocks and funds at a discount broker might be a recipe for panic selling and hysterical buying. Perhaps you'd be better off with a planner or old-style broker.

Knowing when to fold 'em

While the lure of cheap trades and special offers may be pretty hard to resist, discounters aren't for every Canadian, not even close. Some investors should probably stay away from discounters. For example:

> ✔ Nervous investors who are just starting out might be happier opening a mutual fund account at a bank first. They can get at least some personalized help while they learn the basics of investing, before venturing into the discount world.

✔ Those who plan to trade frequently in and out of the stock market might be better off going with a competent traditional stockbroker who'll give them a break on commissions. A full-service broker is more expensive, but he or she can often provide better "execution" of your orders — that is, they can buy and sell stocks at more attractive prices.

Maybe I'm being too hard on the discount brokers by dredging up their service problems of 1999 and 2000. The industry is fairly new, after all, and its rapid growth caught everyone by surprise. Firms have moved quickly to improve standards, and regulatory changes should also speed things up. Keep your eye on this industry as it evolves, and as you develop as an investor.

Chapter 7

Banks: The Fast Food of Funds

· ·

In This Chapter

▶ Discovering why banks are the simplest place to buy mutual funds

▶ Dealing with your bank

▶ Investigating recent improvements at banks

· ·

In the mid-1990s, if you asked an executive at a non-bank fund company why the banks didn't seem to be able to run a decent equity fund, he'd have curled his lip with scorn. "How," he would reply, "can the banks expect to get good stock picking out of their wretched nine-to-five wage slaves who ride the commuter cattle trains every morning from suburban wastes north of Toronto?" Well, those days are long gone. Banks have improved the returns from their stock funds and there are encouraging signs that they are finally reducing the costs charged to mutual fund investors. For one thing, banks have rolled out *index funds* — which simply track the entire market. And the Internet could turn out to be a marvellous device for further reducing costs, marking the dawn of a new age for the small investor.

In this chapter, I explain why banks are a great place to buy mutual funds, especially if you just want a simple option that's also okay value. There are perks to keeping your investments where you keep your cash. No, not that sort of perk, dirty Daniel. If you use a bank to buy funds, your account statement is on the same record-keeping system as your chequing account, which is very convenient, and there are no meddlesome prating salespeople involved. This chapter shows why you can just go ahead and use your local bank branch for mutual funds if you want a quick solution. You won't get the best bargain going, but it'll do the job.

Buying Where You Bank

Banks are the very simplest place to buy mutual funds: Just walk in and put your money into a selection of their house brands. But don't assume they're the best choice. A bank is a great place to start out buying funds, but you should certainly take a long hard look at what they can and can't offer.

Hey, you're busy, what with training your cat to play the xylophone ("No, the *left* paw!") and getting into the *Guinness Book of Records* for growing the longest nose hairs ever officially recorded (that old fool in Sinkiang-Uigar glued them in). So why not just make things easy on yourself and simply grab your mutual funds at the bank? Mutual fund buyers, especially rookies, can do well at the bank for a number of reasons.

One-stop shopping: Update your passbook and buy a fund

It's easy. Even if you don't have an account with a bank you can still walk into a branch, hand over a cheque, and sign up. Okay, it might take a couple of days to arrange an appointment with a *registered representative*, a bank employee who is licensed to sell funds, but after that the process should be painless. Once you've opened a fund account, most banks have telephone services for buying and selling funds, and nearly all offer telephone and Internet services that let you check your account balance and recent transactions.

Banks sell their own funds with no commissions or sales loads. That means all your money goes to work for you right away, and you can cash out at any time with no penalty (although some banks and other fund companies impose a short-term trading penalty, typically 2 percent, on those who sell a fund within 90 days).

You can set up a fairly decent mutual fund registered retirement savings plan — a tax-sheltered account of retirement money — at a bank in half an hour flat by simply buying one of their pre-selected fund packages. Staff are trained to sell these mixtures, and questionnaires are designed to slot you into the right one so you're likely to get a reasonable fit. See Chapter 21 on fund packages for more about this type of product.

Keeping it together: All your eggs in one basket

Now that the banks have devoured the trust industry, you probably have your mortgage, line of credit, and chequing account at a bank. So buying mutual funds from the company that already holds the mortgage on your house means you get the luxury of dealing with the same bank employee for everything.

Offering to move your mutual fund business to a bank can radically improve your bargaining power when seeking a loan or mortgage. Bank employees get little chocolate soccer balls as rewards when their customers bring their investment portfolios to the branch. Use this to your advantage when looking to extend your credit, take a plunge into the real estate market, or buy a car. In today's competitive banking environment, an investor with a portfolio is a sought-after prize.

Not just a watering hole in the Namib Desert

The employees you deal with at a bank branch get wages, so they're not commission-driven jackals. But they usually sell only the house brand. And yes, they receive incentives to attract business, and yes, the banks tend to be vague on exactly what bonuses are paid.

For the most part, you'll find that banks are happy to sell you *index funds* — low-expense funds that simply track the stock- or bond-market index or benchmark. Index funds are such a good deal they should be part of every investor's arsenal, although you should also have between one-third and one-half of your stock market investments in traditional *actively managed* funds, featuring a person who buys and sells investments in search of trading profits.

Banks, unlike mutual fund companies that market their products through commission-paid salespeople, are able to make money from running index funds because they don't have to pay out those big commissions. Most offer index funds with expenses as low as 1 percent, compared with 2.6 percent on the average Canadian equity fund, for example. If you were to simply walk into a branch and open up a mutual fund account full of index funds like that, chances are that you'd do better than millions of mutual fund investors.

Banks fight for the right to serve you

The banks are hungry for your mutual fund business and they're willing to cut prices and improve service to get it. The fantastic growth of the Canadian mutual fund industry, with assets soaring to more than $400 billion in mid-2002 from less than $30 billion in 1990, has represented a migration of cash from bank savings accounts and guaranteed investment certificates into funds. The banks want to hold on to as much of that money as they can.

There's another reason why the banks are fund-mad: Remember that mutual funds are a wonderfully profitable and low-risk business. The management company just keeps raking off those 2-percent fees (plus expenses), no matter how well or badly the fund does. That must be a great comfort to unitholders of the average U.S. stock fund, for example, who lost 9.6 percent of their money annually in the three years ending June 2002.

Dawn of the robots

Competition has forced bankers to come up with some interesting technology-based products and services that should reduce costs for investors. Here are two neat uses of computer technology by the banks:

✔ Late in 1999, Toronto-Dominion Bank launched "eFunds," index funds with extremely low expense ratios that must be bought over the Internet. The funds have annual expenses as low as 0.31 percent, making them almost free for an investor to own. It's too early to say how well the experiment will work, but it's a promising use of the Internet and its efficiencies to bring investors what

looks like a bargain. Check out eFunds at www.tdefunds.com.

✔ ING Direct, a "virtual" bank that deals with its 4 million global clients only over the Internet and the phone, launched no-load funds in Canada in 1999. The funds themselves seem to be ordinary enough fare and their total assets were just $237 million at the end of June 2002, for 41st place in the fund industry. But ING, a unit of Dutch financial empire ING Groep NV, is an aggressive challenger to Canadian banks in other areas so it's interesting to see the company go into mutual funds.

Lending money, the banks' traditional way of making a profit, is more risky than selling mutual funds because borrowers can default and interest rates can jump, leaving the banks stuck with a pile of underpriced loans. So, more and more, banks are trying to become "wealth management" companies, and mutual funds are the name of that ballgame.

Buyer Beware: Shortfalls in Bank Offerings

Nobody's perfect, and buying funds at a bank — either over the telephone or by going into a branch — has its drawbacks. Here, for your viewing pleasure, are the drawbacks of lining the pockets of nasal power-hungry guys from New Brunswick, the sort who become bank chairmen.

Few options

The big problem is lack of choice: The banks have dragged their feet on marketing other companies' funds because a banker likes sharing fees like a lobster enjoys taking a hot bath. That means customers are often stuck with the bank's line of products, which isn't always the strongest. More and more bank employees have personal finance training but most aren't specialists in the field. To get a full analysis of your situation, you may still have to go to a planner working for an independent firm.

The narrow selection of funds at many branches is the biggest problem with buying from a bank. All the big banks offer a full range of funds under their own brand name but that doesn't necessarily mean that their Canadian equity or global equity funds will be any good. And even if you try to build a diversified fund portfolio by buying the bank's index funds and actively managed funds as well, there's always a risk that you're leaving too much money with just one investment team. Let's say that a particular coterie usually tends to get excited about flashy technology stocks — then you're likely to lose money when other investors get tired of such high-priced science fiction tales. You can get around this lack of *diversification* — the annoying word for spreading out your investments — by opening an account elsewhere as well, perhaps with another bank. Or you can at least increase your diversification by buying several of the bank's actively managed funds.

Overworked and underpaid: Not just you, some bankers too

Banks are busily blitzing their branch networks and cutting back on staff in search of higher profits, so it's getting harder and harder to talk to an actual human being unless you've got a whopping balance in your account. That's a drag and it's a disadvantage of going to a bank if you'd rather deal with a person than peck at the keyboard of a machine (what's wrong with you, anyway?).

Lack of pressure to perform

Customers who buy funds from a bank are isolated in the sense that the fund managers don't have brokers and other salespeople breathing in a damp, hot way down their necks, insisting on good returns. If a broker-sold fund's performance goes into the tank, salespeople get angry and embarrassed, because they have to face the clients they put into the loser. That's never a fun session. The sales force demands explanations from the manager. So the presence of salespeople probably serves to impose some discipline on fund companies. With bank funds where no brokers are involved, terrible performance used to drag on for years with little publicity or outcry.

Banks now take funds more seriously, meaning that problems get fixed fairly quickly, but bank fund unitholders arguably still don't have anyone looking out for their interests. Yes, nearly all mutual funds have "trustees" who theoretically are on the side of investors, but I've yet to hear of a fund trustee saying a single critical word about a fund's management or expenses. Most unitholders wouldn't know where to look for the trustees' names and no wonder: the fund companies hardly ever publicize their identities. You have to plow through the obscure "annual information form" for the fund, available on demand from your fund company, to identify the trustees. Securities cops are pushing to have the system fixed, but the fund companies are in no huge hurry to change the rules.

Another problem with buying funds from your bank is that, well, you're forced to deal with a bank. Phone calls get routed to voice-mail hell before they end up in the bottomless pit of general delivery, with Tats in shipping. Branches are being shuttered across the country, forcing customers to dial 1-800-PLS-HOLD or go to an Internet site (which saves the bank a packet). With all the branch cutbacks, employees are overworked. And they usually have to deal with all the other services and products that the bank delivers, and then face the whining, puking, and foot-stamping at home — not to mention the kids. So you won't get the sort of personal attention and time that a good financial planner or even stockbroker delivers.

On the Road to Recovery: How Banks Are Pulling Up their Socks

As recently as the mid-1990s, bank-run equity funds were a bit of a joke as far as serious investing was concerned. Performance has greatly improved since then, but the banks still haven't built much of a record in global equity funds. Their fixed-income funds have long been okay — it's hard to blow it with a bond fund, after all (although some mutual fund companies have managed). But until recent years, bank stock funds lagged the competition by a wide margin. And in the past banks seem to have had difficulty attracting and keeping gifted fund managers (if there is such a thing as stock-picking talent, as opposed to sheer luck).

Explanations varied, but one problem seemed to be that hot fund managers demand lavish paycheques and bonuses — but if the banks were to pay such huge amounts to a few individuals, grey managers elsewhere in their vast dreary bureaucracies would get jealous in a grey, whining way. To some extent, though, the banks seem to have fixed their performance problems, in some cases by spinning off their portfolio management operations into separate companies.

Table 7-1 shows the biggest Canadian equity and large-cap equity funds at seven banks as of June 2002. As you can see, at least half of the bank funds beat or equalled the average Canadian equity fund over five years and ten years — although the average fund number has been dragged down by insurance company funds and the like with even higher expenses than the bank funds. The costs of bank products tend to be middle of the pack. Mind you, the people running bank funds arguably had an advantage in recent years because, wow, bank stocks have done so well they're just the sort of stuff that conservative bank funds tend to hold.

Mutual funds have now become such an important business for the banks that it's very unlikely an equity fund would be allowed to drift along with poor numbers for very long before the manager was reassigned. To checking mortgage applications. In Tuktoyaktuk.

Table 7-1 Getting So Much Better: Bank Funds Are Catching Up

Fund Name	Five-Year Return	Ten-Year Return
Royal Canadian Equity	5.4%	10.4%
BMO Equity	7.5%	–
TD Canadian Equity	5.8%	10.9%
CIBC Core Canadian Equity	3.1%	7.0%
Scotia Canadian Growth	1.4%	9.3%
HSBC Equity	3.9%	10.6%
National Bank Canadian Equity	0.7%	7.5%
Average Canadian equity fund	3.6%	9.3%
S&P/TSX	**3.7%**	**9.9%**

More on the menu: Improving your choice of funds

Banks are also working to improve the problem of limited fund choice by training and registering staff to sell other companies' funds (known as *third-party* funds in the jargon). In 2000, Canadian Imperial Bank of Commerce said it would market more than 1,200 funds from competing companies in its branches, as well as provide advice on those funds. Bank of Montreal has also started selling third-party funds in branches. Toronto-Dominion Bank branches started selling some outside funds back in 1996.

However, these initiatives are still at the early stage and it'll be quite a while before most bank employees are able to give advice on a wide range of funds. And, *mirabile dictu*, it seems that the banks are most keen on training their staff to talk about funds from companies such as AGF Management Ltd., AIM Funds Management Inc., CI Fund Management Inc., Fidelity Investments Canada Ltd., Mackenzie Financial Corp., and Franklin Templeton Investments. Those are all honourable companies, but they also happen to be commission-paying fund managers that sell their products through brokers and planners — which means that the banks are in line for a gush of commission income in return for selling their wares.

Stretching the rules with bank offerings

You should be able to create a widely diversified portfolio from the funds of just one bank by using a bit of ingenuity. In Chapter 4, I recommend portfolios whose equity portion is made up of a Canadian index fund and an international and U.S. index fund, plus a couple of actively managed Canadian and two global actively managed funds. (Global equity funds buy shares everywhere, but international funds stay out of North America.) Achieving that kind of broad mix takes a good bit of work. And using the method is especially tricky if you're sticking to the funds of just one bank, but you can do it by bending your fund definitions a little. By way of example, Table 7-2 shows a balanced portfolio that a Scotiabank customer might have built in mid-2002. This is a cautious mixture, with 55 percent of the assets in bonds and money market instruments and only 45 percent in stocks. Just 30 percent of the portfolio counts as foreign content for tax purposes, so the portfolio is eligible for a RRSP (note that it uses a global bond fund and a U.S. stock index fund that are structured to count as Canadian). Because the bank didn't sell a global equity index fund, I've used a mixture of international and U.S. funds instead. And I've had to use a European fund in place of a global fund. It's a narrower fund because it concentrates on just one region, but a European fund will usually own lots of relatively stable, blue-chip stocks.

Table 7-2 A Conservative Portfolio Using Just Scotiabank Funds

Fund Name	Percentage of Portfolio	RSP Status (Canadian/Foreign)
Scotia Money Market	5%	Canadian
Scotia Canadian Bond Index	35%	Canadian
Scotia CanAm U.S.$ Income	15%	Canadian
Scotia Canadian Stock Index	4%	Canadian
Scotia Canadian Dividend	3%	Canadian

Fund Name	Percentage of Portfolio	RSP Status (Canadian/Foreign)
Scotia International Stock Index	8%	Canadian
Scotia American Stock Index	10%	Foreign
Scotia European Growth	10%	Foreign
Scotia Global Growth	10%	Foreign

A Few Gems from the Banks

Finally, at the risk of seeming like a fund shill, here's a list of seven bank funds, each from a different company, that have produced excellent returns in recent years. Will their good performance continue? There's no way of telling. But I've tried to avoid "hot" funds that have posted chart-topping performance, because such funds have a way of turning into pooches the next year. And I've also tried to stick to funds with relatively low expenses, because modest costs always load the dice in favour of the investor.

Bank of Montreal's **BMO Equity Fund** thrived in 1999 and 2000 by holding Nortel Networks Corp. and Nortel's former major shareholder BCE Inc., when those stocks soared. But manager Michael Stanley seems to have got out before the telecom crash, loading up on bank stocks instead. Pity about the fund's hefty management expense ratio of 2.4 percent, though. Now that the fund has swollen to $1.3 billion, you'd think they could bring the ratio down to 2 percent or less. From 1996 through the first half of 2002, the fund was a consistent performer. In each calendar year, it produced returns that were in the first and second *quartiles* for Canadian large-cap equity funds. First-quartile means a fund generated a return that was in the top 25 percent for its group during a given period. Second quartile means the fund's return was in the next 25 percent down, and so on.

Okay, so the **CIBC Canadian Short-Term Bond Index** isn't the most exciting fund in the universe (try the Venusian Naked Dancing Space Nymphs Appreciation Trust). But people who buy short-term bond funds aren't looking for thrills, just a steady return that's a percentage point or two better than the payoff from a money market fund or guaranteed investment certificate. And this fund is well-equipped to deliver, with a low expense ratio of just 1 percent, compared with 1.6 percent on the average short-term bond fund. Mind you, it would be nice to see them shave those costs a bit more — why not cut the annual expenses to 0.5 percent? CIBC has been one of the most aggressive banks in promoting index funds, and it offers a huge selection. Ted Cadsby, one of its mutual fund honchos, even wrote a best-selling book on the things: *The Power of Index Funds: Canada's Best-Kept Investment Secret.*

Okay, I'm biased: **TD Balanced Income Fund** is run by one of my favourite investment managers, Jarislowsky Fraser & Co. Ltd. The Montreal-based firm is a frequent and loud public critic of corporate executives who may not be looking out for shareholders' best interests. Always nice to hear from people in the investment game who don't subscribe to smug mutual back scratching. And Jarislowsky's returns are good too: This fund made 5.7 percent annually in the five years ended June 30, 2002, when the average balanced fund earned 3.7 percent. Don't mix this fund up with the TD Balanced Fund, though — that lacklustre performer produced a five-year return of just 1.8 percent.

HSBC Canadian Balanced Fund — marketed by the Canadian arm of global banking giant HSBC — is another fund that was lucky and/or smart enough to load up on soaring Nortel. But its performance has been fairly consistent, apart from a minor slump in 2001 and the first half of 2002. The expense ratio is a modest 1.9 percent. Perhaps it's no surprise that the fund struggled a bit when the tech sector crashed. Back in April 2000, its top stock holdings were full of names such as Nortel, fibre-optic innovator JDS Uniphase, and data-base king Cognos. Sort of odd, really, when a commentary at the bank's www.hsbc.ca Web site said the high prices and wild volatility of Internet and tech stocks "leads us to maintain a cautious approach."

National Bank Small Capitalization Fund racked up hot performance numbers in the 1990s, when it was still tiny. Assets were only $24 million at the end of 1999, but they'd grown to $115 million by mid-2002. It's much easier to trade small-cap stocks with a tiny nimble fund rather than a big clumsy one. But the fund has continued to produce strong returns and it's done it the old-fashioned way: by buying a variety of real companies with genuine revenues and profits, as opposed to riding a couple of tech or resource rockets into the stratosphere and beyond.

They don't get much more conservative than this, and that's the way dividend fund investors love it. The Royal Bank's enormous $2.4-billion **Royal Dividend Fund** racked up first- and second-quartile returns from 1996 through 2000, slipping just barely into the third quartile in 2001. Manager John Kellett stuck to super-blue-chip bank and utility common shares. And he avoided the temptation to seek safety in preferred shares, a sort of safe high-income vehicle that offers little or no potential for capital gains. The fund's expense ratio, only 1.8 percent, makes it a relative bargain.

Scotia Canadian Income paid a regular monthly distribution of around 5 cents as of mid-2002. It may not be exciting, but the fund gets the job done: the five-year annual return to June 2002 was 6.1 percent, compared with 5 percent for the average Canadian bond fund. That was partly because the fund takes slightly more risk: it buys some debt issued by corporations as well as government paper. But the low expense ratio of 1.2 percent also helped to boost the performance.

Dave's dilemma

I realized the time pressure that bank staff is under when I carried out an undercover assignment for the *Globe and Mail*. Er, no, I didn't go behind Taliban lines, posing as a hard-line mullah, or even into the heroin salons of East Vancouver. Just walked around downtown Toronto with a friend, Dave, and wandered into various financial institutions to ask what Dave should do with his portfolio. At that stage, he had a confusing mess of RRSPs all over town.

We didn't exactly get the red carpet at the two banks we visited. At Bank of Nova Scotia, we were told to telephone for an appointment. And at Canadian Imperial Bank of Commerce, we encountered a bank employee who proffered a questionnaire but didn't get Dave to fill it out. Instead, we parted with the vague understanding that Dave would call and "talk to somebody." Perhaps the test was unfair in that we didn't set the appointment up in advance, but the banks also didn't impress us with their eagerness to get our business. I mean, I don't think we smelled too strongly of cheap lager or anything.

Who came out on top in this mystery-shopper experiment? In the end, Dave chose a full-service broker from giant BMO Nesbitt Burns Inc., a Bank of Montreal subsidiary. We chanced across the broker in a BMO "Investore," a one-stop shopping location for investments. Dave, a rookie investor without much interest in matters financial, went with the traditional broker because the affable young chap was able to sell him a huge range of investments, from stocks to bonds and funds. But the big factor was Nesbitt's backing from a major bank, which gave Dave a warm, comfortable feeling. The moral of the story — when you're trusting your cash to a bank you should expect decent, if not stellar, service. The banking industry is a dog-eat-dog oligopoly — make sure you go with the bank that throws you the most bones.

Chapter 8

Stockbrokers, Financial Planners, and Advisers Aplenty

*W*e may run out of water, out of brain surgeons, out of Vancouver Island marmots, and out of braying self-important financial journalists. But we'll never run out of mutual fund salespeople. At least 50,000 Canadians hold themselves out as financial advisers or planners in one way or another, and most of them are licensed to sell you mutual funds. They come in a bewildering range of guises, from DKNY-clad smoothies in the downtown core of big cities to hoser types in Molson sweatshirts wolfing down the free sandwiches at fund company lunches. And they give themselves a galaxy of names: financial consultant, investment counsellor, estate planner, financial adviser, investment executive, personal financial planner. Don't get worked up trying to figure out the differences among them. The fact is that the provinces' regulation of the financial planning game is still so spotty, and hampered by power struggles among the competing groups, that outside Quebec just about anybody is free to call themselves anything.

In this chapter, I describe the main types of fund salespeople and tell you about the advantages of using financial planners who charge only an upfront fee rather than collect commissions on the products they sell you. I wrap up with some basic tips on the right, and the wrong, way to pick an adviser.

Alphabet Soup: Figuring Out All those Titles

You could spend a good month or two crafting a long list of all the elaborate titles that financial advisers give themselves. You could then have a couple of gloomy women in leotards read it out on a darkened stage at the Toronto Fringe Festival, to the accompaniment of randomly played cymbals and flutes. Probably be a huge hit — better than the usual dreary one-person show about a failed actor, anyway — but it wouldn't help people much with their financial planning. So how do you wade through all the options and get down to what's best for you and your money? That's the key — your first challenge should be figuring out exactly what kind of financial planning you want rather than trying to decode their titles. In other words, do you need a fast once-over or a harrowing session of soul-searching?

Once you've decided that you need some help drawing up a financial plan and picking the right mutual funds, there are two questions you should ask yourself:

- ✔ **Do I want just a quick solution or a complete financial plan?** If you're reasonably comfortable with your money arrangements as they stand and you just want someone who'll suggest a few funds, then you can keep things simple by going to a storefront mutual fund dealer, a stockbroker, or even a bank employee. They can recommend a package of funds and set up the account for you. If, however, you want help planning your fiscal future, make sure that you deal with someone who has had some formal financial planning training (more on that later) and is also genuinely interested in the subject. And the best choice of all is to go with an unbiased planner who charges you a separate fee for his or her expertise, instead of selling you mutual funds that pay them a commission.

- ✔ **How much money will I be investing?** Don't expect miracles. If you're planning to put $5,000 a year into your fund portfolio, the chairman of RBC Dominion Securities Inc. won't be asking you out to golf. It can be a good idea to tell the adviser upfront how much you think you're likely to save each year. You'll often be able to tell from his or her reaction whether you're likely to get much in the way of attention or advice.

Here's a great way to find out if a fund salesperson is likely to be of much use in drawing up a financial plan: don't just ask about investing. Also bring up subjects such as buying disability and life insurance, estate planning, and minimizing taxes. If the answers are superficial or unsatisfactory, then this person probably isn't the best adviser to help you build a successful plan.

Drawing up a comprehensive financial plan is a complicated process, covering the client's taxes, income, spending, and retirement plans. Choosing investments is only a small part of that, but too many advisers are paid just for selling fancy life insurance or mutual funds, so saving and investing become all they want to talk about.

In fact, as I outline in Chapter 4, every competent financial planner worth his or her salt should emphasize getting rid of high-interest debt as your first step toward sound money management. If they don't look at your whole financial picture, you should look elsewhere for help.

So beware of commission-paid salespeople who encourage you to go ahead and buy funds even though you already have big credit card debts. This is no way to build a sound financial plan or invest for profit.

Basic types of advisers

Advisers can be divided into three main groups according to how they earn their living:

- ✔ Advisers who get paid a commission for selling you investments.
- ✔ Advisers who charge you a separate fee for designing your financial plan.
- ✔ Advisers who earn a salary from an organization such as a bank that markets its own line of investments.

Commissioned advisers

The vast majority of Canadians choose to go with a financial adviser who gets paid by a mutual fund company or insurance company for selling investment "products." In part that seems to be a reflection of the nation's thrifty Scottish psyche: Unlike many Americans, Canadians would much rather have the expense of investing advice hidden from them, buried in the fee of a mutual fund or the cost of insurance. That way, it seems so much less painful than having to cut the adviser a cheque.

An obvious example of a commission-paid salesperson is the traditional *stockbroker*, who makes money when you buy stocks, bonds, or funds. The broker gets a transaction fee or *commission* each time you put an order through.

- ✔ With stocks, the commission is added onto the cost when you buy or deducted from the proceeds when you sell — and your transaction confirmation should clearly show how much was charged. For example, when you buy or sell $10,000 worth of shares, you can expect to pay a sales commission of about $300.

✔ With bonds, the "commission" is normally a profit margin that's hidden in the price, just like buying a pair of jeans at the Gap. That's because brokers usually sell bonds to their clients that they already own themselves. No separate commission is charged or shown on your confirmation slip because the broker has already taken a markup.

✔ With funds, things get more complicated. But the essence of the system is that the broker (or financial planner or insurance salesperson) is paid by the fund company. The fund company, remember, charges an annual management fee — which is deducted from the assets of the fund — and pays roughly half of that out to the salesperson.

Commission-paid salespeople also include life insurance salespeople, whether independent or tied to a particular insurance company. In addition to life insurance, these agents are often licensed to sell mutual funds or the insurance industry's version of mutual funds, which are known as *segregated funds*. Segregated funds — so-called because their assets must be kept separate from those of the insurance company — carry guarantees to refund up to 100 percent of an investor's initial outlay. There's more on them in Chapter 19.

Finally, there are Canada's thousands of financial *planners*, either in franchises, chains of stores, or small independent offices, whose bread and butter is the mutual fund.

Fee-charging advisers

The next group is far smaller but represents an excellent choice for those who don't mind signing a cheque to get advice. They're the *fee-charging* financial planners who aren't interested in selling products. In some cases, they'll help you to set up an account at a discount brokerage in which you can buy low-cost funds.

The drawback of going with a fee-charging planner is the pain of paying the freight, which can be substantial. It might be a percentage of your investments — typically 1 or 2 percent — or it can be an hourly charge that ranges from $75 an hour to a few hundred, depending on the complexity of your affairs.

With a fee-charging planner, you may have to make more choices about the investments you buy and the strategy you adopt. That's because the financial plan produced for each client is different, reflecting individual needs and wants, whereas commission-paid salespeople are often happiest suggesting a predesigned and relatively fixed package of funds that leaves you with few decisions to make.

T.E. Financial Consultants Ltd. claims to be Canada's "pre-eminent" fee-only financial planning firm. Check out its qualifications at www.tefinancial.com.

Investors with substantial assets, in the hundreds of thousands of dollars, should strongly consider going with a fee-charging planner. Your accountant or lawyer may offer the service or may be willing to recommend someone. The fee will often run into several hundred dollars, but that's a bargain compared with the hidden cost of high mutual fund management fees levied by fund companies that sell through commissioned advisers.

A fee-based planner might produce a plan and then refer you to a commission-charging dealer — or even collect commissions on funds that you buy. That kind of double-charging adds another layer of complexity and fees, and it might not be the best deal for you. If the adviser is simply putting you into funds that pay commissions to salespeople, then what did you pay the advice fee for?

Salaried advisers

Thousands of financial advisers are being trained by the banks to take over the "wealth-management" needs of the aging baby boomers. They're generally on salary — plus bonuses if they can persuade you to put your savings into one of the bank's products, usually mutual funds or some other kind of managed-money program.

As I explain in Chapter 7, these bank employees are often limited in the products they can offer, and their training may not be as full as that of brokers or specialized financial planners. That means their advice should always be taken with a pinch of salt: they're employed to push the bank's products or sell funds that pay the bank a fat commission. Still, especially for investors with relatively simple needs and clear financial goals, the bank can be a great place to start off investing. Compared with the hard-driving world of brokers or financial planners, there's often little sales pressure. The product choices are simple, and having all of your money in one place makes for easy record keeping.

But don't forget that you're doing the bank a favour by handing over your savings. That means you're entitled to a helpful and experienced bank employee, not some rookie or sleepyhead. And don't get railroaded into buying one of the fixed arrangements of funds that the banks love to pitch (it makes their administration much easier, for one thing). If you feel that none of the pre-selected packages meets your needs, then insist on a custom mixture of funds.

In general, the bank is the perfect first stop for starting-out investors with only a few thousand at their disposal. The banks are equipped to deal with small accounts and they have handy automated systems that allow you to check your account balance and transactions without waiting for someone to get back to you.

And the banks' employee training in investment advice is getting better all the time as the wealth-management business becomes vital to their future profit growth. Some banks even have qualified brokers available right in the branch who can sell you a range of stocks and bonds or funds from nearly every company.

The blurred distinctions among all these types of commission-paid advisers make the whole business of looking for help confusing. But at least you have one thing going for you: Remember that if you buy mutual funds, your money is reasonably safe because it goes to the fund company instead of staying with the broker or dealer. So if you decide to dump your salesperson and his or her firm, you can simply shift the account elsewhere, after some whinging and delays on the part of the old salesperson. Your money is doubly safe because even the fund company itself has to leave the fund's assets with a separate custodian for safekeeping.

Make sure that you'll be receiving a statement at least twice a year from the fund company (ask to see a sample) so that you can be certain you're on the fund company's books. And make your cheque out to the fund company, not the salesperson. Finally, you should get transaction confirmations for your purchases from the company — alternatively, you can call the fund company itself to double-check that they have a record of your investment.

Fee-only versus Commissions

Your first choice in selecting an adviser is this: Do you want to pay a fee to an accountant or fee-charging planner, or are you happy with a commission-collecting salesperson? Don't rush your decision and just take the easy way out by refusing to pay a fee upfront. I remember the first time I went to a tax accountant and agreed to pay a couple of hundred dollars to have him look over my taxes and file my return. I got back a much bigger refund than I would have on my own, and it felt great to have a professional working for me. And because I was paying the chap a fee, I knew what was motivating him.

Paying upfront

My first choice in hiring an investment adviser would be to go with a fee-charging professional. That way, you've separated or "unbundled" the advice from the sale of the investment product. Long story short, you know exactly where you stand.

Follow the money

Here's a breakdown of how you pay the salesperson and his or her firm hundreds of dollars, directly or indirectly, when you buy broker-sold funds.

Say you invest a total of $10,000, of which $6,000 goes into an equity fund and $4,000 into a bond fund. You usually have two choices:

✔ Buy the funds on a "front-load" or sales-charge basis, in which case you must negotiate the sales commission with the salesperson. However, you're then free to sell at any time with no further charges.

✔ Buy the funds on a "deferred-load" basis, in which case the salesperson gets the commission directly from the fund company but you're on the hook for sales charges if you sell within six or seven years.

If you buy the funds on a front-load basis and agree to pay a 2-percent upfront commission on both, the broker gets $200 from you immediately. But because you bought front-load funds, costing the fund company nothing, the salesperson also gets a richer annual "trailer" commission from the fund manager. That's often equal to 1 percent of your investment in the equity fund and 0.5 percent of your investment in the bond fund, for a total of $60 plus $20, or an extra $80 a year for the salesperson.

If you buy the funds on a back-end basis, the salesperson typically gets a commission from the fund company equivalent to 5 percent of your investment in the equity fund — or $300 in our example — plus 4 percent of your investment in the bond fund — or $160 — for a total of $460. But he or she also gets a trailer of 0.5 percent of your investment in the equity fund and 0.25 percent of your investment in the bond fund, for a total of $30 plus $10, or another $40 annually. Phew.

Use an accountant if you can't find a fee-only planner in your area. More and more accountants are getting into the wealth-management and financial-planning game, and a few phone calls should turn up someone who's qualified. Ask your friends, family, work mates, or boss if they know of an accountant who does this type of work.

Be warned, though, that competent professionals don't come cheap: any fee-only planner worth hiring is almost certain to charge several hundred dollars to produce anything more than a "quickie" plan.

That may seem like a lot, but it could be a bargain compared with the cost of investing in a regular mutual fund that carries sales loads. You often indirectly pay hundreds of dollars to invest in a normal load fund. Say you put $10,000 in a typical broker-sold equity or balanced mutual fund on a "deferred-load" or "back-end-load" basis — which means you pay commissions only if you cash out within about seven years. The salesperson and his or her firm collect 5 percent, or $500, immediately from the fund company.

And they also often get an annual "trailer" commission — an ongoing yearly fee from the company — of 0.5 percent of your account. Those commissions have to be paid for — so most Canadian equity funds hit their investors for more than 2.6 percent of their assets each year. Over 20 years, a seemingly innocuous 2.6 percent management expense ratio means that 52 percent of the total accumulated capital has gone in fees and costs (because $\frac{1}{38}$ of the money is sliced off each year). It would be a lot cheaper to go to an expert, pay a few hundred dollars upfront, and have him or her put you into low-expense index or no-load funds with annual expenses closer to 1 percent.

Going with a commission-paid adviser

Fee-charging advisers who'll also help with investing are still hard to find in Canada — although they're hugely popular in the United States — so Canadians by the millions use commission-paid salespeople. After all, such advisers offer a handy one-stop solution: a financial roadmap of sorts and the glitz and comfort of a mutual fund from a familiar name. All backed up by gorgeous brochures and torrents of advertising in the press and on television. And most of them do a reasonable job for clients, putting them into solid (if overpriced) funds and getting them to save money, the first step in wealth accumulation.

Imagine a confusing, tangled jungle where every plant, animal, and weird fungus is grey. Well, that's kind of like the financial planning scene in Canada, where competing trade associations, duelling regulators, and rival professional qualifications have created a confusing alphabet soup for investors. In the late 1990s, for example, the banks and stockbrokers pulled out of a plan to create a single designation for planner — because the proposed standards were too tough. Except in Quebec and British Columbia, just about anyone can call himself or herself a financial planner — even with no training. But there are signs of progress: In 2002, the Canadian Association of Insurance and Financial Advisors (CAIFA), announced a plan to combine with the Canadian Association of Financial Planners (CAFP).

Commission-paid salespeople and advisers usually fall into one of these three groups:

✔ **Stockbrokers:** They often like to be known by more touchy-feely names such as "investment adviser" and are at the top of the food chain. They work for fairly tightly regulated traditional brokerage firms such as RBC Dominion Securities Inc. or BMO Nesbitt Burns Inc. Because brokerage firms are generally geared to dealing with relatively wealthy clients, a broker usually won't give you too much time unless you have $100,000 or so to invest. He or she may take you on as a client if you have less money than that, but don't expect fawning attention, just a few meetings per year at most. For those with enough money, brokers can be an excellent choice because they can sell anything — including stocks, bonds, funds, and a range of more exotic investments. Another plus: their training and in-house support are fairly good.

✔ **Financial planners:** They are usually only licensed to deal in mutual funds or guaranteed investment certificates. They may work independently or as part of a large chain, and their quality varies greatly. Some are professional, smart, and dedicated, and some are little more than part-timers who can sell you a fund and that's about it. To deal in funds, they must register with the provincial securities commission but regulation of the profession has been patchy. However, things are likely to improve under the new Mutual Fund Dealers Association of Canada, which began accepting members in 2001. The new "self-regulatory organization" will eventually govern all mutual fund dealers who aren't already covered by a similar body. It will admit members, check that they're complying with the rules, and publicly discipline offenders, imposing fines, suspension, or termination of membership. You can reach the MFDA at 121 King Street West, Suite 1600, Toronto, ON M5H 3T9, or go to its Web site at www.mfda.ca.

✔ **Insurance agents and brokers:** Both will sell you insurance, but a broker usually deals with numerous companies while an agent generally has a relationship with just one. As the lines blur between financial institutions, insurance salespeople are registering to sell mutual funds. And life insurance companies, which once had a lock on the retirement planning market, have been forced to launch their own mutual fund families to hang on to customers' money. They've also been smartening up their traditional *segregated funds,* mutual fund–like products that usually promise to refund your invested capital if you hold them for long enough (see Chapter 19). In general, pick an insurance agent or broker to help you with financial planning if they are able to sell mutual funds as well as insurance products. If the salesperson is limited to insurance, then you're narrowing your options.

The Advantages of Using a Salesperson

We've all got hectic lives, so it can be a nice feeling to have someone take us by the hand and deal with our investing dilemmas. The stock and bond markets are confusing, scary places and millions of people find it reassuring to have an ally looking out for them.

Brokers or planners, especially if they're experienced, will usually know some neat tricks and handy shortcuts when it comes to investing. For example, they may suggest ways of minimizing your tax liability by setting up a simple trust for your children or grandchildren.

A good adviser imposes discipline on his or her clients by inducing them to save money — and should prevent them from making rash decisions, such as selling after the market turns down sharply. Without an arm's-length person imposing some sort of structure on our finances, it's easy to let debts mount up and our money problems drift.

Finding the Right Professional

To fix yourself up with a well-trained and professional planner, make sure that he or she meets one of the following tests:

- **Membership in the Canadian Association of Financial Planners:** This national association and lobby group for financial planners had 2,700 members in mid-2002. To join, a planner must complete some fairly tough planning courses or have a professional designation such as Chartered Accountant. The requirement to take courses probably discourages complete incompetents from becoming members of the CAFP. The group at least has a code of ethics — although there's no guarantee you won't end up with a bad apple — and it imposes follow-up "education" on members each year. You can contact the CAFP at the CAFP National Office, 1 St. Clair Ave. East, Suite 700, Toronto, ON M4T 2V7; Tel: 416-593-6592 or 1-800-346-2237; E-mail: planners@cafp.org; Web site: www.cafp.org.

- **Membership in the Canadian Association of Insurance and Financial Advisors:** An association of life and health insurance agents and brokers, this is one of Canada's most powerful lobby groups. Once again, there's a code of ethics and liability insurance for members. You can contact CAIFA at 350 Bloor Street East, 2nd Floor, Toronto, ON M4W 3W8; Tel: 416-444-5251 or 1-800-563-5822; E-mail: info@caifa.com; Web site: www.caifa.com.

  Making life simpler for investors, these two financial planning groups said in early 2002 that they plan to merge, creating a giant organization that will include a good chunk of the independent planners in Canada.

- **Completion of a recognized industry course:** These include courses that lead to the Certified Financial Planner (CFP) and Registered Financial Planner (RFP) designations.

- **Employment by a chartered bank or by a stockbroker who is a member of the Investment Dealers Association of Canada:** If the person works for a bank, you can be sure of some supervision, although you should take nothing for granted. The banks have set up their own personal finance training system, but there's no guarantee that the person you get is particularly knowledgeable. If the broker works for an IDA brokerage firm, he or she could be incompetent or greedy, but at least you know that he or she has passed the Canadian Securities Course, the educational course given to all new stockbrokers. Members of the public are also welcome to take this excellent course, virtually all of which has been useful to me as a reporter and investor. Call the Canadian Securities Institute, an IDA affiliate, at 416-364-9130 in Toronto or dial toll-free 1-866-866-2601 (English) or 1-866-866-2602 (French). The Web site is www.csi.ca. The IDA is a lobby group and disciplinary body for stockbrokers. If the person who wants to sell you mutual funds doesn't work for an IDA firm, then his or her employer should be in the new Mutual Fund Dealers Association of Canada — which was set up to catch mutual fund dealers who "fall through the cracks" with no industry-run body to keep an eye on them.

Unfortunately, you can easily come across bad planners, brokers, and advisers who have impressive qualifications or reputable employers. But at least you know that if they've gone to the trouble of getting trained, or they're under some kind of supervision from a large organization, then you're less likely to be stuck with a complete turkey.

The right way to pick an adviser

Finding an adviser is very like picking a building contractor or nanny: word of mouth and your own gut instincts are among the best methods to use. So your first move should be to ask friends and relatives what they've done and whether they're happy with their advisers. And then go to see several candidates. Apart from qualifications and membership in a professional association, you should also check out a few more things.

Does the adviser seem curious about you and willing to answer questions frankly?

A good adviser will ask you questions about your income, life history, assets, financial goals, health, marital status, pension, and investment knowledge. If that doesn't happen, then you could be dealing with a sales-driven hotshot who's just looking to make commissions quickly. Shop elsewhere. And ask about sales commissions as well as the adviser's experience and training. Vague answers are a bad sign.

Does the adviser work for a firm with an adequate back office for client record-keeping and supervision?

Jargon alert — having an adequate "back office" is just a fancy way of saying that they are set up to administer clients' accounts and orders. Ask to see a typical client statement and ensure that the firm has a *compliance officer*, an employee who keeps an eye on the salespeople and the way they treat clients.

Does the adviser sell a broad range of products?

A planner who wants to talk about funds from just one or two companies is probably lazy. Nobody can be familiar with the products from every company, but you want someone with a good idea of what's out there. You also want an adviser who's knowledgeable about life insurance, or who can at least hook you up with an insurance expert.

Are the adviser's office, grooming, and general image professional?

Nobody's looking for Armani or marble halls, but sloppy-looking premises or a scruffy appearance are signs of someone who hasn't been able to attract many clients.

Check out Chapter 25 for some tough questions you should ask any adviser before hiring them. I talk more about warning signs in Chapter 26, which includes ten sure signs it is time for you and your adviser to part ways.

The wrong way to pick an adviser

Unfortunately, a lot of what passes for investor education is just a giant sales pitch. So-called "seminars" that purport to enlighten you on a particular topic such as preparing a will or taking early retirement are really just a way of getting lots of sales targets into a room. Wandering around a glitzy "exhibition" or "forum" for investors may be fun and even informative. But these events are also a lure for getting "prospects" — potential customers — into a nice concentrated bunch where they can be picked off easily. In fact, be careful about attending seminars if you're the excitable or gullible type. The colourful celebrity speakers who work the investment circuit are often masters of making their audience both greedy and afraid — and easy targets for the inevitable sales spiel from the salespeople who paid for the event.

If the phone rings with a broker, adviser, or planner offering to help, decline politely and hang up. Always. Such "cold calls" are a time-honoured method of drumming up business for brokers, and the salesperson calling may be perfectly legitimate. But responding to a random phone call out of the blue is an awful way of picking someone who's supposed to help you manage your money — such an important aspect of your life.

The telephone is still a favourite tool of those creatures that occasionally crawl out from under the rocks — the dishonest salespeople pushing "unlisted" and "over-the-counter" stocks or other "unregistered" investments that promise fantastic returns. Do yourself a favour and have some fun. Rent two wonderful movies about these crooked sales reptiles: *Glengarry Glen Ross*, based on David Mamet's play about sleazy real estate marketers, and *Boiler Room*, a movie released in 2000 that tells the tale of some Long Island junk-stock pushers. After watching those two great films, you'll be better equipped to deal with telephone sales pitches.

Minding your As and Bs

Glance down the mutual fund listings and you'll notice that quite a few broker-sold fund families market their funds in different *classes* or *versions*, often listed as A or B and even C through F. Alternatively, some, such as Guardian Group of Funds, sell funds labelled classic mutual or adviser.

What do these labels mean to you, the potential unitholder? The difference is in the sales loads: One edition of the fund carries lower expenses, usually because investors in that class of units have paid the sales charge themselves or because they bought the fund directly from the company, bypassing the salesperson. The difference in annual expenses is usually between 0.5 percent and 1 percent per year. Here are a couple of examples:

- Trimark (which was taken over in 2000 by AIM Funds Management Inc., a subsidiary of British–U.S. fund giant Amvescap) has for years long sold its funds in two basic versions. Its original funds, such as the Trimark Fund SC and the Trimark Canadian Fund SC, can only be bought on a front-load or "sales charge" basis (hence the SC). Then there are the "Select" versions that can be bought with a back-end load. The back-end load is expensive for the company to finance — because it must dish out the sales commissions to the salespeople itself — so the Select funds carry higher expenses. Just to make things even more confusing, the original SC funds can also be bought with a back-end load — and higher expenses for the investor.

- Guardian sells its funds in two basic classes, classic and mutual. The classic units must be bought with a front-end load, whereas the mutual units, which carry a higher management fee, are available with a deferred load.

It all becomes bewildering, but treating investors differently according to how they buy a fund is arguably fair. That's because the front-load buyers have saved the company a lot of money by paying the load themselves, so they deserve a break on the management fee. In the United States, investors have long been accustomed to funds that are sold with different classes of units, but the idea has never really caught on with Canadians.

If you're buying a fund that comes in more than one class, do everything you can to get the one with the lowest management fee, especially if you plan to invest for a long time. Sometimes even paying a small sales load is a good idea — but remember that with a front-load fund, your adviser often gets a bigger trailer, so don't put up with any whining at the bargaining table. Over the years, a difference of only 0.5 percent in management fees really adds up. For example, say you put $10,000 into a deferred-load fund that produced an average annual compound return of 10 percent over a decade: You'd end up with $25,937. But say the fund was also available in a front-load version with a management fee that was 0.5 percentage points lower. The fund would be likely to give you an annual return of 10.5 percent instead of 10 percent. If you managed to buy that version of the fund with no sales load, your $10,000 would grow to $27,141 — or $1,200 more! Even if you had to pay an upfront sales load of 2 percent, reducing your initial investment to only $9,800, you would still end up with $26,598, or $661 more than an investor who chose the rear-load version.

Chapter 9

Buying Direct: Fund Companies that Sell to the Public

*B*uying your funds directly from a fund company instead of from a bank or through an adviser is one of the more enjoyable and profitable ways of investing in funds. The company is directly answerable to you when you call or e-mail, and you can pull your money out with no strings attached if the managers don't make the fund go up. And best of all: There are no sales charges or *loads* to increase your expenses — companies that sell directly to the public without imposing sales commissions are called *no-load* fund marketers. In this chapter, I look at getting rolling with buying direct, go through the pros and cons of this style of investing, and take you through a list of the top no-load players.

Getting Started with Direct Sellers

It's easy to get started — just call the companies or company you're interested in. They'll be pleased to send you the information about their funds. Table 9-1 lists the biggest no-load fund companies on the Canadian scene, their Web site addresses, and their assets. All are independent companies except for big Altamira Investment Services Inc., which was bought in 2002 by National Bank of Canada. No-load fund managers treat you rather like discount brokers do. They have anything from one to dozens of telephone-answering staff who will handle your orders but don't know much about you. All you have to do to invest is call their number (often toll-free) and transfer some money or send a cheque. There's no wheedling, pawing salesperson in the shape of a broker, planner, or insurance agent, which means there are no fiddly and costly commissions to worry about. No-load companies are generally fairly big businesses and they can usually be relied on to send pretty reliable statements of your account. Sounds perfect, doesn't it? But first up, you have to make a choice between these two alternatives:

- The no-load direct sellers that offer truly low expenses but also come with a narrow selection and higher minimum investment. The exception to this is Altamira. Or,

- Altamira, with its wonderfully wide selection and low initial investment but higher expenses (which are in line with mutual fund industry averages).

In the rest of the chapter, I look at the advantages and drawbacks of going either route.

Table 9-1	No-Load Direct Sellers in Canada	
Company	**Web site**	**Assets ($Thousand, as of mid-2002)**
Phillips Hager & North	www.phn.com	8,929,000
Altamira Investment Services	www.altamira.com	4,486,000
McLean Budden	www.mcleanbudden.com	726,000
Mawer Investment Management	www.mawer.com	522,000
Sceptre Investment Counsel	www.sceptre.ca	365,000
Saxon Group of Funds	www.saxonfunds.com	320,000

You pay to play

Expect to face stiff minimum investments of $5,000 or more with some companies that sell directly to the public. The fees they charge are low, so they can't afford to fool around with tiny accounts. By contrast, most banks and fund companies that sell through advisers let you invest as little as $100.

Direct sellers impose these high minimum purchases because they have pretty small mutual fund operations. Their main business is usually managing money for institutions such as pension funds. These companies are not equipped to deal with thousands of unitholders, so to avoid attracting lots of small and unprofitable accounts they often impose the required minimum investments.

Take Phillips Hager & North (PH&N) of Vancouver and Toronto, for example. It's the largest mutual fund company (excluding banks) that sells its funds directly to the public, instead of through salespeople such as financial planners. PHN says the people in a "household" have to have at least $25,000 in a combination of its funds. Still, that minimum isn't all that onerous when you consider that the size of the average registered retirement savings plan in 1999, according to a survey by the Royal Bank, was $55,280. An investor who's just getting going but wants to use a fund company that sells directly to the public may have to build up a pile of cash elsewhere before transferring money to the company.

Should you use a direct seller?

Many Canadians are still in love with their banks and brokers, not no-load fund companies. They continue to seek out the reassurance of a salesperson or the comforting embrace of a giant institution. That means no-load direct sellers have yet to really catch on in this country. Even mighty Phillips Hager is only the 15th biggest fund company in Canada. That said, direct sellers are an excellent choice for investors who like to follow their investments closely or seek out funds with low costs. If you can belly up to the bar with the minimum required investment and don't mind the lack of a personal touch, take a good look at this chapter to see if you're really a fit with this type of investing. Direct sellers of no-load funds are best suited for:

- ✔ **Investors looking for simplicity:** People who are very keen to get a simple solution, with all of their investments on one clear account statement. Direct sellers are easy to deal with because you can simply call up and ask questions or make changes to your account without having to go through a broker or other adviser. The same advantages apply to holding your funds at a bank — but a direct seller is much smaller than a bank, so it's easier to talk to.

- ✔ **Savvy market trackers:** People who are interested in investing and want to follow the process closely. Such savvy investors love the low annual expenses and often-excellent performance that no-load fund sellers offer. Many choose to leave a portion of their money in an account with a direct seller while investing the rest elsewhere. People who enjoy watching the markets often find that the information given to investors in direct-sold funds is more complete — that's because no-load companies deal directly with the investor and see him or her as the customer; there are no fund salespeople to muddy the picture. And the simplicity of a no-load account held at a fund company, instead of through an adviser, makes it easy to move money from fund to fund. Active investors who track the markets closely often do more switching around.

The Advantages of Dealing with an Independent No-Load Company

Using a no-load company that sells to the public is a halfway house between the lonely course of picking your own funds at a discount broker on the one hand and the comfy warm blanket of getting help from a bank employee or a salesperson who earns commissions on the other. When you go to such a salesperson (the option I deal with in Chapter 8) or a bank (see Chapter 7), you get lots of assistance and help — but you usually pay for the advice in the form of higher annual costs imposed on your fund. And the selection that a bank or commission-paid salesperson carries is often limited to only a few dozen funds. At a no-load company, the people answering the phone will offer some advice and the expenses on their funds may be low. But the selection of funds on offer is once again limited to the company's own products, and that might be just a handful of funds. Discount brokers (Chapter 6), whoopee, have lots of funds. They're the amusement park of funds. But you'll be riding that roller coaster alone, because you'll get hardly any help.

When you contact any fund company, no matter how it sells its products, ignore all of the marketing blather and ask for an application form and prospectus. Those two usually set out the stuff you need to know, such as minimum investment and annual costs. You can always slip 'em in the recycling bin later. Or toss them in that old rusty oil drum you use to burn garbage. (Don't the people next door complain about the choking greasy plume of smoke, by the way?)

There are important advantages to going with a no-load direct fund seller if you want a hassle-free solution. Here are the main ones.

More money in your pocket

The biggest plus of buying from a no-load company is the fact that you cut out the intermediary. No-load companies can charge you lower fees — although they don't always choose to do so. Because they don't have to pay an army of brokers — or cover the expense of running a sprawling network of bank branches — some direct sellers offer Canadian stock funds with annual expenses of 1.5 percent or less. That's much cheaper than most domestic equity mutual funds, which have total annual costs and fees closer to 2.6 percent. The more expensive fund is taking an extra 1 percent annually out of your mottled hide — over ten years, that difference adds up to 10 percent of your money.

Why one percentage point matters to you

If you were to invest $10,000 and earn a tax-free average annual return of 9 percent for a decade, you'd end up with $23,674. But the same $10,000 invested at a 10-percent rate of return, because the expenses were one percentage point lower, would grow to $25,937 — more than $2,200 more (see Table 9-2). That's why it's better to have a fund with a 1.5-percent annual expense ratio, rather than one with 2.5 percent in annual expenses. You can check a fund's expenses under "Key Facts" at the *Globe and Mail*'s mutual fund site, www.globefund.com, or look at your newspaper's monthly fund report.

Table 9-2 Think 1 Percent Doesn't Matter? That'll Be $2,263, Please

Year	Value at 9-Percent Return	Value at 10-Percent Return
Initial investment	$10,000	$10,000
1st	$10,900	$11,000
2nd	$11,881	$12,100
3rd	$12,950	$3,310
4th	$14,116	$14,641
5th	$15,386	$16,105
6th	$16,771	$17,716
7th	$18,280	$19,487
8th	$19,926	$21,436
9th	$21,719	$23,579
10th	$23,674	$25,937

Advice for adults

Another advantage of going directly to a fund company is that you're treated like an adult rather than simply as a faceless consumer of the fund product. In other words, the company's Web site and mailings to investors often are more candid about performance. That's because many of the investors who use no-load companies tend to be independent souls who relish the low costs and are happy with the lower level of advice. They're the sort to demand complete reporting of performance.

If you're not satisfied with the performance of your no-load funds, or if you have queries, it's simple to just pick up the phone and call. You may not get the errant fund manager or a senior executive, but the representative who answers the phone will probably be able to give you some answers.

And best of all, buying no-load doesn't mean you have to give up getting advice altogether. Direct sellers often have staff who can advise you on choosing funds and even help you shape your overall investment strategy.

Make mine simple

Dealing with a fund company directly is simpler than buying a fund through a salesperson. You're not forced to relay your order or request via someone else, potentially causing confusion or delay. You can call up the company and buy and sell funds in your account right over the phone as well as asking for forms or other administrative help. Your relationship as a customer is clearly with the fund seller, not with an intermediary like a broker. That's great for you because:

- You have just one company to deal with and complain to if there's a mistake in your account. Or did you say you enjoyed muttering endlessly into voice mail, like a doomed character in an abandoned Samuel Beckett play?
- You get just one annual and quarterly statement of account.
- If you own several funds, it's handy to be able to check on their performance if they're all included in one company's mailings.
- You can switch money easily from fund to fund as your needs or assets change.

Allowing frequent trades

It's often tempting to move your money frequently from fund to fund in an attempt to catch rising stock markets and avoid falling ones. Just like it's hard to resist swerving really close to cops carrying out a roadside check to make 'em jump and scramble (they always see the funny side, bless them). Naturally, frequent traders love using no-load companies because there are no charges to switch their money in and out. That makes a no-load fund company the perfect choice if you fancy yourself someone with the ability to time movements in stock and bond prices — for example, every time the Canadian stock market goes up 20 percent in a year, you might decide to pull out of stocks. But no-load fund companies don't appreciate it when customers move their money around constantly, because it greatly increases the company's administration costs (all of those transfers must be accounted for). So they'll eventually crack down on you by limiting your trades. And you'll often get slapped with a charge of 2 percent of your money if you switch out of a fund within three months of buying it.

Still, if you want to try to outguess the markets and trade some money around every few months (even though it's often a bad idea), then direct and no-load may be the way to go. Here's why:

- ✔ The companies have people on staff to move your money from fund to fund quickly and easily.

- ✔ There are no sales charges to complicate the transfer of money or add to your costs.

- ✔ Buying the fund directly from the no-load fund company rather than through a discount broker or commission-paid adviser means your sale orders go directly into the fund company's system instead of through a discount brokerage employee. That speeds up the process and reduces the probability of mistakes in your order.

- ✔ You get an account statement and transaction confirmation slip in the mail directly from the no-load company and not through the discounter. That's simpler and more convenient for investors who are closely tracking their own performance.

Switching into and out of no-load funds through a discount broker can in fact cost you commissions, because discounters often impose small fees of around $40 each time you sell a no-load fund. A conventional broker won't welcome your business if you plan to chop and change your portfolio all the time, because of all the troublesome paperwork you create. Heavy and constant trading won't thrill even a no-load fund company. That's because trading raises administrative and mailing costs, which have to be paid by other investors. So with many companies, expect to pay a 2-percent penalty when you move money out of a fund within three months of buying it. And if you really go over the top, you may be banned from switching your money around or limited to a certain number of trades — say, one a month. How many trades are too many trades? There are no firm rules on what counts as heavy trading, but here are a few guidelines:

- ✔ An investor who moves some of his or her money from fund to fund twice a year or less would count as a light or infrequent trader.

- ✔ Someone who made between 2 and 12 trades a year would count as a medium trader.

- ✔ More than a dozen trades a year indicates that the investor is a heavy trader who thinks he or she can outguess the market.

A fund company is unlikely to cut off your buying and selling privileges unless you're trading very frequently — making changes to your portfolio every few days or every week. If you do get cut off and you can't resolve the situation, you may have to move your money to a discount broker that allows constant trading. But even if you buy through a discounter, the funds you're buying may well levy that 2-percent penalty if you sell a holding that was bought fewer than three months ago.

The penalty seems small but it reduces your return. Let's say I decide that the Canadian stock market is set to boom because oil prices are rising (foreign investors see us as resource producers in toques, so they tend to buy into our market when prices for commodities, such as lumber, energy, and metals, are going up). I put $10,000 into a no-load company's Canadian equity fund, a fund that invests in stocks and shares (which in turn are a tiny slice of ownership of companies). The Canadian market goes up 10 percent in two weeks and my fund matches the rise in the broad market, boosting my investment to $11,000 — at which point I sell half of my holding in the fund, or $5,500. If the company slaps a 2-percent fee on investors who leave a fund after less than 90 days, then I'll receive a cheque for just $5,390, which is $5,500 minus 2 percent. Of course, my other $5,500 is still sitting in the fund.

How many trades are too many? Well, research seems to show that almost any level of chopping and changing reduces overall returns because most investors let emotion distort their judgment, leading them to do things at the wrong time. People sell when the market has slumped and is about to bounce back. And they buy after it has already shot up and is about to go on the slide.

Over time, share prices may tend to rise remorselessly as good companies thrive and the world economy grows, but the stock market also advances in sudden starts. If you happen to have sold your equity funds, following the dictates of your brilliant can't-lose trading strategy, just before one of those days, then you miss out on the profits. That said, there are a few times when it's a sensible idea to move money out of a fund, and holding the fund directly at a no-load company makes the process easier. Good times to move money include:

- ✔ When the fund has gone up so much that it now represents a huge portion of your portfolio. For example, if you've decided to keep just half of your money in shares, but one or more of your equity funds have produced a 100-percent return over the past year, then you probably have too much money riding on equities. Time to sell some of those stock funds.

- ✔ If you're foolhardy enough to bet on a *specialty* fund that invests in just one narrow section of the market, such as South Korea or financial-services shares, and you've been lucky enough to score a big profit. Such one-flavour funds tend to post huge crashes soon after their big wins — as investors go cool on the kind of stocks they hold. So think strongly about selling at least some of your units in a specialty fund as soon as it has a good year. No, don't just think about it: Pick up the phone and do it immediately.

✔ If your reason for holding the fund no longer applies. For example, a fund manager you like may have quit, or the fund may have changed its investment style.

Check your portfolio once or twice a year, and if it's out of line with your ideal mix of investments, then readjust it by moving money from one fund to another. For example, say you've decided that you want one-third of your $10,000 mutual fund collection in sure-and-steady government bonds — certificates issued by the government that pay interest and can be cashed in again at the issue price after a set number of years. The other two-thirds is in lucrative-but-dangerous stocks, those tiny pieces of ownership in companies. See Chapter 5 for more on bonds and stocks.

So your setup is:

$3,300 bond funds	33 percent of portfolio
$6,700 stock funds	67 percent of portfolio
$10,000 total portfolio	100 percent of portfolio

Say the bonds hold their value over the next year, remaining at $3,300, but the stocks rise 30 percent to $8,710, which gives you a mix of:

$3,300 bond funds	27 percent of portfolio
$8,710 stock funds	73 percent of portfolio
$12,010 total portfolio	100 percent of portfolio

This means you have too much riding on the stock market in relation to our original plan — almost three-quarters of the total pile. You can fix it easily by moving $663 out of your stock funds and into the bond funds, leaving you with a portfolio that looks like this:

$3,963 bond funds	33 percent of portfolio
$8,047 stock funds	67 percent of portfolio
$12,010 total portfolio	100 percent of portfolio

If you hold a super-volatile fund that invests in a narrow sector or region, such as a technology company or Latin America, it's a good strategy to move some money out of the fund if it shoots up in value. That way, you lock some profits before the inevitable crash. Holding such funds forever is of dubious benefit because they're at risk of losing money for long periods, as explained in Chapter 12.

The Drawbacks of Going Direct

Most no-load mutual fund companies offer too few funds to really give you a diversified portfolio — that means an account with many different types of investment. Here are the main drawbacks to using a direct seller.

Significant levels of cash required

As I mentioned at the start of this chapter, not everyone can go direct. As attractive as it seems to investors who are serious minimalists in terms of their need for guidance and their interest in paying fees to invest, you need a minimum amount of cash to play. This is obviously not the case with novice investors, or those in the process of building their portfolio. Although this type of investing may not be the right choice for you now, it is something to keep an eye on as your investing savvy, and your portfolio, grows.

Lack of choice

The main problem with direct purchase of funds is the narrow selection. Few direct sellers have more than one or two funds, so if you leave all of your money with the company you're at risk of seeing the market turn against that particular investment style.

A typical no-load fund company sells just a couple of funds of each type. Generally, there'll be:

- One or two stock funds
- One or two bond funds
- One or two global equity funds
- Perhaps a few specialty funds, such as one that buys only U.S. stocks

That's a small selection compared to buying from a broker, insurance salesperson, or financial planner, who can often sell you at least a dozen funds in each category. At a discount broker, you can buy hundreds of each.

You can avoid this lack-of-choice drawback by buying the direct seller's funds through a discount broker instead, if they're available. That lets you use the no-load seller's funds, with their nice low expenses, in combination with index funds or funds from other companies. However, your discount broker may not even carry a low-expense company's funds (because the discounter gets little or nothing in sales commissions).

Doing it through a discounter

Yes, you can often buy no-load mutual funds through your full-service broker and discount broker, instead of going directly to the fund company. But brokers often hit you with a commission or "transaction fee" to let you buy or sell low-expense no-load funds.

That's because these funds often don't pay the brokers much or anything in ongoing annual commissions — known as *trailers* in the colourful argot of the fund world. But the low costs and fees charged to unitholders in many no-load funds usually make it worthwhile to buy them despite the small charge imposed by the broker, especially if you plan to hang on to the funds for a few years.

Be warned, though: If you buy the funds through a broker, discount or full-service, the fund company probably won't have any record of your investment, so you lose the advantage of being able to deal directly with the company.

The only direct seller with a genuinely wide range of funds is Altamira, which pioneered the mass marketing of no-load funds in Canada. Altamira has yet to build a strong record in global equities, but it has a vast selection of specialty funds and Canadian equity funds along with index funds that offer wafer-thin expenses of 0.5 percent a year. But there's a flaw to some of Altamira's other funds: Their expenses tend to be well over 2 percent.

The Dawn of Direct Sellers in Canada

No-load funds from independent companies are a huge business in the United States, with companies such as Janus Capital, T. Rowe Price, and Vanguard Group attracting tens of billions of dollars. But Canadians have never really fallen in love with the concept. However, selling funds directly to the public instead of through advisers is much more efficient, because there are no sales commissions to pay or brokers to mollycoddle, and it allows fund companies to reduce radically the annual charges imposed on funds. As Canadian investors become more aware of the management fees and other costs that reduce the returns from their funds, they'll show more interest in the independent companies.

Let's look at the minimum investment imposed by the three largest direct no-load sellers and go through their selection of funds — highlighting the winners, of course!

Phillips Hager & North

The Vancouver-based firm, which is a big money manager for institutions such as pension funds, posted rapid growth through the 1990s to become Canada's biggest independent no-load company. It offers rock-bottom expenses — just 1.1 percent on its main Canadian equity fund, for example. Those low fees have helped to keep returns above average. The company's performance tends to be steady and above the median, but not spectacular. In fact, low key is the motif of the whole firm. It rarely if ever advertises, doesn't publicize the names of its managers, and barely talks to the press. Money managers seem to stay there for years and blue-chip companies invariably dominate the portfolios. The main drawback of investing with PH&N is its high minimum of $25,000 per household, which can be divided among the company's funds. And the fund menu is limited, with no specialty or regional funds (apart from a well-respected U.S. equity fund). However, the company does offer some extras: It has people on staff who can offer advice with your whole investment portfolio, not just the PH&N funds you own.

The firm is a great choice for conservative investors who realize the importance of low costs. But putting your entire portfolio into PH&N funds carries a couple of risks. All of your money is riding on just one team, for one. To diversify more completely, it would be a good idea to buy a couple of equity funds elsewhere. And the firm also offers no index funds, which are a vital component of just about any prudent investor's portfolio.

The company's PH&N Bond Fund, stuffed with high-quality corporate and government bonds, has long been a thing of beauty. It carries annual expenses of only 0.6 percent, compared with almost 2 percent for the average Canadian bond fund. Remember that the returns from bond funds tend to be modest, so it's particularly important that their costs are kept low. Those modest fees and expenses helped the PH&N fund to generate a hot average annual compound return of 8.4 percent in the ten years ended June 2002, compared with just 7 percent for the average bond fund. The PH&N Balanced Fund, with its rock-bottom expense ratio of 0.9 percent, compared with 2.5 percent for the average Canadian balanced fund, has been another stellar performer. As of June 2002, it was up 8.6 percent annually over ten years, compared with 7.9 percent for the average balanced fund.

Altamira Investment Services

Altamira is the flashy, glitzy rock-and-roller of the no-load fund world — and it has made a lot of investors rich over the years by posting above-average returns. In fact, its vast product line and big selection of aggressive funds make it Canada's closest thing to one of the great U.S. no-load sellers, such as T. Rowe Price. In 2002, National Bank of Canada took over the company, laden with debt after a messy internal struggle for control among the owners. The plucky little No. 4 bank wants to expand its fund business outside Quebec — so far, it has left Altamira intact.

Altamira's expense ratios are higher than those of the other big Canadian independent no-load sellers — 2.6 percent on the giant $1.7-billion Altamira Equity Fund, for example — which is in line with the average Canadian equity fund. But the company's minimum initial investments are low at just $1,000 for most funds. Other no-load sellers keep costs down by avoiding advertising and offering simple service. But Altamira tends to be a heavy advertiser, employing squadrons of employees who are ready to answer questions — hence the higher expenses. The company also offers ready-mixed portfolios of its funds and it even has a discount brokerage arm through which you can hold a self-directed registered retirement savings plan, a tax-sheltered account in which you can own a huge range of investments.

Altamira markets some hyper-aggressive specialty funds that track just one industry or region. These specialty funds include the company's Altamira e-Business Fund, specializing in Internet companies, which had a mighty $311 million in assets at the end of 1999. Launched in late 1998, the fund earned an incredible 190.2 percent in 1999, the fifth best return of any fund in Canada. Then came the crash — by mid-2002, unitholders who were in the fund at the end of 1999 had lost 80 percent of their money in two and a half years.

Altamira has long published superb information for its unitholders. Back in the 1990s, it was one of the few fund companies in Canada that was candid enough to compare the returns on its funds with those of market benchmarks. Regulators are now forcing all other mutual fund companies to do likewise. Altamira's Web site, at `www.altamira.com`, is still one of the best fund company sites in Canada.

The company came under a cloud in the late 1990s after superstar Frank Mersch, who ran Altamira Equity, fell behind rival fund managers because he missed out on soaring bank stocks. Investors yanked hundreds of millions of dollars out of the company's funds and Mr. Mersch departed. Ian Ainsworth, the fund's new lead manager, racked up hot numbers by riding the technology-stock wave in 1999. Altamira Equity surged to 47.8 percent that year, compared with a return of just 20.7 percent from the average Canadian equity fund. But then the rain set in: Tech stocks slumped and Altamira Equity slipped to the bottom 25 percent of Canadian equity funds in 2000 and 2001.

That sounds alarming, but don't worry, the Altamira Equity Fund and the e-Business Fund were just two of more than 50 funds and fund mixtures on sale at Altamira in mid-2002. The Altamira range of funds is so huge that you can build a pretty nicely balanced mix of funds out of its wares — with one drawback. As of 2002, most of the company's Canadian stock funds were moderately aggressive in strategy. That means chasing the shares that will go up the most, soon. In other words, leaving all your stock market money with the company's funds was a bet that the stock market would come bouncing back before long. So if you're an Altamira investor who's pessimistic about the market (and who in their right mind isn't?), here's a solution: Leave some cash in a Canadian equity and a global equity fund bought elsewhere.

The great news is that Altamira gives investors a big break by selling a range of low-expense index funds as well as a selection of actively managed portfolios. So by combining the company's index funds and regular funds, you could build an excellent portfolio using just Altamira products. Its expenses on conventional funds remain on the high side, however, when you consider that Altamira isn't paying commissions to brokers.

Altamira is the only non-bank direct seller to offer a full range of *index funds,* which give you a return in line with the entire stock or bond market (in other words, they just track a well-known benchmark, such as the Standard & Poor's/ Toronto Stock Exchange composite index). Altamira's index funds have bargain-basement annual fees and expenses that are as low as 0.5 percent. The company sells an impressive range of index funds, including funds that track stock markets in Asia and Europe. Because Altamira markets both index funds and conventional *actively managed funds,* which attempt to make money by trading shares and bonds, the company's lineup is varied enough to include all of the funds an investor needs.

Putting a good chunk of your stock market money into index funds — I recommend one-half to two-thirds — is a sensible course for just about any investor. It's an easy way to insure against the damage you suffer by owning one or more submarine funds that drastically lag the market benchmark, the ones that sink when just about every other fund is sailing ahead. (Oh, take it from me, clever Cathy, you'll own funds like that.) At least with an index fund, even if the rest of your money is in a weak fund, you keep up with the stock market as it rises over time, minus the fund's modest annual expenses — usually 1 percent or less. A typical retail mutual fund gets a lot scarier if the manager flails around for years — as they often do — and you also have whopping annual expenses of about 2.6 percent eating into your nest egg like a rabid vole.

Fund companies like to wipe out the unpleasant record of their sick and limping funds — oh how humane! — by simply combining them with healthier members of the pack. That cleaning up of history conveniently polishes the so-called long-term returns produced by the industry (because dying funds and their awful numbers disappear). But even so, over the ten years to June 2002, the average Canadian equity fund underperformed the local benchmark, the Standard & Poor's/Toronto Stock Exchange composite index. The index produced an annual return of 9.9 percent for investors, while funds made 9.3 percent. And that's despite the crash of big-name stocks such as Nortel Networks Corp. that once dominated the index and thus made it easier for fund managers to beat their benchmark.

The message is that loser funds abound. So own at least some index funds as insurance. That way you won't leave too much of your cash languishing with a mumbler who has a damp excuse involving "unrecognized value."

The smaller no-load sellers

Other no-load direct sellers include Mawer Investment Management of Calgary and Toronto-based McLean Budden, Sceptre Investment Counsel, and Saxon Group of Funds. All are conservative firms with good reputations, low expenses, and generally strong returns (although Sceptre has had some performance problems). But you may not be able to buy their funds directly from the company in all parts of Canada. That's because registering to deal with the public in every province is expensive and troublesome, especially if your company is small. For example, Saxon sells through dealers everywhere (the dealer may impose a fee to buy or sell, remember), but it will sell directly only to Ontarians. It mandates a minimum investment of $5,000 per household.

McLean Budden is a long-established institutional manager that imposes a $10,000 minimum investment per account. Sceptre has a minimum of $5,000 per account. Mawer funds can be bought directly from the company with minimum investments of $25,000 or $100,000 per account, depending on your province, or through brokers with a minimum investment of $5,000 per fund.

Once again, the problem with buying from these low-cost no-load sellers is that they don't offer enough funds to give you a truly diversified portfolio. They might argue the point, but I can't help feeling that just one Canadian equity fund or one global equity fund isn't enough to spread your risk adequately because a single manager or management team can go into a prolonged and nasty slump. McLean Budden offers two Canadian equity funds — a _growth-style_ fund and a _value-style_ fund — so its lineup is a little more diversified. Funds that use a growth style usually load up on hot companies, whose profits are expanding quickly, in an attempt to ride their shares higher. Value funds normally seek out companies whose shares have fallen out of favour with other investors, in hopes of big profits when the stocks bounce back. Mind you, in the wacky Nortel Networks Corp.–dominated market of 1999 and 2000, such distinctions tended to blur. Both McLean Budden funds listed Nortel and its then-major shareholder BCE Inc. as their top holdings in late 1999. The bottom line for investors: Don't just rely on a fund's name, check the top holdings with your own beady blood-shot eye to find out what really makes the manager's little heart flutter.

Investors Group: A special case

Investors Group Inc. of Winnipeg is Canada's biggest fund company. It had a huge $40 billion in assets at the end of June 2000, 10 percent more than its nearest rival, Royal Bank of Canada. And that doesn't even include another $32 billion in mutual fund assets in Mackenzie Financial Corp, which Investors Group bought in 2001 for $4.1 billion, but continues to run as a separate operation.

Giant Investors Group got to be that size by giving about 1 million investors exactly what they want: An all-in-one solution to their financial planning needs.

The company sells directly to the public, but it does so through dedicated salespeople who work exclusively for Investors Group. That means it is rather like a regular "broker-sold" company, such as Mackenzie or Fidelity Investments Canada Ltd., that market their funds via advisers. If you buy into an Investors Group fund, you face sales commissions, although they're buried in the management fee charged by the fund. Investors Group is unique on the Canadian scene because its army of more than 3,000 salespeople is tied to the company. That makes it a hybrid between broker-sold fund companies that market through independent salespeople and no-load companies that sell directly to customers. Investors Group representatives are also trained and equipped to provide other financial services and products, offering a cradle-to-grave money-management plan for the customer.

The company levies annual costs that are in line with or slightly higher than fund industry averages. For example, the enormous $2.3-billion Investors Canadian Equity Fund has annual costs of nearly 3 percent, substantially higher than the 2.6 percent levied by the average Canadian equity fund — although the company has a rebate system under which clients get fee reductions as their holdings get bigger. I wish you good luck figuring out the Byzantine system from the information provided at the company's Web site (www.investorsgroup.com), though. I got nowhere.

Investors Group funds are generally middle-of-the-pack performers. Some of its big Canadian equity funds lagged the market and their competitors in the 1990s, but manager changes have led to an improvement. Investors Canadian Equity posted a miserable average annual return of only 7.7 percent in the five years ended December 31, 1999, compared with 13.7 percent for the average Canadian equity fund. But its annual return in the three years ended June 2002 was a respectable 3.9 percent, in line with the 4.1-percent return from the average Canadian equity fund. Faced with defections by customers who wanted a wider selection of funds, the company has launched a truly bewildering selection of new offerings, many run by outside mutual fund companies and other external managers. By mid-2002, there were 87 different funds and versions of funds on its shelf — and that didn't include another 248 products at Mackenzie. But there's a big gap in the lineup: No sign of any index funds. It's impossible to make them profitable if you're paying commissions to salespeople, remember.

The company's enormous financial clout and partnership with sister company Great-West Life Assurance allow it to offer a wide range of non-fund products and services. But dealing with Investors Group is essentially the same as buying funds from other broker-sold fund companies that market through commissioned salespeople — in other words, the expenses on its fund are higher than those imposed by the cheaper independent no-load companies.

Part III
The Fund Stuff: Building a Strong Portfolio

The 5th Wave   By Rich Tennant

"I read about investing in a company called UniHandle Ohio, but I'm uneasy about a stock that's listed on the NASDAQ as UhOh."

In this part . . .

Relax. Have another family-sized bar of candy. Most mutual funds are a waste of your time — so you don't have to use up any time worrying about them. In this section, I talk about the different types or categories of funds you can buy. I recommend the sort of funds you should concentrate on — there are only about six — and I warn you against the dozen or so types of risky, expensive, or confusing funds that you should avoid. I also dig into the bewildering varieties and wrappers that funds are sold in, separating out the useful features from the gimmicks and hype.

Chapter 10

Equity Funds: The Road to Riches

. . . .

. . . .

Equity mutual funds, which buy stocks and shares of companies, are perhaps the best route to riches that you and I will ever find. Okay, marrying a 95-year-old hang-gliding suicidal millionaire in poor health might be quicker. But then there are all those whining rival heirs to fend off. Equity funds are a wonderful invention because they hold shares in a huge variety of (usually) great companies. So wide is the selection of holdings in most equity funds that if some of the businesses fail or stagnate, there are nearly always enough winners in the fund to pull you through.

Equity funds should be the core of just about anybody's investment portfolio, assuming he or she is investing for at least five years. Because the economy and well-run companies are almost certain to grow over time, stocks and shares can be the engine of growth for your money. If you want to earn decent returns on your cash over the long term, and you've decided to buy mutual funds, you're pretty well forced to buy equity funds. That's because they're the only type of fund that's likely to produce big returns, possibly 10 percent or more annually, in the long haul. And those are the types of returns that you need to defy inflation and build a substantial nest egg.

Yes, the stock market and the funds that invest in it can drop sharply, sometimes for years — I'll provide some scary examples in this chapter. So make sure you've a good chunk of bond funds in your holdings as well. But there's strong evidence that equity markets pretty well always rise over periods of ten years or more, so equity funds are a relatively safe bet for buyers who are sure they can hold on for a long time without needing the money back at short notice.

In this chapter I give you a crash course on how the stock market works and explain why funds are a great way to profit from it. I show why you're best off buying equity funds that invest in big and stable companies, especially businesses that sell their wares all over the world. I also make clear why you should hold six or seven equity funds — three Canadian and three or four global — and I give you simple tips for selecting great funds.

Why Investing in Stocks Is Simple

Believe it or not, making money in the stock market is easy — in theory. You just buy *shares* — which are a tiny slice of ownership — in well-managed companies and then hold on to them for years. As the businesses you've invested in thrive, so do their owners, and that includes you as a *shareholder*. But when you actually try to select wonderful companies, things get complicated. For one thing, it's hard to tell which companies have genuinely bright prospects, because the managers of just about every corporation do a great job of blowing their little brass horns and making everything look wonderful in their garden. And like everything else, the stock market is subject to the whims of fashion. When investors decide that they love a particular company or industry, the shares usually go to fantastic heights. At that point, buying stocks turns into a risky game — because there's no point buying a great business if you pay four times what it's really worth.

Being fallible human beings, we constantly sabotage ourselves in the market. When everything is going well and shares are climbing to record highs, we feel all warm, fuzzy, and enthusiastic — and we stumble into the market just in time for the crash. And when the economy or the stock market is slumping, we get all depressed and sell our shares at bargain-basement prices — just when we should be grabbing more. But perhaps the biggest problem with investors is our innate belief that we're smarter than everybody else. Everybody else thinks the same thing, which means that lots of us are going to end up losers. Don't let me stop you: You can try to make pots of money buying speculative technology companies or penny mining stocks or companies consolidating the pallet industry (don't laugh, I did), but that's really gambling. True investing in stock markets is simply buying well-established, well-run businesses and holding the shares, ideally for years.

Mutual funds are one of the very best and easiest ways to make money from the stock market. That's because:

- ✔ They're run by professionals who are trained in the art of checking out businesses.

- ✔ They're set up to make it easy to put your money in and get it back.

- ✔ Best of all, funds hold a wide variety of companies, spreading your risk and giving you the chance to benefit from growth in a huge range of industries.

By handing your money over to a mutual fund company, you're saving yourself from yourself — if you aren't making the decisions, then you can't risk your savings on wild bets or crazy dreams.

The real kicker in stock market investing is figuring out whether a company is genuinely good — a quality outfit worth putting money into — and whether the price you're being asked to pay for shares is too high. Unfortunately, though, there may be no such thing as a true value for a company, because the numbers all vary so wildly according to the assumptions you make about the future. In that case, a stock is simply worth what people decide to pay for it on any given day. And that may not be very much: Stocks can dive for no apparent reason. It has happened to me, painfully, in my own personal investing. But there's one thing about the crazy volatile stock market that we should care about because it makes stocks and shares wonderful for ordinary people like us saving for the future. A gift, in fact, from the gods. Good companies thrive, their profits go up, and their stocks gain value over the long term.

Sometimes selecting a good company to invest in can be almost embarrassingly simple. I remember shopping for a cordless phone in the early 1990s and noticing that only two companies offered phones that could be described as beautifully designed, Canada's Nortel Networks Corp. and Japan's Sony Corp. High-quality design, like reliable service or clever marketing, is no accident — it requires talented people, and they don't stay long with badly run companies. Sure enough, an investor who bought either Nortel or Sony shares in early 1995 multiplied their money more than sixfold over the next five years.

In for the long haul

Based on experience in the past century, you almost always win in the stock market over periods of at least ten years provided you stick to big, high-quality companies and you spread your risk by owning at least a dozen of them in different industries. Most equity mutual funds play it even safer by holding at least 50 different stocks (many hold 100 or more) so they can be sure of buying and selling their holdings easily.

Remember, too: It's hard to lose money in the stock market as long as you buy well-run, large companies and hold them for long enough. Studies that looked at every ten-year period in the market during the 20th century found that stocks produced a profit in 99 percent of the periods, although that falls to 86 percent if you take inflation into account. Still, odds of six-to-one in your favour aren't bad.

Look at nearly any professionally run equity portfolio, such as a mutual fund, and you'll notice that it contains dozens and dozens of stocks. Why so many? Why doesn't the manager just buy his or her favourite half-dozen shares and run with that? One reason is that when the market turns sour on a company its stock tends to drop like a rock. So exposing a huge proportion of your fund to a single company is a bad idea. Getting stuck with a stock that nobody else wants is a fund manager's most ghastly nightmare. Whenever he or she offers the shares for sale, rival investment managers make sympathetic faces and gentle cooing noises — and then refuse to buy the garbage at anything but sub-bargain prices. Under provincial securities law, in order to protect investors, a mutual fund can have a maximum of one-tenth of its assets in a single stock. And most funds limit their exposure to single shares to 5 percent or less.

A test case for capitalism: Meet Angus and Bronwyn

Let's take an equity fund apart and figure out just what it's made of. The "equity" in equity funds is just a fancy word for stocks and *shares* (two words that mean the same thing). Just like stocks, shares are tiny portions of ownership of a company, imaginary certificates that represent ownership of the business. Until the 1980s, some investors hoarded elaborately printed stock certificates in their safety deposit boxes, but it's just about all done electronically now.

Let's use a grossly simplified example (don't worry, there'll be no animal diseases or stuff like that; I don't mean that sort of gross) to see how the stock market works. Suppose you and your Welsh sister-in-law start a dry cleaning business and you each invest $5,000, while your Scottish boyfriend puts up $10,000. That means the store has three *shareholders*, or owners, and a total of four shares: One each for you and Bronwyn, your sister-in-law (in return for your $5,000 each), and two shares for Angus, because he put up twice as much. Now, say people's silk blouses get wrecked and the business doesn't do well. Bronwyn realizes that Angus wants to get out of this mess, even if he has to take a loss. So she buys both of his shares at only $3,000 each, giving her ownership of three shares, or three-quarters of the business. The important point here is that the price of the shares has fallen because the prospects of the business are poor. But the fact that Angus sold the shares to Bronwyn has no direct effect on the store itself. People are still coming and going, beefing about their spoiled clothes, while the stock trading takes place entirely separately — behind the scenes, as it were.

A real-life example of equity investing

Now, mutual funds usually aren't allowed to buy dry cleaning stores (don't laugh, I know some wild-eyed fund managers who probably would if they could) because investments in tiny companies are too risky. Instead, they trade stocks on the stock market, a vast organized exchange system. To see how this works, let's look at Canada's now-fallen stock market star Nortel Networks Corp., a giant global maker of equipment for sending signals over the Internet, phone lines, and just about anything else you care to name. In late 2000, Nortel had about 3 billion shares — that's 3,000 times 1 million — outstanding (that is, in the hands of investors), and they were trading in Toronto at about $70 each. That means the stock market placed a value on the company of about $210 billion — 210,000 times $1 million. You'd have to destroy quite a few shirts to create that kind of wealth. The significant thing in this snapshot, though, was that Nortel shares had soared more than threefold over the previous year. Does that mean that Nortel's real value had increased by $140 billion in just a year? Probably not, but Nortel shares climbed because investors went crazy for technology stocks, sending the stock ever higher. In other words, investors kept *bidding*, or offering high prices for Nortel, and as the mania to own the company's shares grew, the stock price continued to rise. But don't forget that the opposite is true, as Nortel investors discovered to their detriment in 2001 and 2002. If investors turn sour on a company, the stock normally drops like a dead donkey. During the summer and early autumn of 2000, Nortel shares had climbed as high as $122, but they slumped to the $70 range by the fall as investors went cool on the Internet. At that point, you might think Nortel was a great value, with the shares down 40 percent from their peak. Many investors did. Wrong. Nortel just kept dropping as the market for telecommunications gear imploded and fears for the company's very solvency increased. By summer 2002, the shares had collapsed to less than $2, dragging down the whole Canadian stock market with them.

"Equity" sounds nice and rich — but what does it mean?

The term *equity* means "fairness" or "equal treatment," and it's used as a shorthand for stock to indicate the fact that each share is as good as another (in the real world, controlling shareholders sometimes run companies for their own private benefit, but that's another story). In other words, if I own 100 shares in a company and you own 1,000, then you're supposed to get ten times as much say in choosing the directors and you're also supposed to get ten times as much in dividends, no more and no less. Basically, it comes down to who picks the directors, because they call the shots. "Who cares?" I hear you ask.

Well, that little fact — the rule that holders of shares get exactly the same treatment in proportion to how many they own — is one of the great things about the stock market. If you hold 100 shares and a mysterious, scary British pension fund that seems to be a front for the Queen owns 1 million, you both get exactly the same dividends per share and potential increase in share price. The stock market is often rigged or brutal, but it's also a very democratic and fair place — you either sell or buy, your call, with no sort-of's or might-do's.

Deciding How Much to Bet on Equity Funds

Now that you're a regular market whiz, understanding the ups and downs of stocks, it's time for the really tough decision: How many of your loonies are you going to dedicate to equity funds? Finding the right balance here is critical. As I mention elsewhere, stocks, in the form of quality equity funds, are the place for the lion's share of your long-term savings. But not everyone has the time or nerve to be a long-term investor.

Equity funds are not a good place to hold money that you're going to need in the next couple of years. And stocks and equity funds are not suitable investments when you can't afford to suffer any short-term losses. That's because even though stock markets rise over time as the economy expands, share prices can go into vicious slumps for a year or more. For example, as of mid-2002 the average global stock market fund had suffered an annual loss of 3.9 percent over three years. So the money you allocate to equity funds should be cash that you can let ride for several years — that way your funds have time to bounce back from one of the market's periodic funks.

In Chapter 4, which is all about using mutual funds in your financial plan, I suggest three basic portfolios, depending on what sort of investor you are. The allocation of stocks and bonds in these packages is based on professional portfolios designed by banks and fund companies, but it's not infallible. That's because nobody knows what will happen to the world economy and interest rates in years to come. And besides, everybody's different: If you have a fat pension from your job, you can afford to take far more risks with your mutual fund portfolio in search of higher returns. If the funds lose money, at least the regular pension cheque will keep you fed.

By contrast, if your mutual funds have to supply all your retirement income, then risking the whole wad in equity funds would be reckless. For example, the Standard & Poor's/Toronto Stock Exchange composite index — a collection of Canada's biggest companies — slumped almost 15 percent in calendar-year 1990, almost 25 percent in the third quarter of 1998, and almost 13 percent in 2001. For someone who had his or her entire savings tied up in the stock market, that would have been a hair-raising experience.

Investors can logically be divided into three types, each with a very different need and desire for equity funds. Chances are that you don't fit neatly into any of the categories, but you'll almost certainly feel closest to one of them:

> ✓ **Savers** are people for whom investment losses are either unacceptable or unbearable. Typically, a saver is someone who will be using his or her money to make a major purchase, such as a home, within the next couple

of years. So all that savers want is a steady and guaranteed return, even if it's less than 5 percent a year. The group also includes people of modest means who will need every penny they've saved to live on, and thus can't afford to take any risks. Investors like this probably shouldn't own any equity funds because the risk of loss is just too great.

✔ **Balanced investors** are like most of us — we just want a steady return year after year, without too many stomach-turning drops along the way. After all, life plans change, and we may find it necessary to dip into our savings long before retirement. Avoiding huge losses means owning lots of bonds, which are loans to governments and investors that have been packaged into tiny slices so investors can trade them. In Chapter 4, I suggest that investors in this balanced group limit equity funds to only 45 percent of their portfolio.

Only 45 percent in stocks is a very cautious mixture: Most balanced mutual funds in Canada in mid-2002 had about 56 percent of their assets in stocks, so most people feel happier increasing the equity weighting in their portfolios to 50 percent or more. But remember that as you chase higher returns, your risk of loss climbs.

✔ **Growth investors** are the aggressive or "long-term" types who don't mind double-digit losses in their portfolios as long as they, ideally, earn 10 percent or more over the long term. In other words, they're investing for at least five years. In Chapter 4, I suggest a portfolio for growth investors that's 75 percent in stocks. If you have many years to go before you'll need the money in the portfolio — that is, you can tie the money up for a decade or more — then you may be happy putting even more of your money into pure stock funds. But before you decide to roll the dice on equities with compete abandon, remember that nearly all professional investors make sure that they own a good dollop of guaranteed investments, in the form of bonds and cash, in the portfolios they run.

For most of the second half of the 20th century, no other type of investment performed as well as stocks. Real estate went into big slumps. Cash or bonds were safer, but they pay much less, meaning that their returns are often wiped out by inflation.

How good have stocks been in the long run? Well, sorry to give you a weasel-like answer, but it depends what period you want to look at.

At the end of the 1990s, stocks looked unbeatable. The famous MSCI World Index, a collection of the world's biggest stocks, returned an incredible average of 17.1 percent to Canadian investors annually during the 1980s and 1990s. Investing in U.S. bonds, as measured by broker Lehman Brothers, earned you just 11.1 percent over those 20 years. Canadian stocks, as measured by the TSX/S&P index, didn't do nearly as well as global shares did, producing a return of only 11.4 percent from 1979 to 1999. But that was mostly because we have a small economy with a narrow selection of shares. But let's fast-forward to a few years later (sorry, Alanis). After the almighty stock market slide of 2000 through 2002, how did the returns stack up? Well, global stocks were still ahead, but by a much narrower margin. Over the 20 years to June 2002, for an investor who socked away an equal amount each month, the MSCI World Index produced a more modest return of just under 11 percent for Canadian investors, while U.S. bonds earned 10 percent in U.S.-dollar terms and Canadian stocks made 8.6 percent annually. And if you take away the currency gains earned by holders of the MSCI World Index, the return from global stocks falls to only 9.5 percent. In other words, you could have just held U.S. bonds and earned essentially the same return as you would have in the ever-wild stock market.

There are two vital lessons to be learned from these numbers:

- ✔ To get really big growth in your money over many years you almost certainly have to own at least some stocks — but as the time approaches when you need to dip into your savings, sell your equity funds to protect against a market slump.

- ✔ You also have to move lots of your money outside Canada and into big global companies to realize real growth.

Take a great-grandma out to lunch — and ask what deflation was like

The big hope is that inflation is completely under control and that we won't return to the days of double-digit price increases, last seen in the 1960s and 1970s. Runaway inflation means money itself is losing value at a brisk pace, and that's scary news for investors — who depend on their financial assets *growing* in value, not shrinking. From 1970 onward we had a recession about every ten years that was sparked in part by overheating in the economy and the resulting inflation. Oil price increases also hurt. But inflation hit only 8 percent during its 1990s bout, and as of mid-2002 it was still a benign 2 percent or so in Canada and the U.S. In fact, there was even talk of *deflation* — falling prices for goods and services because of global oversupply. Very few adults alive today have lived through that, but the resulting despair and relentless contraction in the economy could make inflation look like a walk in the park. The last time prices fell in Canada in a sustained way was the late 1930s. Lots of people had outdoor washrooms then, and lots of kids in Canada didn't get enough to eat. Not a good time to own stocks. If you know someone who was an adult in the 1930s, take the old girl or boy out to lunch. Ask them what they remember about falling prices — but also look them in the eye and ask them about the poverty and stagnation of those times.

Remember, the time period that you choose to compare investment returns can make all the difference. At the end of 1999, we had just come off a quarter century of soaring stock markets, which propelled the average global stock market fund sold in Canada to an annual average return of 12.3 percent in the 1990s. By mid-2002, the ten-year annual return on the average global equity fund had dropped to a much more modest 8.1 percent.

Stock markets can produce losses over many years, meaning that it's unwise to risk every penny of your retirement savings there. For example, investors in the late 1960s and early 1970s saw the entire stock market in the United States and Canada stagnate for a decade as inflation and recession sapped confidence in the future of equity investing itself. The inflation-racked period from 1967 to 1977 presented the worst possible conditions for stocks because interest rates that soared above 20 percent simply tempted investors to put their money into guaranteed deposits. No mutual fund, and practically no type of investment, will be able to get through catastrophic inflationary times like those without losing money, but it seems that central bankers have finally figured out how to run the economy without slipping into inflationary spirals. For now.

The point of all of these silly warnings about stock declines is that most of the people who are running and selling mutual funds don't remember the grim 1970s either. So they'll often spin you a cheerful yarn along the lines of "the stock market always goes up over the long term." Maybe it does, but they won't be around to refund your money if the market goes into a 1970s-style collapse, either. As of summer 2002, most global equity funds looked set for a third year in a row of losing money — so much for chirpy salespeople.

What Return Should You Expect on Your Funds?

During the 1990s, the average U.S. stock market fund produced a sizzling annual compound return of 20 percent, while the average Canadian stock fund made 9 percent. But by mid-2002, the average 10-year return on U.S. equity funds had dived to 8.7 percent while the average return on Canadian equity funds had held relatively steady at 9.3 percent. So can you ever rely on 10-percent-plus returns in the future? No, no, and no. And no again. Yes, you may be able to earn that sort of return over the long term if you take big risks in volatile markets. Hong Kong produced an annual compound return of 23 percent during the 1990s, after all — but get ready for some harrowing down periods along the way. By mid-2002, the 10-year return on Hong Kong stocks had fallen to just 8.1 percent.

If you look for about 8 percent a year, you may achieve your goal by buying shares in large and stable companies, but you're still stuck with a lot of your money at risk in the ever-choppy stock market. If you settle for a 6-percent annual return, you're being pretty conservative, meaning that you can afford to hold less volatile investments such as bonds and cash; only a major recession or a triumphant return of the dark forces of inflation are likely to give you major losses.

How to Minimize the Damage from Bad Funds

So let's recap: Stocks generally go up over time, as the economy grows and companies become more efficient at creating wealth for their owners (which means the people who own their shares, remember). Does this mean that any equity fund you get your hands on will line your pockets over the long haul? Not so fast — for mutual fund buyers, the problem is that individual funds *can* go into long slumps if the fund manager gets it wrong.

It might seem inevitable, with your bad luck, that you'll be the one stuck with a fund that's a mutt. But I'm now going to show you some simple ways to avoid that possibility, or at least reduce the risks. You should review the method I outline in Chapter 4 for structuring your portfolio — that is, owning six or seven equity funds, including two or three *index funds*, funds that track the entire stock market instead of trying to pick individual shares (and possibly getting it wrong).

The bottom line is this: At all costs avoid having more than one-third of your money in any one stock market fund. That way you won't expose too much of your capital to a pig of a fund. Fund companies and planners might tell you differently, but I really can't think of an exception.

Avoiding Being Bitten by a Dog

As a mutual fund buyer, you can really miss out on returns if you're stuck with a hound. I can't emphasize this point enough: Spread your holdings among half a dozen funds to help ensure that they don't all rot away in something that never really comes back to life.

Fund companies and brokers (with some justification) argue endlessly that buying stocks and shares is a long-term game because the market can drop for no good reason. (Of course, that doesn't prevent them from taking out huge ads trumpeting their short-term numbers, but we'll let that go for the moment.)

In fact, there's an old joke in investing: Everybody says he's a long-term investor as soon as his stock goes down.

The fund industry says you should ride out losses and that the market always turns, meaning that you should be happy leaving money in an equity fund for at least five years. And the industry advises against selling a fund when it becomes a dog, arguing that it's simply having an off year. Well, perhaps, but a fund can take an awfully long time to recover. And it's impossible to tell whether its slump is temporary or long term.

Just ask the unfortunate investors in the Industrial Growth Fund (now renamed Mackenzie Growth), which was once one of Canada's hottest performers. Then the fund loaded up on old-fashioned industrial and natural resource stocks, which were as popular as sandpaper bikinis for most of the late 1990s. That meant Industrial Growth generated a rotten return of 3.2 percent annually in the ten years ended December 31, 1999, representing a lost decade for the people who owned it. In fairness, some resource shares and old-fashioned industrial stocks took off in 2001 and 2002, propelling Mackenzie Growth to the top of its league. But as of June 2002, the fund's ten-year return was just 6.6 percent, still well short of the 9.3 percent return from the average Canadian stock fund.

In some cases, a brief period of bad returns is not the manager's fault. The market just hates the type of companies that the manager likes to buy.

Let's look at the flops and eventual triumph of the managers at Trimark, whose parent, AIM Funds Management, was Canada's third-biggest fund seller in summer 2002 with $36 billion in assets.

Trimark's rock-steady crew, inspired by company co-founder Bob Krembil, use a distinctive style of picking a few companies that they get to know *intimately* (pipe down there at the back of the hall) and hold for years (stop it). Besides, they also often buy lesser-known names. That's all fine — I'll show you how it has produced big returns — but the eccentric style often means the company's funds go in a different direction from most others. That's because most other managers like to thunder herd-like into the same globally famous shares. I mean, how hard is it to grunt "1 million Coke"?

A manager with a distinctive style — as long as it isn't too, ahem, weird — is a great person to invest with. That's because he or she often makes lots of money on a violent turnaround in the market when other managers are losing their pricey embroidered shirts. But when the odd stocks the manager likes fall out of favour themselves, unitholders in the fund miss out.

Here's how the up–down syndrome worked with Trimark. The Trimark funds sold their bank stocks in the late 1990s after financial shares climbed to record highs because the managers reckoned the shares were trading at inflated prices. Turned out they were right — but they sold too soon. Trimark was one of Canada's biggest fund companies, boasting an excellent long-term record in both Canadian and global equities. But the market went against Trimark's team in 1997, and bank stocks went on climbing (although they finally slumped in 1999). That meant Trimark underperformed the broad market and its rivals, and investors pulled more than $1 billion out of its funds. The Trimark saga included another humorous pie-in-the-face — the fund giant missed out on the upside of the insanity in tech stocks. The $3.6-billion Trimark Fund, normally a nice way to invest in global equities, made only 6.4 percent in 1998 while most global equity managers were up 17 percent or more. But then, for two and a half years straight, from 2000 through summer 2002, Trimark ruled the earth. Its funds, featuring established solid companies instead of head-banging greedy telecom executives, took off as the tech scene turned into shabby figures huddled around a fire in an oil drum. As of June 2002, the Trimark Fund had made its unitholders richer by a wondrous 15.4 percent annually over ten years, among the best return for any fund of any type.

The moral of the story: If possible, try to make sure the funds you buy are run by managers with a clearly stated style or method of picking stocks. Then try to choose managers with different styles. That way, when one manager is doing badly, the other could be doing well, smoothing out your returns.

But what if your manager, who was good in the past, keeps posting bad returns year after year? Unfortunately, there's just no quick answer to the question: When do I dump a good manager? Just follow your gut. And ask a few questions if your salesperson seems all puppyish and keen to do a switch. She or he could be indirectly getting a cut of 5 percent of the money you switch to another firm's funds because the new firm pays out sales commissions.

Looking for Hot Funds and Other Ways to Waste Time

Now, I'm going to make your life a lot easier. If you've been worrying about which equity fund among the 3,000-plus on sale in Canada has the best chance of beating the market, forget it. You're better off looking for UFOs in the evening sky (at least you'll be out in the fresh air and you might meet a fellow Space Cadet to start a new life together and bring little Star Pups into the world). There's really no point trying to pick a fund that'll beat the market, because only a tiny group of managers are likely to do so consistently, based on experience over several decades.

The best plan is to take the money that you've set aside for equity funds and simply buy an index fund that tracks the Canadian stock market, another that tracks the U.S. market, and yet another that tracks stock markets in the rest of the world. Or you may someday simply be able to buy a Canadian index fund and a global index fund that follows markets everywhere, including the United States.

Put between one-half and two-thirds of your equity money into those two or three index funds. Then, with the rest of your stock market money, buy two high-quality "normal" or "actively managed" Canadian equity funds and two high-quality global stock funds.

By normal or actively managed, I mean funds whose managers actually buy and sell stocks in pursuit of extra profits — instead of, as an index fund does, simply buying every stock in the market and giving you returns in line with an index or benchmark, such as the Standard & Poor's/Toronto Stock Exchange composite index or the MSCI World Index of big-company stocks around the globe.

Drum Roll: The ABCs of Picking a Fund

How do you pick those high-quality conventional funds, the ones that try to buy and sell stocks? Here are my three basic rules, what I call the ABCs of selecting a great equity fund.

- ✔ First, look for a fund that's full of companies from **A**ll industries — and, in the case of global funds, **A**ll major regions of the world.
- ✔ Second, insist that your fund holds lots of big, stable, and conservative companies — the type that investors call **B**lue-chip (because the blue chip is traditionally the most valuable in poker).
- ✔ Finally, look for a fund that has a habit of producing **C**onsistent returns over the years that aren't out of line with the market or with its rival funds. Later in this chapter, I show you how to do that.

Let's take a closer look at my ABCs for picking core equity funds for your savings: Think **A**ll industries, **B**lue-chip holdings, **C**onsistent performance.

Select from all industries

A fund should hold companies from all, or nearly all, major industries, in order to spread risk — and to give unitholders a chance to profit if the stock market suddenly falls in love with a particular type of company. Here is one way to break down the industry groups:

- Banks and other financial companies, such as Citigroup, Royal Bank of Canada, or Deutsche Bank

- Natural resource processors, such as Imperial Oil Ltd., Alcan Inc., or Slocan Forest Products Ltd.

- Technology companies, such as Microsoft Corp., Intel Corp., or southern Ontario e-mail pager maker Research in Motion; cable-TV companies like Shaw Communications Inc. also fit in this group because they're battling the phone companies for control of the Internet access market

- Manufacturers of industrial and consumer products, such as drug maker Pfizer Inc. or General Electric Corp.

- Dull but steady utility and pipeline companies such as Alberta power generator TransAlta Corp. or pipeline system TransCanada PipeLines Ltd.; telephone companies such as AT&T and BCE Inc. also officially fit into this group, although in 1999 and 2000 they frantically tried to become Internet and entertainment companies, only to get caught in a financial vice as prices plunged for telephone calls.

- Retail and consumer service companies such as Canadian Tire Corp. and Wal-Mart Corp

Not every group has to be represented in the top holdings of every fund, but a portfolio without at least one resource stock, financial services giant, or technology player among its biggest ten investments might represent a dangerous gamble. Why? Because of the ever-present chance that share prices in that missing sector will suddenly and unpredictably take off, leaving your fund in the dust. Avoid funds that make bets like that.

Hold blue-chip winners

Glossy mutual fund brochures often promise the sun, moon, and stars . . . but just look at the fund's top holdings. Whether the fund is Canadian, U.S., or international, at least two-thirds of its ten biggest investments should be big blue-chip companies that you or someone you trust has at least heard of. A list of the top stocks in any fund is readily available on the Internet — see Chapter 22 for details. Look in the fund's marketing material or in the reports and documents given to unitholders — see Chapter 3. What you're looking for are big and stable firms, the type that offer the best prospect of increasing their shareholders' wealth over the years.

Talk is cheap and fund managers love to drone on about how conservative they are. But managers of supposedly careful funds can sometimes quietly take risks: They put big portions of the fund into weird stuff like resource stocks or Latin America to jazz up their returns and attract more investors. The list of top holdings is one of the most valuable pieces of information an investor has about a fund because it can't be faked or fudged (ruling out pure fraudulent reporting). If you don't see at least a few giant names — companies like BCE Inc., Coca-Cola Corp., Bank of Montreal, New York Times Co., General Motors Corp., GlaxoSmithKline PLC, Toyota Motor Corp., or America Online Inc. in the fund's list of its biggest holdings — then the fund manager may be taking undue risks, fooling around with small or obscure companies.

Check out past performance, with caution

After you've satisfied the first two of these conditions, you should look at the fund's past performance. Begin by filtering out funds that have been around for fewer than five years, unless it's quite clear that someone with a record you can check has been running the money. Then look for consistent returns that aren't too much above or below the market. We all want to make lots of money, so leaving past returns until last may seem crazy, and exactly opposite to one's natural inclination. But it's the way sophisticated professionals do it. If the people in charge of a multi-billion dollar pension fund are interviewing new money-management firms, for example, they'll ask first about the expenses and fees the money managers charge and also about the style and method the firms use to select stocks and bonds (more on that topic later). Only then do the pros examine the past record of the managers — it's just assumed that they'll be near the average.

Measuring past performance is almost as impossible as determining the true value of a company's stock — it depends entirely on complex and varying assumptions and conditions. Here's an example: Legendary money manager Frank Mersch of Altamira Investment Services thrashed his competition for most of the early 1990s, playing resource stocks masterfully. He was a journalist's delight, always returning phone calls and providing pithy quotes. Everybody loved him, especially people with money in his fund. It soared more than 30 percent each year from 1990 through 1992, far ahead of the average Canadian stock fund. Who could blame you for deciding that Mersch was good — and for putting money into his fund? But then resource stocks slid when commodity prices fell, and Mersch missed out completely on the climb in financial stocks, which rose more than 50 percent in 1997 and again in 1998. The market and his once-beetle-like rivals left him behind, and by 1999 he had departed as manager of the fund. What happened? Did Mersch suddenly become dumb or did the market turn against him through no fault of his own — or was it simply that his luck changed? Such questions probably can't be answered accurately, so let's not bother debating them. But let me repeat, yet again: Betting too heavily on yesterday's hot performers, hoping that they'll outrun the pack again tomorrow, is a good way to end up in a dud fund.

Don't get too hung up about hot results in the past. Mutual fund companies like to offer lots of funds so they can have a few big performers to bray about in the ads, but those returns are always partly a result of luck. And mutual funds, incidentally, are managed more recklessly than pension funds. There's always the temptation to jack up the risk and returns a little to get the money pouring in. With a pension fund a manager is expected to stick to a certain set of goals and investing style, and the penalties are severe for taking unauthorized flyers. That's because you have a bunch of actuaries, pension experts with thin lips and no sense of humour, keeping a watery eye on a pension fund's portfolio. But retail investors usually don't have the knowledge or resources to check or worry whether a manager is sticking to the fund's prescribed style — say, lots of fast-growing companies with high-flying stocks.

You should find out what a fund's past performance has been and, above all, compare it with that of rival funds and the market as a whole. The simplest place to start is the *Globe*'s monthly fund report, published on the third Wednesday of each month. Remember to stick to funds that have been around for at least five years. There's more on using the *Globe* report in Chapter 2.

Newspaper reports supply the annual compound returns for every fund as well as for the average fund in its category and for the market as a whole. If you're interested in a fund, its compound returns should be above the average for its group, but if they're way above — for example, an annual return of 15 percent over five years while the average fund made less than 10 percent — then the manager is probably a risk-taker. Above all, though, be wary of funds whose returns over five and ten years are below those of the average fund: Such pooches have a dispiriting habit of continuing to bark and dig holes in the garden.

What's in a name?

A fund's name may not tell you much about what it invests in. But if you're looking for equity funds in the monthly fund report of your newspaper, the fund you're interested in should be listed under

    Canadian equity

    Canadian large-cap equity, or

    Global equity

If it isn't, then it may be a volatile fund that's suitable only for aggressive risk-takers or those who don't mind riding out losses. At the very least, it will be ignoring important areas of the stock market. For example, "international" funds, which stay out of the vital U.S. stock market, are intended only for those who already have plenty of money in the United States.

Who is running your fund? Managers on the move

Equity funds offer endless sources of amusement. One of the fun games you can play with a fund is figuring out who exactly is running it. This is often so difficult that investors shouldn't get too worried about it when they start out buying funds. It's impossible with some companies that use a vague "team" to pick stocks. And remember that a superstar manager is extra likely to go cold because he or she gets too much money to run. Remember that what is actually in the portfolio is far more important than any amount of talk of wizards running your money.

If you get more interested in mutual funds, you'll no doubt start wondering: Why not just put my money with guys and gals who have been successful in the past? One problem is

that managers move around so much. As soon as a stock picker builds a strong reputation, all too often he or she jumps ship to another fund that offers a fat signing bonus. And remember the warning that I've been repeating endlessly, in a smug nasal drone: Star managers invariably fall to earth. Sometimes, they go inside themselves and sometimes they seem to . . . well, they always go inside themselves. Don't get excited about the past history of the manager running your fund. And pay even less attention to fawning newspaper articles proclaiming them a genius. Just look at the fund's main holdings and its track record. If these meet the ABC tests outlined above, then it's probably a high-quality fund.

You should also use the *Globe and Mail*'s fund Web site at www.globefund.com to check whether the fund has been near the top or bottom in each individual calendar year, to detect big swings in performance over time. There's more on using the site in Chapter 22.

Pining for the Middle of the Pack: Good News for the Average Achiever

Here's another piece of good news. Most mutual funds are pretty good, and if you end up with a middle-of-the pack performer you'll be fine. Of 36 global equity funds with a ten-year record at June 30, 2002, only nine funds had produced an annual compound return of less than 7 percent. And the average fund made 8.1 percent. Yes, those figures are on the rosy side because the fund industry quietly buried plenty of underperformers along the way by merging them into funds with better records. Your chances of ending up in a total dog are manageably small, however, as long as you follow the simple three ABC rules.

The people running the fund want you to do well, remember, and they'll happily work 18-hour days to make sure that happens. That's because, when your units increase in value, they win in two extremely profitable ways. First, you're happy, which means you're inclined to stay with the fund and invest even more money. But just as important, good stocks in a fund increase in value, increasing the market value of the fund's total assets. Management fees, the rake-off for the fund company, are calculated as a percentage of the fund's assets, which means it's in the fund sponsor's interest to have the fund grow as fast as possible. That way, they get to build weird, oversized houses that are simply jammed into a street of much smaller homes in a good area, like invading spaceships. That's what makes a little fund manager really happy.

Kicking the Tires: Checking Out Your Investments

Remember, though, even if a brochure, ad, or salesperson tells you or at least implies that a fund is the sure route to riches, always make sure you kick the tires yourself. The people who design and run mutual funds are master marketers and they often sincerely believe that their fund is a magic lamp that will reliably outperform the market. If you go to a broker, financial planner, or insurance agent to buy your funds, they too will trot out the same line.

These people are salesmen and saleswomen and, to do a good job, they have almost certainly convinced themselves that the fund they're selling you is a world-beater. They'll use reassuring phrases and labels such as "conservative" or "growth at a reasonable price" to convince you that their fund is a way to achieve that impossible dream: Big returns at almost no risk. They'll even talk about the fund's "black box" (a cynical expression used in the investment industry) in the shape of some impressive-sounding formula or method that purports to maximize returns while reducing the danger of losses. Think of witch doctors brandishing painted bones and you'll get the idea. Yes, you might get lucky and seize on a manager who outperforms the pack for a while, but they always fall to earth, Dudley. Of 150 Canadian equity funds with a five-year track record as of mid-2002, only two managed to beat the return from the S&P/TSX index in each of the five calendar years from 1997 through 2001. And only half managed to outperform the wretched 3.7-percent average annual return from the S&P/TSX over the same five years.

Chapter 11

Heirloom Equity Funds: The Dull Stuff that Will Make You Wealthy

. . . .

In This Chapter

▶ Deciding how many equity funds you need

▶ Picking the best types of funds

▶ Taking a look at global equity funds

▶ Checking out Canadian equity funds

. . . .

This is the most important chapter in this book if you're a long-term investor who's able to commit money to mutual funds for at least five years. That's because *equity funds* — funds that buy stocks and shares in companies — are such powerful investing tools, offering the potential to grow your money many times over. If you pick a sensibly varied portfolio of high-quality funds, and this chapter will show you how, then you're almost certain to do well as an investor. I refer to these funds as "heirloom" funds because that's what they should be — treasured possessions that you can hang on to indefinitely. Sorry if you find these funds a little dull. This chapter isn't about crazy technology funds that soar 80 percent in a year and then crash just as quickly. And it isn't about finding somewhere safe and predictable to hold the cash that you're saving up for a car. It's about the "core" mutual funds that account for most of your long-term money, funds that you can buy and hold forever if necessary. Yes, they may have bad years, perhaps several in a row, but over time their top-quality stocks and varied holdings are almost sure to pay off. In Chapter 10, I outline the basic steps you need to take to identify a good equity fund. In this chapter, I provide more details of the things you should check, I'll suggest some excellent funds, and I show you how to select your own mixture of mutual funds.

How Many Equity Funds Do You Need?

Building a great portfolio of mutual funds is simple. All you have to do is make two decisions:

- ✔ How much risk you want to take — in other words, how much you want riding on equity funds.
- ✔ How much you like Canada's long-term economic prospects.

I wish I could tell you to simply buy a single stock market fund, using the techniques that I suggest, and forget about it. Some salespeople will even insist that you're safe with a single wonderful fund. But that course is just too dangerous.

Putting all of your money into just one equity fund, even if it's a great one, can lead to periods of harrowing underperformance if that fund goes into a slump — and nearly all funds do from time to time. Consider, for example, the fate of investors in the renowned Templeton Growth Fund, Canada's biggest fund as of June 2002, with assets of $8.7 billion. The fund, which gave investors a glittering return of 14.1 percent annually from its launch in 1954 to the middle of 2002, went into a funk in 1998 when it missed out on climbing tech and telecom stocks (the same problem afflicted the managers of the giant Trimark funds). Templeton Growth's return that year was less than 1 percent — basically nothing — while most global equity funds jumped more than 17 percent. The fund, with its conservative holdings, came roaring back in 2000, 2001, and early 2002, posting returns in the top half of the global equity fund group. But for investors with large amounts of their wealth tied up in Templeton Growth back in 1998, it was frustrating to say the least to miss out on the gains that just about every other fund was reporting.

Own more than one equity fund. That way, if one of your funds sags, you have a shot at doing well with the others. But how many funds should you buy to ensure that you've assembled an adequately varied collection? Before I answer that, it's important to look at the only two types of funds you should consider for your serious long-term money.

- ✔ **Global equity funds** buy stocks and shares everywhere, from Taiwan to Tupelo. In practice, they usually end up investing in large companies in the rich economies of the world because, to paraphrase the bank robber, that's where the money is. In other words, giant corporations have proven to be just about the most profitable and most stable investments you can make.
- ✔ **Canadian equity funds and large-cap equity funds** buy Canadian stocks. The difference between them is that Canadian equity funds are free to buy both medium- and large-sized companies, while large-cap equity funds are supposed to concentrate on the very largest corporations, such as the big banks or global manufacturers like Bombardier Inc. In practice, they end up holding pretty well the same companies because the Canadian market offers a limited selection.

In Chapter 12, I look at a host of dancing unicorns and dogs in tutus that the fund industry has come up with to entice money from investors. By that I mean the "specialty" or "regional" equity funds that hold only a certain type of shares or shares in only some countries, the idea being that a concentrated fund will produce huge profits when share prices in that particular industry or part of the world take off like little rockets.

These riskier funds include technology funds, small-company funds, developing country funds, resource funds, U.S. equity funds, and Asian funds. Some have produced great returns and many hold excellent stocks. But they all suffer from one insurmountable handicap: Because they can invest in only a small section of the world's stock markets, they don't give you the variety and stability that your long-term money requires.

So, the only two types of funds you truly need for the portion of your money you've decided to have in equity funds are global equity funds and Canadian equity/large-cap equity funds. Go ahead and buy some of the risky specialty and regional funds if you must, but limit them to just 10 percent of your total portfolio. There's no hard-and-fast rule here, but that's the advice you'll get from many pros.

Deciding how much you should put into equity funds

In Chapters 4 and 10, which deal with using equity mutual funds in your financial plan, I state that all of us as investors fall into one of these three groups:

- ✔ **Savers**, who need to use their money in the next couple of years, shouldn't own any equity funds. The risk of loss in the short term is too great, so savers should just buy investments that pay regular interest.

- ✔ **Balanced investors**, who want only modest drops in the value of their funds in any one year, often put 45 percent or slightly more (up to about 60 percent) into equity funds. With the rest, they buy bond funds, which invest in loans to governments and corporations, leaving a small portion of their money sitting in cash or cash-like investments. Or they buy special balanced funds, which consist of a mixture of stocks and bonds.

- ✔ **Growth investors**, who want the maximum return on their money and plan to let it ride the ups and downs of funds for five years or more, often put about 75 percent of their money into equity funds. If you're investing for periods of ten years or more, and definitely don't mind big slumps in the value of your mutual fund portfolio along the way, you might want to put even more into the stock market with its allure of higher returns.

Dividing your money between Canadian and foreign equity funds

There's no definite answer here, but most experts would advise moving the majority of your stock market money out of Canada, because there are so many wonderful opportunities around the world. For example, Canada is too small to have great consumer-products makers such as Japan's Sony Corp., global oil companies such as Royal Dutch Shell of Britain and the Netherlands, or technology giants such as America's Microsoft Corp. However, most experts would also advise keeping at least some of your money in Canada if you plan to go on living in this country, because you'll need to have assets in Canadian dollars to pay for your expenses here.

And there's a practical difficulty: RRSPs and other tax-deferred retirement savings plans limit your foreign content to just 30 percent. Chapter 20 deals with "clone" funds — global funds that count as Canadian for tax-sheltered plans — that you can use to increase the foreign content in a registered retirement savings plan. If you're convinced that Canada's in trouble, then you may want to move 80 percent or more of your mutual fund money, including equity funds, into non-Canadian stocks and bonds.

How do you split your money among equity funds?

In Chapter 4, the financial planning chapter, I describe a method of dividing your money up among equity funds. Put one-half to two-thirds of your stock market money into *index funds*, funds that simply track the entire market at low cost to the investor, instead of trying to pick the stocks that will go up the most. For much more on index funds check out Chapter 15. Index funds' reliability and low expenses mean index funds are one of the very best deals out there for investors.

Canadian stock market index funds usually track the Standard & Poor's/ Toronto Stock Exchange composite index. Global index funds are rare, so you usually have to buy a combo: a U.S. index fund that gives you the same return each year as a list of giant U.S. companies such as the Standard & Poor's 500-stock index, and an international index fund that tracks all the major global markets except for the United States and Canada. Put a U.S. index fund and an international index fund together, and you've got a pretty damn good global equity index fund. So all you need to buy is a Canadian, a U.S., and an international index fund.

Just a reminder on terminology: In the newspapers' monthly reports on funds, you'll notice that funds are listed as either global or international. Here's the difference. *Global equity funds* are free to invest anywhere, including the United States, while *international equity funds* avoid the U.S. market. The idea behind international funds is that many investors already have plenty of money in the States by owning stocks or other funds, so some fund companies offer funds that stay out of the U.S. market. That's logical thinking, but I think it's just too fancy. In keeping with the ABC rules, I believe that when picking your non-Canadian stock funds you're better off sticking with a fund that's free to go anywhere that the manager anticipates getting the best return.

With the rest of your equity fund money, just buy four equity funds — two global and two Canadian — that have a person or team trying to select winning shares. Those are called *actively managed* funds because they buy and sell holdings in an attempt to beat the market and other fund managers instead of just trying to keep up with a market benchmark. The managers, in other words, are trying to pick the few stocks that go up the most.

Often, though, managers fail. But at least if you buy a few actively managed funds as well as index funds you have a portfolio that isn't just tied to one market benchmark. It has enough variety to ensure that at least one of your funds is probably doing relatively well, even if the others are sagging — as long as the whole stock market isn't crashing. In the event of a wholesale decline in stocks, just about all equity funds — both Canadian and global — will be losers anyway.

Picking Equities: From First Move to Last Hurrah

As I explain in Chapter 10, your first move when picking Canadian equity funds for the core of your portfolio is to make sure they're classified as a "Canadian equity fund" or a "Canadian large-cap fund," the two categories that the newspapers use.

Large-cap companies are the very biggest businesses in Canada — generally the huge banks, manufacturers, and so on that make up the Standard & Poor's/Toronto Stock Exchange index of 60 large companies (the broader S&P/TSX composite index has almost 300). Canadian large-cap equity funds — the "cap" is short for "capitalization" or stock market value — generally buy companies like that. "Canadian equity" funds are free to buy more medium-sized and smaller companies. But, as usual, don't get all hot and bothered by fancy-sounding definitions. Fund classifications are hazy (partly to give fund managers the freedom they need to manoeuvre), and in practice the two groups hold many of the same stocks.

If the company where you hold your mutual fund account offers only one conventional actively managed Canadian stock fund, then use it for half of your Canadian stock money and put the rest into a Canadian index fund. If there's no index fund available (and there should be), then open an account elsewhere for at least part of your money.

Stockbrokers, financial planners, and discount brokers give you a full choice of hundreds of funds, so you may think you have the problem of too much choice. But just ignore the hype, insist on the ABCs that I explain in Chapter 10, and you'll be fine.

Keep it simple, sexy. There's no point worrying about which equity fund manager is going to thrash the competition because such an outcome is impossible, or at least very, very difficult, to predict. Canada's tiny stock market, which accounts for less than 3 percent of the world's publicly traded shares, offers a limited number of companies. In fact, for a big-company fund, there are few suitable names outside of the S&P/TSX 60 index. So most Canadian equity funds tend to be pretty similar.

Global Equity Funds: Meet Faraway People and Exploit Them

Global equities are the Boeing 747s of the mutual fund world, huge magic carpets that offer the best chance of steady, high returns on your savings over many years. They should make up about two-thirds of the money you're putting into the stock market if you're investing outside an RRSP or RRIF. Within your RRSP, you're limited to investing only 30 percent of your cash in such foreign stuff. But don't forget that there are new funds, described in Chapter 20, that allow you to go above the limit.

Global equity funds have earned steady, attractive returns over the years, which makes them the very best type of fund to own. You should put most of your money here because:

- They tend to own multinational blue-chip companies, the best growth asset of all.

- They invest all over the world, spreading your risk and smoothing out your ups and downs — when one country is up, another is often down.

- Sure, the executives running multinational corporations often foul up (remember "new Coke"?) but the companies are usually large enough and sufficiently sophisticated to recover from errors.

Investment styles: Bargain hunter or Champagne Charlie?

The following is detailed stuff that's likely to interest only investors who enjoy peering into mutual funds. It talks about the different styles of investing managers use. You really don't need to know about this if you simply remember to buy two or three funds. That way, when one manager's style isn't working, you'll probably have money with another manager who's having a better year.

Value investors like stocks that are out of favour with the market, maybe because the company, its country of origin, or its industry has run into a temporary setback. So they look for shares that are good value and trading at cheap prices, and they hope to hold them until the shares bounce back.

Growth investors argue that the real way to make money in the market is by buying businesses that are already doing well, so they concentrate on buying shares in companies whose sales and profits are growing fast, even if their shares have already gone up. Growth investors believe that so-called value shares are cheap for a reason, because the company is a pooch.

There's no evidence that one style is superior — for many decades until the 1990s value managers had stronger long-term returns, but in the last five years of the 1990s investors became obsessed with fast-growing companies, meaning that the growth style did much better. But the collapse of overpriced technology and telecom stocks, just the sort of shares that value managers hate, means that value managers were back on top in 2001 and the first half of 2002.

> ✔ Best of all, your mutual fund company is just one of dozens of big international money managers owning shares in these firms — between them, all of those sharp lassies in DKNY and lads in Hugo Boss keep an eye on the companies. When their hangovers aren't too bad, that is.

Many of Canada's biggest mutual funds fall into the global equity class and there are some large ones that have also produced excellent results over the years. They're hugely profitable for the companies that run them, so the managers are intensely motivated not to let the performance slip too much. Most global equity funds hold high-quality, blue-chip companies and they spread their risk over numerous industries and countries, so they also meet our ABC test. But remember to buy at least two, because an individual fund can go into a slump for a year or more. The essential point is that different managers are hot and cold at different times.

Applying the ABC rules to your global equity funds

Be sure to apply the ABC rules that I describe in Chapter 10 when selecting a global equity fund:

✔ Make sure the fund invests in **All industries** and **Anywhere** in the world. All of the important economic regions (that is, North America, Europe, and Asia) should show up in the top ten holdings.

✔ Insist on **Blue-chip** companies, some of which you've at least heard of.

✔ Demand **Consistent** performance that isn't wildly out of line with the other funds in the group.

Investors who just go to a bank branch to buy their funds or who deal with another company that sells funds directly to the public will have a problem: The bank or company may offer just one suitable global equity fund. And there may be no index funds. There's no easy way around this problem. If you can't or don't want to go somewhere with a wider selection of funds, just buy the global fund with half of the money you've earmarked for global stocks and then hedge your bets by putting the rest into one or two narrower funds that invest in a single region such as Europe or Asia.

Check any global equity fund that you buy to make sure it offers plenty of variety. If the top holdings contain no European stocks, for example, or they seem to be all technology companies, then look elsewhere.

Five global equity winners

Here are five conservative and well-run global equity funds that have produced decent results in recent years. I've included one bank fund and four that must be bought through independent investment advisers such as stockbrokers or financial planners, or through a discount broker. The funds in this group all have annual charges and expenses less than or equal to 2.8 percent, the average for global equity funds.

CIBC Global Equity is one of the larger bank-run global stock funds, with assets of more than $230 million. As of June 2002, the top holdings were a healthy mixture of big-name European companies, and oil and gas producers. Looks like manager Maxime-Jean Gerin is a stock picker who can see the attractions of very different types of companies and doesn't get obsessed with just one or two industries.

Investors in the giant $6-billion-plus **AGF International Value Fund** got an unpleasant shock in 2002 when San Diego–based manager Charles Brandes announced he was stepping down to start his own Canadian fund company, Brandes Investment Partners & Co. (after all, why split those lucrative management fees with fund sponsor AGF Management Ltd.?). AGF International Value produced a stellar annual average return of 10.6 percent in the five years ended June 30, 2002, blowing away the 1.7-percent return from the average global stock fund. AGF brought in a relatively obscure replacement, Harris Associates of Chicago, to run the fund. Is it still a buy? Harris's track record is respectable and the firm, like Brandes, uses a value style that may do well when overpriced growth stocks tank. For the moment, this fund deserves the benefit of the doubt.

Run by America's gigantic Fidelity Investments, which is renowned for its relentless research into the markets, **Fidelity International Portfolio** goes heavy on U.S. stocks. In fact, as of mid-2002, nine of the ten biggest holdings were U.S. companies. But the fund held more than 450 companies around the world and only around 53 percent of its total assets were in the U.S. market. If you buy this fund, though, make sure you counterweight it with at least one other global equity fund that has more European and Asian stocks in the top holdings. Note that this so-called "international" fund, like AGF International Value, is free to hold U.S. shares even though the term *international* usually denotes a fund that stays out of North America. This is yet another example of a fund with a potentially confusing name — be sure to always look at a fund's holdings.

Just about every investor should probably have a bit of cash in the famous **Trimark Fund**, now marketed by AIM Funds Management, which produced a stirring average annual return of 16.7 percent in the 20 years ended June 2002. As I point out in Chapter 10, the fund went into a brief slump in the late 1990s, but its managers' style of picking a few great companies and holding on to them for years seems to win out in the long run. Note: Be sure to buy the "sales charge" version of this fund, which may oblige you to pay an upfront sales commission, rather than the similar Trimark Select Growth Fund. Trimark Select Growth is available with a "deferred" commission that's payable only if you leave the fund within six years, but it comes with higher annual expenses of 2.4 percent versus 1.6 percent for the Trimark Fund.

A Mackenzie Financial Corp. fund, **Universal Select Managers** was launched only in late 1998 but it uses five very different managers from all around the world. That means it automatically gives you a diverse mixture of stocks and investment ideas. In fact, you could simply hold this one plus a U.S. and international index fund and get a complete global portfolio. Other companies have launched these "multi-manager" funds, and they can be a handy way of instantly varying your investments. But their annual costs can be high, at up to 3 percent. This Mackenzie fund has expenses of 2.6 percent.

Canadian Equity Funds: Your Turn to Become a Bloated Capitalist

One of the annoying things about being a business journalist is that your stories are almost always about rich white men in suits. Yes, there are hugely successful businesswomen, and there are wealthy entrepreneurs and executives who belong to other racial groups. But in Canada and other Western societies, politics and business are still largely run for the benefit of red-faced white guys in their fifties and sixties. Still, at least if you buy a blue-chip Canadian equity fund, you'll end up owning a few crumbs of the stuff that has made those guys rich (although they'll always get the lion's share). And like it or not, if you're saving inside a registered retirement savings plan or a registered retirement income fund, you'll have to own some Canadian funds because most of the plans must remain in Canada. Yes, you can fill up your RRSP with those "clone" funds, the new foreign funds that use financial engineering to count as Canadian property. But these still haven't been tested over many years, so it would be unwise to risk all of your stock market money there. That means RRSP investors should own at least two Canadian equity funds and a Canadian index fund.

Applying the ABC rules to your Canadian equity funds

Applying the ABC rules when you buy Canadian equity funds is simple:

- Check that the fund invests in **All of Canada's** major industrial sectors, including technology, natural resources, and financial services.
- Make sure that most of the top-ten holdings are **Blue-chip** companies that you've at least heard of.
- Demand **Consistent** performance that doesn't lag or wildly outpace the other Canadian equity funds.

Five winners in Canadian equities

Here are five well-managed Canadian equity funds with consistent returns over the past few years. I've included a fund from Phillips Hager & North Investment Management Ltd. of Vancouver because of its strong performance and low total expenses and fees of 1.1 percent (compared with 2.6 percent from the Canadian equity group as a whole). To keep its costs low, PH&N imposes a minimum account size of $25,000 per household.

With a fairly modest expense level of 2.2 percent, **CIBC Core Canadian Equity** loads the dice in the investor's favour. In mid-2002, it had a selection of financial and resource companies in its top holdings.

 PH&N Canadian Equity lost almost 9 percent in the first half of 2002, twice as much as the average Canadian equity fund. But the fund's ten-year annual average return at the end of June 2002 was still a strong 10.8 percent, versus 9.3 percent for the average Canadian equity fund. Those low expenses helped, and so did management by a low-profile team that kept the fund invested in every major industry group.

 Renaissance Canadian Core Value was once part of the Canadian fund operation of giant U.S. stockbroker Merrill Lynch & Co. Inc., but those funds were taken over by Canadian Imperial Bank of Commerce after CIBC bought Merrill's retail stockbrokerage business in Canada in 2001. The old Merrill funds, now renamed Renaissance, are sold through brokers and planners (and discount brokers). This fund, a resolute hunter for cheap stocks as the name suggests, thrived in 2001 and early 2002 as the telecom and tech bubble burst.

 A huge fund, **Royal Canadian Equity** had more than $3.3 billion in assets in June 2002 and comes with modest annual expenses of about 2.1 percent. The ten-year return was a respectable 10.4 percent, and it's nice to know that giant Royal Bank has the swollen moneybags to hire sharper managers if performance flags.

 The returns from Mackenzie's **Universal Canadian Growth** lagged those of its rivals in 1999 because the fund didn't ride the soaring shares of Nortel Networks Corp. But the big holdings tend to include some original ideas — for example, U.S. fast-food giant Wendy's International Inc. showed up in mid-2002. (Funds can invest up to 30 percent of their assets outside Canada and still count as Canadian for RRSPs.) This fund would make a good combination with a more conventional Canadian equity fund that's full of the usual boring banks.

Beware of Overwhelming Hype

 There's an incredible amount of hype and hot air about the people running equity funds. Fund companies take the managers on cross-country tours as though they were rock stars. But ignore all the sound and fury.

The people who sell equity funds make a lot of noise about them because this product is their bread and butter as well as their caviar and champagne and bloated drunken evenings (actually, they're quite a sober lot nowadays). A good Canadian equity fund is a fund company's showpiece asset, drumming up business across the board. The Canadian equity category accounts for almost one-quarter of the industry's total assets, or more than $96 billion. Canadian equity funds generate a tidal wave of fees for the people who run and sell them — almost $2 billion per year.

Chapter 12

Las Vegas–Style Equity Funds: Trips You Don't Need

I know it's boring and glib but it's also true: Slow and steady really does win the equity fund race. In other words, you'll almost certainly do best over the long haul with the conservative equity funds I describe in Chapter 11, the ones that buy established companies in all industries and parts of the world. But we're only human and there's always the temptation to chase the really hot returns. After all, the average science and technology fund went up 113 percent in 1999. Well, help yourself — but get ready to be bitten. The average tech fund went on to lose 69 percent of its value over the next two and a half years. Which meant that an investor who bought in at the start of 1999 and held on through the whole three-and-a-half-year cycle ended up losing one-third of his or her money. Mutual funds are a wonderfully convenient and relatively cheap way of playing, say, the Chinese market. But with this type of narrow investing you're essentially gambling. In a nutshell, it's probably a waste of time because of what Nobel Prize–winning economists call "rational expectations."

Crudely put, here's how the theory applies to specialty mutual funds. By the time you or I realize something might be a good investment, everyone else, or at least everyone who matters, will have cottoned on to it too. So there's no point deciding that "well, I think telecommunications is the fuel of the future, Deirdre, so I'll load up on a telecom fund" — because professional investors all over the world have concluded the same thing and have already bid telecom stocks up to high prices. Yes, you might do well in a telecom fund — just ask the complacent, plump investors in the AIM Global Telecommunications Class, who multiplied their money fourfold in the five years ended 1999 — but we're really talking about slot machines here. And the flood of coins dries up eventually. An investor with $10,000 in AIM Global Telecom at the end of 1999 saw that asset wither to less than $2,000, yes $2,000 and shrinking, by

June 2002. Still, hope springs eternal and all that . . . so here's a roundup of the more dangerous types of funds. I've refrained from suggesting candidates when it comes to these wild funds because returns from this gang are largely a matter of luck — a manager looks like a genius when his or her favourite type of company or market is in favour, and a stumbling carrier-bag-toting loser when that type of investment goes out of fashion. There are a few suggested candidates, though, in the last chapter of the book: Chapter 30, Ten Cool Funds.

Small and Mid-Sized Company Funds: Spotty Little Fellows

Unless you really love mutual funds, and enjoy monitoring and fiddling with your portfolio, don't bother with these guys. Life is complicated enough without building elaborate spreadsheets to decide whether tying money up for years in risky or sleepy little companies is worth it. At least with the obscure small companies in labour-sponsored funds (see Chapter 18 for more on this type of fund offering) you get a tax break in return for putting your money in danger. Okay, not all small companies are dozy — lots are macho, growing businesses. But guessing which ones are going to "pop" — market talk for getting their stocks to go up — is a tough game. But never fear, investors have a willing ally in the executives and main shareholders of the company. In fact, they're sometimes *only too happy* for their share price to shoot up. *Cling!* — is that an option bulb lighting up? (*Options* are shares that company management can buy at a fixed low price — that become nicer and nicer to have when the market price of the shares goes up.) But what's left in a hot stock for everybody else once the corporate management and the investment bankers have torn off their giant hunk often wouldn't fill a small McDonald's chocolate milkshake container that's been lying for days on the ground beside a gasoline pump.

First, a vital bit of terminology — a company's *stock market capitalization* is the value in money terms that investors are applying to the business. For example, a company with 50 million shares in the hands of its shareholders and a stock price of $5 has a market value, or "market cap," of only $250 million (or 50 million shares times $5), which still makes it quite a small company.

Here are the three most important things to remember about investing in small and medium-sized companies:

> ✔ Shares in small companies move in their own strange cycles, sometimes sliding when blue-chip stocks go up, which can make them a sort of insurance policy for a portfolio. For example, in the first half of 2002 the average large-cap Canadian equity fund lost 6.2 percent but the average small-company fund rose 7.5 percent.

✔ And yes, when they're hot, small caps can produce rich returns. Of all the wacky fund categories, small-cap funds can best justify their existence. But you don't really need them, either.

✔ Small-company funds can go into long slumps, leaving you with "dead money" that just stagnates — or, worse, saddles you with heavy losses. Most people are better off putting their savings into regular equity funds that buy big companies, a strategy that offers steadier returns.

You should take any recommendation to buy a small-cap fund with a hefty dose of salt. These are volatile investments best suited to investors who keep a close eye on their holdings. Unpredictable rallies and collapses are the way that small-cap stocks work. But you usually have to wait through lean and hungry years for the good times, and disappointments are all too frequent.

Think small: Not a place for serious money

So remember that small-company funds are marked by moves upward that happen only too rarely, a disadvantage that makes them unsuitable for much, if any, of your serious money. "There's evidence that small-cap stocks produce higher returns" over the long term. That's from a mutual fund brochure. But what evidence might that be? The numbers show that small-cap stocks may only have their good long-term record because of periodic crazy bull markets in small-company shares — typically at the end of a great period in the stock market, when investors feel clever and brave enough to start chasing riskier stuff. Otherwise, though, small-company stocks and mutual funds have tended lately to underperform big companies. In Canada in the 1990s, the average small and mid-sized company fund produced an annual return of only 8.3 percent, compared with 9.6 for the average Canadian equity fund. Admittedly, small-cap stocks were spared the worst of the great stock market slide that began in 2000. As of June 2002, the average small-cap fund had a ten-year return of 9.3 percent — but that was identical to the return from regular Canadian equity funds. In other words, investors in small-cap funds didn't get any compensatory extra return as a reward for taking on the risk of buying into smaller companies.

If you insist on buying small-company funds, it's vital that you buy at least two or three. That's because the managers of small-cap funds tend to be eccentric individuals who love poring over obscure little businesses and developing their own methods. It's very personality-driven. Even an excellent manager can do terribly if his or her favourite type of stock is out of fashion. And don't forget that the small-cap sector has plenty of walking dead. Here are a couple of funds that dragged investors over the rocks:

- The tiny $1-million **Cambridge Growth Fund**, a Sagit Management Ltd. fund that specializes in obscure and small companies, generated an average annual *loss* of 15.9 percent in the ten years ended June 30, 2002. Yes, that's a loss of 15.9 percent each year. In other words, an investor who put $10,000 into the fund in mid-1992 ended up with less than $1,800 a decade later. Thanks a lot.

- Mackenzie Financial Corp.'s **Industrial Equity Fund** ended up in the bottom 25 percent of its group — a dank cellar known as the *fourth quartile* — every single year from 1995 through 1999, partly because the fund found itself stuck with a bunch of unpopular natural resource stocks as technology stocks were exploding. For all of the 1990s, the fund posted an average annual loss of 1.2 percent. It was merged into another small-company fund in 2001 with little fanfare.

- The $7-million **Mavrix Growth Fund**, which changed its name from YMG Growth in 2001, soared 59 percent in 1999 but crashed 66 percent in 2001. As of June 30, 2002, its ten-year average annual return was a wretched loss of 2.5 percent.

Regional Equity Funds: Welcome to Turkmenistan

Funds that invest in limited areas of the world sound like they're exciting and a good way to speculate. After all, the average Latin American fund soared 49.4 percent in 1999, while the average Japanese fund made an incredible 80.8 percent. But such specialized funds — whether they invest in European, Asian, or emerging markets — suffer from the curse of all narrow investments: They usually go into slumps, which was amply demonstrated by Asia during the 1990s. Latin American funds went into a two-and-a-half-year decline after their big gain in 1999 — as of June 30 2002, the average fund in the group had lost 10.4 percent annually for its unitholders over five years, the worst performance by any fund category (no Latin American funds have been around for ten years). As for Japanese funds, their moment of triumph in 1999 was just a brief respite from a long remorseless decline. As of June 2002, the average Japanese equity fund had given its unitholders a return of just less than zero over ten years (oh that pared-down Zen aesthetic! I'll have my brown rice and twig now, please). That was the worst return for any fund type apart from Asian and Pacific Rim funds, which are free to lose money anywhere in the region — they left lucky investors with an annual deficit of 1.3 percent over ten years.

If you must go regional, try European funds, with their giant blue-chip companies, and then perhaps all-Asia funds. But you're best off with two or three global equity funds that hold assets in countries just about everywhere. Look at the holdings of nearly any big global stock fund and you'll see European and Asian stocks as well as U.S. names.

The pros aren't infallible, though, and they can easily get the mix of countries wrong. That's why it's important with global equity funds to avoid managers who make big bets on a particular region or country. There are even some "country-specific" funds that invest in only one country. But their performance was so volatile and disappointing in the 1990s that I think you shouldn't bother with this group. That's why I include such one-nation funds in Chapter 27, Ten Gimmick Funds.

The one exception may be India-only funds. India is essentially a continent in its own right, with a potentially giant stock market that moves to its own rhythm. "Getting in on the ground floor" is traditionally a sad myth pitched at retail investors. But India, like the United States, seems to have the huge home market needed to nurture companies that go on to become global giants. Often these companies provide investors with years of steady growth — like Coke, Disney, and McDonald's once did until their stocks became overpriced.

Here's a quick rundown of the main types of regional foreign equity funds. I don't plan to spend too much time on them, because by the time you're interested enough in mutual funds to buy one of these things you'll probably be chasing some strange homemade system such as "the U.S. dollar is finished, and copper futures are in Sagittarius, so I'm going into the yen complex." And you'll be talking in a strong Eastern European accent and calling me up and bugging me about a story I wrote last October. So let's not get too worked up by all this.

And okay, I admit it, these narrow, specialized funds can be lots of fun. Consider the AGF India Fund, which jumped 79.7 percent in 1999. Its top-ten holdings included Hindustan Lever and Punjab Tractor — a bit more exciting and exotic than old Royal Bank of Canada or Canadian Tire. But as the newspapers say about their horoscopes, treat this stuff as entertainment — it has nothing to do with really planning your life. AGF India went on to lose 49 percent in 2000 and 34 percent in 2001. An investor who put $10,000 into the fund at the end of 1999 was down to $3,438 by June 2002.

European funds: Why are all these people so well dressed?

European funds invest almost entirely in major companies in big, stable European countries, so they're a sensible choice compared with most specialty funds. Returns from this group were nice and steady in the 1990s, with the average fund in the group producing an average annual return of 12.7 percent. But that's partly because stock markets worldwide have been helped by low inflation and falling interest rates. And it also turned out that the Eurotrash tech 'n' telecom stock party in 1999 and early 2000 had been just as deranged and overpriced as America's. Most Euro funds dropped almost 7 percent in 2000, 18 percent in 2001, and another 9 percent in the first half of 2002. That left the group's annual return over ten years at a respectable 7.7 percent, although lagging the average 8.1 percent return from global equity funds that were at liberty to go anywhere — a.k.a. the U.S. of A.

A rise in European currencies relative to the Canadian dollar during the 1990s made European holdings steadily more valuable in Canadian-dollar terms. And that gave a major boost to European mutual funds. But a slide in Europe's new currency, the euro, dragged down European funds after its introduction in 1999. The euro fought back against the U.S. and Canadian dollars in 2002 as fears grew over U.S. corporate horseplay, sending investors scuttling out of U.S. stocks. The currency swing lifted the value of European assets in European equity mutual funds sold in Canada, which eased losses for unitholders. But don't bother trying to wager on currencies when you buy mutual funds — stick to rock climbing at night. For investors there's little chance of predicting changes. If Canada keeps inflation low and the economy steaming ahead, the Canadian loonie could bounce back fast, slicing into the profits earned on European and other foreign funds.

As always, if you do go into Europe, buy more than one fund, so that a dog doesn't chew up your portfolio too badly. A simple way to do this would be to buy the Canadian Imperial Bank of Commerce or Altamira Investment Services Inc. European *index fund* and then its sibling *actively managed* Euro fund. Index funds buy every stock in a recognized market index or benchmark so that they earn returns in line with the broad stock market. An actively managed fund, which is the most common type of fund, buys and sells stocks in an attempt to select the best ones — but it runs the risk of making the wrong choices. Both banks say their Euro index funds track the Morgan Stanley Capital International European index, a well-recognized benchmark for Europe's biggest stocks. If you don't want to become a customer of one of those two companies, then European funds are available at your discount broker (see Chapter 6, Discount Brokers: Cheap Thrills).

Asian funds: The dream that died

It almost seems like a dream now, but at one time fund salespeople and even some professional investors thought Asia was a no-lose proposition. The region had a young population, pro-business governments (that is, usually repressive), and an apparently insatiable desire to become as fat and self-satisfied as the West.

The success of many Asian countries in escaping their post-colonial poverty and building modern economies has been a genuine miracle, one of humanity's greatest achievements (that and chocolate-chip ice cream). For a while, it looked as if Asia could do no wrong. The average Asian mutual fund gained an incredible 81.9 percent in 1993. No wonder millions of salivating Canadians threw hundreds of millions into funds that invest in the region.

But interest rates moved up in 1994, hurting stocks all around the world. Investors learned a painful truth: Asian markets tend to catch bubonic plague when Wall Street gets a sniffle. That's because small markets such as South Korea and Malaysia are usually driven up and down by a few foreign investors charging in and out. And when interest rates are rising, money managers get jumpy and stick close to home, hugging their government bonds and good old General Electric shares.

The true reckoning came in 1997 and 1998, when the Asian economic marvel turned rancid. It was a bit like the proverbial butterfly's wings starting a hurricane. The wheels started coming off Asia after the real estate market in the Thai capital, Bangkok, turned down. You wouldn't think a property slump in one developing country could lead to an economic slide that hurt hundreds of millions of people, but it did.

Here's how it works: Real estate agents — that harmless cheery crew! — refer to something called The Fear. Normally, it's that churning feeling you get when you've put a binding offer on your first house and you realize that you're about to go hundreds of thousands of dollars in debt. But it also rears its warty, slimy head in commercial real estate when developers and investors get the uneasy feeling that everyone else is getting the hell out of the market. The Bangkok fear caused a crisis of confidence in Thai banks (never known for their rigorous lending checks). It spread irrevocably to other Asian economies, currencies, and stock markets, sending markets such as Indonesia crashing as much as 90 percent in U.S.–dollar terms (that is, not only did stock prices implode, but the local currency was also vaporized).

The Asian success story turned out to be a fairy tale, at least in part, as years of political cronyism and reckless lending came home to roost. The average Asian mutual fund dropped 29.3 percent in 1997 and another 5.5 percent in 1998. Losses would have been much worse but fund managers clung to each other like shipwreck victims and stayed alive in the relatively honest and stable market of Hong Kong. And to this day, most of the big Asian funds keep a large chunk of their assets there.

The average global equity fund made 12.3 percent per year during the 1990s — the average all-Asia fund made a wretched 6.1 percent. So much for the Asian tigers — Far Eastern fleabags, more like. And then the great global stock market slide set in. By mid-2002, the annual returns over ten years on Asian funds that stay out of Japan (so they were the lucky ones) had dropped to an uninspiring 3.4 percent. You got a higher return (4.1 percent) from Canadian money market funds, which are arguably safer than money in the bank. There's more on them in Chapter 17.

Honging in there

Tiny, frenetic Hong Kong is one of history's great survivors and for years produced hyper-capitalist returns for investors: An incredible 26 percent annually during the 1990s. Observers thought the former British colony would be a write-off when China took it over in 1998, but the city-state has continued to thrive, although the 10-year annual return on its stock market had dropped to a more proletarian 8.1 percent by June 2002. Singapore, which was supposed to become Asia's new economic centre, didn't take over. Perhaps that's because Singapore, a masterpiece of social planning and benevolent dictatorship, is simply too boring and squeaky clean to become a great world city. As the local joke has it: Why don't foreigners get culture shock when they move here? Because we have no culture.

If you buy into Asia, your first choice is whether you want a fund that includes Japan or treats it as a completely separate market. There's no right or wrong answer here. Asian funds that also hold Japanese stocks represent a sort of handy one-stop shopping investment in the Far East, much of which is an economic suburb of Japan anyway. But, arguably, a specialized manager who spends all of his or her time in Tokyo reading pornographic "manga" comic books and picking local stocks has a better chance of getting it right in such a distinctive country. Japan marches to its own very strange Kodo drumbeat: for example, when the average Asian fund jumped more than 80 percent in 1993, most Japanese funds made less than 30 percent. So it's hard to believe a manager sitting in Hong Kong or London can hope to become as knowledge-able about the Tokyo scene there as someone right on the spot. That means that if you insist on buying specialty Asian funds, you're better off buying a specialized Japanese fund (more about them below) plus an "Asia ex-Japan" fund that stays out of the Japanese market.

Japanese, please: Once hot, now not

Finally, Japan, land of fast trains, paper walls, and coffin hotels. And oddly, a place where Wall Street's crash also happened, but ten years earlier. At the end of the 1980s, foreign investors in the then-red-hot Tokyo market reckoned that any price they paid for a stock was okay because the Japanese economy had moved to a new way of valuing assets. So, Nippon Telegraph traded at 100 times its profits in 1989 and people weren't worried — a bit like the way U.S. investors argued in early 2000 that they were being all prudent and care-ful when they paid 50 times earnings for a telephone-company stock because they were getting an "earnings yield" of 2 percent, which isn't far short of the one-year deposit rate. See "U.S. equity funds: Land of the fat" below, for an explanation of earnings yield and similar magic incantations.

But Japan crashed, as insane stock markets always do. By 1992, the Nikkei average of 225 big Japanese stocks had fallen by half from its highs of the late 1980s and it went nowhere for the rest of the decade. There was the occasional nice bounce off the bottom, but over the ten years from 1990 to 2000 the average Japanese fund produced a miserable annual return of 3.2 percent. And as of June 2002, the ten-year annual "return" had turned into an exciting annual *loss* of 0.1 percent. Those grim figures don't even include zombie underperforming Japanese funds that were quietly buried in unmarked graves along the way.

How I blew it in mutual funds —
and how you can do better

The good news is that the only truly hot mutual fund I ever owned, the Altamira Japanese Opportunity Fund, went up 123 percent in 1999. The bad news is that I invested a miserable $200 in it. My own failure at picking shoot-the-lights-out mutual funds pretty well convinced me that it's a crapshoot trying to figure out which volatile specialty funds will do well and which will bark. If you buy a few quality conservative funds from the start, you'll do fine. Or better than I did, anyway. Around 1994, I decided that it would be a good source of stories if I opened accounts with as many fund companies as I could, including banks and direct sellers such as Altamira. So I opened around ten small accounts, putting only about $1,000 in each or opening a $50 monthly *pre-authorized contribution plan*. That's the industry's beloved PAC, where they go into your bank account each month and take out the money. It's actually something the fund companies often lose money on, because the investments are small and administration costs are high, so I reckon there could be something in it for you and me.

I'm a gambler by nature, so I went for pitbull-aggressive funds. I reckoned that there was no gain without pain, stocks always go up, rah rah rah. Altamira Equity (then under the legendary heavy trader Frank Mersch) was my most conservative choice. Otherwise, it was frothy Asian and emerging markets funds, not to mention small-company nightmares and other stuff I prefer to forget, thanks. Needless to say, I took some serious hits. The average emerging markets fund lost 7 percent in 1995 and went down in a fairly straight line from there. Japanese funds delivered three straight years of losses — until the carnage of 2000 to 2002, no asset class had probably inflicted that kind of damage since the stock market died in the 1930s. I also bought an energy fund and a precious metals fund, both of which crawled along the bottom until I dumped them around 1998 and switched to regular equity funds.

Even my Altamira Equity stumbled and fell as resource stocks wore out and financial stocks went up for three years straight. But what was up with old Frank? After all, he had the hottest numbers in the industry. That's why I bought the fund. I remember once being at a presentation by some pension fund suits and they had a survey that showed a single unnamed manager way out in front. I asked who it was and I remember one guy answered, "That was Mersch." But Frank didn't like banks so he and I missed the party. The lesson for you is this: Forget about small-cap junk, weird foreign markets, and managers who abandon large sections of the market — at least for the bulk of your savings. Buy funds that invest in a wide range of companies and countries that are familiar to you.

Then ten years later, stocks all over the world turned Japanese. The great Standard & Poor's index of 500 big U.S. companies topped 1,500 in 2000 only to slump below 780 in 2002, down 48 percent from its peak. The Toronto market dropped more than 45 percent from its own record highs. Let's hope past isn't prologue, with global stock markets producing a miserable decade like Japan did. It's never that simple, anyway. If it were, newspaper reporters might make money in the market. And pigs might fly.

Back to Japan, though. It's still the world's second-largest economy, a power-house of ingenuity and brilliant design. Any country that has people who devote their lives to mastering the art of tea-pouring has to have something going for it. Everybody should have a small portion of their assets in the great Japanese global companies, such as Sony, Hitachi, and Fujitsu. But do it just by buying a couple of conservative global equity funds. As with other major economic regions of the world, most good global stock funds put at least some of their portfolio in Japan.

U.S. equity funds: Land of the fat

Remember the Minimalist artists of the 1960s? They were people such as Donald Judd, who produced work that consisted of metal shelf-like objects. Or Carl Andre, whose *144 Pieces of Zinc* was, you've guessed it, 144 pieces of zinc. But then came the Post-Minimalists. I can't claim to understand fully (or even partly, let's be honest) what they were trying to get at. But they seem to have concluded that people like Judd and Andre went in for too much tomfoolery and fancy decoration. So Post-Minimalist work included one piece that simply consisted of damaging the gallery wall. Or another that involved strewing fabric and broken glass in a corner (I found that one particularly moving. With the addition of a few dead animals and pairs of dirty socks, it would have been a perfect evocation of my bachelor days.)

And what's the point of all this? Simply that beauty depends on who's looking at it and what your vantage point is. Back in early 2000, the U.S. stock market looked like a very beautiful thing indeed — but we were standing on the slopes of a mountain, looking back at a gorgeous landscape, after a decade in which the U.S. market had generated incredible returns of more than 20 percent in Canadian-dollar terms per year. And don't forget just how wonderfully rich 20 percent a year will make you. At that rate, money doubles in less than four years and quadruples in less than eight. It was hard to be impartial about something that had done so well.

The subsequent plunge in U.S. stocks wiped out more than $2 trillion U.S. (a trillion is a *million million*) in shareholders' wealth on paper. And by mid-2002, the return from the average U.S. equity fund was down to a more plausible

8.7 percent annually over ten years, still marginally ahead of the 8.1-percent return from global equity funds. Maybe the good times will come back — or maybe American stocks will become the greatest horror show in the history of investing as U.S shares go on falling listlessly to earth with all the grace of crashing Boeing 747s. Unfortunately, there's no real way to know. But America is the engine of the world's economy, a magic lamp of creativity and intellect. So you must have at least some of your savings there. But you don't have to buy regular U.S. equity funds that try to pick winning American stocks. Any sensible global equity fund will own plenty of U.S. companies, so owning a couple of those will give you American content. Add a U.S. equity index fund — one that tracks the entire U.S. market — and you'll have collected plenty of Americana.

In the U.S. market, it's essential you own an index fund because the managers of U.S. equity funds sold in Canada have done a particularly pathetic job of keeping up with the usual market benchmark, the famous Standard & Poor's index of 500 giant U.S. stocks. The index produced an average annual return of 11.9 percent in Canadian-dollar terms in the ten years ended June 2002, well ahead of the sub–9-percent return from the average U.S. stock fund. Nearly all U.S. index funds track the S&P 500 — but as investors have discovered, the S&P 500 is no perpetual motion machine that always goes up. One of the reasons why the crash was so spectacular was that by the end of the 1990s the Standard & Poor's index had established a virtuous but insane cycle in which the stocks that made up the index kept going higher simply because they were in the index, which induced investors to buy the stocks in the index at ever-higher prices because it was such a good index to invest in, if you get my drift.

Now that's all dandy while it works, but it's also a bit like a Ponzi scheme, a fraud in which late arrivals to the scam pay off the first lucky investors. Or it's like one of those grim "airplane" games people would play in the 1980s: The first group of sharks were the "pilots" who got money off a fresh batch of recruits, who would in turn recruit others. Ever watch music videos or movies from the 1980s and notice how things back then were incredibly depressing and grey? Sort of dark. In some ways, it was kind of a drab decade. I mean Billy Joel, Sting, shoulder pads, *Dallas* . . . or was that the 1970s?

Airplane games are not the sort of investment you want to base your retirement on. So for your U.S. index fund money, I suggest using the **CIBC U.S. Index Fund**, which tracks the Russell 5000 index, a massively broad measure that includes just about every stock that matters in the United States. The idea is that if there's a long-term decline in the huge blue-chip stocks such as Microsoft Corp. and General Electric Inc. that dominate the S&P 500, then you'll be hedging your bets by owning lots of smaller companies.

Remember, though, that U.S. equity funds are like any type of specialty fund: You don't really have to own them. Any well-run global fund will contain a large number of U.S. stocks, because America is just too dynamic to ignore.

Emerging markets funds: And you thought you were corrupt

Emerging markets or developing countries — let's drop the euphemisms and call these nations what they are: poor. At least two-thirds of the world's population lives in places such as Ghana and Malaysia where industrial society and all of its plush comforts have yet to take root fully. But why invest there? The theory is that these economies are growing fast from a low level of activity, as opposed to the "mature" economies of the West. Fast growth means corporate profits that are rising quickly — and that's good for stocks, remember?

So these markets are supposed to give you higher long-term returns, at the cost of bigger price swings because shares in these strange places are relatively unstable and prone to dangers such as currency collapse (which nearly always happens, don't kid yourself).

Usually, shares in these small countries rise and fall in line with Wall Street and Bay Street. But these markets are far more volatile because they're smaller. That means one or two foreign lads with MBAs — a.k.a. fund managers from the rich world — can make the whole index go up and down. So in 1994, when interest rates rose suddenly in the United States and spooked investors in both rich and poor companies into dumping their shares, most emerging markets funds fell 10 percent or more, but the average global equity fund managed a gain of 3 percent. Then in 1999, a good year for the markets, most emerging markets funds jumped more than 53 percent after falling into a pit during the previous two years. There were no emerging markets funds in existence for all of the 1990s, but the group produced a rotten average annual return of 4.4 percent in the second half of the decade, compared with 15.4 percent for global equity funds. And as of June 2002, that five-year return had turned into an annual *loss* of 7.6 percent.

Traditionally, there was another important reason to own stocks in these far-off lands. At times, they have been known to move independently of North American markets, which may sound boring but can be extremely comforting. If your Wall Street shares were tanking, then your Brazilian sewer digger might be doing fine. However, there's still the question of whether you even want to bother with such volatile investments. As brokers are reputed to say about a junk stock, "It's for trading, not for owning."

There are other complications with emerging markets that you should bear in mind. One minor difficulty: Managers don't agree on what constitutes a developing market. The $300-million-plus Templeton Emerging Markets Fund, Canada's biggest emerging markets fund, has a broad definition of developing markets, so its portfolio includes countries such as wealthy Hong Kong. That conservative mixture of investments has protected investors in the fund from some of the nasty drops in emerging markets but it could mean missing out on big rallies. For example, the Templeton fund made a more-than-respectable 43 percent in 1999, but that was well short of the 55-percent-plus gains posted by rival funds.

The big problem for investors in emerging markets funds is the tendency of nervous managers to slavishly buy the same few stocks around the world, usually the local phone company, in whatever emerging markets they like. So buying two or even three emerging markets funds may not spread your risk as much as you might think — the portfolios often contain the same stuff. In fairness to managers, they're often forced to stick to one or two big stocks in a lot of developing countries because at least they know there's some sort of professional supervision of the corporate executives, supplied by the other foreign investment managers who own the stock. Many developing countries, like the United States 100 years ago, are still at a stage of cowboy capitalism in which corruption and sharp dealing are rampant. Well, okay, it turns out that plenty of U.S. companies still do that stuff. I remember writing news stories about poor Noble China, a Toronto-based beer company with Canadian brewing industry veterans on board, that tried to run breweries in China. Only trouble was that Noble's Chinese partner essentially took control, striking deals with local Communist Party types, and cutting Noble China out of the loop.

Don't get me wrong — I love emerging markets funds, but only as a form of amusement. I enjoy the exotic names, the strange companies, and the potential for huge returns. But the evidence seems to be that as the world's markets become linked ever more closely, shares in developing markets are simply going to track those of rich countries. And most well-run global equity funds hold at least a few big companies in developing markets anyway, which further reduces your need to bother with a specialized emerging markets fund. Sure, put a small portion of your portfolio, at most a few percent, in these funds. But don't go banking on double-digit returns — they come along all too rarely.

Latin American equity funds: What do you mean the piñata market has collapsed?

At this point, we're getting very hard-core. Latin American funds are about as dangerous as regional funds get. The main justification for investing in Latin America, as with Asia or emerging markets in general, is that these countries are still in the early stages of their economic growth, which means companies there have lots of room to expand. In practice, most managers in the group end up with nearly all of their assets in Mexico and Brazil because the other countries in the region are too small or too impoverished to offer many opportunities. Yes, Latin America has managed a wonderful transition to pretty good democracy, leaving its brutal military regimes of the 1980s behind. The big problem, though, is that Latin American politicians still have an unpleasant habit of papering over the cracks in their economies until after they have been elected. At that point, they announce the bad news, sending their currency and stock market sliding. Fresh-faced foreign portfolio managers are inevitably brought along for the ride. Sorry, *gringo*. The average Latin American fund produced an annual return of only 4.2 percent in the five years from 1995 through 1999. And as of June 2002, the group had slumped to an annual loss of 10.4 percent over five years, the sorriest performance of any fund category.

Sector Funds: Limitations Galore

Funds that buy stocks in just one industry or sector of the economy — for example, technology or resource funds — are bucking broncos, producing wild leaps and sickening plunges. That's because investors have a long-standing habit, as we've seen, of suddenly falling in love with a particular type of stock and then bidding those companies' shares to ridiculous prices.

For example, in late 1999 and 2000 a craze developed for biotech stocks, which had been flopping around on the laboratory floor since 1995. In no time, investors had $180 million riding on the new CI Global Biotechnology Sector Fund, which doubled investors' money in three months. It was nothing to see obscure biotech stocks in Toronto jumping fourfold in a couple of weeks. Then somebody dropped a jar and biotechs went squelch. An investment of $10,000 in CI Global Biotech in September 2000 was worth less than $4,000 by mid-2002.

Specialized funds are far more volatile than high-quality diversified equity funds that hold *all industries,* the first of our ABC rules in Chapter 10 on equity funds.

So their volatility means these funds are essentially a gimmick, and not the place for your serious money. Still, they can be fun. Those who enjoy trading can use no-load sector funds as a cheap vehicle for jumping aboard a trend (or what they fondly hope is a trend). And some of the ideas that fund sellers have come up with are impressive: At the end of this section, I'll talk about some of the weirder sector and specialty funds.

But there are really only two types of sector funds that most investors should even consider:

> ✔ Resource and precious metals funds may arguably have a place in the portfolios of those who are very worried about inflation.
>
> ✔ And technology funds, post-crash, may be good long-term holdings because at least the companies they own are doing something new (although all too often lately it's dreaming up new ways to entice money out of investors).

Resource funds: Pouring money down a hole

Resource funds buy companies that used to be the backbone of Canada's economy: macho, doughnut-eating types who sell oil, forest products, minerals, and basic commodities like aluminum. For complicated reasons to do with oversupply and furtive men meeting in damp hotel rooms in Belgium, the prices for these commodities tend to be extremely volatile, often doubling or falling by half in a matter of months. That means the shares of resource companies are incredibly prone to swings.

So investors in resource companies must get used to living like manic-depressive motorcycle couriers on crystal meth. Or teenage girls in their first week in junior high. One day they're up, everyone loves them and their shares, and profits are rolling in as commodity prices rock. The next day, prices are down and they're aimlessly skidding their bike from side to side at 120 kilometres per hour while staring wildly ahead through bulging eyes. You're such a loser and everyone in the class thinks you're a freak.

Take oil, for example. Periodically since the 1970s, the producers have been able to get together in one of those Belgian hotel rooms, sip warm beer, and rig prices for a while. Oil company stocks duly rise accordingly. But it's pretty well a mug's game trying to predict when the next oil boom is coming, and oil exploration companies have been abysmal at creating long-term wealth for their shareholders. When their shares rise, they tend to issue a whole bunch of new stock into the hot market to grab as much cash from investors as possible while the going is good, sorry, to raise capital for developing new reserves. Eventually, existing shareholders realize that, thanks a lot, they now must give some of the company's profits and dividends to all of those scruffy new shareholders. Meanwhile, oil prices are usually tanking again. Hey, presto, collapsing oil stocks. From 1999 to 2000 oil prices doubled, leaving energy funds with fat gains. But once again, betting that energy prices are going to go on climbing is just rolling the dice, not investing. No wonder investors in Canada have largely turned their backs on energy shares and now insist on oil and gas income trusts, which at least pay out a steady stream of cash. See Chapter 5 for more on income trusts.

For the second half of the 1990s, resource funds were a rough place to invest, with the average fund in the group posting back-to-back losses in 1997 and 1998, in an era when consecutive yearly losses were still rare. Resource funds delivered an abysmal annual return of just 3.1 percent during the 1990s. But when tech stocks began falling in 2000, investors looked for something else to buy. Many commodity stocks took off — especially in oil and gold, which were lifted by soaring prices for energy and bullion — and resource funds posted gains through 2000, 2001, and early 2002. By June 2002, the group's ten-year average annual return had climbed to a respectable 8.4 percent, not far short of the average 9.3-percent return from Canadian equity funds.

The rise in precious metals funds, which buy mostly gold miners' stocks (the easiest way to bet on gold), was even more spectacular. Bullion prices rose from less than U.S.$260 an ounce in early 2001 to more than $320 in mid-2002, and gold funds took off. The group posted an average gain of 24.9 percent in 2001 and then soared another 57 percent in the first half of 2002.

Why did gold go up like that? Well, conspiracy theories abound when it comes to precious metals prices (there have long been dark mutterings of a plot to keep gold down to protect the U.S. dollar), but the simple answer is that gold tends to rise when the world loses confidence in its paper money as a store of value. The yellow metal is the world's oldest form of money (okay, I know one, um, commodity is a lot older, but I don't plan to waste time writing stuff that'll just be censored). Gold soared, for example, back in 1980, when investors around the world were scared that geopolitics was spinning out of control. Jimmy Carter had just stumbled through the Iranian hostage situation and the Soviet Union had invaded Afghanistan. Inflation is also great for gold prices because it means paper money is losing its value, which makes timeless and readily portable bullion more valuable. But gold slid during the 1990s, after Communism collapsed and America basked in a low-inflation golden age.

The latest rally in gold was really just a partial recovery from bullion's slump in the late 1990s — for most of the decade, the metal traded well above $325. Investors also grabbed gold as U.S. stocks fell, fearing that the U.S. dollar was headed downward as overseas investors repatriated their holdings.

For very conservative investors, there might be a case for putting small amounts into a couple of diversified resource funds, perhaps a couple of percent of one's portfolio in each fund, or even a couple of gold funds. That's because resource stocks can act as portfolio insurance — commodity prices move in their own weird cycles, and sometimes in the opposite direction to stocks in general.

If you do decide to buy resource funds, try to buy two with very different portfolio mixtures of forestry, energy, mining, and other commodities (see Chapter 22 for tips on checking out a fund's asset mix). That way, if one manager crashes and burns, the other might make it. And if you buy into gold funds, make sure you hold at least two, because managers can easily miss out on the very hottest mining stocks that are leading the whole group higher. Consider buying gold industry *exchange traded fund* units, or "iGolds." They're a type of fund that holds all of the major precious metals companies, but their units trade on the Toronto Stock Exchange like a share. There's more on ETFs — an excellent choice for investors because of their low costs, flexibility, and wide diversification of holdings — in Chapter 5.

But remember, if you follow my advice and hold a few actively managed high-quality Canadian equity funds and global equity funds, plus Canadian, U.S., and international index funds, then you're bound to own shares in a few giant resource companies anyway. They'll probably go up nicely if inflation and 1970s-style soaring commodities prices ever return, or the U.S. dollar implodes. You'd better hope so, bro, because everything else you own will be going down faster than a 45-year-old turboprop in an ice storm.

Science and technology funds: But how will you control it, Professor?

Back in 1994, Canada had about five science funds. By the end of 1999 there were at least 35, and by mid-2002 there were more than 100. Incredible returns on technology stocks during the 1990s, which reached a hysterical climax of greed and speculation by 2000, produced 100-percent-plus returns for investors in technology funds who were brave enough to hang on for the whole ride. However, the collapse in tech stocks left the average fund in the group with a brutal average annual loss of 21.8 percent in the three years ended June 2002. The point to stress is that the typical investor who didn't get out in time lost all of the profits that he or she made during the run-up in tech stocks, and then some. The five-year annual return for the group was a loss of 2 percent.

There's no point in my launching into a dull sermon about the danger of investing in wild tech funds. Back in 1999 and 2000, people just had to look at the sort of returns these things had posted and a shifty, greedy look came into their eyes. And for all I know, technology stocks may start climbing again, to as-yet-undreamed-of heights. Doesn't seem likely, though. So if you think the party's going to continue, go ahead and buy these funds, damn the digitally controlled dolphin-brain torpedoes.

Science funds can buy virtually anything as long as it has something to do with computers, telecommunications, biotechnology, or research. But they're really just super-high-growth equity funds that hold fancy companies trading at Versace-type prices.

If you decide to buy a science and technology fund — and I advise against it for most investors because of the excessive risk — limit your investment to less than 5 percent of your total fund holdings.

Some people reckon they've got a pretty sharp tooth when it comes to technology, which lets them predict which industries will do best next. In that case, you could select more specialized types of tech funds, including:

- A telecommunications fund, which gives you "exposure" (money management slang for a chance to profit from something) to phone, computer, Internet, and wireless companies that are revolutionizing communications. Telecom funds went on an especially wild ride. If you invested $10,000 in the CI Global Telecommunications Sector Fund at its launch in July 1996, your holding was worth an incredible $71,734 in August 2000. By June 2000, it was worth $13,407.

- A biotechnology fund, which buys into obscure companies selling strange new drugs and bits of protein in jars. We've already seen how the CI Global Biotechnology fund took a pounding. If you put $10,000 into the fund at its launch in August 1999, your investment had grown to almost $23,000 just over a year later. As of June 2002, though, it was down to $8,500.

Technology fund managers like to put on statesmanlike, long-term faces and predict that the companies in their portfolios today will be the giant household names of tomorrow. As though the kids will be pestering you to take them out to look at the new network routers from Cisco Systems or log on to Sun Microsystems' latest servers.

The high priests and priestesses of tech-forever may have a point, and these companies could have many years of exponential growth ahead of them. So there could be a good case for holding a tech fund if you're investing for long periods of, say, ten years or more. But a few good global and Canadian equity funds, including index funds, will own plenty of the big tech stocks that show up in specialized technology funds — so, once again, you'll probably be well covered by simply sticking with your core equity funds. As with so many other specialty funds, only buy these for fun. And get ready to take some spills along the way.

There's one consolation: Tech stocks seem to have shaken off one of their old weaknesses — vulnerability to rising interest rates. People thought tech stocks would fall once interest rates came back up. That's because people are paying high prices for these stocks, so the return of their money (in the form of earnings or, ha, ha, dividends) is many years in the future. In other words, Boris, you'll be old and grey before you get a decent dividend from these tech guys. Higher interest rates in the here and now mean you're giving up lucrative opportunities by tying your money up for years. So investors were supposed to sell their tech stocks when rates climbed. Well, rates did rise in 1999, with the annual yield on ten-year Government of Canada bonds moving up to 5.6 percent from less than 5 at the start of the year. But tech stocks kept on climbing and the average science and the average technology fund made 113 percent that year, probably the best showing ever by a serious asset class (or any humorous one, for that matter).

So much for the theory, which everyone knew was cock-eyed anyway. That's because nobody who was scooping up tech stocks in 1999 or 2000 gave a rat's behind about interest rates or dividends — they were planning to simply sell the shares at higher prices to some dumb heavy-browed investor who had missed out on the chance to buy it cheap earlier on. But beware of markets in which people buy for trading, not for owning. They have a nasty habit of collapsing.

Miscellaneous sector funds — I didn't know railway wheels were a growth industry

You name it, they've pretty well come up with a sector fund that tracks it. There are funds that track industries from financial services stocks to clean energy. Some, such as Friedberg Commodity Management Inc.'s volatile currency and futures funds, at least offer a play on weird asset classes that are tough to invest in otherwise. But otherwise, we're generally talking gimmicks. Sky-high expenses (almost 3 percent annually on the average specialty fund) and wild price swings mean that this stuff is for dedicated fund fanatics only. For example, at least 12 fund companies offer financial services funds that load up on banking and insurance stocks. Perhaps financial services will prove a long-term growth sector (as baby boomers get older and richer), but bank shares have a depressing habit of sliding whenever interest rates go up.

And somehow, these fancy funds never really seem to work out too well. At the start of 1999, mutual experts and commentators loved the AIM Global Health Sciences fund, which had trebled investors' money in four years after manager John Schroer loaded up on global drug stocks such as Pfizer Inc. and Johnson & Johnson. But the fund proceeded to slide 7 percent that year as investors abandoned high-priced blue-chip pharmaceutical shares and went in for strange little biotechnology outfits cooking up smelly stuff in beakers. As of June 2002, the average health care fund had lost 0.7 percent annually over three years. However, in fairness to the health care category, the average yearly return over five years was 5.7 percent, significantly better than the thin 1.7-percent annual return from global equity funds.

The fund industry loves to preach against the evils of market timing, advocating that you buy and hold, and it's generally good advice. But with the way these narrow funds can tank, you're pretty well obliged to jump in and out of them, hoping to grab a profit along the way. Yes, they're a handy and cheap way to jump aboard a sector such as Internet stocks, which would be expensive and messy to buy on your own. But, once again, this is gambling, not building long-term wealth. Some of these funds are so expensive and so unpredictable that they qualify for the list of ten gimmick funds in Chapter 27.

As I explain in Chapter 5, which deals with investing strategies beyond mutual funds, there's an option that beats most sector funds. On major stock exchanges, you can buy and sell *exchange traded funds* — trusts that are simply collections of the largest stocks in different industries. These ETFs are bought and sold just like shares, so you need to open an account with a discount stockbroker or regular broker to invest in them. For example, there are ETFs for banking, for health care, and so on.

These ETFs are much more flexible than sector mutual funds because you can buy and sell them on a moment's notice instead of having to accept that evening's value. And because ETFs represent ownership of the companies in an industry, they'll rise when the shares are rising, just like a sector fund that invests in that industry.

Best of all, the annual management costs and fees on ETFs are rock bottom, generally less than 1 percent annually. But your big disadvantage is the fact that to both buy and sell them you have to pay a commission that easily runs 1 or 2 percent of your total capital. That means no-load mutual funds (that is, funds with no sales commissions) may be a cheaper option if you plan to trade frequently.

Chapter 13

Balanced and Asset Allocation Funds

*E*ver have a really good roti — a West Indian treat packed with extra spices, tasty meat, and East Indian–style stuff like chickpeas? Remember the wonderful numb feeling of fullness afterward? Balanced funds are supposed to be a satisfying all-in-one meal like that. You hand your money over to the fund company or bank, and they make all of the decisions. A *balanced fund* is a nice broad mixture of many types of investment — the idea being that it'll never lose too much money. The manager usually invests the fund in a cautious blend of stocks, which are tiny pieces of ownership of companies, and long-term and short-term bonds, which are debts owed by governments and companies. Balanced funds are investment products you buy when you want nice steady returns of around 6 to 8 percent per year while avoiding losses as much as possible. They're one of the mutual fund industry's most useful inventions and an excellent place for the nervous beginner to get going. In this chapter, I introduce you to the main types of balanced funds, explain why they're a great way to start off in investing, and warn you about the problems you may run into.

Understanding Balanced Funds

Balanced funds are for busy people who want a one-decision product that they can buy and forget about. Imagine your family had a trusted lawyer or accountant who took care of all of your investing needs — the professional, if he or she was at all prudent, would end up putting the money into a judicious blend of bonds and stocks, with a healthy cushion of cash to further reduce risk. And that's the essence of a balanced fund — it includes a little bit of everything so that losses can be kept to a minimum if one type of investment falls in value. Balanced funds, which have been around since the dawn of the fund industry in the 1920s in one form or another, have attracted billions of dollars in recent years as confused investors decide to let someone else pick the right mix for their savings. As of June 2002, they had total assets of $67 billion, making them the fund industry's third most popular product after foreign equity and Canadian equity funds. Investors shaken by the stock market slide put $2.2 billion in new money into balanced funds in the first half of 2002, the highest sales posted by any type of fund.

Reviewing the asset mix of balanced funds

Want to have some fun? Call up a balanced fund manager and during the conversation suddenly shriek, "Watch out! The market's crashing." You're bound to get an entertaining reaction. That's because the people running balanced funds tend to be nervous types who loathe losing money. That's great for you if you're a worried investor who can't afford to take big hits. So put your money in a balanced fund if you want someone watching over it who also hates to see things drop in value. In mid-2002, most balanced funds in Canada had about 55 percent of their assets in risky-but-lucrative stocks, but the majority had about 40 percent in dull-but-sure bonds. The rest was sitting on the sidelines in cash.

Remember the old rule that your portfolio's weighting in bonds plus cash should equal your age? If we assume that the average Canadian balanced fund has 55 percent in stocks and 45 percent in guaranteed investments like bonds and cash, then most balanced funds are suitable for investors aged about 45. So if you're younger, look for a slightly more aggressive mix, and if you're older, try to find something with more bonds.

A balanced fund should be a ready-made cautious investment portfolio. Yes, it might lose money — nothing is absolutely safe in investing — but it's unlikely to drop as much as 10 percent in a year. Just check the fund's mix of assets at the fund company's Web site or in its handouts. If there are plenty of bonds and cash, it's probably safe enough to buy.

Profitable plodders

The good news is that Canadian balanced funds have done a pretty good job of avoiding losses. The average fund in the group lost less than 2 percent annually in the grim two years ended June 2002, while the average Canadian stock fund fell 5 percent per year. Over ten years, Canadian balanced funds produced a respectable annual average return of 7.9 percent compared with 9.3 percent for equity funds. Now, I know that a few weaklings got lost in that shuffle after they were merged into better funds, but that's not a bad showing. The fund industry, always remember, has a habit of quietly folding under-performers into its stars, cancelling the dogs' years of terrible returns. For example, Fidelity in the mid-1990s took a weak balanced fund and popped it inside its huge Fidelity Canadian Asset Allocation Fund. The old fund's poor returns vanished forever. It lives on for a while in the fading memory of strange people like me who love funds. But when we go to our cheap government-provided burial plots, the dud will be gone. It's always possible that you'll find yourself stuck in a similar underperformer. To minimize that risk, the best solution of all is to hold two balanced funds so that your entire portfolio doesn't suffer from weakness in one fund.

Don't worry: Balanced funds are all about simplicity. Until you make up your mind about your long-term investing plans, you'll almost certainly do fine over three to five years by simply buying a regular balanced fund, or two for more safety, and then forgetting about them.

Retiring with balanced funds

If you really want to adopt a simple approach, it's a great idea to use balanced funds in your *registered retirement savings plan* — a special account in which investment gains add up without being taxed until you take them out, usually at retirement. Balanced funds are a nice cautious mix, just the thing you want for your life savings. Younger investors can be more aggressive, putting nearly all of their money into stocks, but above the age of 35 it's a wise idea to own bonds as well. Nothing is forever. If you decide later that you want something else in your RRSP, maybe because the balanced fund you picked turned out to be a dog, then it should be a simple matter to shift the money to another fund or funds within the same RRSP or to another RRSP account without incurring taxes.

So if you just want a simple investment to buy and forget, go for one or two balanced funds. A balanced fund has a single unit value that's published daily in the newspapers and on the Internet, making the value of your holdings easy to check. Its return appears in the papers every month and on the Internet every day. And the performance is also published clearly by the fund company, or should be. As with any regular mutual fund, if you've bought a pooch the whole world can see, there'll be some pressure on the fund manager to improve it.

Steering clear of potholes: Consistently strong returns

Balanced fund managers' scaredy-cat caution has served investors well. As stocks slid in the first half of 2002, the average balanced fund escaped with a modest loss of 3.1 percent. The worst loss the group suffered in a recent full calendar year was back in 1994 when the average fund in the group slipped 2.4 percent. Even that loss wasn't really the fault of the managers. Interest rates jumped suddenly that year, slashing the value of the bonds they held. Otherwise, balanced funds have generated nice steady returns, just as they're supposed to. But remember that balanced funds and all other investors who own bonds have had a gale at their backs since the early 1990s, because the drop in inflation has made bonds steadily more valuable. (See Chapter 14 for more on bonds.) That's unlikely to happen again in coming years. With inflation so low — at less than 3 percent in Canada in mid-2002 — bonds will have a tougher time going up at the same pace. And that means balanced funds could have difficulty keeping up with their flashier equity rivals.

If we move into an era of deflation (that is, falling prices), bonds will almost certainly become increasingly more valuable because the value of their steady payouts of cash rises consistently. In that case, which unfortunately could involve a very painful recession, balanced funds could easily outperform stock funds. But whatever happens, the point remains: A balanced fund is like "home safe" in a kids' game of tag in southern Ontario (the centre of the universe, as you know). It's a safe spot for your money, leaving you to get on with your life. (Okay, okay, what do you call it in Newfoundland? Squishy-jig or something, no doubt.)

Taking a Look at One Balanced Biggie

Let's look at Canada's biggest specimen, Royal Bank of Canada's Royal Balanced Fund, to get an idea of how a traditional balanced fund works. Just get a firm grip and lift it onto the table; don't let it wriggle like that. Heavy, huh? In mid-2002, this fund had just over $6 billion in assets. Remember, that's more than a million dollars 6,000 times over — so obviously the bank was delivering something that Mr. and Ms. Canada want: an attractive rate of return while minimizing losses. The fund had 39 percent of its assets in Canadian stocks and another 18 percent in shares outside Canada. It had just under one-third of its giant portfolio in bonds and the rest, about 12 percent, in cash. At 57 percent, the fund was fairly heavily exposed to the stock market, and manager Mark Arthur — the big cheese in Royal Bank's investment management department — sounded a little nervous about the market. "We continue to anticipate a summer rally [in share prices], which we will use to further pare our equity positions," he told his unitholders in a commentary. In other words, he seemed to be waiting for stocks to go up a bit before he sold them. The fund lost 3.1 percent in the year ended June 2002, slightly more than the 1-percent loss posted by the average Canadian balanced fund, but its ten-year annual return was a middle-of-the-pack 7.8 percent. In other words, it was a typical balanced fund: a solid investment that's fine for your portfolio if one of your key objectives is security.

Global Balanced Funds — The Ideal Lover?

For those who want to chase (possibly) higher returns outside Canada while spreading their wealth over a huge range of investments, there are *global balanced funds*, and their more reckless cousins, *global asset allocation funds*. Let's define the members of this colourful family.

- ✔ **Global balanced funds** are funds that buy shares in big, safe companies around the world and lots of government bonds. They attempt to produce nice steady profits for investors while avoiding loss. Most investors probably hope to get a medium-sized return of 7 to 8 percent from these funds.

- ✔ **Global asset allocation funds** are rougher trade altogether. They're allowed to make heavy and risky bets, on Asia for example, in an attempt to earn more. Investors probably expect 9 or 10 percent from this kind of fund. But the danger of loss is increased and a fund like this is much more likely to suddenly slide 10 percent.

As always, check the top holdings in the portfolio of a global balanced fund. If they're not mostly stocks and bonds issued by giant companies that you've already heard of, plus bonds from countries such as the United States, Germany, and Japan, then look elsewhere. Why take a risk on low-quality investments?

Like their Canadian counterparts, global balanced and global asset allocation funds pull off the same trick of buying a bit of everything, but the fact that they do it globally gives you even more diversification and the potential for higher returns. Very few have even been around for ten years, but the group's average five-year annual return as of June 2002 was a thin 1.4 percent, dragged down by the global slump in stocks.

Insisting on low costs is important with any balanced fund, Canadian or global, because so much of the portfolio is made up of steady-but-dull bonds and cash, and that keeps annual gains down. So if you want to be left with a decent return, you can't pay too much.

The average global balanced fund hits its investors for a nasty 2.8 percent in expenses each year. In other words, the fund company helps itself to 1/36 of your money each year. That's $140 annually on a $5,000 investment, increasing as the account size does.

Some global balanced fund investors rack up fees well above the average 2.8 percent. These include funds with fancy features, such as guarantees to refund some or all of your original investment after ten years or to pay at least that much to your heirs (those snivelling jellyfish), even if the fund has in fact produced a loss. These guaranteed or "segregated" funds may give you enormous satisfaction in knowing that your money is protected. For that reason, thousands of people buy them. But like the overpriced extended warranty that pushy VCR salespeople try to get you to take, such guarantees are usually not worth paying for on something as stable as a balanced fund, which rarely loses money. Few funds of any sort lose money over ten years (except for the speculative gamblers' funds I look at in Chapter 12), and that means the guarantee is of limited value. So to keep costs down and returns up, look for a global balanced fund with annual costs that are lower than the average 2.8 percent. There's more on guaranteed funds in Chapter 19.

Going global: A near-perfect investment?

If you had to invest money in a single fund for 100 years without ever moving it or looking at it, some kind of global balanced fund with low expenses would make sense.

In some ways, the dull old global balanced fund is the perfect mutual fund. It usually holds a little something from every major market, both bonds and stocks, and is about the closest thing the fund world offers to a one-size-fits-all solution — a fund you can buy before you head off to a monastery in Nepal.

A big risk attached to a global balanced fund, as with any foreign fund, is the possibility that Canada has a long-term economic boom while keeping inflation low. Our dollar would then climb (everyone loves winners, especially winners that maintain the buying power of their currency). A climbing loonie relative to foreign currencies will slash the value of your foreign holdings in Canadian-dollar terms, an unpleasant prospect for those who plan to retire in this country. That's why it's almost certainly a good idea to own Canadian assets, too.

A couple of world-beaters

Here are a couple of global balanced funds with respected managers and annual expenses near the group average. The global balanced fund has never really caught the imagination of Canadian investors, which means that there's only a fairly limited selection on the market. And, unfortunately, many of the good ones are sold through brokers and other advisers, so the cost to the investor is too high.

We've attached Dummies Approved icons to these funds because they're high-quality investments that are unlikely to lead you far astray. But bear in mind that any fund can go into a slump because the manager made a bad call. And buying a global balanced fund is always a compromise, because it's impossible to know exactly what sort of assets you'll end up owning or how precisely the manager produced his or her returns. A balanced fund is for investors who just want a quick, instant solution. Personally, I wouldn't buy one because I think they're too expensive — neither of these two Dummies Approved funds have low expenses, I'm afraid: Both ding unitholders for 2.5 percent or more annually. Note that you could reduce your risk considerably by buying both of these funds. They use very different investing styles, which means that when one is doing badly the other may be hot.

Run by renowned market analyst Bill Sterling, **CI International Balanced** thrived in the 1990s by loading up on technology stocks, especially in the United States. That gave it a sizzling average annual compound return of 17.3 percent in the five years ended December 31, 1999. The slump in tech stocks left the fund with a hair-raising loss of 13.5 percent annually in the two years ended June 2002, but the five-year annual return was still a respectable 3.2 percent. Be warned, though, that Sterling is free to make fairly large bets on particular countries and types of stock, which may increase the fund's price swings. As of mid-2002, his top holdings were still dominated by big U.S. companies. Don't risk all your money in this one. Incidentally, Sterling is a perceptive and entertaining writer, one of the few fund managers who can craft a cliché-free sentence. For a sample, go to www.cifunds.com and click on "Sterling's World Report" under "Resources."

Templeton Global Balanced is almost the complete opposite. It sticks mostly to the solid but dull stocks that management company Franklin Templeton Investments loves so much — while steering clear of frothy tech shares. That held its average annual return to only 10.4 percent in the second half of the 1990s. But the average annual loss in the two years ended June 2002 was only 2.9 percent. The five-year return was 2 percent, just ahead of the average global balanced fund.

Look at the portfolio of any sophisticated, wealthy investor and it'll almost certainly contain stocks all over the world plus bonds, with the safety cushion of a little cash. That's what a global balanced fund provides for the average person. It offers instant access to a professionally chosen mixture of investments that should produce a consistent return on their money while staying clear of market gambles. Nearly every major fund seller sells some sort of global balanced fund, and it's a simple matter of dumping your money in and forgetting about it.

Reviewing the Problems with Balanced Funds

There are problems with balanced funds, both Canadian and global. Their fees and expenses are far too lavish, which scythes into investors' already modest returns. Fund companies have come up with their usual bewildering variety of products and combinations of products, waving magic wands and muttering incantations that evoke the gods of portfolio theory and the "efficient frontier." It may all be true, but one thing's for sure, Stuart: you're paying for it. All balanced products are basically porridge. Because returns from their different investments are mixed together in a gooey mess, it's hard to judge exactly how well the manager did on which asset.

High fees and expenses

The costs and fees charged to balanced fund unitholders are just too high. Fund companies already run big equity and bond funds, paying the salaries and expenses of the people who manage them, and they usually get those people to help select the stuff in their balanced funds. How much extra work is involved in that? The bond manager basically just does the same job again with his or her portion of the balanced fund, and the equity manager does the same. Some fat geezer in a huge black robe and cone-shaped hat decides what the asset mix will be and you're away to the races. But the average Canadian balanced fund vacuums up 2.5 percent of its investors' money each year, almost as bad as the 2.6 percent charged by the average Canadian equity fund.

Remember that the long-term annual return from balanced funds may be only about 6 percent, or even less. The long term, incidentally, means the rest of our lives, as economists like to say (it's the only joke they know). So, say inflation and taxes combined take 4 percent out of your annual 6 percent — then your real return is down to around 2 percent. So, for a tax-paying account, most of your real return from a balanced fund like Royal Bank's giant may go into fund expenses and fees.

Bewildering brews of assets

Fund companies know that many of their customers just want simple solutions they can buy and never look at again. So they've come up with a bewildering array of balanced combinations in which you can buy their wares. See Chapter 21 on fund packages for more. Many of these arrangements, such as Mackenzie Financial Corp.'s popular "Star" products, have their own unit values, making them look very much like mutual funds themselves. By mid-2002, there were more than 900 Canadian and global balanced products of all types, counting different "classes" of fund units as separate funds. Mackenzie had 24 Canadian and global balanced products in its Star lineup alone. I wonder how many Star investors, or even their brokers, would have had problems identifying exactly which one they owned.

Difficulty judging fund manager performance

A big difficulty with balanced funds, or any kind of casserole that you buy from a fund company, is that it's usually hard to know just what the manager did right or wrong. He or she may have blown it in bonds, or struck out in stocks, but it's impossible to work out from the comfortable-looking (you hope) overall return number that the company publishes. Some fund companies provide a commentary that at least gives you a clue as to what went right and what exploded in the manager's shiny little face. For many customers that's fine, because they couldn't care less what went on inside the fund as long as the return is reasonably good. And that's a perfectly sensible approach to take if you don't have the time or interest to look further into mutual funds. But balanced funds are opaque and mysterious, violating one of the huge virtues of mutual funds — the ability to check on performance easily.

Because it's difficult to check where balanced funds' profits came from, it's harder for you to pick the right fund. In other words, there's often no clear answer to the crucial question: How much risk did the manager take? Here's an extreme example of two imaginary funds to help illustrate the point.

Let's say you're trying to choose between two balanced funds:

- ✔ First, the Tasmanian Devil Fund, which made an average 11 percent over the past ten years, enough to turn $10,000 into $28,394.

- ✔ And then, the Mellow Llama Fund, which made 9 percent a year. That turned $10,000 into $23,674, or almost $5,000 less.

What if the Devil Fund made its bigger profits by buying bonds and shares issued by risky little technology companies, whereas the Llama Fund owned shares and bonds from big and stable companies and governments? Most balanced fund investors would choose the second fund, because the danger of it crashing and losing, say, half of its value in a year — is so much less.

The Devil Fund, with its volatile but high-profit-potential stocks, may be suitable for an investor who doesn't need the money for years and can afford to take risks now. But it's not the right fund for an investor who may need the money at any time.

A Simple Plan for Picking the Right Canadian Balanced Fund

There's no point getting all worked up about this one. Like money market and bond funds, balanced funds resemble each other. They're run cautiously, remember, so you're unlikely to go far wrong.

There is one classic mistake that too many investors make, and it's one that has cost them millions of dollars: Never pick a balanced fund run by the people who also manage your stock fund. You're putting too many eggs in one basket. Naturally, the managers will tend to select the same shares for both funds, and if they get that wrong, then both of your funds will be poor performers.

Be careful with balanced funds that don't include just about every industry in their list of stock holdings. Consider the fate of investors in the enormous Trimark Select Balanced Fund, Canada's second-biggest balanced fund at the end of 1999. Trimark's stock pickers hit a rough patch in the late 1990s, as pretty well all managers do from time to time, and the balanced fund suffered too because it didn't have enough of the financial and tech stocks that were all the rage. The fund produced an annual compound return of 9.2 percent in the five years ended December 31, 1999, lagging the 11.4 percent generated by the average Canadian balanced fund. The type of conservative stocks that Trimark likes recovered eventually, giving the fund a strong two-year annual return of 2.5 percent as of June 2002 (remember that the average balanced fund lost money over the period). But the late-1990s slump wasn't pleasant for investors who also had money tied up in Trimark stock funds.

Relax: Picking a good-quality Canadian balanced fund is surprisingly easy. Easier, anyway, than getting a cranky, tired child into a snowsuit at 7 a.m. when you're suffering from a terrible hangover.

- ✔ Look for a wide asset mix to reduce the fund's risk of loss. Under the industry's agreed definition, balanced funds should have at least 25 percent of their portfolio anchored in cash or bonds. That's low: I'd look for at least one-third in guaranteed investments such as bonds, "short-term" securities, and cash.

- ✔ It's especially important to look for low expenses since returns are relatively modest with this type of fund. Try to choose a fund or funds with annual expenses lower than the average 2.5 percent for Canadian balanced funds.

Here are a few high-quality Canadian balanced funds. Because you should be obsessive about costs when buying this type of fund, I've limited the sample to funds with modest annual fees and expenses that are below or at least in line with the 2.5-percent average for the group. And I've also stuck to managers who've done a good job of throwing off steady returns for their unitholders. Remember, though, if there's an abrupt rise in inflation and/or interest rates, then even these funds will probably lose money. That's because the value of both their stock and bond portfolios will almost certainly go on the slide at the same time.

The **Royal Balanced** fund, a gigantic $6-billion-plus fund, is supposed to be a "one-decision" fund that investors can simply buy and forget, which makes it a classic balanced fund. The expenses are too high for such a big fund, at 2.4 percent — but the fund has kept up with its rivals. Its average annual return over the ten years ended June 2002 was 7.8 percent, only just short of the 7.9-percent average for Canadian balanced funds. Don't expect fireworks, but rest assured that the Royal Bank is very motivated to keep the fund's huge army of unitholders happy — by making sure that the returns stay respectable.

Launched in mid-1998, **TD Balanced Index Fund** is simply an assembly of Toronto-Dominion Bank's "index funds," which are low-cost funds that attempt to give investors a return in line with the entire stock or bond market. This one will never top the charts, and the managers could get the mix of Canadian and international stocks and bonds wrong, but low expenses of only 1.2 percent mean that it's likely to remorselessly overtake and leave most of its rivals behind as the years pass. There's more on index funds in Chapter 15.

The **Scotia Canadian Balanced** fund, a Scotiabank offering, is another solid balanced fund with nice low annual expenses of only 1.7 percent. This is the sort of cautious dull mixture of bonds and stocks that your grandfather might have bought — and he was no fool.

Looking at "Income" Balanced Funds

Throughout my childhood, inflation was a problem. People would look up at the skies during the 1970s, shrug their polyester-clad shoulders, and cluck about rising prices as though they were a plague of locusts. But as inflation and interest rates tumbled in the 1990s, older people who were trying to live off their savings made an unpleasant discovery. At least rising prices also produced high interest rates. As inflation slipped toward 2 percent, the rates seniors got on their GICs and other accounts dropped from 8 percent at the outset of the decade to below 5 percent by 1998. That's one of the drawbacks of low inflation: It leaves those who live on a fixed income high and dry.

So the mutual fund industry benefited from a huge invasion of "GIC refugees" in the mid-1990s. And the companies' little elves soon tried to figure out a way to deliver one of the things that these people held dear: a nice regular cheque in the mail. The problem was that mutual funds aren't really designed for producing a predictable spinoff of cash — or at least enough cash to satisfy investors, especially after annual expenses of up to 2 percent are taken out to pay the managers and provide forage for brokers. It was hard to find top-quality bonds or shares that had a high enough yield to satisfy everyone. All the good stuff had been driven up to such high prices by other investors hungry for a stream of cash.

A fund made of everything and the kitchen sink

Thus was born the *"income" balanced fund*, an odd hybrid that's usually designed not only to throw off plenty of interest and dividends, but also to gain or at least hold its value over the long term. For example, an income balanced fund might try to generate monthly payments of $50, or $600 a year, for an investor who held $10,000 worth of the fund. That's a yield of 6 percent annually, but some funds chase even higher rates of up to 9 or 10 percent. To produce this income while also holding its value in the face of inflation, the fund buys a mixture of bonds, shares, and other sorts of investments that pay out cash. The new fund managers were turned loose like hungry bears to grab and eat anything in the world — animal, vegetable, or mineral — that threw off a decent stream of interest or dividend payments. The shortage of good-quality investments producing a decent yield became so acute that many of these managers have been obliged to move down the food chain. They've had to buy *income trusts* as well as *real estate trusts* and similar funds that invest in other stuff. These trusts are sort of like mutual funds themselves, but they hold a narrow collection of properties, such as a few power stations, gas wells, or other relatively dull and predictable businesses. A whole new category of funds, Canadian income trusts, has sprung up to hold income trusts and pay the cash they produce to unitholders. I deal with them in Chapter 16, where I talk about dividend funds.

Return of capital funds: The fund industry's latest high-wire act

One of the industry's newest marketing brainwaves is funds that use *return of capital* — they keep up a high level of monthly payments by, when necessary, dipping into the assets of the fund and in essence paying unitholders' own money back to them.

Funds that buy funds: Trapped in a hall of mirrors?

Always be wary when you see a fund put money into other funds or investment vehicles, even if the stuff the fund is buying has a fancy name like *closed-end fund, income trust, royalty trust, real estate investment trust,* or *partnership.* The problem is that there are just too many mouths to feed in this whole deal for you to end up with much. Not only does your fund have its own set of guys in suits raking off their take, but the other fund has the same, and they also expect their fees. And don't kid yourself, Katerina: Those charges come out of your hide one way or another.

After some spectacular crash-and-burn abuses in the 1970s, funds aren't allowed to go investing in each other willy-nilly, like iguanas in a scaly, peeling pile in the sun. Otherwise, I might start the Aardvark Fund with a 5-percent management fee and then invest all of its assets in another fund my brother runs, the Boar Fund, which also has a 5-percent fee. That fund would then just invest in the Caterpillar Fund, run by our dad, with another 5-percent fee, and so on until we were skimming off all of the money and spending it on surgical equipment for experiments back at our weird, dark compound. Regulators have learned to put strict rules in place to prevent that sort of thing. (No, not the experiments — we're still doing those. Drop by sometime.) The law now prevents such pyramiding of fund fees, so the combinations of funds that you see touted by banks and other companies are usually designed to avoid it.

It's too early to say how these return of capital funds will work out, but one big fund that uses return of capital, the hugely popular Clarington Canadian Income Fund, found it tough to maintain high monthly payments in a rocky stock market.

The fund was launched by newcomer ClaringtonFunds Inc. in 1996 and by mid-2002 its assets had ballooned to $1.4 billion. For its first five years, the fund achieved its goal of keeping the net asset value steady in the range of $9 or $10 while also maintaining a steady 8-cent monthly payout to unitholders. (The fund has been so successful that Royal Bank launched a copycat in April 2002, Royal Tax Managed Return Fund.) But in August of 2002, with the unit value down to less than $8.50, Clarington cut the monthly payout to 6 cents (on a temporary basis, the company hoped). Clarington gave unitholders more than two months' notice of the reduction, and it warned investors all along that a reduction in the payout rate might be necessary if the net asset value came under pressure.

Be careful when reporting the distributions from this type of fund at tax time — you shouldn't pay tax on the return of the capital portion of the distribution, because you were just getting your own money paid out to you. However, if you eventually sell your units and have to report a capital gain for tax purposes, you have to essentially add those return of capital payouts to the trading profit you report (that's because they're assumed to have reduced the purchase cost of the units). Be sure to get advice from your fund salesperson or the fund company itself. Chapter 24 deals with the taxation of mutual funds. Some companies, such as Fidelity Investments Canada Ltd., have even started selling "T series" versions of their existing, ordinary funds — the T versions pay out a stream of cash to investors who want regular income but allow them to defer paying tax because some or all of the income is classified as return of capital.

A better way to keep cash rolling in

As we've seen, funds such as income balanced funds that use return of capital to keep up their payments offer tax advantages. But if you ask me (and I guess you are!), I think these funds suffer from unnecessary complexity. Critics even call them "phantom yield" funds because some or even most of the stream of payments is just your own money coming back to you. If you need a stream of income from your mutual fund portfolio, a simpler approach is to just start a systematic withdrawal program at your bank or fund company under which the company cashes in a set dollar amount of your funds every month or three months and then mails you a cheque. It may be less tax-efficient, but it won't make your eyes glaze over.

Asset Allocation Funds: Pay Me to Lose Your Money

Asset allocation funds are the unruly younger brothers of balanced funds — given the freedom to raise hell by dumping all of their bonds or stocks, and to chase hot returns with lopsided portfolios. These are funds that move between different types of investments and take bigger risks than regular balanced funds, all in an attempt to earn fatter returns. For example, a fund of this type may sell nearly all of its bonds and seek big profits with a portfolio that's made up almost entirely of shares. Or it might even move heavily into a volatile area of the stock market such as technology stocks. The idea is that the manager is smart and lucky enough to anticipate big swings in the prices of financial assets — history shows, though, that very few people can pull off that trick consistently.

All flash and no pan: Looking at asset allocation returns and management styles

The average Canadian tactical asset allocation fund posted an annual return of only 9 percent in the 1990s. That was worse than the 9.4-percent return from the average balanced fund, supposedly a sedate compromise between low risk and steady appreciation. As of June 2002, the returns from tactical funds were still unimpressive, at 7.3 percent annually over ten years compared with 7.9 percent for balanced funds. (*Tactical*, by the way, simply means that the fund makes short-term bets on moves in the different asset classes every few months, while *strategic* usually means long-term decisions that a manager sticks to for a year or more.) This group has a few stars that have managed to consistently generate returns in the top half of the pack, including the $6-billion Fidelity Canadian Asset Allocation Fund. It posted an incredible average annual return of 18.5 percent in the second half of the 1990s, and as of June 2002 the five-year average annual return was still a relatively strong 7 percent. But this type of fund basically represents an opportunity to watch someone mess around with your money. That's fine if you trust the company and the warty old wizard or witch mixing up the ingredients in the cauldron, but remember that the less balanced a portfolio, the greater the exposure to loss if the main asset class goes into a slump.

Who is running this crazy show?

Much as I'd love to portray asset allocation fund managers as wild blonde Finnish women dressed in leather and thundering down the highway of life on bucking portfolios full of junk bonds and Internet stocks, in reality they're pretty similar to balanced fund managers. Grey folk in glasses, that is. A major fund seller is unlikely to let an asset allocation fund slide off the road completely because the manager took crazy bets. In mid-2002, most Canadian tactical asset allocation funds had pretty much the same mix of investments as balanced funds, at around 55 percent stocks and the rest in cash or bonds — not exactly a night of passion beside a cooling Harley.

The bottom line on asset allocation funds: Put your money in one if you find regular balanced funds too boring, but get ready to lose if the manager gets it wrong.

Chapter 14

Bond Funds: Boring Can Be Sexy Too

*N*ow, don't get me wrong. My gambling nature recoils at the thought of buying a bond or bond fund — but I don't like getting up in the morning much, either. Buying a *bond* means you're lending money to the government or company that issued the thing. The word "bond" means promise, indicating the borrowers have given their word that they'll be around to pay interest and refund the loan. All you're really entitled to get back are the periodic interest payments plus the return of all your money when the debt comes due. Dull, huh? Bond funds simply hold a bunch of these loans, collecting the interest cheques and cashing in the bonds when they mature. That means bond funds tend to plod along with modest returns, while stocks fly and crash from year to year. Equity (or stock market) funds, with their promise of apparently limitless growth, just seem so much more exciting. But remember that bonds along with stocks represent the two main financial assets you can invest in for the long term — while a little bit of cash on the side is an essential safety valve for nearly any portfolio. In this chapter I explain why you should own at least one bond fund, show you how to pick a good one, and help you work out how much you need to invest in bonds.

A Tasty Tidbit about Bond Buying

Almost any sophisticated investor's holdings should include a good leavening of bonds, because betting the whole wad on shares is just too crazy. That's because it bares your entire savings to nasty losses if the stock market turns down. I remember the smooth-as-silk boss of the giant brokerage that was involved in divorce proceedings in the late 1990s. *Frank,* the satirical magazine, stuck its warty nose into the case and listed some of his lavish assets. I was amazed at how the guy seemed to have an awful lot of his money in dull old guaranteed investment certificates and similar bond-type stuff. Here's a chap who lived and breathed investments. A multi-millionaire who knew more about stocks and their habits than practically anyone else in Canada, and he chose to leave lots of his money in bonds in the middle of a raging bull market. Go ahead and ignore me, but take a tip from him.

Some fund salespeople and diehard stock market players used to strut and boast that "I've never owned a bond." In mid-2002, with world stock markets looking set for their third straight year of losses, those former Rambos were hard to raise on the phone.

Some Great Reasons to Choose Bonds

Here's why you must own some bonds or bond funds: Lending your money short-term, by popping it into a bank deposit or account, doesn't pay you enough. Okay, so you can invest most of your money in the stock market, but that's a recipe for losing most of your pile if the market goes into a huge dive. So we all should leave a portion on long-term loan to big, secure governments and companies. And the way to do that is to buy their bonds, which are essentially certificates representing interest-paying loans to the corporations or governments that issued the bonds.

Declining interest rates, a result of falling inflation, have put a tiger in the tank of bond funds for more than a decade. The average Canadian bond fund produced an annual compound return of 8.5 percent in the 1990s, not far short of the 9.6-percent return from Canadian equity funds. And stocks, remember, are supposed to perform much better than bonds to compensate for their extra risk. As of mid-2002, the ten-year average annual return from bond funds had slipped to 7 percent — but that was mostly because the record no longer included 1991, when the average bond fund shot up almost 20 percent as inflation dropped sharply (bond buyers hate inflation because it erodes the value of the money they'll get back years hence when their bonds mature). That 7 percent didn't look too shabby when compared with the 9.3-percent average return from ever-risky Canadian equity funds. And in the scary two years ended June 2002, bonds came shining through: The average bond fund made 5.5 percent annually in the period, while the average Canadian stock fund lost 5 percent per year.

But bonds will have trouble doing as well in coming years. Inflation was less than 3 percent in mid-2002, meaning that it didn't have much more room to drop (unless we slide into scary deflation). That limited the scope for falling interest rates and higher bond prices. And if inflation and rates rise, then bond prices will drop, dragging down bond funds.

Get some sleep with bonds

Psychologically, having your entire savings in stocks is just too frightening for most normal people. The Standard & Poor's/Toronto Stock Exchange composite index dropped by one-fifth, or 20 percent, during one month (August 1998) as the economies of Russia and Asia threatened to go down the plughole. From August 2000 to August 2001, the index fell by more than 33 percent. Watching your life savings shrink at that speed would be no fun at all. Don't believe me? You will when you're sitting bolt upright at 4 a.m. reflecting on the minus signs next to those equity funds you thought couldn't miss "over the long term."

What goes up must come down, even the market

Sure, equities have always bounced back in the past. But stocks can go into a slump for years, just as they did in the inflation-and-recession-prone 1970s. From February 1966 to August 1982, a stretch of 16 long years, the Dow Jones Industrial Average of blue-chip U.S. stocks fell 22 percent in price.

Yes, America's blue-chip companies paid regular dividends during the period, reducing investors' losses. But it was still a horrible time to be in the market, a depressing and endless era of new lows.

Remember Japan and the way its market hit a euphoric peak in 1989 (just as technology and communication stocks all over the world did in 2000)? More than a decade later, the Japanese market was still down from its 1989 high.

Security if you hit a rough patch

You might lose your job, have legal troubles, or run into some disaster right in the middle of a periodic stock market slump. It would be ugly to be forced to tap into your serious money just after it's been carved up by a stock sell-off. So own some bonds. They serve as a giant, reassuring outrigger for your canoe, producing steady returns while holding their value.

Beware of falling prices

Finally, and perhaps most scary of all, companies and individuals all over the world are getting smarter and more efficient all the time. Why is that a problem? It means they're producing goods and services at ever-lower prices. Inflation in most wealthy countries has dropped to less than 3 percent from double figures in the 1980s, and it could keep right on falling until we're in an era of actual *falling prices*. If that happens, bonds and cash are likely to hold their value or even rise in price because the value of money will be rising (*inflation*, the opposite scenario, simply means that money is losing its purchasing power). In other words, deflation is a weird *Through the Looking Glass* world in which cash under the mattress becomes a solid investment that produces a real return.

Does a world of falling prices sound incredible? It's been happening all around us for years in computers, where prices drop and processing power increases every few months. Natural resource prices were in a slump for most of the 1990s as Russia and other poor countries flooded the market in a desperate bid to get U.S. dollars. Granted, there hasn't been an economy-wide slump in prices since the Depression of the 1930s, so nobody knows what it would be like — or what would happen to equity markets. But falling prices squeeze corporate profit margins like a vice, and declining profits are rat poison for stocks. From September 1929 to July 1932, as the Depression got going, the Dow fell by almost 90 percent. I wish that were a typing error, but it's not. The Dow dropped to 41 from 381. So own some bonds.

How Much Do I Need in Bonds?

Take the old rule — that your weighting in cash and bonds should equal your age — as a starting point. Sure, leaving a big 40 percent of one's savings in such dull fixed-income stuff will seem pathetically craven to all you racy 40-year-olds out there. So bring it down to 30 percent, or even 25 percent if you insist. But any lower than that and the volatility of your portfolio — a fancy word for the yearly up-and-down changes in the market value of your holdings — starts going off the scale. In other words, if you own only stocks, you're betting a lot of your wealth on swings in just one asset. Now, all of this will probably fall on deaf ears for people like me who weren't playing the market in the grim days and blacker months and years of the 1970s. We haven't lived through a grinding decade-long bear market in stocks, so we're hazy on the value of a bond and we think that stocks will always pull us through. But the risk of a long-term slump in equities means that 40 percent in bonds, or a bit less, is probably about right for a 40-year-old. At 50, we should probably have half of our dough in cash and bonds. And in our sixties, it probably should go toward two-thirds. In our thirties it's reasonable to have one-third or less in fixed income, and in our twenties it's probably safe to have one-fifth. So begin with the age rule and then take the cash-plus-bonds weighting up or down depending on your personality.

If you already have or will have another source of income, such as a company pension fund, then you can afford to be more aggressive with your independent RRSP money because it doesn't represent your only hope. In other words, own more stocks.

Always remember that bonds are a guaranteed source of income, a mighty comforting port in the gale if equity markets collapse. If you're a self-employed professional and you definitely have to generate your entire retirement income from your RRSPs and other savings, then the asset mix in your portfolio is of life or death importance for you. You almost certainly already have an accountant helping with your taxes, so get her or him to help you choose the amount of bonds in your portfolio or refer you to another fee-charging professional who's knowledgeable about financial planning (see Chapter 8).

Just about any commission-paid broker or financial planner will have an off-the-shelf system or software package to help you choose the amount of bonds to hold. Remember, as always, that the results are only as valid as the assumptions the program makes about inflation, interest rates, and the economy. Professional investors regularly get those conditions wrong, so there's no reason why salespeople or their systems should do any better. But just about everybody will tell you to put a portion of your savings into a bond fund. Even the aggressive Canadian Maximum Long-Term Growth package in Mackenzie Financial Corp.'s Star series (Star is a bunch of pre-mixed cocktails

Do I need all this boring bonds-versus-stocks stuff?

Financial planning and structuring a portfolio are not clear-cut techniques that you can just learn and use. Folks in the investment game make the whole thing even more confusing. They like to conjure up arcane lore and mutter magic spells as they unveil their latest gizmo. Salespeople must have something to sell, after all. But investment theories can't be proved or disproved, in part because they depend on the future. And the future is always unknowable. So investment "research" is more like folk legend or articles of faith.

That means there's no "right" proportion of your wealth to have in bonds — if stocks surge, then almost any amount will seem too much because you'll miss out on returns. But when stocks sink, you'll get a toasty warm feeling from your bonds. If inflation returns, which it easily might, then bonds and cash assets will steadily lose their real value. But if the opposite happens, and deflation hits, bonds may be about the only things that go up in price because money will steadily gain value. Once again, just remember to buy a bit of every asset class and buy quality, and you'll be fine.

of Mackenzie funds) had 20 percent of its assets in fixed-income investments in mid-2002. And that's supposed to be a volatile mixture for somebody who's sure they won't need the money for a long time — for example, investors in their thirties without much left to pay on their home.

Picking a Good Bond Fund in Thirty Seconds

Selecting a superior bond fund boils down to two simple rules. It should hold plenty of high-quality long-term bonds, and it must have low expenses. You can find funds with low expenses, and check their holdings, at www.globefund.com — the *Globe and Mail*'s mutual fund Web site.

Here's more good news: You should own at least two Canadian and two global stock funds, because any equity manager can go into a slump for years. But you'll almost certainly do fine with just one bond fund, as long as it has low annual costs and is full of quality bonds. No big fund seller would allow its managers to make weird bets with a mainstream bond fund, such as buying 20-year paper issued by a bankrupt tin mine. The backlash from investors, the media, and possibly even regulators would be too great.

Insist on affordability

Demand modest annual expenses — less than 1 percent annually — with any bond fund. The returns from this asset class are relatively low, and likely to get lower in coming years because bonds are already trading at fat prices. So fund costs and fees must be kept down for the investor to be left with anything at all after taxes and inflation.

The average Canadian bond fund hits its unitholders for a criminal 1.8 percent annually, and there are plenty of funds in the group that grab 2 percent or more. That's ridiculous and here's why. In mid-2002, ten-year Canadian government bonds were offering a tiny annual yield of just over 5 percent to investors who bought them and held them to maturity. Now, bond managers can sometimes increase returns by a few tenths of 1 percent by fancy trading, but unless interest rates drop rapidly over the next few years, it looks very much as though 5 percent or so is all that many bond portfolios are likely to make annually. Take a 2-percent expense ratio out of that, and you're left with only 3 percent. After inflation and taxes, in other words, bond fund unitholders could easily end up losing money in real terms.

How to lose money in bonds

In 1999, Canadian bond funds produced a modest average loss of 2.5 percent — how could they lose money when they held nothing but a bunch of loans to the government and blue-chip corporations? The reason is that bond funds, like other funds, are obliged to calculate a value for their portfolio each business day at its current market worth. That's so investors can buy and sell units in the fund at a realistic price.

Interest rates increased sharply in 1999, mainly because the U.S. Federal Reserve was worried about inflation, and rising interest rates always reduce the market value of bonds that are out in the hands of investors. Bond funds were thus obliged to mark down the value of their holdings accordingly. A bond falls in value when interest rates rise because investors are willing to pay less for it. To take a simple example, say you hold an 8-percent bond but interest rates increase so that other comparable investments, with the same term to maturity, are yielding 9 percent. If you try to sell your old 8-percent bond, you'll have to cut the price to get anyone interested. For example, you might have to mark it down to 95 cents per $1 of face value (bonds always mature at face value or "par," which is 100 cents on the dollar). When you offer the bond at 5 percent off, the buyer of your cut-price bond will get the regular 8-percent interest payment but they'll also make an extra kick because they've bought it at the 5-percent discount. When the bond matures at its full face value of $1 per $1 face value, that'll be enough to bring its annual yield up to 9 percent.

The exact opposite happens when interest rates fall, as they've been doing pretty well without a break since the early 1980s. If rates in the market drop to 7 percent, then your 8-percent bond becomes a hotcake and investors will be willing to buy it from you at a premium.

Don't worry about all that stuff if you don't want to; however, try to remember this: Longer-term bonds usually pay you more interest but they also drop the most when interest rates go up and they gain in price more quickly when interest rates decline.

Interest rates fall when inflation drops because lenders become confident that their money won't lose its value too fast while it's in the hands of the borrowers. So they're prepared to accept lower interest rates. About the only thing that's likely to send bond prices sharply higher in coming years, giving bond funds more good times, will be an era of falling prices or at least growing confidence among investors that inflation is dead for the foreseeable future. In that case, bond buyers are likely to bid bonds up even higher. The bottom line, though, is that predicting changes in interest rates is a futile exercise akin to forecasting the weather. Just buy a good bond fund and view it as an insurance policy for your entire savings.

To recap:

✔ Rising inflation makes bondholders and other lenders very, very afraid because they become petrified of seeing the real value of their money wither away. So they demand higher interest rates and bond yields. That means they refuse to buy bonds without getting big discounts, so bond prices fall and you'll make less money on your bond funds.

✔ Lower inflation makes bond buyers and other lenders feel more comfortable about tying their money up for years, so they'll accept lower interest rates and bond yields. Lower rates and yields mean higher bond prices, which means your bond funds make extra profits.

So, in general, look only at bond funds with annual expenses of 1 percent or less. The funds with low expenses will almost all turn out to be no-load products that you buy directly from a bank or direct-selling fund company. That's because fund companies that sell through brokers, financial planners, and other advisers have to add on extra charges in order to have something left over to pay the salespeople; expect to pay an extra 0.75 percent annually on most broker-sold bond funds.

Look for quality in provincial and federal bonds

Buy a fund with plenty of high-quality long-term federal government and provincial bonds. A few super-blue-chip company bonds are okay, but remember that with business changing at the speed of Bill Gates's rubbery mind, today's corporate grande-dame could be tomorrow's bag lady. So go easy on the IBMs. If you're a bit nervous that inflation might come back, you want a middle-of-the road solution when it comes to bonds. So just get a bond fund that pretty well matches the SCM Universe Bond Total Return Index, an imaginary basket of typical high-quality bonds, calculated by huge stockbroker Scotia Capital Markets. The SCM Universe pretty well represents the entire Canadian bond market.

Why should you look for long-term bonds? If you have a home mortgage, you probably know that the best thing for you to do as a borrower in recent years has been to keep on renewing your mortgage for short terms at low rates instead of "locking in" for a longer term at a higher rate. But for lenders, such as buyers of a bond fund, the opposite strategy has been better. Lending long, by buying long-term bonds with ten or more years to run before they mature, has been the most lucrative approach because short-term interest rates kept dropping. Now the next ten years may be different, but you should still just buy a plain bond fund that's got plenty of long-term Canadian government bonds.

For the serious money portion of your portfolio, avoid risky "high-yield" bond funds or sleepwalking "short-term" bonds (more on those later in this chapter). The rule you apply should be this: Bet long-term as a lender because that's where the yield is. There's an old saying in the bond market: *Be long or be wrong.* If you want a compromise, buy a plain-vanilla bond fund whose average term to maturity is close to the SCM Universe Bond Total Return Index, which includes both short- and long-term bonds. Many fund companies and bond investors use the SCM Index as the benchmark with which they compare the performance and holdings of their funds.

Index Funds and Bonds: A Marriage Made in Heaven

A bond fund should be like a holiday in upstate New York. Cheap and dull. So index funds with their low expenses and dreary habit of tracking the whole market are just the ticket. In the United States, index bond funds that simply match the market are by far the most common method of investing in bonds. Index funds, you'll recall, are funds that match a well-known market benchmark. In Canada, index bond funds usually track our old friend, the SCM Index. In the United States, index fund giant Vanguard sells funds whose annual expenses go down as low as 0.2 percent — that's only one-fifth of a percent. Canadian bond funds charge an average 1.8 percent — nine times as much as the Vanguard funds. You'll have to go to the hassle of opening an account from a U.S. address or using a U.S. discount broker to buy Vanguard's funds, because they won't sell direct to people up here. Go to their excellent Web site at www.vanguard.com for more information. Good Canadian bond index funds are also easy to buy from banks. They carry expenses of less than 1 percent, making them reasonable value compared with their "actively managed" rivals, but they're still expensive compared with Vanguard's funds.

Here's a way for a retail investor to add bonds to his or her portfolio at very low cost. Just buy five-year or ten-year bond "iUnits" — so-called "exchange traded funds" (ETFs) that trade on the Toronto Stock Exchange like a share. The five-year version is known as an "iG5" and trades under the symbol XGV. It does nothing but hold a government of Canada five-year bond, replacing it when the term to maturity gets too short, in an effort to give holders the same return as they'd get from actually owning the bond. The ten-year version, which is called "iG10" and trades under the symbol XGX, does the same for ten-year bonds. Sponsored by giant international money manager Barclays Global Investors, these bond ETFs come with rock-bottom annual costs of 0.25 percent — that's just one-quarter of 1 percent. There's more on exchange-traded funds in Chapter 5; also check out the Barclays Web site at www.iunits.com.

Three Beautiful Bond Funds

Here are three bond funds with high-quality holdings and relatively low expenses. All are sold with no sales commission directly to the public or through discount brokers.

Altamira Bond Fund carries a hefty annual expense ratio of 1.5 percent, although that's lower than the average bond fund. It posted an excellent average annual return of 9.5 percent in the ten years ended June 2002, blowing away the 7-percent return from the average bond fund because of its strategy of buying lucrative but risky long-term bonds. "Long" bonds make you the most, remember, when inflation and interest rates are low. But they and the funds that hold them also fall the fastest when inflation or rates rise. This is a fund for investors who think inflation isn't a big threat.

Run by Phillips Hager & North Investment Management of Vancouver and Toronto, the **PH&N Bond Fund** is another promising pick: low annual expenses of 0.6 percent and a mixture of government and top-quality corporate bonds. The only drawback is that you and members of your household have to invest a total of $25,000 with the company in a combination of its funds.

A middle-of-the road selection, **TD Canadian Bond Index Fund** tracks the entire bond market. Its expenses are just 0.9 percent a year.

Long Bonds: Grabbing the Lion by the Tail

Unfortunately, there are no clear rules forcing managers to disclose to the public how long-term their bond portfolios are, but many companies voluntarily compare their holdings to the SCM Universe Index. Bond managers revel in bizarre formulas, and one of their favourites is "duration," which measures how much a bond or portfolio of bonds will drop when interest rates rise. A duration of six years and higher is generally aggressive, while five and down is conservative. Aggressive bond managers, you'll recall, are betting that interest rates will fall or at least stay stable. So if you're really worried that inflation will come back, seek out a manager who holds lots of short bonds.

Short-term bonds, those with five or fewer years to run, are less vulnerable to rises in interest rates and inflation. Why? Because the time they have left is so brief that investors don't mind tying their money up in them. An instrument with 30 years left to run on it looks far worse when rates rise.

Managers of bond funds, like their flashier stock-picking colleagues, love to dress up their rather monotonous jobs with fancy-sounding strategies and jargon. They hang pathetic decorations in their dim offices and buy cheap grey cakes that would break your heart if you only saw them. But running a bond fund basically involves deciding how much risk you're going to take and then buying the bonds that suit that strategy. It's a bit like those stolen-car races you used to do when you were a kid, the ones that involve going round and round a pile of bricks. The braver you are, the closer in you go and the better time you get. In other words, bond managers buy as many long-dated bonds as they dare. Investors who can't handle that kind of risk should turn to the next type of fund, which concentrates on short-term bonds with fewer than five years to run before they retire. (Wish I were quitting in five years.)

Playing It Safe with Mortgage Funds and Short-Term Bond Funds

These are the funds to buy with money you'd like to have cruise along, earning modest but steady returns of about 5 percent (but maybe less if inflation stays low) and not exposed to too much risk. It's the sort of fund a church might buy with the money being saved up for a new roof. Nice and stable (the fund, not the old roof, oh dear, no) but flexible and offering higher returns than a money market fund at the cost of slightly more risk. Money market funds, the safest type of all, are an excellent place to hold the cash portion of your savings. Usually they hold nothing but very short-term loans to the government and big companies. There's more about them in Chapter 17.

In the ten years to mid-2002, mortgage funds produced an average annual return of 6.3 percent, while short-term bond funds delivered an average 5.5 percent, beating the average 4.1-percent return from money market funds. All three fund categories are very similar, however, loading up on short-term, high-quality bonds and other debt. But mortgage and short-term bond funds are true mutual funds in the sense that their units can drop below a fixed price, meaning that you can lose money. Money market funds are more like a form of savings account than a real fund because they're pretty well eternally held at their $10 unit price. Special laws governing them have to be written by young fellows in Toronto who bray over barbecues and tasteless beer in the summer.

Your return from a money market fund comes only in the form of cash or extra units, whereas short-term bond funds or mortgage funds both pay out distributions and mark their units up in value when, you guessed it, interest rates fall, and they mark them down when rates rise.

In reality, though, all these funds are pretty darn stable. There's no record since the late 1980s of the average mortgage fund ever losing money over a full calendar year, but short-term bond funds slipped an average 1.6 percent back in 1994 after interest rates rose sharply. However, that was far gentler than the 5.4-percent loss posted by the average bond fund. The main differences between the fund types are:

> ✔ **Short-term bond funds are almost entirely invested in government bonds with fewer than five years left before maturity.** So there's less risk of having your money tied up during an invasion by Attila and all his Huns. Attila, as you know, has never made clear his attitude toward a technocratic and independent central bank. Corporate bonds may show up in these funds, but they should be from big-brother companies that you've heard of, like Bell Canada. The main holdings should all be from the federal government and provinces. But not too much from smaller

provinces — they're great places but they tend to have lower credit ratings. Not that there's much risk of default, but in the bond market perception is everything. A lower credit rating becomes a leaden factor in itself, dragging a bond down to lower prices.

✔ **Mortgage funds are even more stable than short-term bond funds, so they fit in just next to money market funds.** They hold huge quantities of mortgages that have been packaged by math nerds working at a bank in downtown Toronto, who then also calculate a fee to help keep the bank in the comfortable style to which it's accustomed. Still, dull old mortgage funds aren't a huge profit centre for the banks when the costs are all included, so you won't see many ads for them. The funds are bought by hordes of investors who like the stable return, whether they take the distributions in cash or reinvest them in more units. The disadvantage of mortgage funds is that you lose the simplicity of bond funds. Funds may not be able to find mortgages to buy at decent yields, but bonds are always for sale.

Recommended Short-Term Bond Funds

Here are two short-term bond funds and two mortgage funds that offer low expenses and good track records:

Because bonds are perfectly suited to index funds, one of the best ways to invest in short-term bonds is to buy the **CIBC Canadian Short-Term Bond Index**. It has annual expenses of only 1 percent.

The **Fidelity Canadian Short-Term Bond**, sold through brokers and planners, has reasonable annual expenses of 1.3 percent, compared with 1.6 percent for the average Canadian short-term bond fund. Its big holdings in mid-2002 were a mixture of short-term loans to government agencies and provincial governments. That increases the income earned by the fund because provinces have to pay a slightly higher rate on their borrowing than the federal government.

Formerly First Canadian Mortgage fund, **BMO Mortgage Fund** is a famous fund that has been going since 1974, steadily churning out income for its unitholders all the way. Its annual expenses are only about 1.5 percent, compared with 1.8 percent for the average mortgage fund.

Sold by the Canadian arm of global banking giant HSBC, **HSBC Mortgage Fund** has a modest annual expense ratio of 1.6 percent.

High-Yield Bond Funds: Naked Bungee-Jumping

For students of euphemism — the delicate art of sugar-coating the disgusting — war is a delight. One European politician during the 1999 Kosovo conflict proclaimed that the Serb troops were getting "treatment" from NATO's jets. The Gulf War was great too: To "successfully engage" usually involved incinerating people.

But the best place of all to find euphemisms is in the world of investing, where stocks are never overpriced but "fully valued." Companies never have crushing debt loads, but they might be "leveraged." And boring old businesses like food or steel, where it's virtually impossible to increase your profits quickly and sustainably, are "mature."

For junk junkies

Then there's the world of bonds issued by less-than-blue-chip companies in unstable industries such as media or minerals. Brokers and investment managers like to call such risky paper "high yield," because buyers demand fat interest rates before they'll touch it with a kilometre-long pole. "High yield" sounds nice and healthy, doesn't it? Sort of like it's full of fibre, dried fruit, and tasty bits of soy. But American investors have long used the correct term for such concoctions: "junk." Perhaps some bitter type in a Brioni suit at Goldman Sachs came up with the word at 6:30 one morning while struggling with a vicious bout of cocaine withdrawal.

In other words, in the bond market you get what you pay for, and to achieve more yield you have to go down the quality scale. That involves buying riskier bonds from smaller companies, obscure stuff that's often hard to sell at any price if the bond market turns down sharply. For example, during the global financial panic in the summer of 1998, bonds from even the biggest global corporations became difficult to trade as investors fled to the safety of government securities. And as for finding buyers for your junk bonds: well, it was like selling lemon juice to hummingbirds.

In the U.S., hundreds of billions of dollars have been invested in mutual funds that hold junk bonds, with generally good results and attractive returns. But in the U.S. there are huge numbers of junk bonds to buy, making it easy to build diversified funds full of the things. And a diversified fund, holding dozens of junk bonds from different issuers, spreads the risk of disastrous defaults in any one industry.

In Canada, publicly traded junk bonds are far rarer because our cautious pension funds and other investors usually insist on a high credit rating. In the past, riskier borrowers have been forced to sell their junk south of the border. A few mutual fund companies, though, have launched Canadian and foreign junk funds in recent years.

The record of the Canadian high-yield funds is too short to predict how well they'll do over the long term. But lately junk bonds have shown their usual tendency to slip in price when speculative shares fall and investors get nervous. Over the five years to June 2002, the return from the average high-yield bond fund was just 1.1 percent annually, lagging the 5-percent return from regular bond funds.

Junk bond funds have a couple of major strikes against them:

- ✔ First, their expenses average 2.1 percent annually compared with 1.8 percent for normal bond funds and 1 percent or less for bond index funds.

- ✔ And they're also vulnerable in times of investor paranoia and economic jitters, when just about everyone seeks out government bonds and shares in big, relatively safe companies — a panicky rush for the exits known as a "flight to quality." When stock markets fall, junk bonds tend to do the same.

In other words, corporate and junk bonds have a habit of suffering just like stocks when recession threatens — unlike government bonds, which tend to go *up* because anxious investors reckon the government guarantee means they'll always get their money back. After all, bad economic times increase the pressure on small or debt-laden companies, making it more likely that they'll be forced to renege on their debts, including the hand-knit cozy junk bonds they issued.

Some funds in the junk group also hold safe-as-houses government bonds, but they're included in the high-yields because they're also free to juice their yields by grabbing riskier stuff as well.

Deciding whether the bigger potential returns from high-yield funds compensate for the extra risk is up to you. But even the most fervent advocates of junk probably wouldn't advise you to risk all of your bond money in high-yield debt. And your portfolio will do just fine if you shop elsewhere and simply stick to bond funds that hold only top-quality government and corporate bonds. After all, your stocks are risky enough, so why hold a bunch of dangerous bonds as well?

Buying Bonds Outside Canada

I'd love to tell you that your Canadian bond fund will provide the long-term stability and steady returns that your portfolio requires, but I'd be wrong. There's a strong case for buying a fund that holds *global bonds* — a category that is officially called "U.S. bonds" because the funds so often end up investing in the almighty greenback. You need a U.S. bond fund because there could easily be a multi-year scenario in which both worldwide stock prices and the Canadian dollar go down but bonds hold their value — in that case, foreign bonds will be the thing to own. So, unfortunately, for a complete portfolio you probably need to add a non-Canadian foreign bond as well. That's why I include them in the suggested portfolios in Chapter 4, but there I limit global bonds to just 10 percent of the total holdings. If you're nervous about the prospects for Canada and the Canadian dollar, then switch money from the Canadian bond funds to the global bond funds to increase your insurance coverage. Yes, it's yet another asset class, so adding it to your holdings will reduce overall volatility. But it also adds more complexity, expense, and fiddly stuff to worry about.

The average U.S. bond fund sold in Canada levies a nasty 2.2 percent in expenses annually. That hefty price tag left the average fund in the group with a rather miserable average annual return of 5.7 percent in the ten years ended June 2002, compared with 7 percent for Canadian bond funds.

Fund sellers sometimes claim that you need a foreign bond fund to give you currency diversification and protection against a collapse in the Canadian dollar. But you get the same sort of insurance from your global stock holdings, which, of course, are also priced in foreign currencies. That's why you need only a small weighting in foreign bonds.

Here are a couple of U.S. bond fund suggestions with annual expenses below the group average of 2.2 percent. Many of these funds buy bonds issued by international agencies such as the World Bank, so they count as Canadian content for RRSPs (see Chapter 23 for more on RRSP rules). Stinging losses posted by foreign bond funds in 1999, left the average fund down a spine-chilling 10.4 percent. That wasn't the fault of the managers: It was a lousy year for bonds worldwide as interest rates rose. Meanwhile, a slide in many European currencies relative to the Canadian dollar added to the losses.

Recommended Global Bond Funds

Here are a couple of good global bond funds:

CIBC Global Bond Index Fund is designed to give you a return in line with the global bond market, as measured by U.S. broker J.P. Morgan, but it buys financial instruments and bonds from international development agencies and the like that allow it to count as Canadian content for tax-sheltered plans. Annual expenses are a reasonable 1 percent, less than half the bill charged by the average U.S. bond fund.

The **BMO U.S. Dollar Bond** must be bought and sold in U.S. dollars — that makes it more troublesome to purchase and keep track of, but it also offers a good way of protecting some of your money from drops in the Canadian dollar. The annual expenses are a modest 1.4 percent. It invests only in U.S.–dollar bonds, but U.S. bonds dominate the world market so it's a good way to own global bonds. Each month, the fund pays out to unitholders the income it gets. But, as with any fund, this can simply be used to buy more units.

Chapter 15

Index Funds: The Lucrative Art of Owning Everything

*T*his is my very favourite chapter of the book because I get to tell you about index funds, whose low costs and reliable returns make them one of the best deals out there for small investors. Ever notice how things seem to be getting much larger? Monster mansions dot the landscape, movies last for hours, those wretched vans full of dreary Ontario families take up two-and-a-half parking spaces, teenagers tower, and men's razors are as wide as shovels. Well, one of the most effective and profitable investing techniques to emerge in the late 20th century is also a huge idea. It's *indexing*: buying a little of every single significant stock or bond in the market and just holding it, as opposed to trying to pick which one will go up and which one will go down. The name comes from the fact that portfolios managed using this method aim to track a given market index or benchmark. To do that, they buy each stock or bond in the index. For example, a fund designed to follow the Standard & Poor's/Toronto Stock Exchange composite index will buy all (or virtually all) of the shares in Canada's main stock index. Mutual funds that use the technique are called *index funds*.

In this chapter we look at what index funds are, discover why they're a great place to put a lot — but not all — of your mutual fund money, and find out where to buy them.

Buying the Whole Enchilada: The Ups and Downs of Index Funds

The whole idea behind index funds — giving up on trying to pick the best stocks and just betting on the whole market — runs counter to human nature, of course. We all want to believe in the hero fund manager, the Druid who can peer into the entrails of the market and decide which stocks will thrive. So the fund companies run huge ads, and we journalists (I'm afraid) produce fawning stories about how wonderfully perceptive and percipient these stock wizards are. But it's a myth: Managers who can be relied on to beat the market over many years are as rare as vegetarian leopards. And even if they do exist, determining in advance which ones will succeed is essentially impossible.

Why index funds are great for you

Because nearly all managers fail to beat the market over many years, index funds are an excellent way to go for ordinary investors. With an index fund, you don't have to worry whether you made the right choice of manager, because all the fund tries to do is match the market. It doesn't buy and sell stocks or bonds in pursuit of profits but simply buys the shares or bonds that make up a particular index and holds them forever. A computer could run the thing. Index funds make stock-picking expertise irrelevant. That's great for busy people who don't have the time or knowledge to check a manager's credentials and find out whether his or her track record was achieved through luck or skill.

And index funds have another shining virtue. They're cheap for an investor to own. There's no research involved in just buying every stock in the market (although to hear some index funds types pontificate, you'd think it was the hardest thing in the world). That means there are no lobster feasts to buy for greedy fund managers or soggy week-old bread rolls to throw at the wretched junior analysts, so most index funds in Canada have annual expenses of 1 percent or less. In other words, if you have $10,000 sitting in an index fund, you can expect to pay less than $100 (that is, 1 percent of your money) in fees and costs each year. If the expenses get any higher than 1 percent, an index fund starts becoming a joke. It fails to do a decent job of keeping up with the index that gives it its name. Normal non-index mutual funds — which do try to select particular stocks and bonds in an effort to turn a profit — are known as *actively managed funds*. They're far more expensive to own. Most actively managed Canadian equity funds hit their unitholders for about 2.6 percent each year, meaning that they rake off two-and-half times more in fees and costs than index funds do. And that extra 1.6 percentage points is a lot — over 20 years, it adds up to one-third of your money because the fund company is raking off an additional $\frac{1}{60}$ of your portfolio each year.

The dark side of index funds

There is no magic bullet in investing, and index funds carry their own dangers. The big hazard is that the stock market indexes themselves — those seemingly logical benchmarks that index funds follow — often become dominated by just a few high-priced companies. In turn, that means the index funds that track those benchmarks become risky investments because they're tied to the fortunes of just a few companies. In recent years, stock market indexes have been dominated by high-priced *growth* stocks such as Nortel Networks Corp. or General Electric Corp. that left the rest of the market behind. Growth stocks are companies whose sales and profits are expanding rapidly. If investors decide that the companies can go on increasing their revenues and earnings for years, then they'll bid the shares up to high prices. But any sign of a slow-down in a company's growth is likely to make its stock price drop like a rock. In mid-2000, the Canadian market and its indexes danced to the tune of just one company: Nortel. The giant maker of communications equipment accounted for more than 30 percent of the S&P/TSX index, so an investor in an S&P/TSX index fund had one-third of his or her portfolio in a single stock, representing a very risky bet. The same was true, to a lesser extent, of the U.S. market, where a handful of companies such as GE made up a huge chunk of the market. So index funds inevitably had a huge proportion of their assets in a few soaring giant companies. Many of the index funds, in other words, had turned into high-risk, high-priced investments as opposed to cautious mirrors of the whole market. Then came the fall: By mid-2002, Nortel had crashed 98 percent from its 2000 peak. GE had fallen almost 50 percent from its highs. So, did index funds crash and burn compared with regular funds? The short answer is that they often got whacked harder as growth stocks dropped, but their medium-term returns were still respectable. Let's look more closely at the performance of three index funds.

- ✔ The CIBC International Index RRSP Fund ("RRSP" or "RSP" in a fund's name means it's financially engineered to count as Canadian content for retirement savings plans) plunged 17.9 percent annually in the same two years, but that decline was in line with the 17.6-percent loss suffered by the average international equity fund. Over five years, the fund's annual return was a loss of 1.3 percent, while the average international equity fund posted a tiny loss of 0.1 percent per year. International equity funds invest in stocks outside North America — the CIBC fund tracks the widely followed MSCI-EAFE index of big companies in Europe, Australia, and the Far East.

- ✔ The TD Canadian Index Fund, which tracks the S&P/TSX index, lost a painful 14.8 percent annually in the two years ended June 2002, or almost three times as much as the average Canadian stock fund. But its five-year annual average return of 3.2 percent wasn't too far adrift of the average fund, which made 3.6 percent yearly.

✔ The Scotia American Stock Index Fund dropped a nasty 16.3 percent annually in the two years ended June 2002, but that was actually less than the 17.2-percent loss suffered by the average U.S. stock fund. And over five years, the Scotia fund's return was a relatively hot 4.2 percent annually, outpacing the average 1.7-percent return from U.S. equity funds.

No matter how good they may sound, don't put all your stock market money into index funds — because if the handful of giant stocks that dominate the index turn downward suddenly, your portfolio will take a fearful hiding. The essence of wise investing is spreading your risk among a wide variety of holdings. Of the money you've set aside for equity funds, at most two-thirds should be in pure index funds.

Fitting index funds into your portfolio

Treat index funds as you would fruit and vegetables: They're great for you and they should make up most of your diet, but eat other stuff as well. In other words, index funds offer so many advantages that you should put lots in your portfolio — but keep at least one-third of your stock market money in conventional actively managed funds.

The same caution doesn't apply to bond funds, however. There's no such thing as a "growth" bond because a bond is simply a loan, traded among investors, with a fixed rate of interest and period of time before it gets paid back. Because its terms and features are set in advance, a bond is known as a *fixed-income* investment. And because bonds are so safe and stable, the average return you get from a bond or bond mutual fund will almost certainly be lower over several years than the return from a stock or equity fund. But every portfolio should include some bonds, in the interest of stability, and you can safely go ahead and put all the money you've set aside for bonds into two bond index funds, one for Canadian bonds and one for foreign bonds (officially known as a "U.S. bond" fund). Bonds are ideally suited for index funds, mainly because low expenses are so vital in fixed-income investing (more about bond funds later in this chapter).

Evaluating Regular Mutual Fund and Index Fund Performance

But where's the evidence showing that regular mutual funds just can't beat the market? After all, those clever fund managers with shiny well-scrubbed faces and expensive degrees can't be simply wasting their time, can they? The numbers seem to show that many of them are. Returns from the 1990s indicate that when stocks are going up, managers have a very hard time keeping up with the index — which means that most of your cash should be in index funds. After all, if you don't think stocks are going to go up over the long term, why are you investing in equity funds? For all of the 1990s, only one Canadian equity fund in five managed to outperform the S&P/TSX index. And remember that the industry's long-term record was actually worse than that, because some terrible performers were discreetly merged into better funds along the way. As of June 30, 2002, the ten-year annual average return from Canadian equity funds was 9.3 percent, which was still less than the 9.9 percent yearly return from the S&P/TSX — despite the devastation wrought on the index by the collapse of Nortel and a slide in other heavily weighted stocks, such as phone giant BCE Inc. and plane maker Bombardier Inc. As you can see from Table 15-1, in the year ended June 2002, actively managed funds lost less than the index — but that's often the case in a declining market, because funds hold a cushion of uninvested cash in order to pay off unitholders who want their money back. That cash eases the funds' losses slightly because it's not exposed to the dropping stock market. But in rising markets, active managers have trouble keeping up: The average manager fell short of the S&P/TSX index over five and ten years.

Table 15-1	Funds Have Trouble Matching the Market		
	1-yr % Return **(To June 2002)**	**5-yr Annual** **% Return**	**10-yr Annual** **% Return**
Average Canadian equity fund	Down 4.2%	Up 3.6%	Up 9.3%
S&P/TSX returns	Down 6.1%	Up 3.7%	Up 9.9%

It's a similar story with global equities, another main structural beam of any long-term investment portfolio.

During the 1990s, most global stock funds were left behind by the benchmark MSCI World Index, which tracks shares in every major stock market around the world. Only about one in three could keep up with the MSCI index for the whole of the 1990s. And as of June 2002, global equity managers were still behind the index over ten years. The average fund in the group made 8.1 percent annually, but the MSCI World Index produced a yearly return of 10.8 percent.

In the U.S. market, regular fund managers have had an even harder time keeping up with the almighty Standard & Poor's index of 500 big U.S. companies. The S&P generated an incredible annual average return of 20.7 percent in Canadian-dollar terms during the 1990s, but the average U.S. equity fund managed only 15.3 percent. In the ten years to mid-2002, the annual average return from the S&P 500 was down to 11.9 percent — but the average U.S. equity fund made only 8.7 percent.

Unfortunately, it's almost impossible for index fund fans to keep things simple and just buy a global equity index fund. Fund companies usually already offer a U.S. index fund, so they normally sell an international equity index fund, which tracks stocks in countries outside North America. That means you have to buy three stock market index funds: one for Canada, one for the U.S., and one for international stocks.

Want an easy and fast place to buy index funds? Pop into a bank branch and use the bank's index funds. The institution will be happy to deal in its own funds. You can hold your *actively managed* funds — which try to buy and sell stocks and bonds instead of tracking the whole market — in another account at a discount broker.

Not So Easy: The Life of a Fund Manager

It's hard to grasp the idea that no human being can develop the skill to consistently beat the stock market. But this is the foundation on which index funds rest. We naturally want to believe that we'll improve our chances by handing the money over to an expert. History shows, however, that hardly anyone manages to stay ahead of the pack year after year.

Many people don't care about who will be running their money, and they simply put it in the first equity, balanced, and bond funds their salesperson suggests. Weirdly, it's possible that these investors do better than those who assiduously hunt out top-performing managers — because the hot managers so often tend to flop the next year as their favourite stocks go out of fashion.

But why is it so difficult for most fund managers to beat the stock market? Let's take a closer look.

Balancing wins and losses

Fund managers don't just trade in the stock market — they *are* the market. For every winner who beats the index and earns a profit there has to be a loser to supply those profits. Yes, some of the losers may be small retail investors (or so the pros would like us to believe), but the institutional investors that dominate stock trading have their share of losers too. Economists argue endlessly on this point, but it seems clear that the stock market is ultimately a "zero-sum game" or at least resembles one. It's sort of like a bunch of aging, flabby, boomer lads getting together to play poker on a Friday night. If Laurie walks away with $500, then Al or Rob or Justin is going to be down that much.

Why your fund manager isn't a portly guy with a pint of beer and an impenetrable Lancashire accent

The *Wall Street Journal* runs a famous stock-picking contest in which market experts are invited to compete with each other and with darts that are simply pitched at a list of shares. Folklore has it that the darts usually win, but in fact the *Journal* reported in 1998 that since 1990 the experts had outperformed the darts. How come?

For financial reporters, especially those of us who have been singing hymns of praise to the gospel of indexing for years, it was time to get on the phone and demand an explanation from Professor Burton Malkiel. He's the Princeton University researcher who in 1973 published an investment classic called *A Random Walk Down Wall Street*. And he's one of the godfathers of indexing. The courtly Professor Malkiel came up with two reasons for the darts' poor showings. First, there are thousands upon thousands of sad-sack, no-hope tiny stocks in the U.S. market. The darts, with nothing to guide them, often fell on one of those forgotten losers, whereas the human stock jockeys selected real companies with at least some prospects. His other explanation: When the *Journal* reported that a prominent expert had selected a stock in the contest, that news alone was enough to push the share price higher, giving the experts' stocks a leg-up compared with the darts' selections.

Incidentally, Professor Malkiel wrote in 1973 that a blindfolded monkey throwing darts at the stock page would do just as well as professional money managers. In its contest, the *Journal* got reporters to throw the darts. The paper considered using real monkeys but, as reporter Georgette Jasen put it: "various hand-wringers have so far prevailed with concerns

Manager responsibility

Money managers, believe it or not, are responsible souls who don't want their unitholders to be dragged over the hot coals unduly. So they often shy away from loading their funds to the gunwales with the extremely hot stocks that are driving the indexes higher. Remember the advice in the Monty Python sketch about the dirty fork in the restaurant? "Never kill a customer." It's just not good for business. History shows that the public will accept mediocre performance, sometimes for years, but it won't take kindly to losses. Increasingly in recent years, the stock market itself has become an insane place. In the mid-1990s bank stocks in Canada climbed to absurd prices, and in 1999 and early 2000 technology shares reached astronomical valuations. In both cases, managers had trouble keeping up with the index because they cautiously refused to go along with the madness.

Expenses

With the average Canadian equity fund charging its unitholders almost 3 percent a year in fees and expenses, it's virtually impossible for managers to close the gap between them and the market. It's a yawning gap, especially when you're trying to compensate for it every year. That gives a natural advantage to index funds, with their yearly expenses of 1 percent or less. (Some, from companies such as Altamira Investment Services Inc., go as low as 0.5 percent. Now we're talking.) And mutual funds have another hidden expense that's higher for actively managed funds: brokerage commissions. A fund that's constantly buying and selling stocks is naturally going to end up paying more to brokers.

Why Canadians Shy Away from Such a Good idea

Only a few Canadians have purchased index funds, partly because the idea is so, well, strange. If you ranked all of the global, international, and domestic equity funds in Canada by size as of June 2002, the 58 biggest funds were all actively managed. You had to go all the way down to No. 59, CIBC's $759-million CIBC U.S. Index RRSP Fund, to find an index portfolio. The cherished notion of using a talented stock picker, a magician who knows which shares to buy, is so hard to shake. Why do Canadians shy away from what seems like such a great investment opportunity? Maybe it's a cultural thing, but Canadians have so far proved reluctant to pay upfront fees for investment advice. They would rather get hand-holding from a commission-paid mutual fund salesperson. But there's a problem right there: Such advisers have a powerful incentive to recommend actively managed rather than index funds. It's because of the way the fund business works.

Passive aggressive

Jargon abounds in the world of indexing. Because index funds aim to match the whole market, or an important benchmark, by simply buying and holding everything, the strategy is often called *passive*. In contrast, traditional funds, whose managers try to buy the stocks they think are going up and dump those they believe are dropping, are known as *actively managed* or *active* funds.

The debate between proponents of passive investing (who simply buy and hold the index) and active stock pickers will probably never be resolved. But I think indexing has enough clearly demonstrated advantages to make it a suitable strategy for your "core" equity money.

There's a fairly active recommendation for a passive investing style.

Why Your Salesperson Hates Index Funds

Brokers and planners don't like index funds because they don't pay them much or anything in the way of commissions. It's that simple.

A guideline in the fund industry for equity and balanced funds is that the *sales channel* — that is, stockbrokers or financial planners — gets 1 percent of the client's money each year. They may get it through a commission paid by the investor or the fund company at the time of purchase. Or the salesperson may get this commission annually in the form of a regular "trailer fee," an annual sales commission paid by the fund company.

Index funds are an exception because, with their rock-bottom annual expense ratios of 1 percent or less, they can afford to pay little or nothing in commissions to salespeople. The fees just aren't high enough. So guess what? Be prepared if an adviser gives you a long speech explaining why index funds aren't that great after all. A fund salesperson is more likely to try to sell you on how you'll be better off buying an actively managed fund run by a reassuring-looking fellow who's known for his saintlike devotion to achieving high returns at low risk. The annual expenses? Oh, never mind about those. It's the return that matters, silly. Yes, some fund marketers such as insurer Transamerica Life Canada and CM Investment Management Ltd. (a CIBC unit that sells the Renaissance family of funds) offer index funds through salespeople. But their expenses are generally high, at 2 percent and up (Transamerica offers one index fund that tracks the volatile Nasdaq Stock Market in the United States and comes with a crazy expense ratio of almost 5 percent).

Give index funds a shot with at least part of your money. If your broker or financial planner won't sell you any, then strongly consider moving your account elsewhere. There's just so much evidence that index funds are a great deal for retail investors. Any salesperson who refuses to carry them is being unfair to his or her clients.

Where to Buy an Index Fund

If you want to buy an index fund with truly low expenses, you'll have to go to the banks or National Bank of Canada subsidiary Altamira Investment Services. All sell their funds directly to the public with no sales charges. Altamira's index funds are cheapest, with total fees and expenses of around 0.5 percent. Every discount broker should carry at least one family of index funds, with no hassles.

The profit margins on index funds are so thin that some sellers make you put up relatively stiff initial minimum investments — Royal Bank has a minimum investment of $2,500 on some of its index funds, for example — but you can often make small regular investments after that.

Recommended index funds

Here are three great index funds, two with annual expenses of 1 percent or less:

 The **Altamira Precision Canadian Index Fund** is a bargain, with annual costs of only 0.5 percent. It offers a return that matches the blue-chip Standard & Poor's/Toronto Stock Exchange 60-stock index of 60 big shares, not the broader S&P/TSX composite. In practice, though, the two indexes tend to track each other pretty closely because blue-chip stocks also dominate the composite index.

 Scotia American Stock Index, whose annual expenses are 1 percent compared with 2.6 percent for the average U.S. equity fund, follows the S&P 500 Index. That means it holds lots of huge and famous U.S. companies such as Exxon Mobil, General Electric, Intel, and Cisco Systems, just the sort of quality assets you need for your long-term money.

 Toronto-Dominion's **TD European Index** matches the Morgan Stanley Capital International Index of European stocks, a widely recognized list of the continent's biggest companies. It makes a pretty good substitute if you can't find an international fund — a fund that holds stocks from everywhere in the world except the United States.

 If you're with a financial planner or broker who doesn't offer index funds, there's nothing stopping you from opening a separate index fund account at a bank and holding the rest of your money with the financial planning chain. Each of the big bank–owned discount brokers has index funds available, usually from the bank that owns the firm. The simplicity and relatively clear account statements offered by discount brokers make them perfect for holding index funds, especially if you can avoid the fees that some discounters impose for buying and selling other companies' no-load funds. If the discounter is bank-owned, then the bank's own index funds will be free of fees.

 Although a bank or discount broker should let you buy index funds free of all charges, a broker or planner may ask for a fee to cover his or her running costs in lieu of commission. Paying such a fee is your choice. It may not be a bad deal, if you like the salesperson, because you'd be paying more anyway with regular funds that have higher expenses than index funds. For example, on a $10,000 investment, an extra one percentage point in expenses (to pay the broker) is $100 off the top of your portfolio, increasing and decreasing each year in line with the total investment. You may decide that an administration fee for buying an index fund is worth it in return for the convenience, help, and advice offered by a salesperson.

Cashing in or out?

Those sleek brokers (and rather less affluent financial planners) who knock index funds sometimes claim that these funds will plummet when stock markets are bad because index funds don't hold any cash reserves. Part of what they say is true — index funds are all about matching a market benchmark, instead of forecasting the direction of the market, so they nearly always simply hold the stocks in the index with barely any cash. By contrast, most Canadian equity funds had at least 4 percent of their assets in safe-but-dull cash in mid-2002, and some big funds had 20 percent or more.

Although there's no doubt that a fund with lots of cash will probably ride out a market downturn better than an index fund, stocks go up in the long term — which is really the point of the whole exercise. Sticking with cash-heavy investments means you're partly out of the game. And the index fund that drops first because it has no cash is also likely to bounce back to new highs sooner as the index itself recovers.

The fund industry speaks with a forked tongue on the question of cash in funds. On the one hand, fund companies say it's your time *in* the market that counts, not timing the market. By that they mean that history shows you should stay the course, hold on to your equity funds, and avoid jumping in and out of the market. On the other hand, managers are allowed to carry tens of millions of dollars in cash in their funds for long periods.

The Bond Squad

Bond index funds, which track the whole bond market at a low cost to the investor, make it wonderfully simple to invest in bonds; however, they aren't very common in Canada. You may get an active bond manager who outperforms the index, but that could be by taking bigger risks, perhaps loading up on volatile long-term bonds. Just take the portion of your portfolio allocated to bonds and put it into a bond index fund with annual expenses of below 1 percent. Ideally, bonds and bond funds — including bond index funds — should be held *inside* an RRSP or tax-deferred plan because they throw off lots of interest income each year. As with an equity fund that pays lots of capital gains distributions, if you have to pay tax on all of those interest payouts your after-tax return could be slashed. Better to let them pile up tax-free inside the RRSP. Most Canadian bond index funds simply match the entire bond market by tracking the Scotia Capital Markets Universe Bond Index. See Chapter 14 for much more on bond funds.

Putting Your Finger on the Right Index

The problem of which index an index fund should use is thorny and difficult. On the one hand, if you start guessing which index is the best one to match, then you're getting close to picking stocks again, and this is the antithesis of passive investing. On the other hand, if you just let things go and blindly match an index that's ruled by a few high-fliers (such as Nortel, for example), then your index fund has arguably become an aggressive volatile fund. However, there isn't really a simple answer to this problem: just follow the advice in this book and keep index funds to a maximum of two-thirds of your equity funds. That way, if the big stocks in the index turn out to be bubbles that burst painfully, a good chunk of your money will be in regular funds as well.

In the U.S. market, the safest policy would be to buy a super-broad index fund, one that tracks the huge Wilshire 5000 Index, which contains just about every stock in America that's worth buying. CIBC's U.S. index fund tracks the Wilshire, so it would be a good choice. But it seems pretty certain that the better-known S&P 500, which is dominated by fewer and larger companies, will remain the main yardstick for the U.S. market for years to come.

The Tax Appeal of Indexing

Index funds expose you to very little in taxation until you cash them in, making them a great way to defer taxation.

Nearly all mutual funds pay *distributions* to their unitholders — cash payments that most people choose to take in the form of more units of the fund (so the investment continues to compound and grow). Funds make the distributions when they have trading profits or interest (and dividend) income that the manager wants to pay out to the fund's investors.

Say you hold 1,000 units of a fund at the end of the year and the unit value is $10, for a total investment of $10,000.

The fund manager generated $1 of trading profits per unit during the year and pays this out to the unitholders.

The value of each unit drops by $1, reflecting the payment that has been made. You now hold your original 1,000 units, which are worth $9 each, for a total of $9,000. But you've also received $1,000 in the distribution, which you can take in cash or new units, bringing you back to $10,000.

No matter how you receive the units, though, you're liable for tax on the distribution, just as if you had earned it trading stocks on your own. Some funds whose managers trade a lot can make very large distributions. Note, though, that getting distributions isn't a problem if you hold the fund in a tax-deferred account such as a registered retirement savings plan, which lets you delay paying taxes on the money you earn within the account. There's more on taxes in Chapter 24 and on RRSPs in Chapter 23.

Index funds just buy and hold the stocks in the index and they do very little trading. So they tend to pay out very little in the way of distributions. That makes them especially suitable for *taxable* accounts — money that isn't held in a tax-deferred account.

Don't get fooled by RSP index funds

One group of index funds, however, pays out a lot in distributions. The so-called RSP index funds are designed to track non-Canadian indexes, but they still count as Canadian content for RRSPs and other tax-favoured retirement savings plans. You should always hold those within an RRSP or RRIF because such funds often pay out huge distributions, even more than actively managed funds do. That's because they use derivatives to pull off the Canadian-content trick. *Derivatives* are essentially promises to buy and sell financial assets on pre-set terms for a fixed period of time. These are also called *futures* or *options*. These derivatives must be constantly renewed and traded, throwing off a stream of income distributions that count as heavily taxed interest income in an investor's hands.

In Chapter 20, there's more on funds that are foreign but that also count as Canadian for tax purposes.

Why is Everyone Wearing Fanny Packs Again?

Don't you love 1980s and 1990s nostalgia? Those long summer nights sweltering and dreaming of Madonna in her pointy you-know-what. It became clear even to the financial media in the middle of the last decade that index funds were the remorseless end product of investing. Big sophisticated pension funds had known for years. In 1995, the almighty *Worth,* the biggest U.S. personal finance magazine, finally conceded defeat and admitted that "settling for average is good enough."

Making money in the stock market is a gamble. But it's a casino in which your long-term chances are excellent, because good companies grow their profits and share prices over the years. And you improve your odds even more by simply buying an index fund that tracks the whole market — because these big suckers, the successful companies like financial combine harvester Power Corp. of Canada or network empire Cisco Systems, actually *become* the whole market. And it's good to know that with an index fund, you own them.

Chapter 16

Dividend and Income Funds: Confusion Galore

I'm afraid dividend funds, and their newfangled offspring, income funds, are one area where the mutual fund industry has taken a great idea and turned it into a tangled mass of very different funds. The basic theory behind dividend funds is a good one — invest in blue-chip companies that pay a steady flow of increasing *dividends*, and you'll be off to the races. Dividends are the quarterly payments that a company pays to its owners — the shareholders who own its shares. Over the long term, buying into good-quality companies and growing rich as the dividends increase annually has been one of the best ways to build wealth. If you hold shares in successful companies for long enough, then your dividends will increase to the point where they represent a meaningful source of income. Seems simple, doesn't it? Don't count your earnings yet. There's a lot more to this story. In this chapter I demystify the dividend fund, identify who should buy one, review the two main types of dividend fund, and wrap up with some valuable tips on picking a winner. I also look at the new "income trusts" funds that have sprung up to give mutual fund buyers an opportunity to invest in the ever-increasing herd of income trusts — vehicles that pay the cash flow from a business directly to investors.

What Is a Dividend Fund?

When a company earns a profit, it can do only two things with the money: reinvest it in the business or pay all or part of it out as *dividends*, actual cash paid to those who hold shares in the company. That's true for every company — from the dirtiest restaurant in Prince Rupert, B.C. (beware of the chicken fricassee) to the swishest financial holding company in the fanciest marble-clad office tower in Toronto. Traditionally, blue-chip established corporations have lined their shareholders' pockets over the years by regularly paying a nice steady dividend. A *blue-chip* company is a big and stable business, such as Toronto-Dominion Bank or supermarket giant Loblaw Cos. Ltd. The term *blue chip* comes from poker, where a blue betting chip usually has a high value.

Here is some good news for you if you buy into a blue-chip, large company. The other shareholders include big and assertive professional investors, horse-faced people with loud voices, who usually keep management focused. So if you hold shares in big businesses, you can usually be sure that the companies' managers and directors are under at least some pressure to look out for the interests of you and the other shareholders. By contrast, if you invest in small companies, they may not be big enough to attract professional investors, so management will find it easier to neglect shareholders' interests.

Many mutual fund companies sell conservative *dividend funds* that simply buy shares in a bunch of blue-chip mega-companies such as BCE Inc. or Royal Bank of Canada and then pass the dividends they collect straight through to their unitholders. This is investing in dividend funds at its very best — clean and simple. Sounds great so far, doesn't it? You're probably wondering why I'm so cranky about dividend funds. The problem is that sometimes their complexity and lack of transparency (always a bad sign in the world of investing) makes them next to impossible to wrap your brain around. In theory they're great; in action they can be horribly confusing.

It can be hard to tell whether a fund will actually pay you very much in the way of dividends, whether the distributions will actually be dividends or interest income, and whether the manager is really seeking dividend income or is in fact chasing stocks that will go up. But don't worry, later in this chapter I'll show you a simple way to figure out what the flow of dividends from a dividend fund is likely to be — just look at the fund's main holdings and they'll tip you off as to what sort of job the fund will do for you.

A dividend fund is usually designed to meet your needs if you:

- ✔ Must withdraw steady amounts from your savings to live on
- ✔ Face a high tax rate on the money you take out of your investment portfolio

Many big dividend funds perform well, producing a stream of ready cash for their investors. In other words, they collect the dividends from big companies and pay them out to you.

Best of all, the money normally comes from the fund to you as a dividend payment for tax purposes that's lightly taxed (more on that later in the chapter).

Some dividend and income funds boost their flow of monthly payments to unitholders by holding riskier assets such as trusts that buy into oil wells. That'll increase the payments you get from the fund — but the stream of payments that these investments dish out to the fund (and ultimately to you) could get cut drastically when business conditions turn down. These newer dividend funds have been around for only a few years, so it's too soon to say whether they'll really do well for investors.

Why companies pay, or don't pay, dividends

Companies pay dividends to their shareholders because that's how the owners of the business are rewarded. A large and well-established business, such as a bank, usually throws off enough profits each year to cover the cost of acquiring new equipment and other assets and still has money left over for paying out as dividends. But some companies — particularly fast-growing technology outfits with huge needs for cash to research and develop new products — don't earn enough cash each year to come up with a dividend. They offer such good prospects for growth in sales and profits over the medium to long term, however, that investors are happy to buy their shares, even though there's little chance of getting a dividend for several years.

Slow-growing companies

Traditionally, boring businesses whose earnings grow slowly have had to pay out up to half of their profits each year in dividends in order to keep investors interested in their shares. Think pipelines or electricity utilities (companies that pump natural gas to homes or sell electricity are called *utilities* because that's the greyest name anyone could think of). If you bought Alberta power generator TransAlta Utilities in mid-2002, you pocketed a fat annual dividend yield of 5 percent. In other words, the stock traded at around $20 and the annual dividend per share was $1; $1 represents 5 percent of $20, so the yearly yield was 5 percent. Banks are able to increase their profits faster than utilities, partly because they're expanding in new and profitable areas such as mutual funds. But banks are such big companies already that they can't increase their profits as fast as, say, a software company can. So they occupy a sort of middle ground, made up of companies that are likely to increase their earnings at a respectable but not feverish pace in coming years. Banks also pay out a relatively large proportion of their profits as dividends to shareholders. As of summer 2002, most big bank stocks yielded about 3 percent. That might not sound generous but it wasn't bad when you consider that the stocks in the broad Standard & Poor's/Toronto Stock Exchange as a whole yielded just 1.9 percent.

Blue-chip companies are sometimes forced to cut their dividends when their profits fall unexpectedly. TransCanada PipeLines Ltd. did so, to great consternation and dismay among investors, at the end of 1999. But dividend cuts by established companies are rare because shareholders hate such reductions. They hate 'em like poison. Managers are unlikely to establish an annual dividend rate in the first place, if they know they'll have to take the humiliating step of reducing it. A portfolio that holds at least half a dozen blue-chip stocks — such as a dividend fund — will spread your risk, reducing the pain if one of them slashes the dividend.

The big shooters: Growth companies

So-called growth companies, whose profits are expected to increase rapidly, can get away with paying little or nothing in dividends and investors still tend to throw their hat — and their cash — into the ring by buying the companies' shares. Investors are willing to forgo gratification today so the company can use the cash to build its business instead. The idea is that when the dividends do eventually come, they'll be bigger than if the company had paid out the cash to shareholders earlier in the game. And as stock markets climbed in a techno-frenzy in the late 1990s and in 2000, you hardly heard a murmur about dividends. I mean, dude, who cared? Don't-Care was made to care, in this case. The great slide in growth stocks left the average Canadian equity fund with an annual loss of 5 percent in the two years ended June 2002 — but the average dividend fund, typically with a heavy larding of stable stocks that pay dividends, actually made 7.6 percent annually in the same rough period. And over ten years, Canadian dividend funds positively shone. They produced an average annual return of 11.1 percent, the best performance by *any* fund category — except for wild and wacky gold funds, which made 11.4 percent per year.

It's a good idea to hold at least some conservative dividend-paying stocks, even within an RRSP. Because as the popping of the tech stock balloon showed, it's nice to own something that doesn't depend on a weedy teenage software genius staying conscious.

But don't worry. You don't have to take special vitamin pills if your diet is rich and varied, including plenty of herrings' backsides. And by analogy, you don't need to worry about buying a special dividend fund if your portfolio includes some high-quality equity funds. Those funds are bound to hold several dividend-type stocks — and that covers your daily requirement.

Damn the dividends

Here's one reason why dividends were so out of favour in the late 1990s and 2000 (until the crash): Cisco Systems Inc. of San Jose, just south of San Francisco.

Cisco makes equipment for building giant computer networks. By 2000, investors reckoned it was worth more than half a trillion (U.S.) dollars, making it the world's most valuable company. The shares traded at just under $80 each, up threefold in a single year. They were first sold to the public back in 1990 at the equivalent of — don't worry, this hurts me as much as it hurts you — *6 cents* each.

And how much did these very rich Californians pay out to their shareholders in dividends each year? Not a bent penny. In other words, they reinvested all of the business's profits in future growth.

Cisco represented a capitalist ideal of a company at the very start of the 21st century. And it didn't pay dividends. So, that's why there were less than 80 dividend funds in Canada in mid-2000 compared with 170 science funds.

But how did this story end? Well, by mid-2002, Cisco stock had slumped to less than $15. It still didn't pay a dividend (so much for growth). And there were 136 dividend and income trusts funds in Canada compared with 176 tech funds.

Those seemingly insignificant little quarterly dividend cheques are what capitalism and the stock market is all about. Remember that under the law — in the Anglo-Saxon world, at least (and elsewhere, more and more, as the whole world becomes obsessed with investing in stocks *à l'américaine*) — dividends are about the only way that shareholders can legally get any money out of their company. Yes, they get a payoff if the company is taken over at a fat price or if they sell the shares after they've gone up or if the company "spins off" an asset to its shareholders in the form of a special restructuring. But receiving a dividend remains the only fundamental way in which you can actually extract cash from a business (apart from giving yourself a bloated salary or options package). It's the thing that ultimately gives a share any value. Which made investors' obsession with future growth and damn-the-dividends in the late 1990s rather a reckless attitude. What does this all mean to the mutual fund investor? Just that it's fine to engage in torrid flirtation with a technology fund or aggressive growth fund full of stuff like Cisco, but limit it to a dalliance using just a tiny part of your money. Your core equity funds should also hold plenty of blue-chip stocks that pay a meaningful and rising dividend. Because when a market crash comes — and they always do — they're the shares that are most likely to fall the least and recover first.

I didn't know Tom Cruise was that short

Modern investors still don't ask company managers to "show them the money" in the form of a big dividend. They still appear willing to wait years for future profits and dividends — or to gamble on castles in the air, depending on how cynical you are.

Most big companies pay at least some dividends. But there's so much investor money already chasing high-quality stocks that pay a decent rate that prices have been pushed sky-high. Let's say you bought all of the shares in the S&P/TSX index, in roughly the same proportion as the index, in mid-2002. You'd have a portfolio that gave you an anorexic annual dividend yield of only about 1.9 percent — in other words, if you tied $100 up in the S&P/TSX stocks, you got only $1.90 in annual dividends.

In part, that was because interest rates were so low. With ten-year bonds yielding only about 5 percent a year, there weren't many quality investments around that produced any sort of decent income stream, so you might as well have stuck with shares.

Are Dividend Funds Right for You?

A dividend fund will suit you best if you meet one or more of the following tests:

- ✔ **You're a long-termer but you need cash now:** You need the long-term growth prospects offered by shares, but you also need to make regular withdrawals from your portfolio of investments. Many dividend funds are designed to accumulate a steady stream of cash, which they pay out regularly.

- ✔ **You're in a high tax bracket:** You face a high rate of tax on the income and profits earned by your investments. That might be because you already have a high income or because your investments are held in a taxable account, not a tax-deferred plan such as a registered retirement savings plan. Remember that dividends are lightly taxed, which makes them a great way to earn investment income for a taxable investor. That means the payments you get from a dividend fund won't be too badly savaged by the government.

- ✔ **You're not a risk taker:** You're nervous about the stock market and you feel happiest with a stock fund full of conservatively run large companies, the sort that pay lots of dividends.

But dividend funds aren't right for everyone, especially people who don't care if their investments pay out a regular income. Why bother with collecting dividends if it compromises your long-term returns? If your aim is to build your money over many years, then you'll probably do better in a regular stock fund that's free to buy shares in all sorts of companies, including those that pay hardly anything in dividends. That way, you'll own a balanced mixture of shares that also includes some high-flying technology players and natural resource producers, and not just a portfolio of blue-chip, conservative names.

The Appealing Tax Implications of Dividends

In Chapter 24, I take a close look at how the periodic payments you get from a mutual fund are taxed. Dividend funds get special treatment when it comes to taxes. They can be one of the best ways of earning a stream of income that doesn't get too badly mutilated by the tax collector. To encourage Canadians to buy shares issued by Canadian corporations (to help the economy grow), dividends are taxed far more lightly than *interest income*, which is the sort of fixed payment you get from a bank account, bond, or fixed-term deposit such as a guaranteed investment certificate.

As a quick-and-dirty rule, each $1 of dividend income is as good as $1.25 of interest income because the taxes on the interest-income dollar are so much higher. If you earn $125 in interest and only $100 in dividends, you'll end up with about the same amount after taxes. Dividends are *tax-efficient* or *tax-advantaged* investments, because this type of investment actually helps you keep more of your hard-earned income.

You'll know if any mutual fund you own has paid you distributions in the form of *capital gains*, dividends, or interest because it'll be indicated on the T3 or T5 statement of investment income that you get from your fund company each year for mailing in with your tax return. (Capital gains are trading profits a fund earns by buying assets at a low price and selling them at a better price.) The calculation for reporting dividends on your tax form is a little laborious and weird but you soon get used to it (amazing how the prospect of putting more money in one's pocket tends to fire up the old synapses). Essentially the principle is this: You "gross up" the amount of dividends received by increasing them by 25 percent and you report that amount on your tax form. But you then reduce your tax payable by a "tax credit" amounting to 16.7 percent of the dividends actually received. Don't fret: The tax form provides a step-by-step guide.

Fund salespeople have long preached that there's not much point collecting dividends within a tax-sheltered account such as a registered retirement savings plan. That's for two reasons:

✔ All the income earned inside such a plan is tax-deferred anyway. And all withdrawals are heavily taxed as regular income when you take money out of a plan. That means the dividend tax break is no use within an RRSP, so dividend funds — which are designed to take advantage of the tax law — arguably, aren't a good fit.

✔ For your core equity funds in an RRSP, it may be better to buy normal equity funds rather than dividend funds because the managers of regular funds have a freer hand to play the market, rather than trying to maximize their dividend income.

But because many dividend funds hold big familiar companies, they can logically be treated as superconservative equity funds that are well suited for RRSPs. And that certainly seemed to be true in both 1996 and 1997, when most dividend funds soared more than 20 percent as investors went crazy for the banks and utility shares that the funds usually end up holding. But when bank stocks go sour, dividend funds turn positively rancid. The average fund in the dividend group slipped 0.6 percent in 1998 and made only 2 percent in 1999. The bottom line seems to be this: Check the holdings of a dividend fund, and if it's full of regular shares in big companies — as opposed to things like income trusts or other investments that are designed to throw off regular streams of cash — then it can probably be treated as a conservative equity fund.

Looking at Two Types of Dividend Funds

If dividend fund managers went out for a picnic each summer, they'd tend to separate into two groups. One bunch would sit on the rugs, nibbling primly at muffins, while the others would be scampering around, getting in fights with Canada geese and swilling Alberta vodka out of plastic jugs. In other words, there are two main types of dividend funds, although many fall somewhere in the middle.

Conservative dividend funds

These funds fall into the scaredy-cat category that's mainly designed to produce a steady and predictable flow of dividends. In mid-2002, it wasn't easy to dig up quality stocks that paid a substantial dividend (remember that the dividend yield on the market as a whole was less than 2 percent). So the managers of these funds often resort to buying *preferred shares*. Preferred shares pay a fixed and usually high dividend, which is nice, but the dividend doesn't grow over time. In other words, preferred shareholders are more like lenders to a company than its owners. By contrast, an ordinary or common share in a company pays a lower dividend but the annual rate tends to increase over the years, providing an investment whose value should increase over time. Conservative dividend funds usually hold a few common shares, but they're generally shares in super-stable and slow-growing companies such as pipeline operators and electric utilities.

Aggressive dividend funds

This aggressive type of dividend fund loads up on banks, utilities, pipelines, blue-chip industrial companies — and sometimes even growth companies that pay hardly any dividends. These funds try to increase the value of their units as the price of the stocks they hold rises, while also paying out at least some dividend income. Still, their holdings are usually so conservative that they're less volatile than regular equity funds.

Which dividend is which?

To find out which personality type a dividend fund fits, look at the *holdings*, the list of investments that the fund owns. Holdings for funds are listed at independent Web sites such as www.globefund.com, at the company's own Web site, or in the company's brochures and reports to unitholders.

Preferential treatment

If you see a lot of *preferred* or *pref* shares in the top holdings or in the asset breakdown, then you're dealing with a slow-but-steady dividend fund that's almost certainly a dull-but-reliable source of tax-advantaged dividend income.

Preferred shares sound fancy and mink-lined but they're really a sort of cross between a stock and a bond. They suit investors who want predictability but also relish the nice tax break attached to dividends. They pay a high fixed stated dividend, which can be reduced or omitted if the company hits turbulence but in practice rarely is. And preferred shareholders nearly always get their dividends before common shareholders are entitled to receive a cent, hence the name. So why doesn't everyone just buy preferreds? Because the steady predictable payout is all you ever collect, which means that preferred shareholders aren't truly owners of a company, with all of the attendant risks and rewards, but more like debt-holders who have bought a sort of bond.

In return for that lightly taxed and relatively generous stream of income, preferred shareholders miss out on the chance of prospering if the business booms. They "give away the upside," as red-faced young fellows drinking expensive lager in unbearable Bay Street bars like to bark.

Preferred shares nearly always stay close to their issue price, dropping a little when interest rates rise and rising when rates fall, just like bonds do. They're often (but not always) issued at $25 each and they usually stay in a trading range of between $22 and $28, unless interest rates rise or fall very violently. You can spot them in the newspapers by their trading symbol, which always has "PR" in it.

If a stock has a percentage — 4.7 percent, for instance — as part of its name, then it's a preferred share that was set up to produce that percentage yield for buyers of the stock when it was first issued. For example, the CI Signature Dividend Income Fund's biggest holding in summer 2002 was "5.5 percent" preferred shares issued by base-metal miner Inco Ltd., designed to produce an annual dividend yield of, you guessed it, 5.5 percent. By contrast, Inco's common shares didn't pay any dividend at all (thanks a lot). Sure, over the years Inco's earnings are supposed to grow (investors hope) — which might eventually allow the company to pay a steadily increasing dividend on its common shares while the preferreds stay in a rut. But preferred shares were just the ticket for the CI dividend fund's superconservative unitholders, who relied on its steady monthly distribution of 4.5 cents. Six of the fund's biggest ten holdings in mid-2002 were preferred shares.

Common sense

A sure sign that a dividend fund is more aggressive, taking a risk on share prices while also trying to earn at least some dividend income, is a portfolio that holds few or no preferreds and is full of *common stock*. Common shares are the volatile legal slices of interest in the company that trade on the stock market, along with preferred shares. These funds tend to chase trading profits by riding shares whose prices rise — but don't expect much in the way of actual dividends from this bunch. Royal Bank of Canada's $2.4-billion Royal Dividend Fund had only about 2 percent of its assets in preferred shares in mid-2002. The fund produced a blistering average annual return of 10.9 percent in the five years ended June 2002, well ahead of the 7.7-percent return from the average dividend fund. But its payouts of dividends tend to be stingy — only 46.5 cents per unit in 2001 and just 29 cents in the first half of 2002.

The New Income Trusts Funds — The Jury's Still Out

In Chapter 5, I talk about the pros and cons of *income trusts*, which are businesses that have been turned inside out and transformed into a sort of fund that pays out cash directly to investors without the tax authorities getting their claws into it. Income trusts issue units that trade on the Toronto Stock Exchange like shares but nearly always have ".UN" attached to their trading symbol. For example, Keg Royalties Income Fund, which pays out cash from the Keg chain of steakhouses, trades under the symbol KEG.UN. Billions of dollars have flowed into income trusts, naturally attracting the beady gaze of the fund industry. Fund sellers have been quick to launch funds that invest in the trusts.

As of mid-2002, at least 35 funds had popped up in a new "Canadian income trusts funds" category for funds that chase income — that is, a regular stream of payments from their investments — but have less than half of their assets in traditional bonds. That pretty much obliges them to buy into income trusts. It's usually easy to spot funds in this group by their name: they generally include turbo-charged labels like "high income" or "monthly income."

Some of these new funds have been fantastic marketing successes. The Dynamic Focus Plus Diversified Income Trust, launched in July 2001, mushroomed to more than $400 million in assets in less than a year (a whopping 27-percent one-year return sure helped).

But remember that we haven't seen how these exotic new income trusts will perform over a period of several years — there's a danger that they may have to cut their distributions if a nasty recession bites. Critics warn that many of the trusts are as risky and potentially volatile as stocks, not bonds. Even some fund salespeople are wary: supercautious U.S. brokerage firm Edward Jones reportedly told its Canadian clients in 2002 that it won't sell them "income funds" unless most of the holdings are old-fashioned bonds. So go easy on your purchases of these new funds; they're still an unproven product.

A taxing lack of clarity

One late Saturday night I was researching this chapter. Plowing through the small print at the back of a mutual fund family's annual report, I was looking in vain for some clear indication as to whether the distributions from the company's dividend fund counted as dividends or interest in the hands of the customer. Then it occurred to me: Neither I nor any other investor should have to waste time doing this. Why can't the companies make it simple? As I explain in Chapter 24, on taxes, the fund industry's attitude to the taxes its unitholders pay generally ranges from don't-really-care to not-our-problem. And when it comes to cavalier treatment of taxes, dividend funds can be one of the worst examples of all. It's impossible to tell from many companies' brochures, reports, or Web sites exactly what form the distributions take when it comes to taxes. And my e-mails to almost a dozen companies asking where I could find this information in a clear and understandable form met with either blank silence or a vague answer.

The problem is that it's easy to find out how much a fund paid to its unitholders — those payments are known as *distributions* — but it's difficult to ascertain what proportion of those distributions was in the form of dividends, with their attractive tax break.

The best way for you to discover if the fund has been tax-efficient is to insist that your fund salesperson or bank employee check with the company and get back to you. You should be told how much the fund has paid out in distributions per unit in recent years. How much of those distributions were made up of dividends or capital gains (trading profits) for tax purposes and how much counted as interest?

Selecting a Winning Dividend Fund

Don't just grab the first dividend fund you're offered. Make sure the fund you buy comes with reasonable annual costs — certainly less than the 2.4-percent average for the group — and that the stocks that make up its largest holdings are the sort of shares that you want to own: lots of preferred shares, royalty trusts, and utility stocks if you're seeking income, or plenty of high-quality common stocks if you also want some price appreciation.

Fees, please

Hate to be monotonous, but expenses on a dividend fund should be the first thing you check. That's because income-oriented dividend funds aren't likely to earn much more than bond funds. Expect sedate average annual returns that come in at less than 6 percent. So any dividend fund that hits its unit-holders for more than 2.4 percent a year, the average for the group, won't leave much for investors in a flat-to-declining stock market.

Looking for income

After looking at the annual costs, if you want a dividend fund for its stream of income, here are the questions you should put to your salesperson, no-load fund company, or bank employee. If you can't get a straight answer, then consider shopping elsewhere:

- ✔ What distributions has this fund paid over the past year, and how frequently?

- ✔ Is there a stated monthly distribution, and how much is it?

- ✔ Which distributions over the past year counted as dividends from taxable Canadian corporations, entitling the fund's investors to claim the dividend tax credit?

- ✔ Did any of the distributions include a *return of capital* — a partial refund of the investor's own money — to maintain a stated payout rate? Not only are such returns of capital potentially misleading, but they also can be horrendous to account for at tax time.

A few dividend funds have been set up as taxable companies themselves, so their payouts of income nearly always qualify as dividends. (And you thought mutual funds were supposed to make life simple.)

Looking for income and more

If you're more aggressive (that is, hungry), you probably want a dividend fund that tries to buy shares that go up in price as well as generate income for unitholders. In that case, look to see whether the fund's biggest holdings are:

- ✔ Mostly large companies that pay some sort of dividend — if they don't, then it's more like a common stock fund.

- ✔ A mixture of shares from companies in different industries — otherwise you're in for big price swings when one part of the economy turns down.

You can easily check the dividend on a stock by looking up its listing in the *Globe and Mail's Report on Business* section or the investing section of the *National Post*. Find the company's name and see whether it has a dividend next to it. By the way, the papers always give the *annual* dividend rate for a stock, even though the payments are nearly always made quarterly. So the dividend for Canadian Imperial Bank of Commerce common stock, for example, was shown as $1.64 in mid-2002, representing four quarterly payments of 41 cents.

Three strong choices

Here are three top-quality dividend funds that chase very different objectives. One produces income, the other seeks income and price gains, and the third is one of the new generation of funds that invests partly in income trusts. The three funds have reasonable expenses and well-regarded managers, but remember to ask plenty of questions before you invest.

Predictable Pete: Looking for cash

Consider the **CI Signature Dividend Income Fund**. Most of the $784-million fund's biggest holdings as of mid-2002 were preferred shares, which shows that it's designed to throw off predictable dividends. The fund paid a regular 4.5 cents per unit per month, or 54 cents per year. The net asset value was about $12.66, so the fund offered a yield of less than 5 percent. But its blue-chip holdings — both common and preferred — meant a cut in the dividends paid by the stocks was unlikely.

Best of both worlds

Bank of Nova Scotia's Scotia Canadian Dividend Fund buys mostly conservative shares, such as banks and pipeline companies, in an effort to generate income and capital gains. That mixture gave it a stellar annual average return of 8.5 percent in the five years ended June 30, 2002, compared with 7.7 percent for the average dividend fund. (Always be wary, though, when comparing returns from dividend funds because their investment objectives can be so different.) The expenses on the Scotiabank fund are a reasonable 1.2 percent. You can buy it at Scotiabank branches, some discount brokers, and some stockbrokers.

One of the newbies

The tiny $30-million **Saxon High Income Fund**, launched in late 1997, is one of the new generation of funds that seeks a high level of income by investing in just about anything it can eat, including trusts. The expenses are a low 1.3 percent. Small no-load seller Saxon Funds of Toronto, a conservative company with excellent returns and low fund expenses, imposes a minimum account size of $5,000 — there's more information in Chapter 9, which deals with fund companies such as Saxon that sell directly to the public.

Chapter 17

Money Market Funds: Welcome to Sleepy Hollow

Some archaeologists and historians have an interesting theory to explain why the Romans were so successful in war, usually against massive odds (apart from Russell Crowe, that is). Bathrooms. Yes, that's right, bathrooms. The Romans liked their plumbing. Centuries before most of Western Europe had any kind of organized sanitation, the Romans were building bathhouses and sewage systems. Even in the field, they stuck to their clean-living ways. This meant that their armies didn't die *en masse* of typhoid, cholera, and other diseases transmitted by, well, patchy hygiene. Money market funds are a bit like the humble throne in the bathroom, the white porcelain god that separates us from 15th-century Bruges with its pungent odours, annoying Belgian jesters, and unspeakable ditches down the middle of the street. They're dull, they're predictable, they're almost invisible — and they're one of the mutual fund industry's greatest inventions.

Money market funds are simply a safe parking spot for cash, designed to produce at least some sort of return. They generate a modest stream of income — annual returns from the group averaged just 4.1 percent in the ten years ended June 2002. These funds invest in very short-term bonds and other fixed-income securities that usually have less than three months to go before they mature and the issuer pays the holders their money back. Money market funds are different in structure from normal mutual funds, and the way they calculate their returns can be confusing. But just use the same rules to pick one as you do with bond funds: Buy quality and, more than ever, insist on low expenses — 1 percent annually at the very most. As with all mutual fund investing programs, when buying a money market fund you should do more than just insist on low costs. Lean across the table — glaring at the hapless salesperson through bulging, insane eyes — part your spit-flecked, crusty lips, and scream for a reduction in expenses at the top of your voice. Otherwise, you won't make anything off a money market fund. In this chapter, I will show you why money market funds are a great place to hold your cash while you wait to spend or invest it. I'll also show you how to spot a good money market fund.

How Money Market Funds Work

Throughout this book I've given you tons of grim warnings about how you can easily lose money in mutual funds because of a drop in their unit price. Well, at the risk of contradicting myself, that doesn't apply to the vast majority of money market funds because they are held steady at a fixed value, usually $10.

Some money market funds — especially the guaranteed type that promise to refund some or all of your money — have unit prices that do increase over time. There's more on them later.

Keeping the unit price fixed isn't required by law, but it's the practice among fund companies. In theory, if short-term rates were to shoot up exponentially or the government's credit rating collapsed in some kind of unprecedented catastrophe, the fund company would let the value of your money market units drop. But by that time, you'll be too busy pitching bottles at the giant green spacecraft that just zapped your dog to worry much about it. In other words, woe betide the fund company that lets its money market fund units drop below their fixed value. Investors who buy this type of fund aren't known for their devil-may-care attitude to losses. It's more a kind of grim-glare-where's-my-money type of situation. So money market funds are rather like a guaranteed investment certificate: You're certain of getting your cash back, plus extra units that represent the interest you've earned along the way.

The interest is usually calculated daily but it's generally added to your account every month or when you sell your units. Money market funds, like nearly all mutual funds, however, beat the pants off GICs because they're "liquid." That's a bit of investment industry jargon that simply means you can "liquidate" or turn the investment into ready cash at a moment's notice. Unlike GICs, money market funds refund your money without penalty, usually at a day's notice.

As a guideline, the return from money market funds tends to be almost exactly the same as the return from one-year GICs. GICs earned an annual average of 4.2 percent in the ten years ended June 2002, just a fraction more than the 4.1-percent return from Canadian money market funds.

In other words, both fixed one-year deposits at the bank and money market funds gave you an annual yield of just over 4 percent over a decade. That's only about half the 7.9-percent yearly return investors got from the average Canadian balanced fund, though — normally a pretty cautious mix of stuff from the stock market (which is always volatile) and bonds (which usually work in great slow cycles).

The *yield* is just the harvest you get on your money, expressed as a percentage of what you invested. So, a madcap biotech fund might go up 50 percent in a year — at huge risk — turning $1,000 into $1,500 (always assuming you were canny enough to sell out in time before it crashed). A money market fund in late 2000 offered an annual yield more like 4.5 percent, which would transform $1,000 into just $1,045 but at very little risk. But by mid-2002, as inflation stayed low, that yield had slumped below 2 percent, making money market funds much less attractive for investors. We're talking about a return of 20 bucks for tying up $1,000 for a year.

So remember that with a money market fund, you nearly always buy a set of units at a fixed price, usually $10 in Canada and $1 in the United States, and that unit price never changes. Your return comes in the form of extra units paid out to you along the way. You're not going to get wealthy soon with one of these funds. Just like bond funds, they're designed only to earn a steady and fairly predictable return. There's none of the flash, risk, and potential for big gains that you get with an equity fund. And fewer of those annoying broken-teeth incidents.

Checking Up on Your Money Market Fund

Let's say you want to buy a money market fund but you don't know what the yield over the next year is likely to be. The listing for the fund in the daily newspaper will give you a reasonable idea. When you turn to the pages that list mutual fund prices, you'll notice that money market funds are listed separately from the other funds. That's because there's no point in printing their unit prices, which are nearly always fixed at $10. Instead, the paper shows two types of yield for each fund, the *current yield* and the *effective yield*, both of which represent rough forecasts of what the fund, with its current portfolio, is likely to earn over the next year. Each yield figure uses a slightly different calculation, which I outline in a moment. But remember that both of these yield numbers are just estimates.

Money market funds are full of short-term stuff that matures in the next few months, so the portfolio manager can't be sure if he or she will be able to replace those T-bills and other short-term securities with new investments that will produce the same return. If rates are falling, then it will be almost impossible to do so. There's no need to worry about the difference between the two types of yield. Each calculation basically boils down to the same number of dollars and cents in your pocket. But just for the record, here's how to tell them apart:

- **Current yield:** The first number printed in the newspaper is the *current yield* (sometimes called the *indicated yield*). It shows the yield that the fund earned over the past seven days, which is then "annualized" to show what the same rate of return would work out to over one whole year.

- **Effective yield:** The *effective yield* is the same annualized number, but this time it assumes that all distributions are reinvested in more units, thus achieving compounding. Because it assumes that the new units are being added to your stockpile during the year, earning that extra bit of interest, the effective yield is usually a fraction of a percentage point higher than the current yield.

The fix isn't always in

There are some money market funds whose unit value does change, increasing slowly as the fund earns interest income. These are the so-called "segregated-fund" or "guaranteed-investment-fund" versions of money market funds. Seg or guaranteed funds are funds that promise to refund most or all of the holders' original investment, as long as they stick around long enough. Chapter 19 deals with segregated funds.

Mind you, with something as safe as a money market fund, such a guarantee is pretty pointless and almost certainly not worth the higher expenses charged on such funds. Some hit their investors for as much as 1.5 percent annually, which leaves little or nothing for unitholders after taxes and inflation are taken into account. For legal reasons to do with insurance contracts (you'd get too excited if I explained them all to you), guaranteed and segregated funds often don't give unitholders their returns in the form of extra units. They simply reinvest all interest, capital gains, and other income so that holders of the fund own units with a steadily increasing value.

The fund industry is still in the process of inventing such guaranteed funds so there are yet other examples that both increase their unit value and pay distributions, just like normal mutual funds. It's terribly confusing for investors, and your salesperson or bank employee could have trouble keeping up.

Your statement from the fund company should clearly show what's going on, although that's not always the case. Consider switching to another fund company or broker if you can't get a proper explanation — a clear and simple explanation of how your funds work is your inalienable right as an investor. Even if you're an alien.

You can also go to the *Globe's* mutual fund Web site at www.globefund.com and call up the page for any individual mutual fund. That usually shows the latest distributions paid by a fund and it should give you an idea of what system the fund uses.

When inflation and interest rates are low, there's no real gap between the two types of yield. For example, in mid-2002, the huge $6.5-billion TD Canadian Money Market Fund quoted a current yield of 1.9 percent and an effective yield of 2 percent. In times of high interest rates, when compounding means that the new units pile up fast, the effective yield will be quite a bit higher. But the low interest rates in 2002 meant there wasn't much difference at all.

In the early 1990s, when short-term interest rates and the returns on money market funds climbed well above 10 percent, fund companies started making a lot of noise about their "effective yields," which were much higher than the "current yield" (because the money was theoretically going to compound at high rates). But investors became so confused over which yield was which (and who can blame them?) that the regulators eventually stepped in. The fund industry agreed to show both figures in its ads.

Why Money Markets May Not Be All They're Cracked Up to Be

Don't just assume that a money market fund is the only place to park your cash — you can usually earn a full percentage point or two more annually in a low-risk short-term bond fund that has low expenses of 1 percent or less. Chapter 14 on bond funds suggests a few good candidates.

Short-term bond funds can be even better than money market funds

Short-term bond funds posted an annual average return of 5.5 percent in the ten years ended June, 2002 — that's an impressive 1.4 percentage points more than money market funds annually. The drawback, though, was slightly more volatility and the danger of losing money. That's because bond prices fall when interest rates rise, as explained in Chapter 14, although short-term bonds fall the least of all (when interest rates drop, however, they also go up the least). Money market funds, by contrast, are designed never to leave investors with a loss. In 1994, the average short-term bond posted a small loss of almost 2 percent after interest rates rose suddenly.

Before you go plunging into a short-term bond fund, sneering and making rude gestures at the dolts lining up to buy boring old money market funds, remember that the 1990s were marked by a sharp fall in interest rates. That gave short-term bond funds an unfair advantage because bond prices were lifted by those falling rates. If rates start rising again, then short-term bond funds will have a tougher time beating money market funds. In fact, by the fall of 2002, there was talk of a "bond bubble" as investors fled stocks and tried to hide in bonds. Pessimists warned that a return of inflation and the accompanying sharp rise in interest rates could burst that bubble rapidly. Still, short-term bond funds are among the safest of all investments. A portfolio stuffed full of high-quality short-term government bonds with less than five years to go before they mature (just check the top holdings) will ride out nearly anything.

Realistic expectations for money markets

How much can you expect to earn from a money market fund over the next year? Here's a good guideline: Just check what banks are offering to pay on one-year GICs.

Over the 20 years (whew!) ended June 2002, buying one-year GICs produced an annual return of 7 percent while money market funds produced a return of 6.8 percent, almost exactly the same. To compare one-year GIC rates from all the major banks and other financial institutions, just buy the *Globe and Mail* on Monday when the paper lists the rates offered by virtually everyone on all sorts of loans and deposits, including GICs.

Pick Only the Plums: Selecting Winning Money Market Funds

Don't stay up all night picking a money market fund, because you've got a busy day ahead. A long day of sliding through sticky mud, trying to get a grip on infuriated ostriches. Money market funds tend to be pretty similar. In other words, there's no point chasing a big yield, because to get one the manager has to take more risk. If you're buying your other mutual funds at a bank or bank-owned discount broker, simply buy the bank's money market fund. There's enough competition in the industry to make it embarrassing for a bank to have its money market fund turn into a hound. If you're buying through a broker or other commissioned salesperson, his or her office is probably set up to put clients into a particular money market fund, probably from the fund company the salesperson's organization does the most business with. Since money market funds are just temporary holding spots for cash — or they constitute the low-risk, low-return "cash" portion of your portfolio — then one fund is pretty well as good as another.

Just make sure that you can find the money market fund listed in your daily newspaper, in a newspaper monthly report, or on the Internet. That way, you know you'll be able to track your holdings and check the accuracy of your account statement.

Choosing from a mix of money market funds

Some money markets are ultrasafe, sticking to government bonds. Others increase the risk level very slightly, and pick up about one-fifth of a percentage point in annual yield. Either choice is fine — it depends on your personality. Here's how to tell the two options apart.

- ✔ For their very nervous clients, the banks offer a superconservative "T-bill" fund that buys only short-term government bonds and government "treasury bills" (a type of bond with just a few months before it matures).

- ✔ For those willing to take a bit more risk, the banks offer slightly lower-quality funds — usually known simply as money market funds — that are allowed to increase their yield by buying things like corporate "commercial paper"; that is, short-term debt issued by big companies when they need a bit of cash to tide them over. These funds really aren't dangerous at all, because the companies that issue the paper they hold are nearly always blue-chip multinationals or their Canadian subsidiaries.

It would take a very nasty economic cataclysm indeed before any bank-run money market racked up losses big enough to force the bank to let the fund's unit price drop. So there's no significant difference between the two types of funds.

In the end, the extra bit of yield you get from a money market fund compared with a T-bill fund is very small. For example, the TD Canadian Money Market Fund, which is free to buy corporate securities, generated an annual return of 3.8 percent in the five years ended June 2002, only slightly higher than the 3.6-percent annual return from the TD Canadian T-Bill Fund, which must stick to government debt.

World travellers: U.S. money market funds

A handful of companies also offer foreign money market funds, either for investors who want to hold a lot of cash in U.S. dollars or for scaredy-cats who want a low-volatility investment that's safe from a drop in the Canadian dollar. Nearly all the funds in this group are bought and sold in U.S. dollars. The same rules apply to pick a fund. Look for low expenses if you want to end up with anything. Don't believe me? Look what happened to unfortunate investors in the AIM Short-term Income Fund. The fund's class B units came with annual expenses of 2.7 percent — which left investors with an average annual return of only 1.8 percent in the five years ended June 2002, compared with 3.9 percent for the average U.S. money market fund. In other words, investors paid out more to the fund company than they got back in returns.

The average foreign money market fund has expenses of 1.2 percent, so refuse to pay anything more than that.

Is thin in? Watching those pesky expenses

Always remember that because the returns from money market funds are so thin, the slightest increase in expenses can leave you with nothing after taxes and inflation. So refuse to pay a sales commission when buying a money market fund. The broker or salesperson should be able to let you have it commission-free, especially if you're simply parking your money in the money market fund temporarily while you decide on a long-term home for it. Take five minutes to fire up www.globefund.com or check the listings in the monthly fund guide printed with your newspaper to check that the money market fund offered by your bank or salesperson has produced acceptable returns. It probably has. And remember that the average Canadian money market fund has expenses of 1.1 percent — you shouldn't be asked to pay more than that.

Three ways to make money in the money market

Here are three great money market funds, two of them from the big banks. A bank is the simplest place to buy a money market fund because the company is set up to deal directly with the public. Besides, banks' money market funds are large enough to earn the bank a profit, which means the bank is eager to accept money into the fund.

Other "no-load" companies besides the banks (that is, fund companies that don't charge sales commissions) and fund companies that sell through brokers also run money market funds. They're usually fine but they're smaller and generally offered only as a convenience for customers who have cash that they plan to invest later in the company's funds. Beware of higher expenses in some cases.

The $3-billion **Royal Canadian Money Market** fund from Royal Bank of Canada expense ratio of about 1 percent. It underperformed most of its rivals from 1993 though 1996 but moved into the top half of money market funds after that.

The **TD Canadian Money Market** fund is the Godzilla of the business, with more than $6 billion in assets in mid-2002. Its annual expenses were a bargain-basement 0.9 percent, which has helped the fund to beat most of its rivals year after year. Like Toronto-Dominion's other funds, this one dropped "Green Line" from its title in 2000. Green Line was once the name of the bank's big discount brokerage, and that brand was also used for the bank's funds. But TD started referring to its discount brokers around the world as "TD Waterhouse" in 2000, so the funds were simply renamed "TD."

The $480-million **Altamira T-Bill Fund** has a super-low expense ratio of only 0.4 percent, and for nervous investors there's the added security of knowing it sticks to short-term debt issued or guaranteed by governments. Keep an eye on those low costs, though. National Bank of Canada bought Altamira Investment Services in 2002 and insists that it plans to run the no-load fund seller as an independent operation — but the bank could be tempted to started raising expense ratios to squeeze profit out of the operation (many people on Bay Street thought the almost $500-million that National paid for Altamira was too much).

The Lowdown on Expenses

As I keep repeating over and over until readers want to shove me down a disused grease trap, the main thing to look for in a money market fund is *low expenses*. That can be hard in Canada because the cheapest funds, those with expenses of around 0.5 percent, are often "premium" funds from the banks that need big investments of $100,000 and up.

But if you're buying only small quantities of the fund, don't get too worked up about costs, either. If you have, say, $5,000 in a money market fund, representing 5 percent of your $100,000 portfolio, then a 1-percentage-point reduction in expenses on the money market fund means an extra $50 a year for you. Nice, sure, but not a huge deal. For convenience, you may decide just to stick with your fund company's money market product, even if it has higher expenses, and treat the extra $50 as a sort of fee. But remember that all expenses eat into your return.

Beware of empty promises

Don't bother searching endlessly for the money market fund that promises to give you a few more bucks of income. If the performance looks hot, chances are the fund company has doctored the return in some way — no doubt legally but not quite candidly. That's because in the drab world of T-bills and short-term bonds, it's very hard to generate any kind of extra return through fancy trading without taking on more risk. It's very hard to get anyone to play footsie in the cafeteria with you at lunchtime, too, but let's save that for another day. You can be pretty sure that the yield of a high-flying fund will magically revert to the middle of the pack — or worse — straight after you buy it.

Be curious, George

As always, be curious — and cautious — when some kind of "account management" fee or commission is added onto a money market fund's published expenses. If you're thinking about paying such a fee, ask to see a sample statement that at least shows clients how the fee is calculated and charged. Does the statement clearly reveal how much is taken off? Such extra charges may be legitimate and even a good deal, but they make checking on your real return a lot more complicated.

Remember that simplicity is one of the great beauties of regular mutual funds because they publish returns and unit prices after their fees. You have a right to a clear explanation of every fee. If the fund company or salesperson doesn't respect you enough to provide you with one, then shop elsewhere.

Sound fund shopping advice

One last word of warning: Just about every fund seller offers a money market fund — but some may be all coy and shy about the historic rate of return. In his wonderful investing classic, *Bogle on Mutual Funds,* John Bogle cautions that some fund companies don't publish the returns of their money market funds because the performance has been terrible. Bogle founded Vanguard Group, America's leading seller of low-cost mutual funds. His guideline, a good one, is to avoid a money market fund if its yield doesn't appear in the newspapers. Check to see if historic rates of return for the fund are printed in the papers' monthly reports or if they're available on www.globefund.com. If not, keep looking for a fund that isn't shrouded in mystery.

Chapter 18

Labour-Sponsored Funds: Strange Brews Worth Tasting

. . . .

In This Chapter

▶ Checking out labour-sponsored venture capital funds

▶ Evaluating why labour funds can be a good deal

▶ Deciding when to steer clear of labour funds

. . . .

*O*kay, so I've stressed the importance of buying funds that hold a variety of top-quality stocks and bonds. I've also said over and over that you should look for simple investments whose value can be readily checked by picking up a newspaper or firing up an Internet site. And I've harped about keeping management costs low, pointing out that they're one of the few variables in investing that you can actually control. Well, labour-sponsored venture capital funds break just about all of those rules — but they can be a decent investment. In this chapter, we'll get to the bottom of these confusing beasts, assess their value to you, the Canadian investor, and then I offer some warnings about who should, and shouldn't, take a dive into this particular pool.

A Fund Like No Other: Introducing the Labour-Sponsored Fund

So what exactly is a *labour-sponsored fund*? Hold onto your hats — these things are weird. They invest in strange little companies, most of which will probably fail or stagnate. Their holdings often aren't even publicly traded, which means that the true market worth of the stocks that the funds own is impossible to establish clearly. And labour funds' expenses are often obscene.

Oh yes, and there are a few more ugly poisoned spikes sticking out of these beauties. Their investments usually take years to mature and you lose a huge chunk of the benefit from most of these funds unless you leave your money sitting there for almost a decade. So why should you bother with them? The

So are union guys running my money, or what?

No, or at least probably not.

Labour funds were launched in the 1990s, growing out of talks between the federal government and unions on how to back small businesses, which are a major source of new jobs. In return for the lavish tax breaks given to their investors, the funds must have an affiliation with a union or employee association, but in fact the connection between most labour-sponsored funds and organized labour is tenuous at best.

The union movement in Canada is divided over whether to support the funds, mostly because labour fund managers generally don't care if the companies they finance are unionized. "Whether a company is unionized or not does not enter into consideration when making investment decisions," says the Working Opportunity Fund, which is backed by British Columbia's labour federation.

In practice, the funds usually end up being managed by corporate financiers and venture capitalists that simply pay an annual fee to the labour group that lends its name to the fund — or "rent-a-union," as critics put it. "Private financial consultants simply arrange for official sponsorship from some obscure union, in return for an endorsement fee," says the Canadian Auto Workers union at its Web site at www.caw.ca. It adds sarcastically: "Unions involved in this industry include such prominent voices of labour as the [Canadian Football League] Players Association, the Canadian Police Association and the Professional Association of Foreign Service Officers."

answer: because of the attractive tax break available to buyers, representing 30 percent or even more of the investment in some cases, and also because the unknown ventures that these funds invest in sometimes explode in value.

Labour funds are about as risky as investing gets, however, so don't put more than 5 percent of your money here (okay, 10 percent if your idea of a quiet evening out is partying hard at the greyhound track in a low-cut dress or snakeskin suit, clutching a fistful of grubby $20 bills — be sure to give me a call, incidentally).

A Look at Labour Funds

Labour-sponsored venture capital funds (I'll call them "labour funds" for short) are funds that operate under special rules. The main point is that they buy into small Canadian businesses that would otherwise have trouble attracting investors — in return for taking on such a big risk, the unitholders get some generous tax breaks. Sometimes, they concentrate on backing businesses that have a track record of earnings and revenue, and some labour funds even seek out companies that are already listed on a stock exchange, but often the little companies in these funds tend to have a very high failure rate. In general, the small companies backed by the funds are supposed to have fewer than 500 employees and less than $50 million in assets. Here are the main points:

✔ **Receive a tax credit:** With just about all labour funds, the federal government refunds 15 percent of your investment in the form of a tax credit — and your provincial government may also give you back the same amount. The maximum annual investment eligible for credits is usually $5,000 — so investing that amount in a labour fund that qualifies for both federal and provincial credits will immediately net you tax refunds of up to $1,500 ($750 from each government). In other words, you could end up with $5,000 worth of fund units in return for a cash outlay of only $3,500. As with contributions to RRSPs, you can usually make your purchase of a labour fund during the first 60 days of a calendar year and have the money earn tax credits for the previous year. With some even riskier "research-oriented" labour funds, Ontario investors can get yet another $250 in tax credits.

✔ **Be prepared for a long commitment:** To stop people from buying labour funds, grabbing the tax credits, and then simply selling the units back to the fund, the federal government imposes an eight-year "hold period." If you cash out of the fund within that period, you have to repay the federal tax credit. That's up from a previous hold period of only five years. There are exceptions for illness and so on, but reckon on tying your money up for a long time.

✔ **Boost your foreign content:** Buying a labour fund can boost the amount of foreign property in your registered retirement savings plan. One of the problems with RRSPs has long been the rule forcing you to keep most of the assets in Canada. A maximum of 30 percent of the assets in an RRSP can be non-Canadian. However, for every dollar invested in a labour fund, you can increase or "bump up" your foreign content allowance by $3, to an overall maximum of 50 percent.

✔ **Not so unified:** Labour funds often have few connections with the union movement — in fact, many unions want nothing to do with them, complaining that they're a sort of squalid financial mushroom thriving on vastly expensive government tax subsidies, with the money ending up in the hands of Bay Street types and non-unionized companies. Labour funds are a "dubious stock promotion scheme," according to Jim Stanford, an economist with the Canadian Auto Workers.

Reviewing Possible Perks of Labour Funds

So here's a little history — labour funds produced fairly wretched returns for most of the late 1990s. Obliged by law to keep 20 percent of their assets in safe stuff like treasury bills in order to protect unitholders, some left most of their cash sitting in bonds or the bank — while some management companies raked off generous fees and salaries. There was a chorus of criticism from the media and union officials who demanded to know why governments were handing out such lucrative tax breaks to investors who simply had their money in bonds. Ottawa and the provinces responded by slapping penalties on the funds and reducing the tax credits — which choked off the flow of new money to labour funds. So Ottawa eased up yet again, leaving us with the present set of rules. The current regime seems to work pretty well, with most labour funds investing reasonable portions of their assets in the start-up companies they're supposed to be supporting.

Understanding the Rule of 10

Venture capital investing is notoriously risky and unpredictable, meaning that it will almost certainly take several years for the investments your fund has bought into to show any kind of profit. Venture capitalists like to talk about a "Rule of 10." By that, they mean that a portfolio of venture investments will often contain two big winners, two so-so performers, and six that end up being taken down quietly to the river in a black plastic sack. But when venture investing is hot, it can really cook.

It's impossible to predict in advance which labour fund will hit the motherlode, however, so you should improve your chances by buying at least two. Most funds will let you invest as little as $1,000 or even $500, so it's no problem dividing up your money. Your broker may beef about the extra paperwork, and holding multiple funds is more bother for you, but this is an area where it's essential to have plenty of hooks in the water by owning several funds.

Being wary of short-term tech stock successes

The massive rally in small-company stocks and technology shares in 1999 and early 2000 was manna from heaven for labour funds because it produced inflated valuations for many of the tiny companies that they hold. That gave some of the funds blistering returns, but labour funds ultimately soared and sagged very like tech funds. The average labour fund jumped 22 percent in 1999 and another 11.7 percent in 2000 but then fell 12.2 percent in 2001 and another 7.1 percent in the first half of 2002. As of June 2002, the group had a mediocre five-year return of 1 percent annually, significantly less than the 3.6-percent return from Canadian equity funds. Sure, those returns don't take into account the generous tax handouts that labour fund buyers received — but there's an old piece of wisdom in investing that you shouldn't let tax breaks be your only reason for buying into something. Without the tax breaks that investors got, plenty of labour funds have been fairly awful performers.

Going against the grain: Labour funds may not mirror the market

There's another reason, though, why venture capital may be a good addition to a portfolio. It seems to march to its own strange drummer, sometimes producing strong returns even if the broad stock market is tanking, and vice versa. For example, the average small-company mutual fund in Canada soared more than 30 percent in 1996 — but most labour funds made less than 5 percent. So labour funds could offer you diversification, smoothing out scary swings in the value of your total portfolio.

Be prepared for slim pickings

A big problem with labour funds is lack of choice if you live outside Ontario. A few are available for sale in several provinces, giving investors the 15-percent federal tax credit, but some provincial governments don't give purchasers of those funds a matching provincial credit. Provinces such as British Columbia, Manitoba, and Quebec have their own labour funds, offering both federal and provincial tax credits, but putting all your money into one fund is a risky proposition. The big $300-million Working Ventures Canadian Fund offers provincial tax credits in Ontario, New Brunswick, Nova Scotia, and Saskatchewan.

Expensive tastes

Expenses are stiff with this group, at an average 4.8 percent of assets. That's really expensive. At that rate, a labour fund siphons off almost half of your money in just ten years, which means these funds had better earn big returns to earn their keep. And the expenses look even worse when you consider that some funds have invested only half of their money — meaning that some are levying fees and expenses that amount to 10 percent of the money they've actually put into small companies. From an investor's point of view, the only justification for accepting such high expenses is the chance of earning huge returns if one of the funds' venture investments explodes in value.

Labouring toward the Right Fund

Here are the main points to bear in mind when picking a labour fund:

> ✔ **Think small:** Look for a smallish one with assets of less than $200 million. Any larger than that, and it'll be hard for any one super-successful investment to have much of an influence on returns. If you live in Ontario, you're spoiled for choice because more than a dozen funds offer both

federal and provincial tax credits. In the rest of the country, however, you may have to settle for the local provincial fund if you want to get back the full 30-percent refund.

✔ **Remember the risk:** Remember that this is risky investing, suitable for 10 percent of your portfolio at most. Some commentators advise, sensibly, that you take the entire tax refund you get from investing in a labour fund and invest it in a solid common stock fund, a guaranteed investment certificate, or even a bond fund. That way, if the labour fund turns out to be a dud, you'll probably earn a decent return on some of the money.

✔ **Check the fund's baggage:** As always, check the fund's main holdings and read its literature carefully. Even the bland brochures should give you an idea of what the main goal of the fund is — creating jobs or earning big returns for investors. After that, it's your choice as to what you think is more important. If you're buying more than one labour fund, and you should, try to get funds with different styles. Some specialize in technology stocks while others concentrate on relatively mature companies that are close to issuing shares to the public or have already listed on a stock exchange.

✔ **Recognize the reality of the return:** Don't get all worked up by promises of fabulous extra tax savings if you buy the units and put them into an RRSP — RRSP savings are available on any mutual fund, stock, or bond. Labour fund ads tout the tax credits and then, in big black letters, also talk about the extra deduction available for buying the units through an RRSP. But despite lavish ads and eye-popping figures, there's nothing special about labour funds in that regard. Just about every fund can be put into an RRSP.

How one labour fund got lucky

If you're thinking of buying a labour fund because it seems to have a good long-term record, make sure you check just how those returns were actually achieved. In other words, use www.globefund.com to check on the annual returns. Take the Working Opportunity Fund, which is available only to British Columbians, for example. From 1991 through 1998, it produced fairly boring returns, ranging from a peak of 9.9 percent in 1996 to only 0.8 percent in 1998. But in 1999, the fund struck a gold mine — or "bagged an elephant," as crusty old venture financiers like to call it.

Working Opportunity had put about $4 million into a tiny company called HotHaus Technologies Inc., a specialist in zapping data and images over networks. The fund ended up with about one-third of HotHaus. In the tech frenzy of 1999, HotHaus was taken over by U.S. chip manufacturer Broadcom Corp. for more than $400 million. The deal left Working Opportunity with a sudden profit of about $100 million and sent its units surging by 50.5 percent in 1999. That gave the fund a hot five-year average annual return of 9.2 percent as of June 2002 — but keep in mind that the return was turbocharged by that one big score.

Some Potential Winners in the Labour Game

Here are a few high-quality labour funds. I've left some good funds off the list, not because there's anything wrong with them but simply because they haven't yet demonstrated the ability to catch a really big winner. That's unfair, I know, because bagging such elephants is essentially a crapshoot, but remember: you always want lucky people running your money. Some funds such as the Covington Fund and VenGrowth have now been closed to new investors, so that their old unitholders can get the full benefit when the funds' investments mature. But the same management companies have since launched similar "successor" funds.

 The **Canadian Science & Tech Growth Fund** sticks to tech companies — perhaps the most promising area for an investment that really shoots up in value. As of mid-2002, the five-year return was a comparatively strong 4.6 percent — exactly the same as the annual expense ratio. In other words, unitholders gave away half of their return in fees and expenses.

 Headed by Denzil Doyle, a veteran financier of Ottawa-area technology companies, **Capital Alliance Ventures** offers experienced management and the prospect of getting in early on some technology success stories. However, it's sold only in Ontario.

 Vengrowth II Investment Fund was launched in 2000 as a successor fund to the original Vengrowth. The top holdings in mid-2002 were names like Icefyre Semiconductor, Spotwave Wireless, and Bitflash Graphics, which means investors could be in for a wild ride. But as of June 2002, the original Vengrowth fund had produced a relatively hot five-year annual return of 5.5 percent — it shot up more than 20 percent in both 1999 and 2000.

One Final Word of Caution about Labour Funds

 Don't bother with labour funds unless you're absolutely sure you won't need the money back for years. That's because of that eight-year hold period. Remember that if you cash out within that time frame, you'll have to repay your federal tax credits as well as, in some cases, shell out redemption fees to the fund company. And there's another reason why labour funds are suited only for your very long-term money. The value of venture capital investments traditionally forms a "J curve" that's shaped like a hockey stick. In other words, a holding often doesn't increase in value for several years — it may even drop — but it can suddenly shoot up when a deal is struck to either sell the business to a bigger company or take the investment public by listing its shares on a stock exchange. If you cash out too soon, you risk missing out on the payoff, leaving other investors to collect the big profits.

Quebec's Solidarity Fund: Mixed messages

The model for Canada's labour funds is Quebec's huge Solidarity Fund, launched in 1983 and sponsored by the Quebec Federation of Labour. In early 2000, Quebec residents who bought into the $4-billion-plus fund got the standard tax credits: 15 percent from the Quebec government and the same from the federal government. The maximum investment eligible for credits was the usual $5,000.

There's no doubt that the fund has done invaluable work saving and creating jobs in the province, but potential investors should remember that it has social and economic aims that are separate from and perhaps take precedence over making its unitholders rich. At its Web site — www.fondsftq.com — the fund reminds investors that it "calls on the solidarity and savings of Quebecers to help create and maintain jobs in Québec by investing in small and medium-sized businesses. *Part of its mission is also to offer its shareholders a fair return.*" (My italics.) There's an old Irish saying in the county of Armagh — You can't ride two horses with one arse (please excuse the robust language, but they're like that up there). In other words, the fund's laudable goal of strengthening Quebec's economy and backing unionized businesses (a far higher proportion of its investments than

most other labour funds) won't always be compatible with generating the maximum profits for investors. That's in contrast to most Ontario-based labour funds, which have no real involvement with the labour movement. The big Ontario funds are almost entirely concerned with generating the hot returns that will attract more investors and assets, thus boosting the fees and salaries that their managers get to rake off.

The Solidarity Fund seems to be reluctant to publish the straightforward compound annual returns that it has produced for its unitholders, returns that can be compared with those of other funds. I wish you luck finding the information on its Web site. But in June 2002, the fund estimated that its share value as of June 30 would be $22.02. That represented an increase of 9 percent in five years, an annual gain of about 1.8 percent, topping the 1-percent annual return generated by the average labour fund. The vast size and diversified portfolio of the fund make it extremely unlikely that one or two big scores will send its unit price soaring. Buy the fund by all means, grabbing the tax credits and doing Quebec some good, but remember that it's a more conservative investment than most other labour funds.

Chapter 19

Segregated Funds: Investing on Autopilot

. . . .

In This Chapter

▶ Playing it safe with segregated funds

▶ Adding up the extra cost of going the seg route

▶ Deciding if seg funds are right for you

. . . .

I'm sure there's a play in it somewhere — a scene around the kitchen table when the salesperson drops by to push these things. Since 1997, the mutual fund industry has been hawking expensive new "guaranteed investment funds" or "segregated" funds that promise to at least refund an investor's original investment as long as they stay in the fund for ten years or, well, die. Fund salespeople who've gone forth to pitch them to cautious older customers are finding that the super-safe funds are quite popular — with the investors' kids, who don't want to see their inheritance wiped out because Mom couldn't resist the allure of Brazilian junk-bond funds. I can see it now: the family matriarch idly shuffling a deck of dog-eared cards in between slugs of bourbon, stogie dangling from the corner of her brightly rouged mouth. Meanwhile, her prim bespectacled Chartered Management Accountant offspring whine on about how they know that she'll be around for years yet, and that's just so great, and it's her money of course, but couldn't she cut back a little on the over-the-counter dot-com stocks. . . .

Anyway, the new funds have been a hit with Canadians, attracting billions of dollars from customers who just can't bear the risk of losing money they put into a fund. In return, they're willing to pay much higher annual costs, an extra charge that can be more than 1 percent of their holdings every year, for a guarantee that some observers argue is of dubious worth. And the guarantees have been getting even more expensive for investors. In 2000, insurance regulators brought in tough new rules that increase the amount of capital that insurers must set aside to cover the cost of their seg-fund promises. The new regime increased annual expenses on many funds and forced companies to scale back the guarantees. They've also responded by releasing waves of new products with watered-down money-back pledges. As of summer 2002, just over 1,700 or one-third of the 5,000 fund choices on sale in Canada were seg funds. In this chapter, I explain the main differences between segregated (or guaranteed funds) and regular mutual funds, set out some of the main advantages and drawbacks of seg funds, and offer a few guidelines to help you decide whether they're right for you. Throughout, I use the expression "seg funds" for both segregated funds and guaranteed investment funds (*guaranteed* funds is the term that Manulife Financial, Toronto-Dominion, and some other companies use). Both terms mean essentially the same thing: funds that promise to refund most or all of an investor's initial outlay, if held for long enough.

Hang on to Your Hats: The Rise of the Segregated Fund

Segregated funds: What a steamy, exotic name. Surely only those wacky knockabout jesters in life insurance could have come up with such an exciting term. For years, they sold a sort of grey version of a mutual fund, often wrapped inside impenetrable life policies. The funds' assets were kept separated or "segregated" from those of the life insurance company itself, hence the name. In principle, seg funds were much the same as mutual funds: Investors looking for growth from stocks or steady returns from bonds pooled their money in a professionally managed fund and were issued units, representing ownership of the pool, that were supposed to increase in value. Often these funds were marketed as part of frequently incomprehensible "whole life" or "universal life" insurance policies that were supposed to provide an investment return as well as protection for the customer's family.

Security with segs

There was one major advantage to seg funds that their flashier Porsche-driving, model-dating, mutual fund rivals couldn't match. Regulated as insurance products, not investments, seg funds came with an attractive guarantee to refund at least 75 percent of an investor's money, as long as he or she stayed invested in the fund for a set period. This guarantee was passed on to the holder's estate in the event of the investor's death. In other words, when the funds were cashed in at the time of the holder's death, the heirs got at least 75 percent of the amount that was originally invested or the market value, whichever was higher.

A crack in the armour: Segregated funds spring a leak

The rise of mutual funds in the late 1990s, with their easy-to-understand unit prices and relatively strong returns, left life insurers and their dreary complicated seg funds in the shade. Seg funds were usually managed extremely cautiously and they were loaded down with heavy expenses. Another big problem was the difficulty in figuring out what exactly you were buying: an investment or life insurance? The public, tired of carnivorous life insurance salespeople, listened avidly as a host of financial authors and other gurus told them to "buy term and invest the rest." The theory, which is generally a good one, goes like this: Why buy some complicated life insurance product loaded down with weird concepts like "commuted value" and "vanishing premiums" when you have no real way to be sure you're getting value for money? As for comparing the endlessly complex "whole life" policies from different companies — you might as well try to teach raccoons to play rugby (they never seem to be able to do the Welsh accents properly, although the mindless drinking and fighting seem to come naturally).

So, the experts advised, just protect your loved ones by buying straightforward, cheap, term life insurance for a simple monthly premium and use the savings, which would otherwise have vanished into a whole-life policy, to buy regular mutual funds. That way, you're clear on exactly what you own and what you're paying. As you know, I'm a simplicity nut, so I agree with the strategy.

If you're a self-employed businessperson or if you have complicated tax needs, life insurance still can offer some important tax-sheltering and estate-planning benefits. So there still is a place for "whole life" coverage in some cases. Just make sure, though, that you get help in this area from a fee-paid professional such as an accountant, and don't fall for the blandishments of a commission-collecting sales rep.

A fancy fund makeover

In 1997, two interesting things happened. Life insurance companies started selling seg funds that looked like mutual funds — and mutual fund companies started selling seg-fund versions of their mutual funds. Okay, it wasn't the most interesting thing that happened in 1997, but I'm sure you don't want to hear about my trip through the Channel Tunnel.

Manulife Financial got the ball rolling by launching funds that essentially took well-known mutual funds from big partners such as Trimark (now part of AIM Funds Management Inc.), AGF Management Ltd., and Fidelity Investments Canada Ltd. and "wrapped" them in a nice cozy "guaranteed investment fund" blanket that pledged to at least return all of the investors' original outlay if they died or if they held the funds for ten years. I remember that Marnie McBean, Canada's gold-winning Olympic rower, was at Manulife's press conference to launch the GIFs, incidentally. I was hoping she'd be some kind of towering Xena, Warrior Princess–type giant but she was just a normal, nice-looking lass. Not sure what she had to do with mutual funds, either. Anyway, the fund industry soon struck back, with CI Fund Management Inc. of Toronto launching segregated versions of its own funds in partnership with a life insurance company. Other mutual fund players followed suit, launching seg versions of their mutual funds, on which a life insurance company provided the guarantee. Soon, life insurance companies were scrambling to jazz up their stale seg offerings by forming partnerships with fund companies or hiring fancy managers of their own.

In the old days, seg funds were generally grey collections of blue-chip stocks and bonds, run by pallid people who took commuter trains every night at 5:30 sharp to their identical houses in awful far-off places with names like Milton, Ontario. But by early 2000, the sector had plenty of more exciting stuff on offer, including seg funds that invest in emerging markets, health sciences, resource companies, the technology-crazed Nasdaq stock market, and Asian stocks. Government regulators noticed, and started to wonder whether life insurance companies had enough money to make good on the guarantees they had attached to these relatively volatile funds. They got so worried, in fact, that they forced life insurance companies to set aside extra piles of cash to cover the potential cost of providing these risky guarantees to investors.

Here are the main features of seg funds. Note that most of these funds technically count as insurance contracts, which means they involve a whole new set of jargon and concepts. I introduce some of the new terms as we go along (yes, I know it's exciting, but please try to stay in your seat), but remember that this short description can't hope to cover every seg fund from every company.

Guaranteed return of initial investment

The essential point with seg funds is their ten-year guarantee. In insurance lingo, when you buy a seg fund, you've bought a "contract" that "matures" in ten years. It doesn't matter how you hold the fund: in a taxable account or a registered retirement savings plan (or some other kind of tax-sheltered account). The guarantee usually states that no matter what happens to the fund or the markets in the decade following your purchase, after ten years you're entitled to get back at least the amount of money you put into the fund or the market value of your units, whichever is greater. Say, for instance, you bought $10,000 worth of a fund, which proceeded to have an awful ten years, slashing the value of your holding to $8,000. After the period, you can go to the fund company and get your $10,000 back. If, by contrast, the fund does reasonably well, doubling the value of your holding to $20,000, then you get the

$20,000. Under insurance law, the guarantee must be for at least 75 percent of your investment, but many insurers and fund companies have boosted that to 100 percent for marketing reasons. However, the tough rules introduced in 2000 forced many companies to scale the guarantee back to 75 percent again. Some still sell funds with a 100-percent guarantee, but expect to pay a fat premium.

Funds that live longer than you might

The guarantee also applies when the *annuitant* (that is, the person whose life has been insured) named in the contract dies. In that case, the value of the seg fund units is paid to the policy's *beneficiary* (the person selected to get the death benefit). No matter when the policy was bought, the amount paid out to the beneficiary is subject to the guarantee. He or she gets either the original investment or the market value at the time of death, whichever is more. Note that the so-called guarantee is pretty limited. It applies only after ten years or upon death. If you sell your fund units at any other time, you get only the market value, even if it's less than your purchase price. There's no point going whining to the fund company if the value of your units has collapsed after three years. They'll just make a sympathetic little face, give you an attractive key ring, and tell you to come back in seven years.

If you're winning the game, you can press the reset button

A popular feature with most of the newer seg funds was the ability to "reset" the amount covered by the guarantee, often up to twice a year. For example, say you put $10,000 into a technology-based seg fund and saw the value of your investment soar to $13,000 in six months. You could reset the value of your contract at the higher amount, so you're guaranteed to get back at least $13,000 after ten years — or your estate is guaranteed to get back at least $13,000 when you die. The only drawback: Resetting the contract starts the clock ticking again, so that you have to wait a full ten years, not nine and a half, before the contract matures. Reset features — which greatly increase the risk of seg funds for insurance companies — have been curtailed or even eliminated under the new strict capital rules.

Asset protection

For self-employed businesspeople or professionals who might face lawsuits from creditors, segregated funds can be an excellent way to protect assets. Because they're an insurance contract, seg funds are normally out of the reach of creditors, as long as a spouse, parent, child, or grandchild is named as the beneficiary or the beneficiary has been named "irrevocably" (that is, their written consent must be obtained to name a new beneficiary). Watch out, though: The beneficiary of seg funds held in an RRSP must be revocable or the investments lose their registered status. And the protection from creditors doesn't apply where a debtor has cynically shovelled assets into seg funds just to get out of paying obligations. This is a complex area, so talk to your lawyer before making decisions.

Giving to your heir apparent without the hassle

Seg funds are a great way of passing money on to heirs without hassle or fees (apart from redemption charges if you bought the funds on a deferred-load basis). Again, because they count as life insurance, the proceeds from seg funds are paid directly to your heirs when you die; they do not pass through your estate. That means the money escapes provincial probate fees, a sort of death tax that can run as high as 1.5 percent. And the money is usually paid out to the beneficiaries immediately, without the holdups that can plague the settlement of estates. Normal bequests are public documents, but seg fund contracts are private, so you can leave money to a charity or individual without Nosey Parker finding out about it.

Seg funds avoid probate fees, but they can be less tax-efficient than regular mutual funds when the holder dies. Normally, investment assets pass to a spouse with no taxes payable immediately on capital gains that have been earned. But gains earned in a seg fund may be taxable. Be sure to talk to a knowledgeable accountant.

Seg funds are life insurance contracts; therefore, you must buy them from a salesperson licensed to sell life insurance, which means that your usual financial planner or broker may not be able to help you. However, more and more brokers and planners are taking the necessary courses to qualify to sell insurance, or they refer their clients to a colleague or local insurance agent or broker who can sell seg funds.

A Grim Reminder with Some Helpful Hints

Now, I know we journalists are always producing sensationalist scare stories, but hear me out. As you get older, it becomes more likely that you'll die in the near future.

At 30, a Canadian woman has an approximately 0.5-percent chance of dying in the next ten years, while a Canadian man has a 0.9-percent likelihood. At 40, it rises to 1 percent for women and 3 percent for men — still not too bad. But at 70, Canadian women have a 22-percent chance of dying in the next decade, while for men it's 35 percent. And at 80, women have a 50-percent chance of dying before they hit 90 — but for men, well, there's a 66-percent chance that they'll be throwing a seven in the great craps game of life before ten lacrosse seasons have come and gone. Those figures, by the way, are based on 1996 Statistics Canada numbers reported by Moshe Milevsky, a professor at Toronto's York University, in his book *Money Logic: Financial Strategies for the Smart Investor.*

The fact that older investors are more likely to die means that it gets riskier for the fund companies to guarantee a refund of the amount they put into a seg fund. So many companies reduce or restrict the guarantee for older investors. For example, some don't allow resets of the death benefit guarantee once the annuitant has turned 75. And once the annuitant has turned 90, the death benefit guarantee may be reduced.

Mutual funds must obtain their unitholders' consent to increase fees, but seg funds are pretty well free to charge what they like. Companies are still learning how to price and design seg funds — so there may also be extra bonus fee hikes on seg funds if stock and bond markets stay in a prolonged slump, which increases the cost of insuring investors against losses.

Seg funds are complicated beasts, and their "information folders," the prospectus-like documents that set out their features, are tough to read. You have to buy them through a licensed insurance salesperson, so take your time and find an experienced agent or broker whom you trust. You'll need an expert on your side to figure out the often-horrendous complexities.

How Much Does All this Certainty Cost?

How much extra do you pay for the guarantee? For volatile funds, the difference can be several percentage points of your investment each year — slicing into returns like a giant weighted machete cutting rancid butter — but if you shop aggressively and buy sane, high-quality funds, you may be able to get the coverage at reasonable cost. Check out Table 19.1, which shows the median (or midpoint) annual management expense ratio for regular mutual funds and then segregated funds in the industry's four biggest categories (which are the only four types of fund you need, apart from a money market or short-term bond fund for your cash). One of the things that makes insurance companies most nervous is clearly foreign stock investing, with its added risk in the form of currency swings — on global equity seg funds, insurers demand an extra half-percentage point in costs each year. For investments closer to home, they get less cagey. On Canadian balanced funds, normally a fairly stable stew of bonds and stocks, insurers apparently ask only four-tenths of a percent in extra costs each year. They want the same premium for providing the (limited, remember) pledge on Canadian stocks. This method of looking at average costs is actually far too kind to the seg funds because it includes older insurance funds with low expenses that aren't even on sale now. Buy one of the new seg fund versions of a regular mutual fund and you'll be lucky to get away with paying less than 4 percent per year. The survey also doesn't highlight some examples of seg funds with pretty spectacular expenses. How does 4.9 percent annually on the seg version of a Toronto-Dominion Bank health-industry fund sound? That's half of your money in a decade. Thanks, nurse. As for bond funds, charging an annual premium of one-half of 1 percent to guarantee against losses seems exorbitant, given the low volatility of bond portfolios. But buying some kind of guarantee might well be a good idea if inflation returns in a big way, potentially sending bond prices tumbling for years.

Table 19-1	The High Price of Peace of Mind	
Fund Type	*Regular Funds (MER)*	*Segregated Funds (MER)*
Global equity	2.8	3.3
Canadian equity	2.5	2.9
Canadian balanced	2.4	2.8
Canadian bond	1.7	2.2

A Closer Look at the "Deal" with Segs

Many commentators have argued forcefully that those costly seg fund guarantees are ripoffs when it comes to bond funds and of dubious benefit for balanced funds, which are supposed to be sedate portfolios that avoid losses. After all, in the 15 full calendar years from 1987 through 2001, the average Canadian bond fund lost money only twice, a drop of 5.4 percent in 1994 and another of 2.5 percent in 1999. The average balanced fund had only three losing years, falling 1.5 percent in 1990, 2.4 percent in 1994, and 0.8 percent in 2001.

Given the long-term tendency of stocks to rise, it's rare, too, to find any kind of equity fund that loses money over ten years. That makes it unlikely that you'll ever need to collect on the ten-year maturity guarantee (which promises to at least refund your investment if you've held the fund for a decade). As of mid-2002, just under 600 funds of all types had a ten-year record — and only

Reality check for seg funds

Let's see how one segregated fund has fared against the normal mutual funds it's supposed to track. Manulife Financial launched its MLI Fidelity Canadian Asset Allocation Guaranteed Investment Fund 1 in early 1997. The fund was pitched as a conservative way to achieve much the same performance as the Fidelity Canadian Asset Allocation Fund, a fund that switches among stocks, bonds, and cash in an effort to achieve high total returns. At the cost of a higher management expense ratio, currently about 3.2 percent compared with 2.5 percent for the Fidelity fund, investors in the GIF got the usual guaranteed return of at least their original investment after ten years or upon death. The Fidelity fund, by contrast, could in theory lose money over ten years, leaving unitholders in the red. The Manulife GIF funds were a huge marketing success: By the end of 1999, the Manulife Fidelity Canadian Asset Allocation GIF's assets had ballooned to $750 million, making it Canada's seventh-biggest seg fund. The GIF hasn't done a bad job of tracking the Fidelity fund. As of June 2002, an investor who put $10,000 into the fund on inception was sitting on $14,703, representing an annual return of 7.4 percent. The same $10,000 investment in the Fidelity fund grew to $15,281, for an annual return of 8.1 percent. In other words, the Manulife fund has done a reasonable job of tracking the Fidelity fund, with the difference in returns attributable to its extra annual costs of almost three-quarters of 1 percent.

14 had managed to lose money over the period. Admittedly, a lot of flea-bitten funds got buried along the way, as a result of the fund industry's habit of quietly folding underperformers into their better-performing sister funds. This "survivorship bias," the tendency of truly awful mutual funds to vanish from the record, is notorious for casting a rosy glow over the industry's history. For example, real estate funds, grim horror shows for many an investor, were restructured out of existence in the 1990s as property prices collapsed.

Those who argue that seg funds are a scam because funds rarely lose money over a decade may be missing the point. Over shorter periods, mutual funds are perfectly capable of losing money, and lots of it. Some 992 funds lost money over the *three years* ended June 2002. For older investors who are worried about dying just as their funds are going into the tank, taking thousands of dollars off the value of their estate, a segregated fund guarantee is mighty comforting. At least on death the full value of the original investment goes to the heirs (not that I'd give the slack-jawed gum-chewing brats anything, but that's just crusty old lovable me).

To Seg or Not to Seg: Deciding if They're for You

The bottom line with seg funds is almost certainly that they're best suited for older or unwell investors who have a reasonable probability of passing away in the next few years. Their protection from creditors also makes them very attractive to self-employed businesspeople and entrepreneurs.

Here are two examples, adapted from material produced by Trimark, of older investors who seem well suited for seg funds.

The first is a 67-year-old woman with four nieces and three nephews to whom she wants to leave money without legal hassles and probate fees. She puts $50,000 into a seg fund. If she dies after five years and the value of her deposit has risen to $85,000, her beneficiaries get $85,000, minus any withdrawals or redemption fees if she bought the funds on a back-end-load basis. But say the market has slumped and the value of her contract is only $43,000. Then her beneficiaries get the guaranteed amount of $50,000, again minus redemption fees.

The other example is a 61-year-old self-employed engineer who's two years from retirement. He's repelled by the low interest rates available on guaranteed investment certificates but he doesn't want to put his money at risk just before he retires. So he invests $100,000 in seg funds. If it grows to $230,000 in ten years, when the contract matures, he gets $230,000. But if the value of his fund drops to $80,000 at maturity, he gets his original $100,000, minus any withdrawals.

Then there are the estate-planning advantages of seg funds, especially the relative simplicity of passing on money to a beneficiary by simply putting it in a seg fund. You shouldn't get too excited about saving on probate fees, though, because the higher management fees on seg funds will quickly wipe out that advantage.

Choosing a seg fund really comes down to the famous "pillow factor." Just how well can you sleep at night knowing that your money is in danger? If you're really afraid of losses, then seg funds may well be your thing, despite their higher management expense ratio. The emotional security is sometimes worth the higher MERs.

Chapter 20

Clone Funds: Neat but Still New

. . . .

In This Chapter

▶ Understanding what RSP foreign funds are

▶ Reviewing the potential benefits of clones

▶ Cutting through clone confusion

▶ Knowing when to avoid clone funds

. . . .

*T*here's nothing as depressing as sitting in your dim room, staring at the peeling wallpaper while a party rages on next door, complete with excited squeals, smashing glass, and drunken yelling. Especially the excited squeals. Well, in the 1990s, Canadian investors sometimes felt like that when they heard about booming stock markets overseas and south of the border. In the 20 years from the end of 1979 to the end of 1999, if you just invested a lump sum and left it in place, global stocks produced an average annual return of more than 17 percent in Canadian-dollar terms, while U.S. stocks were good for more than 19 percent. Canadian stocks, as measured by the Standard & Poor's/Toronto Stock Exchange composite index, produced a watery return of less than 12 percent.

The slump in overseas and U.S. stocks since 2000 has narrowed the gap. As of June 2002, the 20-year return on global stocks had dropped to 14 percent while the annual return on U.S. stocks had fallen below 16 percent. But the 20-year return on Canadian stocks was still stuck below 12 percent. So the fund industry, ever ready to please, has come up with a new generation of RSP funds called *clone funds* that are designed to give you the benefits of investing in foreign markets, but with a kicker: They also count as Canadian content in your RRSP and other pension plans. In this chapter I explain how these new clone or RSP funds can be a good way to increase the number of foreign stocks in your portfolio — and this both reduces your risk and improves the growth prospects of your mutual fund portfolio. I outline the advantages and drawbacks of using clones and look at the mechanics of how they work.

A Clone by Any Other Name . . .

Clone funds got that scary-sounding name because they're a copy of a normal foreign mutual fund, just as a cloned living thing is a reproduction of the original. However, cloned funds have one important difference from the fund they're modelled on — using financial engineering, the fund company has modified the clone so it actually counts as a Canadian investment even though the returns it produces are similar to those generated by the original mutual fund. The drawback to buying a clone is higher expenses plus all the other risks of foreign stocks. The biggest of those risks is the danger that you'll be retiring after the Canadian dollar has risen sharply against world currencies. If that happens, an investment in overseas stocks will have fallen nastily relative to your Canadian-dollar retirement needs. You don't want to be cruising into Tim Hortons with the momma in tow, clutching a grubby fistful of Turkish lire.

And there's another potential drawback to the clones. To count as Canadian content, they use financial alchemy and over-the-counter risk-swapping deals with banks. That not only adds costs, but it also brings more complexity and the slight danger that, in very unsettled times, the financial techniques used to keep the clones ticking just won't work. For example, there's a remote possibility that the bank or broker partners who help fund companies to build clones will run into some kind of cash flow difficulty, which prevents them from making good on promises they've made. So to cut costs and keep things simple, you should avoid clones and stick to regular foreign equity funds that actually own overseas and U.S. stocks in a straightforward way.

The Risks of Keeping All Your Cash in Canada

Canada may be the best country in the world to live in, but don't put all your money into Canadian mutual funds. For safety and the chance of earning higher returns, it's important that you invest a good chunk of your money in funds that buy stocks and bonds in other countries. By leaving most of your money in just one market such as Canada, you lose in three ways:

- ✔ Increase short-term risk, because the tiny Canadian market is more prone to big swings than an investment in a diversified basket of world markets.

- ✔ Miss out on investment opportunities, such as big global companies in other countries.

- ✔ Lose the opportunity to use currencies to insure against Canadian inflation or a prolonged Canadian economic slump.

The problem is that under the spirit of the tax law (and just hope you don't find *him* pawing at you on a cold night), Canadians must keep most of their tax-advantaged registered retirement savings plans and registered retirement income funds in this country.

✔ Until 1999, only 20 percent of your RRSP or RRIF — as measured by the acquisition cost of all the investments — could be outside Canada.

✔ For the 2000 tax year, the limit expanded to 25 percent.

✔ In 2001, the limit rose to 30 percent, where it looks set to stay for the moment.

The limits on foreign content have long been a source of annoyance for many investors, who chafe at the requirement to tie most of their RRSP money up in one small market. But Canadians really lost their tempers in 1998, when the domestic stock market hugely underperformed markets abroad. The average global equity fund produced a return of almost 18 percent that year. However, a stagnant Canadian market, which was dragged down by low commodity prices and the government's refusal to allow monster (and arguably monstrous) bank mega-mergers, left the average Canadian fund with a wretched loss of just over 2 percent, seriously ticking off investors.

The Dawn of a New Product: The Clone

To let their annoyed customers get more foreign content into their RRSPs, fund companies furiously marketed new clone or "RSP eligible" funds that track a foreign market or fund but still qualify as Canadian for registered plans. These funds were a runaway hit, attracting assets of almost $9 billion by the end of 1999. However, it's unlikely that clones will again become such a hot product until the Canadian market goes into another slump — and lately we've been leaving foreign markets in the dust. The great crash in telecommunications and tech stocks has been surprisingly gentle on Canadian investors. The average Canadian equity fund actually made 4.1 percent annually in the three years ended June 2002, while the average global equity fund fell 3.9 percent.

Clones are similar in principle to the "index-linked" guaranteed investment certificates that banks issued when interest rates plunged in the late 1990s. The index GICs guaranteed to refund your original investment but also promised to pay a return that was linked to, although nearly always less than, a given foreign market. The weird contorted rules on these GICs, including limits on your profits and staggered closing dates for the markets, made it tough to work out if they were a good deal. The guarantee of at least getting principal back (after it had been eaten away by inflation, of course) was attractive to nervous investors. But index GICs had a huge problem: They violated the principle of simplicity because it was so difficult to establish the

---

Mackenzie's giant cloning experiment

In mid-2002, one of the biggest clones on the market was Mackenzie Financial Corp.'s Universal RSP Select Managers. Launched in May 1999, it ballooned to an incredible $4 billion in less than a year, probably the fastest-ever growth for a fund in Canada. It generally takes years or decades for a fund to get that big. This fund was modelled on the Universal Select Managers Fund, a fund with multiple managers, each running a portion of the fund. Normally you would expect Universal Select Managers and its clone to be steady, but not stellar, performers because they have five different managers. Each manager picks about ten stocks, giving the fund a concentrated portfolio of only about 50 names. The idea is this: When one or two managers are in a slump, the others will probably do better, which arguably makes this the only global stock fund you need to own. But because no one investing style will dominate, it's possible that the fund will simply trade in line with world stock indexes, minus its annual expenses of 2.6 percent. However, in practice, the managers running the fund were biased in favour of technology stocks: Universal Select Managers shot up 58.4 percent in 1999 and then crashed more than 24 percent in 2000. As of June 2002, the original Universal Select Managers had posted a three-year annual loss of 8.3 percent, worse than the 3.9-percent loss suffered by the average global equity fund. How closely did the clone track that performance? Universal RSP Select Managers' three-year loss was 8.8 percent, meaning that the clone's return was an average one-half of one percentage point lower each year.

---

value of your account on any given day. And if you don't know how much you're making, how do you know how much you're making?

With clone funds, the fund companies are simply buying a more volatile type of index GIC from a bank or broker, and passing the gains and losses on to investors. In this case, the return from the GIC is the fund or market that the clone is supposed to track, minus a bunch of fees (not for you, though). The clone fund will also lose money when the corresponding index or fund it tracks has problems, unlike an index GIC. The cost to you for all these fireworks and dancing girls is, mainly, expenses.

The real cost of clones

The new generation of clones got going only in 1999, so it's still too early to say exactly how far behind regular funds they're likely to lag over the long term because of extra costs. Clones that track a normal fund will probably carry extra costs equal to one-half of 1 percent of the investor's money each year. Most global equity funds already charge more than 2.5 percent annually, so tacking on an extra one-half of a percentage point gets you up to a Ritz-Carlton–style expense ratio of 3 percent and over each year. That's a lot of bomb damage for your Panzers to take on the way to the front, before they've even encountered the enemy.

Looking for an affordable clone

There are some clones that may be a better deal for investors. The banks and some other no-load companies can earn higher profit margins on their funds because they don't have to pay commissions to brokers. So they can afford to sell clone index funds with lower expenses than clones that track regular funds. Index funds simply give you a return that's in line with the stock or bond market as a whole by "tracking" a stock market index such as the Standard & Poor's 500-share index of America's biggest companies. On some of these clone index funds, the annual management expense ratio is less than

Unclearly Canadian?

The government's exact reason for insisting that most of an RRSP stay in Canada isn't often explicitly stated. But it seems to be a feeling that people who benefit from the handsome tax deferrals that RRSPs provide should keep their money in the country, where it backs Canadian enterprise. After all, RRSPs cost the provincial and federal governments an extremely large amount of lost taxes: about $15 billion by some estimates. And nearly all of it goes to comfortably off people because they're the ones with the big RRSPs. As usual, in other words, the wealthy have done a pretty good job of hijacking the political process. Some economists (but not all) think that handicapping RRSPs and RRIFs by forcing them to keep most of their money in Canada is useless. That's because, they say, the money will just slosh out of the country in some other way. In other words, the costs of goods, services, and capital in Canada ultimately just reflect their true worth on the global market, whatever jiggery-pokery the government does with RRSPs.

The argument goes something like this: By forcing stock and bond market investments to stay in Canada, supporters of the foreign-content limit seem to be trying to reduce the cost of capital for Canadian businesses (and governments too, presumably, since investors' money is also needed for government bonds). But in the Internet age, and in a country with minimal controls on other flows of money, cash sluices in and out through a thousand other uncontrolled channels. That means Canada, with its sophisticated and efficient financial markets, is just part of the global market for money. So putting a dyke on one portion of the beach, in the form of RRSP foreign-content limits, does nothing to lower the overall cost of capital for Canadian companies.

Scrapping the RRSP foreign limit altogether may sound like a good move but remember that the economists who advocate it can sometimes be seen wolfing down seafood in lush restaurants with the investment industry types who pay for their research. Any economic theory depends on the axioms and dearly beloved assumptions of the assumer. The dominant economic dogma of our times is that any kind of control or check on the free flow of capital is a bad thing because, allegedly, it leads to inefficiency. So, for example, there were dire predictions that Malaysia would become an international economic pariah after it slapped on controls during the Asian economic crisis of 1997, to prevent foreigners from abruptly yanking their money out of the country. But Malaysia didn't become an outcast. And free market fanatics also conveniently forget that Chile, one of Latin America's economic success stories, has had controls on foreign investors for years.

1 percent, much better than the 3 percent or more levied by some broker-sold clone funds. So far, most of the banks' offerings track a foreign market index, which at least makes it easy to know what you'll be getting. It's too early to predict just how good these funds will be at staying close to their index, but the modest fees imposed by these funds make them attractive. Just don't go overboard until it becomes clearer how well they'll be run.

Keep it simple and put 10 percent of your cash into a clone that tracks the Standard & Poor's index of 500 big U.S. stocks and another 10 percent into a fund that follows the Morgan Stanley Capital International Index or the MSCI European Index. At least you'll have a conservative investment in high-quality stocks around the world.

Looking at Why Clones Are Great for Some Investors

The bottom line with clone funds is that putting a small portion of your RRSP into one or two of them can't hurt — but don't go overboard. These products are just too new to gamble a large proportion of your life savings on them.

Clones: A couple can't hurt

There are enormous advantages to buying lots of investments outside Canada. The choice of public companies in Canada is relatively limited and stock markets in the U.S. and other countries have at times dramatically outperformed ours, at least when you include *currency gains*. They're windfall profits that mount up when you get lucky with changes in foreign exchange rates. For example, if the Canadian dollar drops 50 percent against the U.S. dollar, then that will double the value of your U.S. assets in Canadian-dollar terms.

Canada has a relatively tiny economy that is considered extremely *open*, meaning that much of what we produce is exported and lots of the stuff we consume is imported. That means we're very dependent on what happens overseas, exposing our economy to imported inflation or slumps in demand. We specialize in just a few industries such as autos, mining, some software and energy. That makes our narrow economy more prone to dangerously big slumps.

The big problem with the Canadian market is that there aren't many Canadian global technology corporations or huge consumer-products companies such Coca-Cola Co. But businesses such as large-scale technology empires and global consumer brands have been one of the best investments out there for

How to send your money on holiday

There's been a lot of math and shifting percentages in this chapter, so let's try using a simple example to illustrate how you as an investor in 2001 could use clone funds to get most of your RRSP into non-Canadian stocks and bonds.

First, you buy straightforward foreign funds with 30 percent of your money. Next, you use another 20 percent to buy clone funds. Now, one-half of your portfolio is in foreign investments. Finally, you look for Canadian funds that themselves hold some foreign stocks and bonds.

A mutual fund can hold up to 30 percent of its assets in non-Canadian assets while still counting as Canadian content. Say, for the sake of argument, that you buy Canadian funds that have the maximum 30 percent in foreign shares and bonds — if they account for the other half of your portfolio, that's another 15 percent in non-Canadian investments.

Hey presto, a grand total of 65 percent of your money is now outside Canada. See Chapter 23 for more on RRSP rules.

the past two decades. And consumer products outfits tend to grow their profits steadily year after year, instead of going into major slumps when the world economy slows or commodity prices drop.

But don't assume clones will solve all your problems. This type of fund has not yet fully proved itself. Because of the extra expenses and the uncertainty over how well they'll ultimately work out for investors, don't put much more than one-fifth of your total money into clones.

Don't forget that professional Canadian investors such as pension funds always keep a large portion of their portfolio in Canadian stocks to match their liabilities, a policy that's probably good for individuals too. In other words, pension funds know they will have to pay out pensions in Canadian dollars so they ensure that most of their assets remain in Canadian dollars also. Otherwise, they're speculating on currencies — a huge run-up in the Canadian dollar could leave them short of cash to pay their liabilities because all the foreign stocks they hold have dropped in value.

Understanding the Role that Currencies Play in Investing

Yes, clones apparently offer an easy way to ride hot foreign stocks to big profits. But remember that Canadian stocks haven't really been all that bad over the years — one of the big reasons they have underperformed is that our dollar has been in a long slow decline versus foreign currencies. But there's no reason to assume that the Canadian dollar will go on declining. In other words, the currency effect means that buying a foreign equity fund has been as comfortable as getting slightly drunk on a cruise ship and toddling off to bed. But the effect of a recovery in the Canuck buck will be like hitting an iceberg for investors who have all of their money outside this country, because the value of their foreign assets will drop.

The main reason for the decline in our dollar was steady erosion of the price of commodities and other goods that Canada sells to get foreign exchange. In fact, keeping our currency from falling even further against the U.S. dollar represented a major achievement for a small economy. That's because our interest rates and inflation have at times been even lower than America's since the late 1990s. Traditionally, when the Bank of Canada tried to bring interest rates below U.S. rates, our dollar collapsed as money moved south of the border in search of a higher return. But from the late 1990s through early 2000, for example, Canadian interest rates were lower than American rates, implying that at least some investors were satisfied that Canadian inflation would stay low and that our dollar was a good bet for stability.

In the good old days, when the Canadian dollar kept falling, you didn't even have to think about currencies. Investors just bought foreign equity funds, and if Canada and/or the Canadian dollar ran into trouble, then the foreign-currency holdings acted as insurance. If virtually all of your RRSP is in Canadian-dollar assets, then you're vulnerable to a homegrown crisis, such as a major row over Quebec independence.

But Canada's achievement in slashing inflation and interest rates, arguably at the cost of lower living standards for millions of people, means our currency could be in for a turnaround. Global inflation might return, for example, sending the prices of Canadian commodity exports higher. Or Canadian technology companies might thrive and grow worldwide, which could also be enough to lift our currency as money from export sales flows into this country.

It all means that you shouldn't send every last cent out of the country, where it will be exposed to foreign exchange losses. Because when you take out currencies, the Canadian stock market hasn't been such a bad performer.

Most of the clones offer full exposure to the foreign currencies they invest in. And that's as it should be: One of the reasons why investing in foreign countries provides such valuable diversification is that it puts some of your portfolio into guilders, lire, and yen. But fund companies are often far too vague when it comes to explaining the foreign-currency policy of their clones. It's one area where they could do a much better job.

To make absolutely sure that you're getting foreign-currency exposure, always check that the clone's structure doesn't eliminate the foreign-currency effect in some way. For example, a clone fund that tracks the U.S. market but hedges away U.S.-dollar exposure could end up watering down your returns if the Canadian dollar falls. Say the value of the fund's U.S. stocks rises 20 percent and the Canadian dollar drops 5 percent against the U.S. greenback. A regular U.S. equity fund would give a return of about 25 percent, representing the stock appreciation plus the currency gain. But if the clone has no exposure to foreign currencies, then 20 percent is all you get. Yes, a currency-hedged clone will do well when the Canadian dollar rises against other currencies, but you're narrowing your portfolio unnecessarily. Insist that the salesperson, bank teller, or fund employee check into the currency question and get back to you. And if you've bought a clone that's based on an existing foreign fund, look at the monthly mutual fund report in your newspaper, or log on to www.globefund.com, the *Globe and Mail*'s mutual fund Web site, to check that the clone is doing a reasonable job of tracking the original fund.

Taxes: Don't Get Skewered by Clones

Clones or RSP funds are designed to be held within RRSPs or registered retirement income funds — and putting them into an account that has to pay taxes can be seriously damaging to your wealth. That's because the structure of these funds, with their constant rolling over of stock futures and other bits of financial engineering, means that they often generate a lot of income and capital gains that must be paid out to investors in the form of *distributions*. Distributions are simply payments that a fund makes to its unitholders — they're taxable in your hands, even if you simply take them in the form of extra units. (See Chapter 24 for more on how mutual funds are taxed.)

Never hold a clone fund in a regular, taxable account. They're intended for RRSPs, so keep 'em there.

Getting lots of distributions from a fund isn't a problem if you're holding it in an RRSP, where taxes are paid only on money that's taken out of the plan. But if you have to pay tax on each distribution as you get it, you'll end up sharing a lot of your return from the fund with the government. Even if you reinvest the payout in more units, you're still on the hook, just as if you'd taken the distribution in cash.

Chapter 21

Fund Packages: Nutritious Stew for Investors (if a Little Dull)

*W*e don't go to McDonald's to be challenged. We go in there to be soothed and babied in a corporate version of the womb, taken into a nice sparkling maternity-hospital-like environment where choices are limited and everything is relentlessly predictable and monotonous. Best of all, we can order by number — just point your hoof at the food combination you want and grunt "No. 4." After all, we're always being hassled and badgered to think for ourselves in our exciting and empowered workplaces — so isn't it nice to just regress to a vegetative state once in a while? Well, mutual fund companies and stockbrokers are keen students of human weakness and they've noticed that many investors like to be presented with simple one-decision products that they can just buy and forget about.

Hence the birth of fund packages. Brokers, bank employees, and financial planners enjoy selling them too. They're nice and simple to pitch, and they help prevent those annoying phone calls from clients who want to know why their Rust-Encrusted Highly-Indebted Declining Heavy Industry Recovery Value Fund is bottom of the performance table once again. Typically, before you're sold a fund package, you'll be asked to fill out a questionnaire that establishes how much risk you can stand and what sort of annual return you're demanding. Then, the salesperson or bank staffer will suggest that you put your money into a collection of funds with an impressive-sounding name such as "aggressive growth portfolio" or "conservative savings asset allocation service." A "long-term" or "aggressive" package, for example, will usually contain lots of stock market funds while a "conservative" product will be full of bond funds. The bottom line, though, is that these fund portfolios don't really make investing simpler. They have so many confusing names and rules that I think, for reasons I set out later, you're better off buying individual funds. In this chapter, I describe the main types of preselected fund packages and list some of their advantages and disadvantages.

The Flavours Fund Packages Come In

Fund companies, stockbrokers, insurance companies, fund managers, banks, and financial planning chains have come up with a bewildering range of fund combinations that claim to take care of your every need, eliminating the need to pick and choose your own funds.

When banks and other fund sellers pitch these packages what they're really trying to do, of course, is eliminate the need for you to pick any other fund seller's wares. They'd much rather you stuck to their product line than mix and match funds from different sellers. So they offer their super-simple off-the-shelf packages that relieve you of the need to choose your mutual funds, and that tempt you to go with their stuff. More recently, some companies have come up with packages that also include other companies' funds. For example, Royal Bank of Canada in 2000 started selling Royal Select Choices Portfolios, collections of funds that included offerings from other companies. You'll notice that where such bank-sold packages include *third-party funds* — funds from other managers — they're usually from companies such as Fidelity Investments Canada or AGF Management that pay a sales commission to the people who put the package together. These packages may include good funds, but they also carry the same disadvantages as other pre-mixed fund selections. That is, their costs can be high and it's hard to know which fund is doing well for you and which is sinking like a lead submarine.

These mixtures of funds come with glorious glossy brochures and pseudo-scientific titles such as "portfolios," "asset allocation services," "portfolio management programs," or "wrap accounts." Some use the company's own funds, known in the jargon as "proprietary products," while others include "third-party" funds. But all have one thing in common: The fund company or brokerage house provides an all-inclusive solution that's supposed to save you worry and trouble in return for handing over your cash, and sometimes parting with an extra fee. In nearly every case, you're asked to fill in a questionnaire that helps to establish how much risk you're willing to take on, ranging from none-at-all to full-speed-ahead-riverboat-gambler. From there, the salesperson, bank employee, or fund company representative simply takes your money and sticks it into a suitable package, usually straight off the shelf, but sometimes supposedly designed for your needs. You'll probably be offered something that falls into one of these three risk categories: conservative, moderate, or growth. And the packages usually come in "registered" (or "RSP") versions for tax-sheltered registered retirement savings plans, whose foreign content is subject to limits, and "investment" (or "non-RSP") editions for taxable investors. Non-RSP packages can contain unlimited foreign content.

✔ The safest packages of all are usually dubbed "conservative," and that's what they're all about: conserving capital while offering a reasonable flow of income from bonds or treasury bills, and perhaps the chance of some capital gains from stocks. (Remember that "income" in this context doesn't have to mean money you take out of the account and use to buy skateboard pants and miniature Russian wolfhounds. It can also refer to the steady interest payments generated by bonds, money that you simply plow back into the same kind of investment.) These conservative packages are usually full of funds that invest in bonds — which are debts owed by governments and big companies — and *money market* securities — which are short-term borrowings by the government and large corporations.

✔ The next step up on the volatility scale is usually dubbed "moderate," "balanced," or "medium." These packages are pretty similar to the typical balanced fund. They're for investors who don't mind the occasional loss in return for the higher returns that stocks and long-term bonds offer. Generally, their mixture of stocks and bonds will be close to one-half each, with a cash anchor of about 5 percent.

✔ Finally, there are the "growth" or "long- term" mixtures that own mostly stocks. These typically have only a small portion of their assets, usually 25 percent or less, in bond and money market funds, with the rest in equities. You'll be steered into these mixtures only if you've indicated on the questionnaire that you won't be needing to cash in any of the investment for several years. If your "horizon" is long-term like that, the theory goes, you shouldn't be worried by a nasty dip in the value of your holdings in the short term. The most entertaining growth packages, naturally, are those with "aggressive" in their name. Much as I love to think of these being bought by shaven-headed former paratroopers with drinking problems, it simply denotes a mixture that puts as little as 10 percent of your assets into bonds and holds lots of volatile stuff such as emerging markets and technology companies.

Canadian Imperial Bank of Commerce offers index-fund fund packages that are among the better buys. They impose no extra fees beyond the charges and costs of the underlying CIBC funds. Index funds track the entire stock or bond market at a low cost to the investor. Everyone should own some. (See Chapter 15 for more on index funds.)

Before choosing a fund package, work out what you want it to do for you.

Okay, you've got your own unique challenges and obsessions, but we all pretty well fit into one of these groups:

✔ You're really just getting by or you plan to spend your savings in the next year or so, perhaps on a house or car, and you just want something safe to hold it with a bit of appreciation. In that case, your goals are said to be "short term." Then go with the "short-term" or "money market" package. You'll find those packages listed under Canadian Money Market or Canadian Short-Term Bond in the monthly fund reports in the newspapers and on Web sites such as www.globefund.com.

The money market is just that — the place where you can deposit cash for short periods and get it back in less than a year with a modest return that was only about 2 percent annually as of mid-2002. Packages in this short-term group will hold the most conservative mixtures of all, consisting mainly of funds that buy high-quality bonds and other loans that come due in a few months.

✔ You want to tie your money up for something like three to seven years and you expect a reasonable return of around 6 to 7 percent while minimizing risk. In that case, you should buy a "balanced" package that's a combo of bonds and shares in big, safe companies. Look under Canadian Balanced and Global Balanced and Asset Allocation in the newspapers or on the Internet. There's a choice of Canadian or global packages. These balanced products might suit you even if this is very long-term money but you just hate risk.

✔ Finally, you're interested in chasing returns in the 8- to 10-percent range or even more, and you don't mind tying your money up for five years or longer. Then buy an "aggressive" or "long-term" package. You'll find it under one of the main categories of equity funds in the newspapers or on the Web. The packages consist mostly of shares, and you can choose among products that invest in Canadian or global stocks.

Should you buy a Canadian or global package? It depends partly on what you think will happen to currencies. If the Canadian dollar tanks, then it would be better to have your money outside the country. If it soars, then it's better to keep a lot of your investments Canadian. But it's impossible to know in advance what will happen to foreign exchange rates. For short-term and medium-term savings, an all-Canadian package of investments is probably fine because you plan to spend the money relatively soon and you'll be spending it in Canadian dollars. But with long-term equity packages, you should make sure you get at least some global stock action. It spreads your risk by giving you a more mixed bag of investments, and there are great companies to invest in all around the world. And you also need to protect yourself against a drop in the Canadian dollar.

What to Find out before You Buy

Be sure to pose these stumpers to anyone who tries to peddle you a fund portfolio. This section reviews the two essential questions to ask.

How much will this cost me?

With some of these preselected mixtures, you have to pay the regular fees and expenses of the funds included in the service — plus an extra fee for the package itself that can run as high as 1 percent annually. Adding another 1 percent in yearly costs is a heavy weight to put on your portfolio, especially if some of the equity funds in the package already have management expense ratios (MERs) of more than 2.5 percent. Some brokers and financial planners sell their own private *wrap* or *asset allocation* products that use funds that charge low or no management fees. But in this case, the client pays a separate fee — often listed directly on her or his statement — to cover the asset allocation service.

In theory, costs you incur trying to earn investment income are tax-deductible, so you may be able to claim fund management fees against taxes — some vendors like to make a big song and dance about this advantage. But that applies only to fees that are charged separately to the investor and not simply deducted from the fund. Ordinary mutual fund charges and fees are quietly taken out of the fund's assets by the manager and can't be claimed as a cost. However, though they're not directly deductible, ordinary fees do reduce your taxable capital gains and income by cutting into the return you get from your funds, so the fees are ultimately deductible also.

Yes, it's great to see fees broken out openly on your statement instead of having them buried in the management expense ratio, but make sure you realize what you're paying — because it can be confusing. Funds that charge you expenses separately, instead of taking them out of your annual return, present another problem. Because they ignore expenses and costs when they report those returns, they'll often seem to be doing better than funds that handle fees and costs in the normal way, by extracting them before they report performance.

How do I know how well I'm doing?

Things can get extremely confusing here. Many of these services don't publish their returns publicly, and even if they do the names are often so similar that it can be hard to remember what you own. Some fund companies even establish a sort of imaginary unit price, simply for the purpose of calculating performance. That's mostly because the newspapers and Internet mutual fund reporting services use special software for working out a fund's returns. Essentially, their systems determine performance by calculating the changes in the price of a unit, taking into account any distributions for unitholders along the way. For example, if you check out the portfolios available from CIBC in the monthly fund reports in the papers, you'll notice they have unit prices. In fact, when you buy into these services, you sometimes buy each fund in the package separately with its own unit price, in the normal way.

The units shown for the package may simply be there for ease of calculating returns. The account statement you receive semi-annually, quarterly, or monthly for any service should make your returns absolutely clear, so ask to see a sample before you sign up. Don't be fobbed off by vague excuses such as "we're changing the system so we don't have any of the new ones." If the salesperson or bank employee can't demonstrate that your returns will be clearly reported, avoid the product.

The Pros and Cons of Packages

Many people are perfectly happy with the returns and risk protection provided by the predetermined mixture of funds that they bought. While they are not for every investor, there are some pretty solid reasons to be satisfied. Stay tuned for the highlights.

The upside of fund packages

The idea of simply handing over your cash to let professionals decide the asset mix is wonderfully attractive psychologically. And fund packages offer a number of other important advantages:

- **Dealing with only one fund company:** You don't have to juggle account statements and tax slips from several sellers. Most investors, with their busy lives, loathe getting piles of mail from fund companies.

- **Automatic rebalancing:** You don't have to rejig your funds if strong returns or big losses throw the asset mix of your portfolio out of whack. Many packages are periodically rebalanced by the company so that clients don't end up with too much of their money riding on just one type of investment. For example, say you've put $100,000 into a sedate portfolio made up equally of bond funds and stock funds. If the stock market slides by 20 percent but interest rates stay unchanged, your stock funds will probably be worth only $40,000 while your bond funds are still worth $50,000. To maintain your 50–50 mix, the portfolio service will redeem about $5,000 worth of bond funds and put the money into stocks instead, to restore the equal balance.

- **Reasonable fees:** Because they use regular mutual funds that are subject to public scrutiny and fairly tight securities laws, the widely available fund packages charge fees that are usually reasonable, at least when you compare them to the charges that trust companies or lawyers can levy for looking after assets.

The downside of fund packages

There are drawbacks to letting someone else pick your funds for you. Here are a few:

- ✔ **An unexciting way to invest:** It's boring and Big Brotherish. All you get is the same gruel-like return earned by everyone else who buys the same package, with no real clue as to which fund did well and which one barked your money away. It's more interesting to be an informed consumer who can tell that, for example, bonds were up while international equities were down, just by looking at your account statement.

- ✔ **Beware of extra costs:** If extra costs are levied, they eat into your return, especially when tacked on top of the underlying mutual funds' fees and expenses.

- ✔ **Look out for tax implications of rebalancing:** The regular portfolio rebalancing by the fund company can trigger taxable capital gains distributions for investors holding the package of funds outside a tax-deferred account such as an RRSP. Fund companies maintain that these distributions will generally be small because they're simply readjusting the asset mix rather than turning the fund inside out, but taxable payouts add unpredictability and can cut into your real, after-tax return.

- ✔ **Make sure returns are reported:** Be very wary before you buy into any fund or managed investment whose returns and unit price aren't published regularly in the newspapers. Remember that sunlight disinfects: If the performance isn't publicly reported alongside that of big regular mutual funds, making comparisons simple, then you can never really be sure you're not stuck with a dog.

- ✔ **Don't get stuck with their funds:** Worst of all, if you're in *pooled* or *house-brand* funds that are sold only through a particular brokerage or financial planning firm, then moving your money elsewhere can be troublesome. You might even have to sell your holdings, incurring a nasty tax hit if the funds are held outside a tax-deferred account. Such limited-availability funds have snob appeal and they may offer extra features such as fancy personalized reporting. But I personally stick to widely available funds and I think I always will. Not only are their returns easy to discover and compare, but also if I get tired of my brokerage or salesperson I can simply move the funds to another account at another firm, without having to cash them in.

- ✔ **Great potential for confusion:** Working out how you're doing or even what package you own can be tricky, given the confusing multiplicity of products with similar names. The brochures I've seen are often vague on how the systems actually work and salespeople are hard-pressed to keep up with the flood of new offerings. And a whole bunch of transactions may be reported to you on your statement, just as though you had ordered them, when the portfolio is automatically rebalanced or a fund is dropped from the mixture. If you're not completely sure you understand what you're buying, better to steer clear.

Down, boy

If the salesperson has sold his or her clients a pre-mixed package containing a selection of funds holding cash, bonds, and stocks, chances are that at least something in the casserole will be doing all right — so a dog's slimy wet nose won't stand out so much. And there's another advantage for fund sellers: It's easy to tell if an individual fund you own is an underperformer but it's pretty well impossible to tell if your pre-mixed fund package isn't doing its job. That's because packages are virtually impossible to compare with each other. These things use so many different rules and structures that they're like lobsters and cantaloupes. Meanwhile, quite a lot of nonsense gets said about the magical results of combining funds in these packages. I once wrote this about a fund: "You could travel to the worst-run Canadian Tire store in the country, root around at the back of the filthy warehouse and dig out the wettest and most disgusting bag of salt. Then you could dress up the salt in a suit and tie, and give it an expense account, a pair of wire-rim glasses, and a nice office in Winnipeg. And it would do a better job of picking U.S. stocks than these guys." Someone from the company called to gripe that I was being unfair, because the fund fitted in some mystical way with the rest of the seller's funds. But bad returns are bad returns, no matter how you cut 'em.

Just about every fund seller claims that its asset allocation strategies are best, and comparing them is just about impossible. That's because the returns produced by any system tell only half of the story. The other half is how much risk did the portfolio take on and how violent were the swings. To provide a crude example, a portfolio that made 20 percent a year for five years might look superior to one that generated a return of just 8 percent annually. But if it turns out that the first portfolio was exclusively invested in super-risky early-stage biotechnology shares while the second held mostly government bonds, then the second portfolio probably did a better job — earning a good profit relative to the low level of risk it incurred.

Before buying a fund package from a bank or other seller, look at the newspaper's monthly fund report (the *Globe*'s is printed on the third Thursday of each month) or get a printout from www.globefund.com of the fund package you want. Before you hand any money over, make sure you can find the package in the newspaper's monthly report or on the Web. That way, you'll be able to track your returns easily from month to month without relying solely on your account statement from the company.

Don't worry too much about trying to figure out the difference between one company's Nervous Nellie Never-Lose-a-Penny-of-My-Money Portfolio and another fund seller's Shaky Sue Can't Stand the Slightest Suspicion of Suffering a Slump Asset Allocation Service. The big thing, as usual, is to look for low costs, so you know you're getting reasonable value, and clear reporting, so you at least know how you're doing.

Long-Term Capital Management: The Suits Have No Clothes On

Just about every fund company that sells predetermined fund mixtures will give you a riveting — well, pretty dreary actually — song and dance about the wonderful way they knead the dough, sprinkle it with fairy dust and confectioner's sugar, and bake it to a cute golden crispness.

They'll talk about the "efficient frontier," that magical place in asset allocation land where you can find cappuccinos for less than 50 cents and earn higher returns while taking no more risk. But take all such claims with a big swig of salty vinegar. Investment wizards are only infallible until they blow it, and the explosion can be spectacular. The truth is that the market and economy have a delightful way of throwing weird slimy curveballs that completely fool the number-crunchers. No system is perfect.

That was proved in a spectacular way in late 1998 when the Nobel Prize–winning geniuses running Connecticut-based Long-Term Capital Management had to be rescued by the U.S. government and a cabal of U.S., Swiss, German, and British banks because the fund's losses threatened the world's financial system. The private fund had lost $2 billion (U.S.) in a month — its ultimate losses topped $4.5 billion — and it had about $1.25 trillion worth of complicated bets outstanding on stocks and bonds around the world. Less than a year before the near-collapse, two of the eggheads behind Long-Term Capital, Robert Merton and Myron Scholes, were awarded the Nobel Prize in economics for their work on playing options, a risky way of betting on stocks. In collaboration with fellow mathematician Fischer Black, they produced work that led to the famous Black-Scholes formula for deciding what price an investor should pay for an option. (An *option* is essentially a bet that a stock or some other financial assets will fall or rise in price.)

Their excuse for the collapse of Long-Term Capital? They didn't realize that financial markets just about everywhere would dry up after Russia defaulted on its debts in the summer of 1998 (the Toronto Stock Exchange collapsed by 28 percent in a few months). The worldwide near panic blew Long-Term Capital's careful formulas and intricate financial dealings out of the water. Mr. Merton and Mr. Scholes should have listened more closely to boring old Mr. Black, who died in 1995. According to some accounts, he had warned that big plunges in markets would throw a wrench in their theory but the other two ignored him and went on to win the Nobel Prize with their faulty work.

Preselected packages of funds are convenient, but there's no guarantee that the fund company, bank, or broker has got the mix right. And the packages can make it hard to know how well you're doing or even what exactly you own. Better to buy a varied selection of high-quality low-cost funds, monitor the mix yourself, and adjust it when one asset class either soars or falls out of bed.

Part IV
The Nuts and Bolts of Keeping Your Portfolio Going

"My portfolio's gonna take a hit for this."

In this part . . .

Okay, brains, so you usually don't bother reading instruction manuals. I promise to keep this tight. In this part, I supply some maintenance tips to help make sure your fund portfolio ticks over nicely. I introduce you to the odd cackling symphony of voices on the Internet and in the media, all of them trying to talk to you about funds. But don't worry: I also suggest ways of cutting through the cant to find valuable information. I describe the wonderful RRSP, with its ability to keep the tax hounds at bay. And, for your funds that are exposed to taxes, I show you the basic methods of working out how much you have to pay.

Chapter 22

What's Going on? Using Books, Media, and the Internet

. . . .

In This Chapter

▶ Reviewing books on mutual funds

▶ Assessing the media — can you believe what you read?

▶ Harnessing the power of the Internet to make the most of your funds

. . . .

*O*h, I'm under no illusions as to what'll happen when this book comes out. The phone will ring like a funeral tocsin during a cholera epidemic and my spluttering competitors in mutual fund journalism will demand to know how I dared to distort their brilliant work. But anyway, here goes: a guide to what's worth looking at amid the gushing tide of mutual fund reporting, analysis, and general guff. After a while, you'll discover your favourite sources and commentators. But here are a few places to get started. I haven't listed newspapers because I assume everyone knows that they carry lots of fund stories — as do magazines. In Chapter 2, I show you how to use a newspaper's daily report and monthly mutual fund survey to check on returns. In this chapter, I look at just some of the stacks of books and magazines that deal with mutual funds. I also offer some suggestions as to where to go for the best and most critical analysis of funds. And I take you on a quick tour of the Internet, visiting four of the most useful Canadian sites for selecting and keeping track of your funds.

From Classic to Cutting: Books on Funds

By the time you read this, stores will be jammed with a fresh crop of mutual fund books for 2003, each at least implying that it's the key to finding the very best funds to put you on the road to eternal wealth, peace, security, and lithe massage therapists. Here's a sampling of promises made by these books:

"Consistent top performers."

"State-of-the-art selection methods to help investors choose the best performing funds in Canada."

"This indispensable guide clearly explains the upside potential of a fund while disclosing its downside risk."

"Find the Heavy Hitters. Avoid the Underachievers."

"Sort through the hundreds of alternatives to pick the ones that suit your growth and income needs."

For all their posturing and fancy formulas, none of these authors knows which funds will outperform their peers over the next few years and which will turn out to have four paws, a tail, and a not-so-cute wet nose. To be sure, they do their homework. They can tell you which funds have low expenses, which managers have great track records, and what the investing style of each fund may be. And that's a valuable service, making many of these books worth more than their purchase price. Some authors have attempted to come up with interesting methods to analyze fund performance, which try to eliminate distortions that arise when a fund has just one or two good years, inflating its long-term record. Again, that's useful.

But when it comes to picking which funds will be winners, take the experts' claims, promises, and fancy talk with a big grain of salt. Until their fund-picking skills are evaluated by an independent third party — someone who can verify that the funds these books recommend actually do outperform the pack — we only have the authors' word for their forecasting prowess. In general, they play it pretty safe: The same old funds tend to be recommended year after year in these guides.

Here are my thumbnail reviews of the most popular books that you'll see in the stores.

Bogle on Mutual Funds

This U.S. book doesn't recommend individual funds, but it's a classic — the bible of index funds — and the only mutual fund book you'll ever really need: *Bogle on Mutual Funds* by John Bogle. Bogle founded the Vanguard Group in 1974 and he has made millions of U.S. investors rich with his low-cost no-load mutual funds. The book is well illustrated and entertaining. And Bogle sets out the case for *index funds* — low-cost funds that simply track the whole market — with devastating clarity. At least take this one out of the library.

Gordon Pape's Buyer's Guide to Mutual Funds

This hefty volume (more than 650 pages in 2002) is the original Canadian mutual fund guide and it's still the most comprehensive, rating and describing hundreds of funds. Veteran author Gordon Pape is a one-man publishing industry. He produces truckloads of books and newsletters on everything from buying a car to speculating on stocks. He also publishes an annual guide to registered retirement savings plans and registered retirement income funds. I don't know where he gets the energy. Pape is a clear and down-to-earth writer and this book contains plenty of (rather dull) news about the fund industry and investing tips. So, for novice investors at least, it's a good place to start.

Chand's Top 50 Mutual Funds

Author Ranga Chand, an "independent economist" and fund analyst, has a regular slot on ROBtv, so he's a colleague of mine. His book is a lightweight compared to Pape's because it recommends just 50 funds — which Chand calls "heavy hitters." Chand says he's kept the selection small so the reader can "cut to the chase." And yes, it's nice to come across some brevity in mutual fund writing, an area where we commentators do seem prone to go on and on and on.

Top Funds

Both authors of this guide, Riley Moynes and Nick Fallon, work for the Assante Inc. empire of fund salespeople and financial planners, so don't expect them to thump the tub for the low-expense funds and index funds that are the best bets for investors. However, commendably, they have a policy of refraining from recommending Assante funds (the products are sold under the brand names Optima Strategy and Loring Ward). Moynes used to produce a book each year with Duff Young, a fund commentator and author who offers an analysis service for fund salespeople at www.fundmonitor.com. Damn, I miss Young's outspoken style (I've long been trying to get him to come on ROBtv but he hasn't bitten yet). He was a lovely writer — very colourful — and could he ever dish it out. Here's a past gem from the Duffster: "Mackenzie runs this confusing clone for a bunch of marketing half-wits at Great-West." I mean, I wouldn't dare write that.

Some books such as *Top Funds* used to print tables of data showing funds' returns but that's largely been abandoned now. If you have Internet access, you can get much more recent information from the Web. And tables in a book are always long out of date. Anyway, the newspapers print monthly fund reports that show fund returns up to the end of the previous month. The *Globe* produces its report on the third Wednesday of each month.

The Media — The Curse of the Cover: Magazines and Newsletters

Yes, the media may be a good guide to picking funds — as long as you do exactly the opposite of what journalists (like me) and other self-appointed experts recommend. In other words, as soon as you see a fund manager grinning from the front cover of a magazine, over a headline that reads "market wizard" or "magic lamp," head for the hills.

Consider this:

- ✔ In "Stalking the Wild Gurus," an article for *MoneySense* (www.money sense.com) in 1999, Kelly Rodgers reviewed Canada's best-selling mutual fund guides over four years. She found that none of the fund pickers produced results that were better than the returns one would expect from random selection.

- ✔ Then there's the curse of Mutual Fund Manager of the Year, a prize awarded by a pack of Canadian mutual fund writers and other know-it-alls. Since 1996, managers who've received the prize have tended to go into a slump almost immediately afterward.

Why are the experts so often wrong? The big reason seems to be that most fund managers post fantastic returns only when the market is going their way and the type of stocks they favour are going up. Journalists lionize them and hail them as geniuses. (Well, we have to write something. And you wouldn't believe how hard it can be to get underperforming managers to come to the phone. Or out from underneath their desk.) But when the direction of the market changes, and the former stars' investing styles don't work anymore, they slip to the back of the pack.

The stories in personal finance magazines are usually thin stuff, with little or no direct criticism of individual companies. That means they're not really giving you the dirt you need by naming names. But writers sometimes snipe at the investment industry as a whole over rip-off charges and poor service. Magazines often avoid critical stories that seriously roast individual industry players because they have tight budgets compared with big papers such as the *Globe*. That makes it hard or impossible for a small mag to finance the time-consuming research needed to attack someone. And magazines usually can't afford to fight libel suits.

Canadian Business

Canadian Business is a big mag that gives only a portion of its space to personal finance and mutual funds — but the stories about funds and investing can be hard-hitting and critical. So grab a copy, especially if it features an interesting-looking investment story on the cover. Go to www.canadianbusiness.com to check it out.

Canadian MoneySaver

This is a pretty low-budget production, with no glossy colour pictures and few graphics. Most of the pieces offer advice written by financial planners and other non-journalists. Still, with two decades of publishing experience *MoneySaver* must be doing something right. It's nice and compact (at about 40 pages). Go to the Web site at www.canadianmoneysaver.ca for more information.

The Canadian Mutual Fund Adviser

Edited by the courtly Peter Brewster, this Toronto newsletter is a conservative advice sheet that comes out 26 times a year and generally discusses high-quality funds. Recommendations are also on the cautious side, covering the medium and long term.

You're bound to get one or two useful suggestions a year from the newsletter, potentially making it worth the hefty price — the official subscription rate in mid-2002 was $127 a year, although there are discounts for new subscribers. But much depends on the value of your mutual fund holdings. If your portfolio is $10,000, then the advice you get should add 1.3 percentage points to your annual return to make a $127 subscription worthwhile. But the cost as a percentage also falls as your nest egg grows. At $50,000, it's only one-quarter of a percentage point.

The *Adviser* prints a list of recommended funds. But without an easily checked record of returns it's hard to say how well its favourite funds have performed. And how would you even measure that track record? Over one year or three or five? Mind you, that's also true of newspaper journalists and our watery predictions.

The newsletter is too advanced for a beginning investor, although a diligent rookie would soon figure it out. I personally wouldn't pay the rather stiff subscription price, but you might find the ideas useful enough to make it a bargain. The Web site is at www.adviceforinvestors.com.

The bottom line on any type of investment newsletter that covers either stocks or bonds is this: If you get a couple of good ideas from one, it may pay its way. But in the absence of independent checks on the authors' predictions, it's hard to say how valuable the information is. In money terms, I think you'll do better spending the money on a few good books and then searching the Web for information.

Newsletters generally cost between $100 and $200 per year, but that's cheap compared with the hidden cost of ending up in a high-expense mutual fund that performs badly, because you didn't do your research. An error like that can run into thousands of dollars over the years.

MoneySense (for Canadians Who Want More)

Launched by media giant Rogers Communications — yes, the cable guys — in early 1999, this is *the* glossy magazine in the Canadian personal finance market. There's plenty of dull stuff, but the overall writing is smooth and well edited and the advice is up-to-date. There are piles of flashy ads from big fund marketers and consumer-products companies. *MoneySense* prints articles about funds because they're so important to many people's planning. But there are also plenty of good advice pieces on other aspects of running the money side of your life. *MoneySense* is recommended. Reading it will prod you to get out of denial and into doing something about your money management. Just about anyone will find excellent ideas here.

The magazine also has a good Web site, at www.moneysense.ca. It offers past stories from its archives on topics including investing, family, home, and leisure.

The Internet: Free at Last?

This is a truly exciting period to be an investor because, for the first time, high-quality information on stocks and mutual funds is available to everyone on the Internet. But cutting through all of the noise and marketing blather to get something you can use is often hard at first. There's no point just going to the great search engine at www.google.com, typing in "mutual funds," and blasting away. I'll give you a few excellent spots to start. They'll make your life a lot easier.

The Internet has revolutionized the mutual fund industry by blurring the lines between customers and companies. As an investor, here's what you can now do:

- ✔ Check your account or accounts every day.

- ✔ Sell, buy, and swap mutual fund units over the Internet or sometimes by e-mail.

- ✔ Rank and compare the returns from funds sold by different sellers.

- ✔ Talk to other mutual fund buyers in chat groups — pages where you exchange comments with other investors.

- ✔ Look at a fund's main holdings, as well as its legal documents and full reports.

A Golden Age for the small investor?

The Internet doesn't guarantee that you'll make money from your portfolio — the same old rules of buying quality funds with low expenses and conservative holdings still apply. So don't worry if you're not using the Net to invest. It's perfectly possible to build an excellent portfolio of funds without ever firing up a browser. In fact, as some hapless investors have found, the Web has given birth to a whole new generation of scam artists. And it's certainly created a tidal wave of confusing marketing clutter. But the Net also gives you far more control over your portfolio by allowing you to check and adjust your holdings almost instantly.

- ✔ To get the real benefit of the Internet, you need to hold your mutual funds at a big discount brokerage. Then you can look at your account online and place orders via the broker's Web site. It's easy to combine funds from different companies.

- ✔ The next step down is buying funds directly from a bank or other no-load seller — that is, a company that markets its funds directly to the public without sales charges. In that case, you can also check your account over the Internet, but it'll show only the funds from that company.

- ✔ Finally, many fund companies that market through brokers and financial planners haven't yet given investors a way of checking their holdings over the Internet — although big players such as Fidelity Investments Canada at www.fidelity.ca and CI Fund Management at www.cifunds.com have already done so. In the case of such "broker-sold" funds, you have to relay your buy and sell orders through the salesperson, who may or may not let you place orders by e-mail.

Here's a quick way to find a mutual fund company's site. Go to the site run by the Investment Funds Institute of Canada, the industry lobby group and trade association, at www.ific.ca, and click "Related Links." There's a comprehensive and extremely useful collection of links to fund managers and dealers.

Checking your account online

The ability to monitor the value of your mutual fund investments easily and quickly is one of the most revolutionary benefits of the Internet. Some sites even show you what your return has been in percentage terms over various periods. If you're holding the account with a traditional stockbroker or planner who doesn't yet offer Web access to your portfolio, then you can easily set up a simulated portfolio at a site such as www.globeinvestor.com, the *Globe*'s stock market Web site, or www.globefund.com, the *Globe*'s mutual fund site. Such virtual portfolios allow you to enter the price you paid for each fund and the amount you own, and then they automatically update your holdings each day to reflect their current value plus the return you've earned.

Buying and selling online

More and more companies now let you make changes to your fund portfolio online or by e-mail, instead of by phone or regular mail. The speed appeals to people who demand instant gratification (yes, Drooly, that means you), but it isn't likely to benefit you much unless you're constantly changing your holdings. And if so, why are you using mutual funds — why not just trade stocks yourself instead? Before you can make changes to your portfolio online, by e-mail, or over the phone, your fund company, broker, or planner will almost certainly get you to sign a "limited authorization" form allowing the company to take orders without a signature. The Investment Funds Institute, the industry group that represents all of Canada's big fund sellers, released guidelines for the practice in early 2000.

Researching and comparing funds

Services that let you "slice and dice" through funds from hundreds of different sellers to find the ones that suit you best have been one of the most important tools created by the Internet. The *Globe and Mail* site (www.globefund.com) or its rival www.morningstar.com offer some of the best fund-sorting engines. You can rank Canada's more than 5,000 mutual funds and versions of funds by their performance over periods ranging from one day to 15 years. You can also search for funds with low expenses, large assets, and a host of other qualities. The *Globe* is an affiliate of ROBtv, where I work.

Chat groups

Discussion rooms and chat groups about funds tend to be full of hot air and short on hard information. And they're not as interesting to hang around in as chat rooms on stocks — those forums are often full of rumours that make share prices move up and down rapidly. But mutual fund chat groups can be valuable sources of ideas because the investors who post comments are often well informed. The other participants in a chat room don't have a crystal ball that reveals which funds are going to do well — nobody can make that claim. But they may suggest effective tax-saving techniques or interesting investment strategies.

Start with the rooms at `www.fundlibrary.com`, a comprehensive site offering news and data on Canadian funds.

Checking out funds' holdings

Before the Internet age, it was notoriously difficult to even find out what your fund held. However, just about every fund seller now has a Web site that at least shows you the returns posted by the company's funds. And most report the top holdings and asset breakdown of each fund. Many also carry fund managers' comments on the markets and outlines of their strategy. But these are usually so vague and out of date that they're of little use.

The information on funds' major holdings is also available from independent sites such as `www.globefund.com`. For investors who want to know everything, there's `www.sedar.com`. This is a site run by Canadian securities regulators that contains every public document, report, and filing a fund manager (or any publicly traded company) produces. The name stands for System for Electronic Document Analysis and Retrieval. Sedar can be slow and not particularly easy to use, but every single factoid is there.

Very few sites — apart from the *Wall Street Journal*'s, at `www.wsj.com` — have as yet succeeded in getting people to part with a subscription fee. And no, we're not talking about the type of site you're thinking of, Smutty Sue. So all their content must be paid for through advertising revenue. That means you need to labour through a lot of screens that look like financial brochures and weed out tonnes of outdated mutual fund profiles and insipid promises.

The impact of the Internet has been most obvious so far on the no-load side of the business. No-load funds have no sales charges, commissions, or "loads" — they're marketed by companies such as the banks and Altamira Investment Services, which sell to the public directly instead of through commission-paid salespeople. People who buy no-load funds tend to be happy making their own investing decisions, so they often enjoy checking their portfolio and tracking the market over the Internet.

By contrast, investors who use brokers and financial planners to buy their funds are happier leaving the paperwork and even fund-purchase decisions to the adviser. That reduces their need to check their holdings instantly over the Internet, so fund companies that sell through advisers have been slower to offer services and information on the Web. Mutual fund companies that sell through advisers traditionally shy away from making contact with investors directly because their systems are geared to dealing exclusively with the brokers and planners. That keeps things simple and reduces their own costs. In any case, the independent salespeople see their clients as their property and they don't particularly relish seeing other people sniffing around their accounts.

A few great Web sites

Most of the mutual fund advice and information on the Internet is either marketing blather or bland generalities. But there are a few sites that give you news "with blood on it," as a cranky old editor at the *Globe* used to say. And best of all, most of this advice is free — as long as you can tolerate all those ads. Here are a few sites that I use regularly as a journalist.

www.globefund.com

Yes, I'm biased. But the *Globe and Mail*'s mutual fund site is my favourite. I like the way you can rank funds by short-term and long-term returns, quickly set up a temporary basket of funds to compare them, and also check a fund's performance against its rivals and a market benchmark. Other sites offer similar fund-ranking tools, but I find globefund's the easiest to use. You can even combine data from globefund and from www.globeinvestor.com, the *Globe*'s stock site, to set up a portfolio that shows your holdings of both funds and shares on one screen. The site also carries recent *Globe* articles on funds, including pieces that are critical of the industry. And there's a paid-for service at www.globeinvestorgold.com — it costs $9.95 a month and up — with even more features. It includes exclusive columns on stocks and funds as well as data that shows whether big investors are buying or selling a stock. You can compare the financial results of more than 9,000 companies, monitor a steady stream of financial news (even watch ROBTv right from the site), and use powerful tools to analyze your own stock and fund holdings.

www.bylo.org

This is a truly sophisticated site on low-cost investing, put together by a long-time Internet message-poster who goes by the handle Bylo Selhi (say it out loud). There's a breathtaking amount of news and of information on index funds and exchange traded funds — both excellent solutions for investors.

www.fundlibrary.com

This was one of the first mutual fund Web sites in Canada, and it still offers one of the widest range of services. There's a huge selection of educational material, tools for recording and monitoring your fund holdings, and e-mail notifications for news affecting the funds you're interested in. The chat groups on funds at www.fundlibrary.com can be active and lively, so check them out.

www.morningstar.ca

The U.S. fund-rating giant offers mutual fund news and fund-analysis tools at its new Canadian site. I find it clumsy for sorting funds by returns, but the site carries excellent information on funds.

There are high-quality articles and a rating service that awards between one and five stars to funds according to their past returns (www.globefund.com has a broadly similar ranking method). But don't pay too much attention to such rating systems, because they can address only what's happened in the past — and past performance is no guide to the future. But at least if a fund has four or five stars, it may be a good place to start looking.

Chapter 23

RRSPs: Fertilizer for Your Mutual Funds

In This Chapter

▶ Making your money grow like crazy in a registered retirement savings plan

▶ Figuring out where to buy an RRSP

▶ Falling in love with self-directed RRSPs

▶ Deciding which funds should go in your RRSP

Coffee and cigarettes, Saturday night and fighting, tight leather and fun — some things just go together. And mutual funds are a powerful combination with Canada's beloved *registered retirement savings plan* (RRSP), a tax-deferred account in which your investments pile up without molestation from the government. In this chapter, I explain why it's a great idea to fill up your RRSP as a first step when buying funds and I also look at the sort of funds you should put into your plan. There's a brief rundown of the rules of RRSPs. They can be horrendously complex, but in essence they're simple — just stick your money in, buy top-quality funds, and watch your nest egg grow and grow.

Pour It in and Watch It Grow: Understanding RRSPs

An RRSP is like a sticky, steamy glass case for growing plants, offering the perfect lighting, oxygen, and moisture conditions. In legal terms it's a holding tank for investments and assets in which they can pile up *tax-free* until you take the money out and spend it. At that stage, you have to treat the withdrawals as income, and pay taxes on them. But the idea is that you won't care about having to share some of the loot with Ottawa at that stage because the money will have grown tax-free to such a huge pile and also because you'll be in a nice low tax bracket (because your income will be lower in retirement).

So an RRSP isn't an investment in itself — you don't "buy" an RRSP — but a tax-privileged account in which you hold investments and assets. Don't even think about it too much. Just go ahead and open up an RRSP. It's one of the great tax breaks Canadians get, for two reasons:

- ✔ **The money you put in comes off your income for tax purposes:** The government's attitude is that money you put into an RRSP is cash that you've diverted from your income for the moment — or *deferred,* in the jargon — so you don't have to pay tax on it. That's why taxpayers who've contributed to their RRSPs the previous year get back tax *refunds,* or returns of taxes they already paid.

- ✔ **Your investments accumulate tax-free within the plan:** This is the real reason why RRSPs are so powerful. The dollars in there are super-charged because the interest, dividends, and capital gains they attract are free of tax. Added to the pile, those earnings go on to earn their own cute little baby earnings, which in turn produce their own offspring, and so it goes. And tax-free compounding of investment returns — along with lightweight bicycles and movies by Ridley Scott (*Alien, Blade Runner,* and *Gladiator*) — is a wonder of the modern world.

Claiming a tax refund for the cash you put into a plan is wonderfully simple and perhaps the most enjoyable thing about an RRSP (although watching your balance climb steadily is also fun). And the refund can be a fair amount of money. If your top tax bracket is 40 percent (that is, the government takes away 40 percent of the uppermost portion of your income), then a $5,000 RRSP contribution can earn you a refund of $2,000. Even the saddest and least organized financial planner in Canada (poor old Vern, I wonder how he is) can open an RRSP for you and handle your contributions. Ottawa makes it simple. Your tax return clearly asks if you've contributed to an RRSP and then invites you to deduct the amount from your income. And, helpfully, the government mails you a slip along with your tax refund or tax bill each spring showing exactly how much you can contribute for the current year.

How much can you put in your RRSP

Actually, it's a good thing that the tax authorities tell you how much *room* — or maximum possible contribution — you have. That's because for people who are in a pension scheme at work, the RRSP contribution limits are complicated to calculate. If you're in a pension plan, you're already getting tax relief on the money you contribute to that scheme, and your employer may also be helping out, so policymakers water down the amount you can plow into your RRSP.

If you're not in a pension plan, the maximum contribution is up to 18 percent of the income you earned the previous year, to a maximum contribution of $13,500. The limit is currently scheduled to stay the same until 2004, when it goes up to $14,500, and then it will climb to $15,500 in 2005. After that, it's supposed to be *indexed* to inflation — that is, the maximum contribution will increase each year in line with the general rise in prices. If you are in a pension scheme, then your maximum contribution is reduced by something called the *pension adjustment*, which is reported to you each year on the T4 tax slip you get from your employer. The T4 shows the income you earned and the tax paid during the latest year.

The very phrase "pension adjustment" sounds steamy and exciting but, no, it's not about spending six months on Martinique, lolling under palms while lusty young . . . ahem. It's the value that the tax authorities assign to the value of the pension benefit you build up each year — and it's then used to reduce your maximum RRSP contribution. For the example (as we say in Cairo), if your income is $75,000 then you're entitled to contribute the full $13,500 — as long as you're not in a pension plan. But if you are, and the tax people decide that the value of the pension benefit you build up is, say, $5,000, then your maximum contribution is reduced by that amount, to $8,500.

It all sounds a bit daunting but don't worry: The institution, broker, or fund company holding your RRSP will deal with most of the paperwork. This service is covered by the administration fee you'll pay. It isn't too bad; you should expect to pay a maximum of $100 for most plans annually, but lots of fund sellers and discount brokers waive the charge altogether if your account is big enough. Be sure and ask them to do so if you're investing $10,000 or more. For example, at Royal Bank of Canada's discount brokerage firm, Action Direct, there was no administration fee for a *self-directed RRSP* if your balance was above $25,000 in mid-2002. Otherwise there was a fee of just $25 every year. A self-directed RRSP is a plan in which you're free to hold just about anything. There's much more on self-directed plans later in this chapter.

Getting help from the tax folks

Here are some other ways in which Ottawa makes it easy to put money into an RRSP:

- ✔ For the first 60 days of every year you can make contributions and have them count against income for the previous year. Being procrastinators, millions of people leave their RRSP contribution until those two months, and that's why you see a hysterical flood of RRSP advertising and hype in January and February.

> ✔ You can *carry forward* any unused contributions since 1991 to another year. In other words, if you don't have enough money to put anything into your RRSP this year, you can use up that contribution in a subsequent year; it's not just wasted. The slip that comes with your refund or tax bill each year, which is known as the *notice of assessment*, tells you how much unused room you have left.

It's nice to get a tax refund for contributing, but the even more powerful attraction of RRSPs is the way that income earned within the plan is also *tax-deferred*. It piles up year after year without Canada Customs and Revenue Agency (the exciting new name for Revenue Canada) sticking its claws in along the way. Given long enough, money that compounds tax-free grows at a frightening pace. But it's a good sort of scary, if you know what I mean. To use an example from the Canadian Imperial Bank of Commerce:

> ✔ Let's say you invested $6,000 each year in an ordinary account that earned 10 percent annually, but you also had to pay 40 percent of the return each year in tax. The money would grow to just under $350,000 in 25 years.

> ✔ If you invested the same $6,000 in an RRSP, where it built up tax-free, then you'd have almost $650,000 after 25 years.

So, investment income such as interest and dividends, as well as *capital gains* — a fancy name for trading profits — can pile up tax-free inside an RRSP — which makes an RRSP the ideal place to put your mutual funds. That's because, as I explain in Chapter 24, funds throw off their income and capital gains to unitholders each year in the form of *distributions*. Most people take the payouts in the form of new units but it doesn't matter; the distributions are taxable just the same — unless they're earned in a tax-deferred plan such as an RRSP.

How much growth can I expect?

You can be sure that a bond or other income-oriented fund will generate a steady stream of distributions (that's what they're designed to do), and equity funds have a habit of suddenly producing big capital gains for their investors — which can be painful if you don't hold the fund in a tax-deferred account. Distributions are payments that your fund makes to you. You can take them as a cheque (thanks) or as more units. Imagine you invested $10,000 in Templeton Growth Fund in the summer of 1977, and held on to it for 25 years, to June 2002. If you owned the fund in an RRSP, the money would grow tax-free to just over $260,000. But say you'd been paying tax on the distributions each year — settling the tax bill directly out of the account — at a rate of 44 percent on income and 33 percent on capital gains. In that case, the money would have grown to less than $181,000, or one-third less (see Table 23-1).

Table 23-1 $10,000 Invested in Templeton Growth Fund in 1977 for 25 Years, Untaxed and Taxed Values

Period End	Untaxed Value	Taxed Value
Dec. 1982	$26,590	$24,485
Dec. 1987	$59,659	$50,343
Dec. 1992	$105,321	$83,184
Dec. 1997	$235,797	$174,197
June 2002	$263,329	$180,679

Now, the $181,000 in the taxable account is not too shabby, and the example is a little misleading. You see, the money in the tax-paying account is free and clear — you're at liberty to do whatever you want with every cent because the tax is already paid. By contrast, money in an RRSP isn't really normal capital — in legal terms, it's more like deferred income that you haven't yet declared for tax purposes. Sort of frozen earned income hovering in space, like the doomed characters in a Beckett play or at one of your Christmas parties.

So when you take the money out of that whopping quarter-million-dollar RRSP, you'll want to avoid having to pay tax on every penny of it. The idea, of course, is that by that stage you will have quit working, so you're in a low tax bracket. But always remember that while the magic of tax-free compounding within an RRSP does produce wonderful growth, the dollars inside the plan have annoying little strings attached.

Where to Buy Your RRSP

Buying an RRSP is simple because banks, brokers, and fund companies just love them. The money tends to be long-term retirement savings that won't be withdrawn for years, so it sits there producing a stream of fees for the lucky firm that gets to hold it. And it's a massive industry: In early 2000, Canadians had about one-quarter of a trillion dollars — or around $250 billion — sitting in RRSPs. Contributions to the plans in 2000 topped $29 billion for the first time. The growth in contributions has slowed since 1996 as the wealthy use up their carry-forwards and run out of contribution room, but we still put around $25 billion a year into our plans. And there's one-third of a trillion dollars out there — that is, more than $300 billion — in unused contributions because wage slaves can't or won't find the dough.

There are three basic choices when setting up an RRSP. Here's the triple play:

- ✔ **Basic banking:** You can stumble into a bank, trust company, or credit union and ask for a basic RRSP account that holds that particular institution's mutual funds and other offerings, usually guaranteed investment certificates. Limited choice of investments is the problem with doing this, but the simplicity and convenience make it ideal for investors who are just starting out. So if you're looking for convenience, fire ahead and open up a simple plan at a bank. As you learn more and your assets grow, it's pretty simple to move the holdings later into another RRSP at a full-service broker or discount broker plan for a fee of about $100 (the delighted institution that's getting your money will often pay the fee for you). And remember that banks now offer a wider selection of *index funds* that track the entire market at low cost to the unitholders; an RRSP full of index funds with a smaller portion of ordinary actively managed funds is a wise choice for nearly any investor. There are also some good *no-load* fund companies — fund managers that sell directly to the public with no sales commissions — that offer funds with low expenses. They, too, will be happy to set up an RRSP on their books for you.

- ✔ **From your planner:** If you go to a commission-paid financial planner, he or she may put your investment into a fund company's RRSP. That's an RRSP set up on the books of the fund company, which almost always holds just that company's funds. It's an easy option for the salesperson because the fund manager handles all of the administration and registration of the plan with the government. Once again, though, limited choice is a problem from your point of view. But a fund company RRSP is handy for investors who don't want to fiddle around too much with their portfolios because the fund company does all the bookkeeping. Not all planners will limit you to a fund company–sponsored RRSP. Some have arrangements with an outside trust company or other service provider that let them offer independent RRSPs and normal taxable accounts that can hold funds from a variety of fund companies.

- ✔ **Self-directed:** The final, best, and increasingly popular way to do it is to start up a self-directed RRSP at a discount brokerage company. This is the very finest type of RRSP because you're free to hold virtually anything, instead of limiting your portfolio to the wares of just one company.

The Beautiful Garden that Is the Self-Directed RRSP

Just about everyone should have a self-directed RRSP because, well, these things are marvellous. The traditional RRSP offered by a bank or fund manager is basically a vehicle for holding just their stuff. But with a self-directed plan, you're free to roam the world. It's about the only way to own stocks or bonds within an RRSP and to load up on funds from a multiplicity of companies.

Foreign discontent

One of the big flaws of the RRSP is Ottawa's rule that most of its contents must be Canadian. There's nothing wrong with Canadian stocks or bonds, but ours is a relatively tiny stock market that doesn't offer enough global companies and technology giants to build a really good equity portfolio. After years of lobbying by the investment industry, which ultimately wants the limit eliminated altogether, the federal government expanded the foreign content maximum in the February 2000 budget. From 2000 onward, an RRSP could hold up to 25 percent of its assets in foreign stocks, up from 20 percent previously. In 2001, the percentage rose to 30 percent. One of the advantages of having a self-directed plan is that you can roll everything into one account, making it simple to ensure that you're maximizing your foreign content. If you had, say, three RRSPs at institutions all over town, it would become tiresome to keep monitoring them. Each RRSP has to stay within the rules on its own: You can't have two equal-sized plans with 50 percent foreign content in one and 10 percent in the other, even though the average foreign content averages out at 30 percent. Each plan must individually come in at 30 percent foreign content or less.

The foreign content is based on the *book value* or acquisition cost of the investments in your portfolio. Say you have a Hungarian marzipan fund that cost you $1,000, while the rest of your RRSP is made up of Canadian funds that cost you $9,000. Now, say the candy stores of old Budapest do a roaring trade and your Hungarian fund soars to the point where it accounts for half of your RRSP's market value — you're probably still not over the limit. That's because the marzipan investment still accounts for just 10 percent of the book value of your RRSP. Distributions by the fund can complicate the picture because they may count as fresh purchases of units, but that's the general idea. By the way, don't get any smart-alec ideas about deliberately exceeding the foreign-holdings limit. Ottawa will hit you with a sky-high penalty tax of 1 percent of the excess foreign content *every month*. Investors have been getting increasingly annoyed at the foreign-content limits in RRSPs, so the fund industry has come up with flocks of "clone" products that are foreign but use financial witch-craft to count as Canadian. Chapter 20 deals with clone funds.

Setting up a self-directed RRSP is easy — remember that brokers welcome this type of business, because it tends to represent long-term money that'll be on their books for decades. And the term *self-directed* often doesn't apply, because many investors have a full-service broker who helps them pick what should go into their plan. However, self-directed RRSPs are ideally suited for discount brokerages because discounters tend to have a large selection of funds, available for low or no sales commissions. See Chapter 6 for more on discounters.

Don't get worried that opening a self-directed plan means you have to become a stock market wizard. Stick to the rules for fund selection in this book and you'll almost certainly do okay. There's nothing that says you have to start playing stocks directly: Lots of investors hold nothing but conservative mutual funds in their self-directed plans. And don't be shy about transferring assets from other plans into your self-directed plan. The old brokerage firm or bank, that is seeing your money depart its coffers will sometimes drag its feet on the paperwork (getting nasty shoe marks all over it). In fact, they like to store written requests to transfer out money in an old tar barrel in the parking lot. But after a few weeks, if a delay drags on that long, you can simply threaten politely to call the Investment Dealers Association of Canada, the Toronto-based lobby group that regulates the industry. That usually speeds things up a bit.

If you're moving assets from an existing plan over to the self-directed RRSP, the new brokerage firm may tell you that its systems won't accommodate some or all of your old funds. In that case, you may have to sell the funds in the old account and just move the cash proceeds over. That's a hassle, but it shouldn't cost you anything in taxes because the transaction is taking place within an RRSP, shielding any capital gains.

Planting the Most Fragrant Flower: Choosing Funds for Your RRSP

The overriding rule for investments inside your RRSP should be Insist on Quality — leave the wacky speculative stuff for the money that's not earmarked to support you in your annoying dotage. That means buying conservative equity and bond funds, while going easy on emerging markets funds, volatile single-industry funds, and small-company funds. The dollars inside your plan should be treated as sacrosanct — all incense and white cloth — because they're irreplaceable. There's a limit on the contributions you can make to your RRSP in your lifetime, and once a magical compounding RRSP dollar has been lost on a slump in the Brazilian market it can't be restored. In Chapter 4 there are two suggested RRSP portfolios; just about any bank or mutual fund now has a proprietary system for suggesting the asset mix in your plan.

Just remember, though, that with this type of long-term investing, the costs and fees charged by the funds and fund mixtures assume ever-greater importance. So own at least some index funds in your plan. Your RRSP is too important to have it spoiled by some BMW-driving turkey who can't keep up with the market.

What happens to my RRSP when I retire and beyond?

At 69, everyone has to convert his or her RRSP into something called a *registered retirement income fund* (RRIF). An RRIF is similar to an RRSP in that investments grow tax-free and you can also hold the same range of assets in an RRIF. But there's one crucial difference: You can't make regular contributions to an RRIF and you have to steadily withdraw the money that's there accord-ing to a specified timetable. And as the money comes out, year after year, the government gets to take a bite out of it.

Mixing the right assets

As with other forms of investing, your asset mix is almost certain to get more cautious as you get older and closer to taking money out of your plan rather than putting it in. For nearly everyone, that means more bonds and cash and fewer stocks.

Many experts say you should put your bond funds into your RRSP if you're a long-term investor, and the numbers seem to indicate that they're right. That's because bond funds earn and throw off a constant stream of interest, which attracts murderous rates of tax.

Funds usually pay distributions in the form in which they receive the money from their investments. So interest earned by a fund is paid as a distribution that's taxable as interest in the investor's hands. Capital gains — the polite term for trading profits — are paid out as *capital gain distributions,* and dividends earned by a fund are paid out as *dividend distributions to the investor.*

Equity funds are mainly about buying and selling stocks so they generate capital gains distributions — and, since October 2000, only one-half of a capital gain is taxed in the hands of the investor. Equity funds also produce dividends from Canadian companies — payouts of the company's profits to shareholders — which are also lightly taxed. So, funds that produce distributions in the form of dividends or capital gains are reasonably *tax-efficient,* or lightly taxed, making them more suitable than bond funds for an *open* or taxable account. In other words, equity funds are often better than bond funds when it comes to investing outside your RRSP. Here's an example: Say you'd invested $10,000 in the Dynamic Income Fund, a Canadian bond fund, in 1992. If you held the fund for ten years in an RRSP, you'd end up with $18,956, just about doubling your money in a decade. But if you'd been paying tax along the way, you'd have ended up with $13,962, or 26 percent less than if your investment were tax-free. Take a look at Table 23-2 for the actual figures.

Table 23-2 $10,000 Invested in Dynamic Income Fund in 1992 for 10 Years, Untaxed and Taxed Values

Period End	Untaxed Value	Taxed Value
Dec. 1994	$12,678	$11,297
Dec. 1996	$15,434	$13,017
Dec. 1998	$15,858	$12,657

(continued)

Table 23-2 *(continued)*

Period End	Untaxed Value	Taxed Value
Dec. 2000	$17,170	$13,049
June 2002	$18,956	$13,962

But say you'd done the same thing with the Dynamic Value Fund of Canada, a large-cap Canadian equity fund. In an RRSP, the $10,000 would turn into just over $23,000 in ten years. If you'd invested the money in a taxable account you'd end up with just under $20,000 — that's only about 16 percent less than the tax-deferred account. In other words, you take a smaller haircut for holding an equity fund outside an RRSP because it pays fewer distributions (usually), and the distributions it does pay are made up of dividends and capital gains, which are far more lightly taxed than interest income. Table 23-3 shows the figures.

Table 23-3 $10,000 Invested in Dynamic Fund of Canada in 1992 for Ten Years, Untaxed and Taxed Values

Period End	Untaxed Value	Taxed Value
Dec. 1994	$14,353	$13,293
Dec. 1996	$18,278	$16,511
Dec. 1998	$17,967	$15,113
Dec. 2000	$25,002	$20,801
June 2002	$23,761	$19,768

Now, there are always exceptions to every rule, and quadruply so when it comes to taxes and investing. So an equity fund that pays big distributions year after year, while producing solid returns as well, may be an excellent candidate for your RRSP because you'll be shielding those payouts from tax. You can get an idea if the fund manager is in the habit of paying out lots of capital gains by looking at one of the new fund prospectuses or by checking with your salesperson.

But don't get all bogged down in theories: Remember to put top-quality stuff into your RRSP and you should do fine, whether it's bonds or stocks. There's an old saying in the market that you should never let tax strategies blind you to the merits or faults of an investment. Nobody's ever wished she'd had more to drink the night before (especially you) — and nobody's ever regretted holding a well-managed equity fund in an RRSP over many years, no matter how small the distributions.

Chapter 24

Taxes: Timing Is Everything

. . . .

In This Chapter

▶ Paying taxes on distributions from your fund

▶ Paying taxes when you sell your fund

▶ Reduce your tax load

. . . .

A lot of investment writing and theorizing seems to take place in an airy-fairy world in which everybody is beautifully dressed and articulate, no one ever eats with her mouth open, all decisions are perfectly rational, and nobody ever has to pay taxes. In fact, the stock and bond markets are rather squalid places driven by terror and avarice, in which nondescript people swap sleazy favours. And taxes end up grinding us all down remorselessly. Unless mutual fund unitholders are investing through a tax-deferred plan, the government often goes after them mercilessly. In this chapter, I outline how to count the cost of taxes and I look at a couple of methods of reducing the pain.

The Wacky World of Fund Distributions

Now this stuff will get a little complicated, but bear with me because it's worth knowing and we should be able to cut through it pretty quickly. Mutual funds, as you know, hold all kinds of company shares, bonds, and cash — and sometimes *derivatives*, those strange financial deals based on *options* and *futures*, which are promises to buy or sell something at a certain price.

All the time, cash is piling up in the fund from three main sources:

✔ Every year, the stocks pay *dividends* to the fund — which are payouts to the shareholders of a portion of the company's profit.

✔ Meanwhile, the bonds and cash, which are loans to government and big companies, keep earning *interest income*.

✔ The fund also earns *capital gains* — which are essentially trading profits generated by buying low and selling high — when it sells stocks, bonds, and derivatives.

In general, no fund hangs on to these streams of income and capital gains because, if it did, the fund itself would have to pay tax on them, reducing its total return. So just about all mutual funds pay out the interest and dividend income and capital gains to their unitholders in the form of so-called distributions, letting them deal with the tax.

The investors have to pay tax on the income and gains at their own personal rate. It's more sensible to have the unitholders, rather than the fund, pay the tax because many of the unitholders may not even be taxable personally. Those investors can collect the distributions and not owe a penny to Ottawa. And investors who hold the fund in a registered retirement savings plan (RRSP) — a tax-deferred holding tank in which investments can grow tax-free — don't have to pay tax on the distributions immediately, so it would be a waste of money for the fund to pay taxes on their behalf. Other unitholders may have low incomes, meaning that their tax rates are low or zero.

Here is where things begin to get Druidical — when a fund pays out a distribution, it reduces the cash value of each of its own units. Let's say the fund has total assets of $100 million and 10 million units *outstanding*, or in the hands of investors. Then each unit has a *net asset value* per unit — or price — of $10 ($100 million divided by 10 million). Now say the manager was lucky enough to sell the notorious fraudulent stock Bre-X Minerals Ltd. before it blew up (yeah, right) and she pays out $20 million in capital gains to the unitholders. That's $2 for every unit ($20 million divided by 10 million units outstanding). If all of them took it in cash, then the value of the fund's assets would drop to $80 million. It still has 10 million units — outstanding, though, so the value or price of each falls to $8 ($80 million divided by 8 million), after taking away the value of the $2 distribution.

Let's say you're a unitholder in the fund and you have 100 units; take a look at Table 24-1 to see what happens to your cash.

Table 24-1	What if You Take the Distribution in Cash?			
Units Held	Unit Price	Value of Units Held	Cash in Hand	Total Holding
Before distribution				
100	$10	$1,000	Zero	$1,000
After distribution				
100	$8	$800	$200	$1,000

In other words, you start out owning 100 units, which are worth $10 each, for a total holding of $1,000.

The fund declares a distribution of $2 a unit, which you elect to take in cash.

You then still hold 100 units, but the value of each has dropped by $2, to $8, which leaves you with $800 worth of units. But you also have the $200 in cash ($2 for each of your units), which means you still have a total holding of $1,000.

But most people just put the money back into the fund. One of the great advantages of mutual funds is the fact that you can automatically reinvest your income and capital gains in more units, which go to bolster your account and earn even higher streams of income and gains in the future. It's a no-brainer, as we like to say in frontal-lobe surgery. That's what long-term investors do — take their distributions in the form of more units.

So let's say you follow that course. You don't get cash but more units. Their value has dropped by $2 each, but that's fine because the investor now owns more of them. This scenario is shown in Table 24-2.

Table 24-2	What if You Reinvest the Distribution?			
Units Held	**Unit Price**	**Value of Units Held**	**Cash in Hand**	**Total Holding**
Before distribution				
100	$10	$1,000	Zero	$1,000
After distribution				
125	$8	$1,000	Zero	$1,000

You get an extra 25 units valued at $8 each, which increases your unit total to 125. The units are now worth just $8 each, though, so you still have a total holding of $1,000. As you can see, a distribution isn't really a windfall or a payout to you. It reduces the value of each unit you hold, so it's more like a reshuffling of your investment in the fund.

In fact, a fund can easily lose money during a calendar year (because its unit price dropped) but also pay out distributions to unitholders because the fund manager earned interest or dividend income or made some capital gains by selling a stock or bond. Taxable unitholders find themselves in the galling position of having to pay taxes on their investment in a fund, even though it lost them money. Gee, thanks.

Many equity and balanced funds pay out their capital gains distributions in December, while bond funds and other income funds usually pay out interest income quarterly or even monthly. Funds that seek bond interest, dividends, and other regular income nearly always pay it straight out to unitholders. So, bond, dividend, and other income funds by their nature pay a lot of distributions every year, exposing taxable investors to lots of tax on the income. So hold them inside a tax-sheltered plan when you can, unless you need the regular payments.

By contrast, equity funds can go years without paying any distributions at all because the manager hasn't generated enough trading profits. That can be for a number of good reasons, though. The fund may have simply bought a bunch of good companies and hung on to them without selling the shares, nicely increasing its value per unit.

The taxation of funds is cruelly complicated because a host of factors can influence it. But with stock funds the basic rule is this: The more trading done by the fund, the bigger the distributions and the higher your tax bill (again, if investing outside an RRSP). However, sometimes the need for distributions is eliminated because of the way investors move into or out of the fund. Or a fund manager can sometimes sell shares and then buy them back immediately, again reducing the tax liability of the fund.

Fund companies often make a song and dance about the fact that a fund hasn't paid much in distributions in recent years — reducing the tax bill for unitholders — because its manager tends to hold stocks for long periods. Instead of selling shares and earning trading profits that must be paid out in big distributions, some managers try to simply hold good stocks for long periods, increasing the fund's unit value. But always be wary: A takeover bid or drastic change in a company's fortunes might force the manager to sell the stock, forcing the fund to pay out a big distribution.

Fund companies say the lack of annual payouts helps you to defer paying taxes until you sell the fund's units. That may be true, but remember that taxation shouldn't be the first thing you consider when making an investment — the fund should be suitable in other ways, too. However, if you're deciding which fund to hold in a taxable account — that is, an account that isn't an RRSP or some other tax-deferred plan — then a fund that doesn't do much trading is often the best choice. If the fund uses a definite buy-and-hold style, the fund company's literature will usually say so. And as I explain later, equity index funds — funds that simply track the whole stock market — are a great buy-and-hold investment.

So if you're trying to decide which funds you should put *into* your RRSP, the income fund is often the best choice, because the distributions can just pile up in there tax-free until you take the money out.

Because a big capital gains distribution produces an apparent abrupt fall in a fund's unit price at the end of the year, mutual fund investors sometimes get a fright. Every year, fund companies get worried phone calls from investors asking why their fund's units seem to have plunged. However, they needn't worry: Yes, the unit price has fallen, but the investor has received more units.

It's easy to find out what distributions your fund has declared. The newspapers' monthly mutual fund reports list distributions made by each fund during the previous month. Many fund company Web sites also carry the information, and you can check a fund's distribution history on www.globefund.com, the *Globe*'s mutual fund Web site.

Note that if you hold funds in a discount brokerage account, you may have an alarming experience when you get your statement for December 31. Your fund units may have fallen sharply, reflecting the value of a distribution, but there might be no sign of any extra units in your account to make up for it. So it sometimes looks as though the value of your investment has slumped. That's actually just an administrative glitch: The lines of communication aren't always very good between discount brokers and the fund companies at the end of the year, when the fund industry is scrambling to calculate the distributions. Your broker's system may not record the distributions until mid-January or so, after you've gotten your December statement. However, the error should be fixed by the time you get your statement for January 31.

Paying Taxes on Fund Distributions

Here's the rub. It doesn't matter if the investor takes the distributions in the form of cash or reinvests them in more units. The distribution is taxable just the same — as long as the fund is held in an *open* (that is, taxable) account and not a tax-deferred plan such as an RRSP. Always remember that none of this stuff applies if you hold your fund in an RRSP, but the distributions are ultimately taxable when you start taking money out of the plan. At that stage, any money you withdraw is taxed as income, just as though you earned it at your normal job, dancing topless in a Turkish sailors' bar.

The fact that RRSP withdrawals are taxed like normal income can be a disadvantage because the money gets no special treatment, even if it was originally earned as capital gains or dividends from a Canadian company. That's a pity, because normally dividends from Canadian corporations and capital gains are eligible for special tax breaks:

- ✔ Canadian dividends received by investors get the "federal dividend tax credit," essentially a reduction of the tax you pay, to encourage investment in Canadian companies and to reflect the fact that corporations have already been taxed. That means taxation of dividends is relatively low. As of mid-2002, an Ontario investor with $60,000 in annual non-dividend income faced a tax rate of only 16.9 percent on each extra dollar of dividends earned compared with 33 percent on interest income, according to accounting firm Ernst & Young.

- ✔ You must include only half of a capital gain in your taxable income. That makes it even more attractive to hold equity funds outside your RRSP, because their capital gains distributions aren't heavily taxed in the hands of investors. As of 2002, the Ontario taxpayer with a $60,000 income had to pay tax of only 16.5 percent on each extra dollar of capital gains.

Don't worry: Your fund company will send you tax slips each year showing how much in interest income, dividends, and capital gains distributions you should report on the appropriate place on your tax form. Note that if you hold the fund in an RRSP or other tax-deferred plan, you don't get tax slips because you don't pay tax on the distributions. There are two types of tax slips you may get:

- A T3 if the fund you hold is a mutual fund trust, which most funds are. If you hold several funds with one company, you'll probably get just one consolidated T3 but it should have a breakdown on the back showing which fund paid you which sort of distribution.

- A T5 if your fund is itself a corporation, issuing shares instead of units. That's a less flexible type of structure, and most funds these days are trusts.

Paying Taxes when You Sell or Exchange

If you sell or *redeem* some of your fund units at a higher price than you paid, and the fund is held in a taxable account, then you're liable for capital gains tax on the profit you made. The same applies even if you just do an *exchange* or switch — moving money from one fund to another. As far as the tax authorities are concerned, an exchange is the same as selling Fund A and then buying Fund B. It's irrelevant what you do with the proceeds of the sale — if selling the first fund generates a capital gain, then you have to pay taxes on it.

An ever-weirder parade of tax-skirting fund structures

A few companies, such as CI Fund Management Inc., Mackenzie, and AGF Management Ltd., have set up funds that are organized in "classes" or versions that are designed to let you switch from fund to fund without generating capital gains for tax purposes. Technically, they're actually units of the same fund, although one is the Canadian equity class, the next is the bond class, and so on, each with its own cute baby unit price. You can use this fund structure and jump from fund to fund, avoiding taxes on any capital gains along the way. After all, a capital gain is produced when a fund has gone up — and that's why you bought it in the first place.

Since the start of 2001, other fund marketers have jumped on the tax-free switching bandwagon. But they've gone much further than that, bringing out ever more complicated products. Here are just a couple:

✔ Fidelity Investments Canada, Mackenzie, and Franklin Templeton Investments started selling classes of existing funds that make a steady payout to investors who want to gradually withdraw their money from their funds — but a lot of the distribution is in the form of "return of capital" or a refund of the investor's own money. That means no tax is payable right then — but it's added to the investor's profit for capital gains purposes when the units are sold. In Chapter 13, I talk about the new balanced funds designed to throw off income that also use this technique. I wonder how many investors have trouble telling the difference between having your cash in one of these programs or in one of the return of capital balanced funds. Everyone?

✔ Things get more . . . alien and strange. Don't you miss old Scully and Mulder? Mackenzie (and no doubt others) has launched bond funds that throw off interest that normally would attract a heavy tax rate — about one-third in the Ontario example above. But by swapping a lot of e-mails with another chap who went to Upper Canada College, they've figured out a way to turn the interest payments into capital gains for unitholders — and those are often taxed at just 16 percent.

These new tax-managing structures may turn out to be great deals for investors, but they add a level of complexity. Make sure you understand before you buy — or at least get an adviser who you're sure knows which number goes where.

Working through capital gain calculations

Let's go into more detail about the tax hit you face when you sell units of a mutual fund in a "taxable" account that's not an RRSP or similar tax-deferred plan. We'll look at the example of the investor who holds 100 units of a fund — say she paid $8 a unit. If she sells half of those units for $10 each, then her account will look something like this:

Purchase 100 units at $8 for total investment of $800

And six months later

Sell 50 units at $10 for total proceeds of $500

Hold 50 units at $10 for total holding of $500

Calculating the capital gain: The units that were sold for $500 cost the investor $400 originally, so she has to report a capital gain of $100, only half of which must be included in taxable income for the year. The investor also still holds another 50 units.

When the investor was working out the capital gain on the sales, it was necessary to establish the *cost base* or original cost of the units. That was simple to do because it represented just half of the initial investment. But when you've made more than one purchase of the fund, things become more complex and you have to work out an *adjusted cost base (ACB)*. Here's an example:

Purchase   100 units at $8 for an investment of $800

Purchase   Another 100 units at $10 for investment of $1,000

The investor now holds 200 units, which cost a total of $1,800, so her adjusted cost base is $1,800, or $9 per unit ($1,800 divided by 200).

Sale   100 units at $13 for proceeds of $1,300

Calculating the capital gain: The 100 units that were sold at $13 have an adjusted cost base of $9 each. That means they were sold for a profit of $4 each, so the investor has generated a capital gain of $400. And she also still holds 100 units, whose adjusted cost base remains at $9 per unit.

If you get distributions and reinvest them in more units, then that represents yet another purchase of the fund — so you add the value of the distribution to your cost base. And always make sure that you do increase the ACB by the value of reinvested distributions, because if you don't you could face double taxation.

One more complication: Say the investor incurs a "back-end" commission when she sells the fund — that's a sales charge that's levied on the proceeds of the sale or redemption of the fund.

Sale   50 units at $13 for proceeds of $650, incurring a 5-percent redemption charge

The investor's proceeds from the sale have been reduced by 5 percent, to $617.50. That means, for tax purposes, she's received only $12.35 per unit.

Unfortunately, fund companies say they don't have the systems or information necessary to provide you with an accurate adjusted cost base for your units for tax purposes. That means the unit cost shown on your account statement may not be an accurate guide, so you should keep full records of any reinvested distributions or purchases or sales. Things can get horrendously complex if you have a regular purchase plan, which involves buying units at different prices at different times, or you've done a lot of switching around. But the basic principle remains: The cost of your units is any money you spent to buy them, plus the value of reinvested distributions. And selling some of your units doesn't affect the adjusted cost base per unit of the ones that remain.

The Web site of Mackenzie Financial Corp. at www.mackenziefinancial.com features helpful information on taxes, including clear examples of how mutual fund investors are taxed.

Avoiding fund purchases near year end

If you're tempted to celebrate the holidays by throwing a few thousand into an equity mutual fund in a taxable account, it might be a good idea to hold off until you're struggling through your blinding hangover in early January. That's because many funds pay out big capital gains distributions at the end of the year. Even if you buy the fund just before the distribution, you're on the hook for capital gains tax on that distribution. Here's an exaggerated example:

Purchase   100 units at $8 for total investment of $800 on December 10

Receive distribution: If the fund pays out $2 a unit a few days later, its unit price will drop to about $6. If you reinvest the distribution, you'll end up with 133 units. But you'll also have incurred $200 in taxable capital gains.

In a sense, you're simply paying the tax early because the reinvested distribution is added onto your adjusted cost base, which reduces your eventual capital gain when you sell. But most people would rather defer paying tax, thank you very much, so it would have been better to wait until after the distribution was made and then buy the fund. That way, your $800 would have got you the same 133 units, but you wouldn't have faced that annoying capital gains bill.

Also remember that foreign funds that use derivatives to count as Canadian content in a retirement plan can be lethal for tax purposes. That's because they keep rolling over their strange collections of options and futures, throwing off a stream of distributions that attracts a vicious tax bite. So only hold these "clone" or "RSP" funds in the account for which they're intended — a tax-deferred RRSP or similar plan. There's more in Chapter 20 on this type of fund.

Taxes and Index Funds

In theory, an equity fund that does lots of trading will throw off more distributions because the manager is constantly scoring capital gains (or at least that's the idea). So if you're worried about distributions, it may be a good idea to seek out "buy-and-hold" managers who hang on to stocks for a long time. They usually trumpet the fact in their handouts, as if it were an especially virtuous way of life.

For example, imagine a manager who never traded a stock, ever. If the market price of the shares in her portfolio doubled every seven years, you could simply buy her fund at $10 and then watch it climb to $40 after 14 years, without collecting any taxable distributions along the way. But in practice, the whole business of predicting taxable distributions is devilishly complicated. It's influenced by so many factors, including the timing of the manager's purchases and sales and the numbers of investors who sell and buy the fund, that making forecasts is difficult.

But there's one type of fund that's virtually guaranteed to produce very little in the way of distributions, and that's the equity index fund (bond index funds throw off piles of income, just like regular bond funds). Index funds don't try to buy and sell stocks in pursuit of capital gains; they just hold every stock in the index. So their stream of capital gains distributions is usually small or non-existent. Yes, they may flow through some of the dividend income they receive and they may have to declare capital distributions if a major company in the index is taken over or dropped from the benchmark, forcing the index fund to sell it and book a gain. But just like buying good stocks and holding them for years, putting index funds in your non-RRSP portfolio is a highly tax-efficient strategy.

Taxes are a blind spot for the fund industry. Most investors probably find it virtually impossible to calculate the adjusted cost base of the units accurately. And the performance published for funds invariably shows only the returns earned by a non-taxable investor. Both problems may be insoluble because everybody's tax situation is different; however, once again, buying an index fund solves a lot of your problems. See Chapter 15 for more on index funds.

A Few More Ideas for Tax Savings

For the average Canadian, the RRSP is the Rolls-Royce of tax planning. Not only does money grow tax-free within the plan, but you also get to write each year's contributions off against your taxable income. The write-off is known as a *deduction*. There's much more on RRSPs in Chapter 23. There are some other pretty simple methods of shielding your investments, including mutual funds, from taxes. Two of the most popular are used to build capital for a child — often to go to college or university — so they're useful for parents and grandparents.

Informal trusts or in-trust accounts

These are investment accounts set up for the benefit of a child or *beneficiary*. The person who supplies the money is called the *donor*. Income earned by the account, such as dividends, is still taxable in the donor's hands. But capital gains can be taxable in the child's hands, and the child presumably has such a low income that he or she pays hardly any tax. The fact that capital gains are taxable in the child's hands makes in-trust accounts ideal homes for equity mutual funds, because they usually produce capital gains distributions rather than interest income or lots of dividends. Contributing money to the account doesn't give you a tax deduction. When the child reaches 18 or 19 (depending on the province), he or she is free to do anything with the money.

Brokers and mutual fund companies have offered informal trusts for years. You should be careful when setting them up to make sure that the "trustee" — the person overseeing the account on behalf of the beneficiary — is not the same as the donor. Otherwise, the tax people may refuse to have the capital gains taxable in the child's hands. And don't forget that money put into the in-trust account belongs to the child forever: You can't get it back. That means the kid might just choose to squander it at 18 or 19. By law, you can't do anything about it.

Registered education savings plans

Registered education savings plans (RESPs) are more formal government-registered schemes in which investment income and capital gains add up tax-free. As with informal trusts, there's no deduction for contributions, but the plan can hold unlimited foreign content, unlike an RRSP. And there's a major plus in the form of a federal government *Canada Education Savings Grant* (CESG), which Ottawa adds to the RESP. The grant is 20 percent of the first $2,000 contributed per child annually, so it's a maximum of $400 per year. If the child doesn't go on to post-secondary education the money put into the plan is refunded, but taxes, and even potential penalty taxes, apply to the accumulated income. RESPs have become hugely popular since the government introduced the education grant in 1998. The limit on contributions is $4,000 per child each year, to a lifetime maximum of $42,000. The maximum grant for each kid is $7,200 and the grant money must be refunded if the child doesn't go on to third-level education. There are three basic types of RESP:

- ✔ A so-called scholarship trust where your money is pooled with that of other parents by a money manager. The fees, complicated rules, and superconservative investments (mostly bonds) of these trusts mean that I would avoid them.

- ✔ Then there are the RESP accounts offered by mutual fund companies, aimed at getting you to buy their funds. They're fine, but the selection is limited.

- ✔ Also, there are self-directed RESPs offered at brokers and discount brokers, which can buy stocks, bonds, and cash. Because of flexibility, I would go with the self-directed option, but investors who want simplicity often stick to a fund company RESP.

With an RESP, if the child doesn't go to university or college, you can get back your contributions, but you must refund any CESG grants. You then pay tax on any accumulated investment income, but you can move $50,000 of it into your RRSP if you still have the *contribution room*. Contribution room is the limited amount you can put into an RRSP each year, and any quota you don't use can be made up in a subsequent year. For much more on RRSPs see Chapter 23.

Part V
The Part of Tens

The 5th Wave   By Rich Tennant

"All right, ready everyone! We've got some clown out here who looks interested."

In this part . . .

Feeling intimidated by a salesperson — or even an office bore, the lad with the protruding teeth who claims to be the all-knowing oracle of investing? Whip out this part, and you'll find enough ammunition to blow 'em away permanently. Here are six collections of factoids, each with ten entries. There are handy checklists that you can turn to when you're hiring a salesperson, wondering whether to dump one, or considering buying a fund. For history fans, there's a gallop through ten low points in the epic story of mutual funds. There are ten suggested funds that you can do perfectly well without — but what the hell, they're fun or useful. And there are ten investing blunders that just about everyone makes. Including me.

Chapter 25

Ten Questions to Ask a Potential Financial Adviser

● ●

*L*ots of us are uncomfortable with haggling and being assertive with sales-people. Hey, we're North Yorkers, not New Yorkers. But there are some things you get straight before you hand over a penny to an investment adviser. Ask each of these ten questions and jot down notes to look over later. If the answers you receive are hazy or otherwise unsatisfactory, think seriously about looking for somebody else.

How Do You Get Paid?

This is the first thing to find out from an adviser, because it usually dictates where you'll hold your account and what kind of investment he or she will suggest. If the adviser is paid by the hour (not common in Canada), then his or her advice should be reasonably impartial and you will have at least an idea of how much you'll be paying. And your adviser will probably be happy to help set up an account at a discount broker to hold your investments. But if the adviser makes a living by earning sales commissions — usually from a mutual fund company — then getting you to buy a product is his or her bottom line. A commission-paid planner or broker will try to get you to move your money over to his or her firm or to a mutual fund company account on which the firm earns commissions — that's known as *asset-capture*. Some commission-paid advisers won't want to discuss the subject of how they get paid. It's not that they're being dishonest. It's because skilled brokers often avoid depressing topics (such as commissions) and confusing statistics (such as rates of return) until they believe that they have won the *trust* of the customer. They will first sell you on the concept of the fund — investing in big, stable, undervalued companies, for example — and then get down to the mechanics of how to buy it. The same thing happens on the car dealer's lot — the salesperson will try to dodge the issue of price until you've picked out a car you like. But don't fall for the line. If you don't get a straight answer on commissions, then go elsewhere.

What Do You Think of My Financial Situation?

Toward the end of the meeting, ask for a quick version of the sort of financial strategy the adviser recommends for you. Listen carefully to the way he or she expresses ideas.

Even after a brief interview, an experienced adviser should have a reasonable notion of your financial health and priorities and should be able to make a couple of sensible suggestions. Clearly, the adviser can't give you a definitive financial prescription without knowing your goals, assets, income potential, and liabilities. But the sort of questions that he or she asks, and the interest shown in your problems, will tell you whether the planner or broker is comfortable with you as a client.

Will You Sell Me Index Funds and Low-Cost No-Load Funds?

This is one of the most important questions you can ask, because funds with low expenses are the very best way to accumulate wealth. Unfortunately, too many stockbrokers and planners won't sell them because the bargain-priced funds don't pay enough in commissions. That's not necessarily because the salespeople are greedy: They have to make a living. But a good planner or broker should be prepared to fix you up with a mixture of low-expense no-load funds and regular *load* or commission-charging funds.

Some planning firms and brokers don't even carry low-cost funds, claiming that their administrative systems can't handle them. In that case, try a firm with a full range of products.

What Will You Do for Me?

"Financial planning" is such a nebulous but complex topic that the term means something different to everyone. Get a clear idea of what your planner or adviser will do for you and how many times a year you can expect to meet. Ideally, there'll be an organized calendar, so that tasks such as making a registered retirement savings plan contribution and reviewing your portfolio are dealt with in a predictable way. If you go away from the initial meeting with the impression that all this person wants to do is sell you a few mutual funds, then that's probably all you'll get.

Can You Help with Income-Splitting and Tax Deferral?

Canadians pay a lot of tax, but there are many opportunities to lessen the burden through simple *tax deferral* and *income-splitting* devices, such as spousal registered retirement savings plans. An adviser who's not a tax enthusiast isn't worth hiring. Tax deferral is postponing payment of taxes, usually by diverting income into a tax-sheltered account such as an RRSP. Income-splitting usually involves shifting income to a spouse or child who's in a low tax bracket. Make sure that the adviser is able to set up a registered education savings plan and that he or she is happy talking about *tax-avoidance* methods in detail. Avoidance is the legal practice of minimizing the tax you pay, while *evasion* is illegal tax-dodging.

Can I Talk to Some of Your Clients?

The best reference is from someone you know, but asking to talk to satisfied customers never hurts. Confidentiality rules will probably prevent an adviser from giving out names, but he or she should be able to get someone to call you. If the adviser can't think of a single customer (known in the trade as an *account*) who'd be willing to do that, then how much loyalty does he or she inspire?

Okay, an unscrupulous salesperson might ask a relative or crony to fool you. But aren't we being a bit paranoid by this stage? It's more likely that an incompetent salesperson will simply reject your request.

What Do You Think of the Market?

Believe it or not, the ideal answer to this question is: "I don't know." You're hiring someone to help manage your savings here, not to accompany you to Las Vegas. One of the good things about mutual funds is that they enable brokers and advisers to do what they're good at — selling investments to people — while relieving them of the need to pretend that they know how to pick stocks. After all, why should they? It's far more honest for an adviser to admit that he or she can't beat the market and then sell you a "managed-money" product run by someone who is trained to do the job.

All right, there's nothing wrong with a potential adviser having an opinion on share prices, and it's not a crime to enjoy talking about the market. But if you get a stream of investing theories and stock tips, then you're talking to a frustrated portfolio manager and not someone who's necessarily going to help build your financial future.

What Training Do You Have?

Financial planning is so complex that you should insist on some kind of specialized training. All mutual fund salespeople have to pass a basic funds course to obtain the licence, but that's fairly bare-bones. You should also check that the planner has obtained a specific financial planning qualification. There is a danger that an underqualified planner or adviser could miss out on some tax-deferral or wealth-building techniques that he or she has not heard of.

If the salesperson doesn't have much in the way of training, he or she could try to bamboozle you with bewildering talk of designations and obscure trade associations — "Oh, you have to have your associated affiliated estate-planning-wealth-building-pigeon-shooting certificate before they'll let you join." Unfortunately, there's not much you can do about that. But if a planner isn't a member of the Canadian Association of Financial Planners or the Canadian Association of Insurance and Financial Advisors, then ask why.

How Long Have You Been Doing This?

I know it's unfair, but let someone else give a beginner his or her first big break. Like any sales job, financial planning and stockbrokerage takes in hordes of people every year, chews 'em up, and spits lots out. You don't want to hire someone who shouldn't have been in the industry in the first place.

It's better to go with a veteran with at least a few years of experience. An adviser who's dealt with scores of clients is far more likely to know some neat tricks and ways of cutting red tape.

Can I See a Sample Client Statement?

If you're buying through a financial planner or mutual fund dealer, then you should always get a twice-yearly account statement from the mutual fund companies you're dealing with. It's the best way to ensure that your investment is correctly recorded on the fund companies' books. But the salesperson's firm should also give you a consolidated account statement showing all of your holdings. Check that it's professionally produced and easy to read. Many aren't.

If you invest with a traditional stockbroker, then you may just get a statement from the brokerage firm, and not the fund company. Ask to see an example of a statement.

Chapter 26

Ten Signs You Need to Fire Your Financial Adviser

• •

Maybe they just say this to fool us into thinking they're human, but senior executives often claim that firing someone is the hardest thing they have to do. And for an investor, dumping an adviser is also tough. A salesperson's ego and livelihood are tied up in getting and keeping clients, so loosing your account can feel like he or she has been punched in the stomach. The circumstances are rarely cut-and-dried. Most investment advisers are a mixture of good and bad, just like the rest of us. But there are some clear signs that it's time to move on, and here are ten classics. You'll notice that these apply mostly to commission-paid salespeople — because they have the greatest potential for conflict of interest — but drop a fee-only adviser if he or she develops any of these bad habits.

Produces Rotten Returns

It's amazing how many clients hang on with a broker or planner through years of poor investment performance, often languishing in mutual funds that consistently lag the market and rival funds. Yes, measuring performance is tricky, especially if you've been sold a confusing package of funds that can't be compared with other investments. Your funds should show up fairly consistently in the middle of the pack or higher. One year of poor performance is acceptable because good managers often hold stocks that are out of fashion. But develop itchy feet if it happens again. Fund managers can be left behind by the times, after all. There's evidence that hot funds may fall to the bottom of the league — but bad funds stay that way. If you have an awful year in which most or all of your funds are near the back of the pack, then ask for a clear explanation from your adviser. If none is forthcoming, consider moving your account.

Nobody expects a broker or planner to be a genius at picking funds. But all too often, poor returns are caused by simple mistakes such as putting too much money into funds with the same style, betting too heavily on one asset class (stocks or bonds), or chasing risky specialty funds that are too volatile for an investor's core savings.

Pesters You to Buy New Products after the Firm Is Taken Over

Be wary if your adviser's firm changes hands and your salesperson suddenly starts pushing a new line of funds, possibly an "in-house" brand or other limited-distribution product. These funds may be excellent — and you can be sure there'll be a fancy sales pitch — but the firm's new owners may be pressuring your adviser to switch as many clients as possible to the new lineup. You may pay extra costs. In general, stick with widely available mutual funds that can be transferred later to a new brokerage or financial planner if you decide to change. Alternatively, the new funds may be available everywhere but the firm's new management may have struck a special distribution deal. Remember, if you switch you'll probably be on the hook for commissions.

Switches Firms Frequently

An adviser who doesn't stay put is usually someone whom employers aren't happy with — and that's a sure indication of trouble. The problem may be fairly innocent — poor record keeping, for instance — or it could be as serious as putting clients into unsuitable investments. Whatever it is, by the adviser's second or third move, you should probably part company.

Financial planners and stockbrokers are independent business people with their own book of clients. They join a brokerage firm or mutual fund dealership because it provides an office, administrative support, and credibility. So your adviser will almost certainly try to take you and your account along if there's a move. But there's no reason why you should follow blindly. Talk to the firm's office manager to see if there's another broker or planner who suits you and your investing style. Be warned, though, that things can get tangled here. The firm will also want to hang on to your business, so the salesperson's old boss may falsely imply that there was something not quite right with the departing employee. In other words, investors often find themselves in a tug-of-greed, with both parties battling over "who owns the assets" — yes, that's the industry phrase, even though we're really talking about *your* money here. I'm afraid you'll just have to use your judgment. If the adviser has provided excellent service, then move your money to his or her new firm. Good brokers are hard to find.

Keeps Asking for Power of Attorney or Discretionary Authority

Be very wary if an adviser seems excessively keen to get *power of attorney* or *discretionary authority* over your money — legal terms that denote giving him or her the ability to make decisions without consulting you. Even if you find the whole investing process overwhelming, it's often much better to give the job of choosing and selling securities to a trusted friend, relative, or even your lawyer instead.

Cases of fraud, exploitation, and deception by brokers almost always involve abuse of discretionary authority over clients' accounts. In fact, it's questionable whether you should ever give such sweeping powers to a salesperson.

Doesn't Listen to You

People in the investment game tend to come out with a spiel, while brushing aside or ignoring questions. To some extent, they have been trained to do this. Clients often ask questions just for the sake of saying something, the reasoning goes, and if the query is genuinely important they'll raise it again later.

But advisers who just don't want to hear from you are all too common. I've sat in rooms and heard brokers set out a plan for a prospective investor after asking only one or two questions. If you feel that your adviser isn't listening to you, then he or she probably isn't. Time to find someone who will.

Doesn't Return Your Phone Calls

I couldn't begin to count the number of phone calls I've fielded from confused investors who can't even get through to their brokers to obtain answers to simple questions. Brokers and planners are salespeople, remember, which means that they're fuelled by new conquests. According to some astute observers, people who go into sales are in fact approval junkies: Every time they get a prospect to say "yes," it represents validation of them and not the product.

Junkies are annoying, though. Brokers and planners often neglect their former clients, perhaps because the accounts are too small to generate much in the way of commissions and perhaps because the thrill of the chase is gone. You deserve better. If you can't get hold of your adviser easily, then look for someone else.

Suggests "Unregistered" Investments or Other Strange Stuff

This is a sure sign that you should head for the hills. If a fund doesn't come with a regular *simplified prospectus* — the legal document setting out the dangers and potential of the fund — then you're probably going into the deal unprotected. If the investment is offered by an insurance company, however, it should be from a company you've heard of and it should come with a prospectus-like document called an *information folder*. There are a few "high net-worth" funds for the rich that generally require a minimum investment of up to $150,000. These are sold more like stocks, with the risks and terms set out in a document called an *offering memorandum*. They may be good investments, but always check with an accountant or a lawyer. A professional's fee of a few hundred dollars can save you lots of grief.

One of the most common frauds involves offering unlisted stocks, usually with the promise that they'll soon be trading on a proper exchange and that the price will shoot up when that happens. Or an unscrupulous broker will offer "notes" that purport to carry lavish rates of interest. The scam nearly always contains the implication that you're being let in on the deal in a slightly seedy way — "I shouldn't be telling you this, but . . ." In fact, there's an old saying among fraud artists: "You can't cheat an honest man." So if your salesperson even hints that buying into a deal involves bending the rules, then move your money immediately.

Keeps Wanting You to Buy and Sell Investments

Excessive trading — known as *churning* in the investment industry — is one of the classic signs of a greedy salesperson who views you as a lucrative source of commissions rather than as a long-term customer. If your adviser moves your money to a new fund company and if you buy the funds on a *back-end load* basis — incurring a sales commission that applies only if you sell within a set number of years — then the salesperson gets up to 5 percent of your investment. That's $1,000 if you move $20,000. So always ask why when the adviser suggests that you sell. You can be less suspicious about moves between funds sold by the same company because they don't usually generate a commission for the adviser, although some fund salespeople charge a "switch fee" of 2 percent. There's no real justification for such transfer fees, so refuse to pay them.

Remember that funds are supposed to be long-term holdings — and this means at least five years for an equity fund. That's because the stock market often dips for extended periods and because a good money manager's investment style can easily stop working for a year or longer. Perhaps your adviser can present a compelling reason to sell — a loss of a fund manager or a drastic change in a fund's holdings, for example. In that case, it may be wise to go along with the suggestion. The adviser's knowledge is what you're paying for, after all. But remember that when you move money to a new fund company or buy a new stock it's payday for your adviser.

Keeps Making Record-Keeping Mistakes

The investment business is so sales-driven that paperwork and reporting of transactions is often far down the priority list. Every investor (including me) encounters mistakes and incorrectly executed orders. It's vital that you check your account statement and transaction slips religiously.

The profit margins in the financial planning business aren't huge, so many small firms can't afford elaborate *back offices* or administration systems. But why should that be your problem? If you find that your adviser or firm is constantly getting things wrong, then don't accept the frustration. Move your money to someone who's more professional. And act quickly if you notice that money is missing from your account. Don't be fobbed off with claims that the money is in transit or tied up in red tape. If you can't get written confirmation of the whereabouts of every penny, then talk to the adviser's manager.

Won't Abandon Pet Theories

Some investment advisers are gold fanatics, some are bond nuts ("I don't like to see anything in an RRSP but fixed-income securities"), and some think they're all-knowing about the stock market. If your salesperson keeps repeating the same mantra, no matter what's happening to your portfolio, then consider a change.

The history of the market is littered with those who hung on for dear life, insisting that their particular stocks or ideas "will come back." Advisers and brokers become incredibly attached to these beliefs, even at the cost of losing clients. If you think that your adviser has a one-track mind, then get off at the next station.

Chapter 27

Ten Gimmick Funds

••

*T*here may be some great funds on this list, and there are certainly some that will produce fantastic returns. But there are also plenty that will end up costing their unitholders dearly. The bottom line is that these are funds that you don't need. They have fancy features that add excessive costs, or they invest in volatile narrow markets that collapse as often as they rise, or they have vague goals and blurred investment restrictions that make it impossible to figure out what kind of funds they really are. The companies that sell these funds do so in good faith, and they can produce reams of statistics that show that the concepts are wonderful. And maybe they're right. But complexity, vagueness, and extra costs are strikes against any investment. Stick to high-quality stocks and bond funds with low expenses and you'll do fine.

Funds that Hedge Currencies

If you see a manager boasting about his or her astuteness in *hedging* currencies, then be very wary. Hedging is essentially buying insurance against currency losses, usually by buying and selling promises or options to either deliver or take delivery of a currency at a future date. It sounds prudent and risk-free but it usually costs money, reducing your returns. There's no guarantee that the manager will be right about moves in currencies. And hedging adds another level of complexity to a fund, which is generally a bad thing. The most common form of hedging is buying insurance against losses caused by a drop in foreign currency assets. But one of the points of diversifying outside Canada is to spread some of your wealth into non-Canadian currencies: Hedging muddies the picture. Many well-respected mutual fund managers such as Fidelity Investments usually avoid hedging because they reckon it's hard enough to pick good stocks without being right on currencies as well. They're right.

Closed-End Funds

Funds that issue a set number of shares (unlike ordinary *open-end* funds that are constantly buying and selling units) and then list them on a stock exchange just like stocks are *closed-end funds*. In other words, once a fixed number of units have been sold, then the door is "closed" — no more are sold and none are bought back. The big problem with some of these funds is that they typically slide to a *discount* to the value of their holdings; for example, a fund might own assets that are worth $20 per share, but its stock might trade at only $15, representing a discount of 25 percent. It's impossible to predict what kind of a discount or premium investors will decide to put on a closed-end fund, so they are doubly difficult to invest in. Not only do you have to be right about the value of the underlying assets, but also you have to guess what discount the shares are likely to trade at. You don't need that complexity. Current versions of closed-end funds offer periodic buybacks of units by the manager at the net asset value or at a slight discount, to stop the units falling. Although that may help support the price, you're still better off in a regular open-end fund that's always ready to repurchase your investment at its market value.

Single-Country Funds

Single-country funds are just too risky for most investors, and this is why they're rarely launched nowadays. Investing in just one market means you're not only exposed to swings in the stocks that the manager picks — you're also at risk of losing money if the country's currency tanks or its political system goes off the rails. There are a couple of exceptions: The U.S. market is so vast, accounting for 60 percent of the world's stock market value by some measures, that a U.S. equity fund can count as a reasonably broad-based investment. And perhaps there's a case that India is distinctive and huge enough to merit launching funds that buy just Indian stocks. But if you're going to start picking and choosing among narrow-based single-country funds, you lose one of the main benefits of a global mutual fund portfolio — having a professional do the country allocation.

Single-Industry Funds

Much the same criticism applies to funds that invest in just one industry, such as financial services or biotechnology. They're just too prone to dips and crashes when investors decide that the shares in that particular sector are overpriced. Admittedly, these funds thrive when the industry they invest in is hot. And yes, they're a convenient way to spread risk if you feel that a particular sector is going to boom but you don't have enough cash to buy half-a-dozen stocks. But the volatility of such "specialty" funds — plus their high annual expenses — makes them unsuitable for your serious money. Their wild price swings make them seem like good candidates for buying and selling — but if you think you're such a great trader, why are you buying mutual funds?

"Enhanced" Index Funds

Enhanced index funds are more common in the United States, but they have popped up in Canada and probably will continue to do so as fund sellers strive to dress up their index funds. Index funds simply mirror the whole market, making them rather dry fare. Therefore, fund companies have tried to soup them up, giving the manager a bit of latitude to overemphasize or go light on certain stocks as he or she sees fit. The problem is that this strategy defeats one of the main goals of indexing — to track the entire market as accurately as possible instead of trying (and usually failing) to outguess it. Enhanced index funds are neither fish nor fowl.

Commodity Funds

Every so often a fund seller will launch a fund that invests in just one commodity — currencies, say — or a fund that tries to jump among commodities in an attempt to rack up trading profits. Often, the marketing campaign will include fancy charts that show how commodity prices move up when stocks are falling — mostly because inflation is bad for share prices but good for the prices of hard goods, such as commodities. Although that may be true, the expenses on these funds are high and their returns volatile. The only exceptions, arguably, are gold funds and oil funds, because these are two economically important commodities that have risen sharply in the past when inflation flares up. Oil is the energy that fuels the world and gold is the ultimate currency and store of value. But a broad-based Canadian equity fund will probably hold companies that produce both energy and bullion — and an index fund certainly will (now are you beginning to see why so many people, including me, are index fund nuts?). So, there's no real reason to clutter up your portfolio with yet more exposure to these two industries, unless you're truly terrified of inflation.

Woolly Concept Funds

Some of the best-respected fund companies in Canada — including banks — have launched funds that can really only be described as marketing exercises. They include funds that purport to profit from an aging population or funds that try to profit from a vaguely defined "new economy." There's nothing wrong with these funds, but the manager is free to buy pretty well anything he or she likes — making the fund's purported mission almost meaningless.

Wannabe Socially Conscious Funds

"Ethical" funds have clear rules on what they can buy, and prohibit investing in certain types of stocks. But if you look closely at the companies that some "socially conscious" funds invest in, you'll often find that these rules are lax. Funds with a conscience are a healthy development and they're perfect for investors who don't want to make money by harming others or the environment. But stick to funds with definite black-and-white rules — for example, portfolios that exclude all companies that produce tobacco or arms or liquor or pornography, according to the fund's mandate. Forget about guidelines that are poorly defined and simply try to take advantage of the socially conscious investing movement.

Funds of Funds

Companies have been trying to make things easier for customers by introducing funds that combine other funds into one supposedly simple package. In Chapter 21 I discuss this further and explain that these collections can end up being more confusing than the individual funds they replaced. Expenses are hard to figure out and it can even be difficult to establish which product you've actually been sold. You're better off buying your equity and bond funds individually — that way, you can monitor managers' returns easily and dump the perennial underperformers.

"Market-Neutral" Funds

A manager's stock and bond selection may be excellent, but if the whole market is tanking, the fund will probably drop, too. A few companies have tried to get around this market effect by introducing *market-neutral* funds, funds that attempt to make money by picking individual shares but are structured to shake off the effects of a rise or fall in stocks as a whole. But the whole thing ends up adding complexity — and anyway, why bother? The long-term appreciation in stock prices as a whole is one of the reasons why equity investing has been so lucrative. Why give away the benefits of that rising tide? Trying to eliminate the market effect is likely to add costs. Just stick to regular equity funds that offer the prospect of winning both ways — from gains in individual shares and also from the long-term tendency of stocks as a whole to rise.

Chapter 28

Ten Famous Foul-ups in Funds

This chapter was fun to write. Funds have made millions of investors rich over the decades, but the industry's occasional greed and shortsightedness have produced memorable fiascos and farces. Here are just some of the better-known jackpots. In a couple of cases, I've cited whole classes of funds that produced awful returns for investors, or even no return at all. In the case of commodities and real estate, that was arguably because inflation fell so sharply in the 1990s — but the losses raise the question of why the fund industry ever sold such stuff in the first place. And the list of fund foolishness is a lot longer. I never even got around to mentioning the funds that got caught with Bre-X Minerals, or the long dark ordeal of unitholders in Japanese funds, or the drawn-out living death of investors in gold funds in the late 1990s, or . . .

Magellan: Its Bonds and the Fall of Jeff Vinik

Open a personal finance magazine and chances are you'll see the reassuring white-haired mug of Fidelity Investments' mutual fund guru Peter Lynch. The guy hasn't run money in more than ten years, but when he did it was fairly spectacular. He steered Fidelity's enormous Magellan Fund in the United States for 13 years, increasing its assets to $13.3 billion (U.S.) from $20 million. From 1980 to 1990, when he left the fund, he produced an average annual return of 28.5 percent, compared with 17.5 percent from the broad Standard & Poor's 500-share index. But one face you won't see in the ads is that of Jeff Vinik, a subsequent manager of Magellan. He got scared by soaring stock markets in early 1996 and put almost one-fifth of the $53-billion fund into bonds. But the market went on roaring — and unitholders in the world's biggest mutual fund, who'd thought they owned a stock fund, discovered that they owned lashings of bonds and cash as well. The S&P 500 soared more than 22 percent for all of 1996, but Magellan, weighed down by those bonds, gained less than 12 percent. It was history's most spectacular example of *style drift* — a nefarious practice on the part of fund managers who stop buying the type of investment that they're supposed to buy. They either go into more dangerous investments to boost returns, or, as in poor Mr. Vinik's case, they retreat to overly safe holdings. By the end of 1996, needless to add, Mr. Vinik had drifted out the door. And Fidelity put handcuffs on its managers, banning them from fooling about in cash or bonds when they were hired to buy stocks. (For you *Star Trek* fans, incidentally, giant Fidelity is apparently known on Wall Street as "The Borg" because of its incredible ability to regenerate fund managers after one is destroyed.)

The Fidelity North American Income Debacle

This one happened right here in Canada — and fund salespeople will tell you that it held back Fidelity's invasion of the Canadian market for years. The U.S. behemoth came to Canada in 1987 and by late 1994 it was making steady progress, grabbing market share from Canadian fund sellers. One of its hits was the Fidelity North American Income Fund, billed by brokers as a conservative income-producing fund that paid a couple of percentage points more in yield each year than government treasury bills. Trouble was, the fund juiced up its yield by piling into Mexican treasury bills. Fidelity made this perfectly clear in its prospectus, reports, and other documents, but it seems that a lot of salespeople and investors weren't listening. The Mexican holdings collapsed in value when Mexico lurched into one of its regular currency crises in December 1994. Unitholders in the $600-million fund, some of them elderly and new to mutual funds, were horrified when it dropped 13 percent in a year. It was quite a few years before brokers forgave the company, but Fidelity's strong performance since then has made the unpleasant memories fade. Money has a way of doing that.

Bernie Cornfeld and His Infamous Fund-of-Funds

Renowned swindler Bernard Cornfeld was a master of the *fund-of-funds* — a fund that doesn't hold real stocks or bonds but rather units of another, usually related, fund or funds. The structure was ripe for fraud and multiple layers of fees — up to 20 percent annually in Cornfeld's case — as investors soon discovered. Cornfeld was born in Istanbul and grew up in New York, where he was a taxi driver before going into mutual fund sales in the 1950s. He then moved to Paris, where he and his rapacious salesmen intoned the famous phrase "Do you sincerely want to be rich?" He shifted his offshore fund empire to Switzerland, attracting money from expatriate Americans and investors who wanted to avoid taxes. But as the 1970s bear market hit, European and American investigators started sniffing around. They suspected that Cornfeld was essentially running a giant *Ponzi scheme* — a scam that depends on attracting ever greater numbers of victims, using money from the latest arrivals to pay off the original investors. Cornfeld spent 11 months in jail in Switzerland, although the charges were later dropped. There may be a lesson for today: Recent years have seen a fearsome spawning of confusing packages of funds that purport to fix the investor's every need. The companies offering these products are ethical and everything is disclosed. But by their very nature, these latter-day funds-of-funds make it hard to work out what expenses you're paying and what returns you're getting. Sometimes it's even hard to tell which package is which. Stick to individual funds so that when things go wrong, you know which manager messed up.

The Go-Go Funds of the 1960s and 1990s

The go-go funds of the 1960s turned into burst balloons, just like the red-hot tech funds of the 1990s. The most famous go-go fund of the late '60s was Gerald Tsai's Manhattan Fund. In 1967 he made 39 percent, while the broad market gained just 15 percent, by loading up on frothy tech stocks like Teleprompter, Deltona, Telex, and Polaroid. How quaint those names sound now. The media worshipped Tsai. By the end of the year, the Manhattan fund swelled to $559.5 million (U.S.) in assets. But in 1968 the losses began, culminating in the great bear market of the 1970s: The fund lost 30 percent in 1973 and 36.49 percent in 1974. It ended up with an annual loss of 7.6 percent over a decade and its assets fell to $57 million. The Manhattan Fund's plunge was eerily like the fate that befell the Internet-heavy funds of our era. Most of the 45 stocks it owned in late 1969 had either plunged by 90 percent or gone out of business in less than a year. As of June 2002, the average science and tech fund sold in Canada had lost money over one, three, and five years.

The Fall of John Kaweske

In early 1994, the mutual fund industry was shaken when Invesco Funds Group of Denver said it had fired superstar manager John Kaweske for alleged "substantial" unauthorized trading of stock in personal accounts. Mr. Kaweske co-managed the $3.6-billion (U.S.) Industrial Income Fund, one of America's largest and hottest funds. There was no evidence that unitholders were ever harmed, and Mr. Kaweske later reached a settlement with regulators where he paid $115,000 while neither admitting nor denying wrongdoing. But the news caused a shockwave in the fund industry, especially when it turned out that personal trading by fund managers was widespread and that many companies had lax rules. Investors were angered to learn that there was little preventing managers from *front running* — the practice of buying up stocks cheaply in advance of huge purchases of the same shares by the very funds that they ran.

The Costly Ethical Dilemma of Veronika Hirsch

Canada had its own minor personal-trading circus in 1996. Fidelity, desperate to get a Canadian equity fund with decent performance, had wooed high-profile manager Veronika Hirsch from rival AGF Management Ltd. She got a brand-new fund to run, Fidelity True North, and the defection caused a blaze of publicity because poor AGF had built a massive TV advertising campaign around her. But Ms. Hirsch soon parted company with Fidelity when it emerged that while at AGF she had invested in a junior gold stock and then bought it for her fund. She paid $140,000 to regulators to settle the case and is now running her own fund company, Hirsch Asset Management. The fiasco embarrassed the Canadian fund industry and cast a cold light on the often-cozy relationships between fund managers and brokers. Companies tightened up on personal trading and agreed to an industry code of ethics, although the pension fund industry was slow to catch up. In early 2000, Royal Bank of Canada parted company with several managers of pension fund money and other institutional accounts at its RT Capital unit after they turned out to have been manipulating stock prices to make their performance look better.

The Rancid Alphabet Soup of Financial Planning

More than six years ago, Ontario Securities Commission member Glorianne Stromberg came out with a report on the mutual fund industry in which she criticized excessive fees and managers' scant regard for the best interest of unitholders. She also lambasted regulators for failing to impose controls on fund salespeople who called themselves "financial planners." Progress has been slow. A national self-regulatory body for fund dealers is finally up and running and there are signs of progress toward establishing a national standard for financial planners, but turf wars and squabbling among the banks, brokers, insurance companies, and planning profession led to an unacceptable delay in reaching an agreement. Registered Financial Planner (RFP), Certified Financial Planner (CFP), Personal Financial Planner (PFP), Chartered Financial Planner (ChFP) . . . can you figure out the difference? The public deserves better.

Real Estate Funds

It's not often that you get a chance to witness the demise of an entire class of fund, but that's what happened in the 1990s. One by one, as the real estate market collapsed, funds that held buildings and other properties had to ban unitholders from taking their money out. Many eventually converted themselves into stock-exchange-listed real estate investment trusts. Investors who thought they had the right to their cash back at any time had to take their chances on the open market, hoping that a buyer for their units would come along. It wasn't the fault of the managers — the real estate slide brought whole trust companies down as well. But the fund industry had misled investors. They were sold a fund that purported to give their money back on demand — a so-called *liquid* investment. The funds turned out to be *illiquid* because they owned pieces of buildings that nobody wanted to rent or buy. There are a few latter-day real estate funds that buy shares in real estate companies and units in real estate trusts — not parts of buildings — and some have done well. But if you're a homeowner, why would you want to tie more of your wealth to this fickle asset class?

Altamira's Downward Slide

Altamira was once the golden child of the mutual fund industry, attracting billions of dollars to its no-load funds. The company sold its funds directly to investors, meaning it didn't have to pander to brokers and planners with fat commissions and other goodies. The marquee attraction was the Altamira Equity Fund, run by fast-trading Frank Mersch. Mr. Mersch became one of Bay Street's most powerful players, generating millions of dollars in commission income for brokerage firms that did his bidding. For five solid years in a row, from 1990 to 1994, his fund generated returns that were in the top 25 percent of its group, an incredible feat. From 1991 to 1993, it never made less than 30 percent a year. Altamira's fund empire thrived, with assets peaking at $6.4 billion in late 1996, making it Canada's 12th-biggest fund company. But Mr. Mersch, a dedicated trader of resource stocks, missed the explosion in bank shares as interest rates dropped in the late 1990s. From 1996 to 1999, the fund posted returns that were in the *bottom* 25 percent of Canadian equity funds. Investors fled and Mr. Mersch stepped down. By late 1999, Altamira's assets had slumped to $5.3 billion, leaving it in the No. 20 position. Performance recovered in 1999 — Altamira Equity caught the tech-stock wave nicely — and the company's assets bounced back to $6.8 billion. But as the tech tide ebbed, Altamira Equity foundered yet again — and the company was swallowed by National Bank of Canada in 2002. Altamira is now a more balanced company that's less dependent on just one star. But the magic of those Mersch days can never be recovered.

Resource Funds

If ever there were a perfect illustration of why you should stick to broadly based funds, this is it. Resource funds sound plausible at first — they're funds that buy commodity producers and other companies that pull stuff out of the ground. But stop for a moment and ask: Why would you want to tie your money up in companies like that, with their violently fluctuating profits, environmental black holes, and gyrating shares? The funds were one of the most wretched letdowns for investors during the 1990s, posting a miserable average annual return of 3.1 percent. That's only just higher than the group's average expense ratio — a whopping 2.7 percent or so. In other words, for every dollar that investors made in these funds, they handed over 87 cents in fees and expenses. Yes, the decade was marked by falling inflation, which dragged down commodity prices. And a surge in gold and oil stocks after tech shares faded in 2000 lifted the average natural resource fund. The group had a respectable ten-year annual return of 8.4 percent as of June 2002. But do yourself a favour and stick to index funds and well-managed diversified funds — they hold all the resource stocks you need.

Chapter 29

Ten Mistakes Investors Make

. . . .

I think I've been guilty of every blunder on this list, so please don't accuse me of lecturing you. Investing is hard because we not only have to conquer inflation, endless sneaky expenses, and taxes — but we also have to master our own innate fear and greed. Here are ten warning signs that your personal demons are sabotaging your quest for wealth.

Diversifying Too Much

There's no point buying 20 different funds and assuming that you can't lose because you've covered all the bases. Sure, you're certain to own something that's going up — but a chaotic portfolio like that is also bound to contain lots of funds that hold very similar investments. And the more funds you own, the closer your returns will be to the index or market in general — so why not just buy index funds and have done with it? Keep things simple by limiting yourself to a few index funds (one Canadian, one U.S., and one international) plus a few conservative equity funds. That way, you won't be paying multiple management fees to everyone and his beagle in return for mediocre returns that track the market, minus expenses.

Diversifying Too Little

It's so tempting to roll the dice and bet the whole lot on one pony. But look at what the professionals do and you'll notice that they always own lots of different stuff. If your portfolio isn't a broad mixture of top-quality bonds and conservative stocks, then you're probably going to come off at the first fence. Remember the old rule: Own your age in bonds and cash. So, according to the traditional saw, a 40-year-old should have just 60 percent of her money in stocks. That seems overly conservative to many people in our go-go age, where retirees can look forward to 25 years or more after quitting work. But if you don't own at least some bonds, then you're walking a tightrope — with a noose around your neck.

Procrastinating

Invest $200 a month for 20 years at an 8-percent annual rate of return and you'll end up with more than $113,000. But wait five years before starting, and you're looking at less than $69,000. So get going now. Ten years hence, you don't want to be looking back at today . . . and regretting that you didn't pick up the phone.

Being Apathetic

It's so easy to allow your portfolio to slide into mediocrity — by ignoring your awful funds, perhaps, or letting the cash component build up too high. Personal finances aren't exactly a blast, so we're all tempted to leave things to the forces of continental drift. But just a few dull hours of work once or twice a year can make all the difference between a well-adjusted, balanced portfolio and a neglected mess.

Hanging on to Bad Investments

Refusing to sell a bad fund or stock is the true mark of the hopeless amateur — I should know, because I've done it many times. Unfortunately, no green light comes on when it's time to get out. But one thing's for sure — the price you paid is completely irrelevant. Waiting "until it's back where I bought it" is one of the most damaging things you can do to your wealth. Sell it, absorb the lesson, and move on.

Taking Cash out of Your RRSP

Once contribution room to an RRSP has been used up, it can't be replaced. Just like brain cells. So think long and hard about cashing in any of those supercharged dollars nestling within your plan. Not only will you pay taxes, and high ones at that, on the withdrawal, but you'll also be giving up years of tax-free growth. Withdrawing money for a down payment on a house under the Home Buyers' Plan is a little less harmful, because Ottawa lets you put the cash back in. But you're still probably giving up years of tax-sheltered income within the RRSP because the money isn't there to earn it.

Ignoring Expenses

Those extra one or two percentage points in mutual fund fees and costs seem so unimportant — but they ultimately represent a huge chunk of your retirement savings. Remember that over 20 years, an extra one percentage point in annual expenses eats up one-fifth of the total accumulated capital. Do yourself a favour and go with some low-cost managers — look for a maximum expense ratio of about 1.5 percent on equity funds.

Failing to Plan for Taxes

Remember that the mutual fund returns that appear in the papers were earned in a magical tax-free land of hugs, kisses, and happy pixies. In the real world — hellish places like your neighbourhood, for example — people have to pay taxes. So beware of holding bonds, bond funds, and other income-paying investments in a taxable account. To minimize the taxes you pay it's almost always a good idea to pay for professional advice, unless your finances are extremely straightforward. Tax accountants know perfectly legal tricks that you or I don't.

Obsessing about Insignificant Fees

If you're happy with an adviser or fund company, then don't get all irate about a $75 RRSP administration fee. Just pay it if your returns are good and your other expenses are low. People in the fund business will tell you that clients happily pay out hundreds or even thousands in management fees without even noticing — but they fly into a rage if presented with a $25 bill for transferring an account. Remember that the fund company or broker who's truly the cheapest may also be the one who nags you for a "nuisance fee" — but at least it's out in the open. By contrast, a fund that's dinging you for huge expenses each year might seem to be absorbing all of those annoying charges itself. But don't worry, you're paying.

Waiting until the Market Looks Better

Ignore this one if you're a psychic. But for the rest of us, attempting to divine the direction of the market is like trying to catch the wind. The movement of share prices is as intangible and random as the weather, or it may as well be.

The fund industry will tell you that "the time to invest is when you have the money." In other words, trying to jump on and off stocks is pointless. And, for once, the fund sellers' homilies are right on the mark. The evidence is overwhelming that market timing is a futile exercise, so grit your teeth and invest. As they used to say in an annoying Irish lottery ad: "If you're not in, you can't win."

Chapter 30
Ten Cool Funds

∙∙∙

*T*his chapter is unfair, I'll admit. For every fund listed here, I could have picked two others that probably would have fit the bill just as well. But this is an arbitrary and unscientific selection of ten funds that all have genuine good qualities to make any investor take a second look. In some cases, it's a unique investing style. In some cases, it's low expenses. And in others, it's just the sheer high quality of the portfolio. Nobody's guaranteeing that these funds will do well or even keep up with the average fund in their group. At least some will flounder and underperform in their categories. But in mid-2002, all had something to recommend them. (Some of these funds are in volatile groupings such as small-company stocks, which makes them unsuitable for the bulk of your long-term core holdings. But hey, they're also fun.)

Mackenzie Cundill Value

This global equity fund is a classic. It's a Mackenzie Financial Corp. offering that uses the bargain-hunting techniques of Peter Cundill, a world-renowned buyer of beaten-up "value" stocks. The fund had a tough time in the late 1990s as investors flocked to glamourpuss growth companies. But it had a great year in 1999, jumping more than 33 percent as its Japanese holdings finally soared, and it blew away the competition again in 2000 and 2001. As of mid-2002, the fund had a glittering ten-year annual average return of 12.8 percent, compared with 8.1 percent for the average global equity fund.

PH&N Balanced Fund

Balanced funds are a murky mixture of stocks and bonds — it's hard to establish which parts are doing well. But this no-load fund makes up for that with its bargain-basement expense ratio of less than 1 percent. From 1992 through 2000, this fund was in the top half of the balanced fund group every single year. If you can afford the $25,000 minimum account size and you only want to buy one fund, here's a good candidate.

Saxon Small-Cap Fund

There's a minimum account size of $5,000 with the no-load seller, but the expense ratio is a reasonable 1.8 percent. If you like small-company funds (they're not to everyone's taste), then this one practises the time-honoured art of buying well-run growing companies as opposed to jumping aboard technology fads. As of June 2002, the ten-year return was an impressive 16.3 percent.

Scotia Canadian Dividend

No flash, no dancing lizards in sequinned leotards. Just low expenses of 1.2 percent and a nice varied mixture of blue-chip holdings. Oh yes — and a stellar five-year annual return of 11.2 percent as of mid-2002.

Talvest Global Health Care

Slumping biotech shares and big drug stocks have left unitholders in health care funds feeling queasy — the average fund in the group produced a sickly annual return of less than 6 percent in the five years ended June 2002. But this fund rode out the slump by holding some booming health-service companies: Its five-year annual return was 28.2 percent.

TD U.S. Blue Chip Equity

Managed by U.S. mutual fund giant T. Rowe Price Associates Inc., this fund is a top-quality way to play America's giant corporations. Its biggest holdings in mid-2002 included go-go growth names such as drug maker Pfizer Inc., but there were plenty of more sedate companies too, such as mortgage lender Freddie Mac.

Templeton International Stock

Who knows if the once-amazing American stock market machine will keep sputtering and stalling out? But if it does, this fund could be a refuge. The superconservative portfolio, which is light on high-priced tech stocks, holds blue-chip names from just about everywhere except the United States.

Trimark Discovery

Yet another tech-flavoured fund, this one at least thinks for itself. Other science fund managers load up on the usual dreary names like Microsoft, but this fund also owns smaller companies you've never heard of. And that's what you're paying a tech manager to do.

Trimark Fund

Buying quality is never a mistake . . . just ask long-time unitholders in this classic global equity fund, now sold by AIM Funds Management. Like other cautious funds that refuse to overpay for inflated stocks, it slumped in the late 1990s as tech ruled. But as of June 2002, the ten-year annual average return was a giant 15.4 percent.

Universal European Opportunities

Regional funds have a way of breaking investors' hearts, but this one seems to keep coming up with candies and flowers. Veteran manager Stephen Peak loves to hold obscure European stuff, so at least he's not chasing the predictable names. If you're looking for a way to diversify your global holdings (after buying a few mainstream conservative funds), this would add spice to your stew.

Index

• N •

• *S* •

FOR DUMMIES®

The easy way to get more done and have more fun

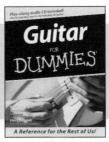

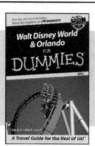

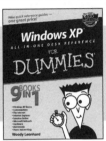

FOR DUMMIES®

Helping you expand your horizons and realize your potential

GRAPHICS & WEB SITE DEVELOPMENT

Photoshop 7 FOR DUMMIES

0-7645-1651-5

Creating Web Pages FOR DUMMIES

0-7645-1643-4

Macromedia Flash MX FOR DUMMIES

0-7645-0895-4

PROGRAMMING & DATABASES

C++ FOR DUMMIES

0-7645-0746-X

Visual Studio .NET ALL-IN-ONE DESK REFERENCE FOR DUMMIES

0-7645-1626-4

XML FOR DUMMIES

0-7645-1657-4

LINUX, NETWORKING & CERTIFICATION

Red Hat Linux 7.3 FOR DUMMIES

0-7645-1545-4

TCP/IP FOR DUMMIES

0-7645-1760-0

Networking FOR DUMMIES

0-7645-1677-9

Available wherever books are sold.
Go to www.dummies.com or call 1-800-567-4797 to order direct

 **WILEY**